Unpacking Globalization

Unpacking Globalization

Markets, Gender, and Work

Edited by
Linda E. Lucas

LEXINGTON BOOKS

A division of
ROWMAN & LITTLEFIELD PUBLISHERS, INC.
Lanham • Boulder • New York • Toronto • Plymouth, UK

LEXINGTON BOOKS

A division of Rowman & Littlefield Publishers, Inc.
A wholly owned subsidary of The Rowman & Littlefield Publishing Group, Inc.
4501 Forbes Boulevard, Suite 200
Lanham, MD 20706

Estover Road
Plymouth PL6 7PY
United Kingdom

British Library Cataloguing in Publication Information Available

Library of Congress Cataloging-in-Publication Data

Unpacking globalization : markets, gender, and work / edited by Linda E. Lucas.
  p. cm.
 Includes bibliographical references and index.
 ISBN-13: 978-0-7391-2157-3 (cloth : alk. paper)
 ISBN-10: 0-7391-2157-X (cloth : alk. paper)
 ISBN-13: 978-0-7391-2158-0 (pbk. : alk. paper)
 ISBN-10: 0-7391-2158-8 (pbk. : alk. paper)
 1. Women—Economic conditions. 2. Globalization. I. Lucas, Linda E.
 HQ1381.U57 2007
 303.48'2—dc22   2007008655

Printed in the United States of America

™
⊖ The paper used in this publication meets the minimum requirements of American
National Standard for Information Sciences—Permanence of Paper for Printed Library
Materials, ANSI/NISO Z39.48–1992.

Table of Contents

Part III: Engendering the World of Commerce

Part IV: Out of the House: Entrepreneurship, Savings and Networking as Empowerment

List of Tables

List of Figures

xiii

Foreword

One of the challenges to gender analysis today is the lack of empirical information and theorizing with which to guide policy and practice at national and international levels. This book provides that theory and data along with insights into the dramatic effects of globalization on economies, culture and governments. The focus is on how these changes impact individuals within their economic and gender relationships.

This book addresses the practicalities of gender mainstreaming as well as a number of other critical policy issues. The research indicates that gender systems are changing as economic lives change. Women are learning new skills and new strategies for communicating with each other in villages and across oceans. These changes lead to new negotiations in the gender systems. On the international level, channels are opening for economic and cultural flows. Gender plays an important role in the development of all these channels.

The volume is unique both in its perspective and in its coverage. Contributions come from both developed and developing countries, from the global North and South, and from Africa and Asia. The chapters are in dialogue with one another and thus develop a complex picture of what is happening under globalization regimes. The research presented here indicates that the benefits of globalization although very powerful and positive are uneven. The voices in the text are clear and original and very much on the ground with their research. They answer the question: How well are people doing under the conditions of globalization? The answers have to do with quality of life issues within the family as well as economic survival concerns. This volume could serve as a supplemental text in several types of courses covering issues of globalization, women's issues, gender mainstreaming and economic development.

The authors in this volume came from across the globe (Burkina Faso, Canada, India, Israel, Malaysia, Mexico, Mozambique, the Netherlands, Norway, Swaziland, Sweden, Tanzania, Uganda, United Kingdom, United States and Uruguay). They presented early versions of these papers at an international conference sponsored by the Department of Women's and Gender Studies at Makerere University. This conference, the Eighth International

Women's Worlds Congress: Gains and Challenges 2002 was held in Africa for the first time under the Department's sponsorship. More than 2,000 participants presented papers and contributed to expanding knowledge of gender relationships and multiple other exciting topics. The Department sponsored a series of volumes of proceedings, The Gendered World Series. We are grateful to the many sponsors of the Congress as well as the women and men who attended and participated.

Grace Bantebya Kyomuhendo
Chair, Department of Women and Gender Studies
Makerere University
Kampala, Uganda
http://womenstudies.mak.ac.ug

Acknowledgments

Many assisted with this book and to all of them I am very grateful. I acknowledge the intellectual talent, patience and goodwill of the authors in this volume; and the professionalism of the staff at the Women's Worlds 2002 Secretariat at the Department of Women and Gender Studies, Makerere University, Kampala, Uganda. The U.S. Fulbright Commission awarded me a grant in 2001–2002, which first took me to Makerere University to teach and research. The Department of Women's and Gender Studies provided a warm environment for this work to be done. A second Fulbright grant in 2003 and a grant from SAGA/USAID facilitated editing this volume. I received excellent support from Eckerd College in St. Petersburg, Florida: Linda O'Bryant, of the Collegium of Behavioral Sciences, Elizabeth Jadus, of the Collegium of Letters, and several students and graduates of Eckerd College including Malene Alleyne, Sarah Sieloff, Andrew Valdespino, and Katrine Vinita. Each one, with commitment and skill added considerable value to this work. Sarah Hudgins, Zachary Hudgins and Patty Callaghan read, gave feedback and support at critical times during the editing process.

Part I

Gender Perspectives on Economics, Solidarity and Survival

Chapter 1

Unpacking Globalization: Markets, Gender and Work

Linda E. Lucas

This volume explores the consequences of globalization for women, for gender equity and for quality of life. The focus is on markets, gender and work and how women and men are making their ways through these changing systems. The authors theorize globalization's consequences and contribute a gender analysis to the literature describing globalization (Friedman 1999, 2005; Mittelman 2000; Sassen 1998). Each chapter also builds on a large literature that tracks women and men through economic change and development, through shifts in thinking about poverty alleviation and through implementation of Structural Adjustment Policies (SAPS)[1].

When studying the effects of globalization, Lourdes Benería asks if the move to a market economy and increased trade is an improvement for women and gender relations. In order to answer this question, we need a lot more information and in order to get this information, we need to unpack the gender effects, the market effects, the work, income and welfare effects of globalization (Benería 2003).

The book is unique in offering so many voices from diverse theoretical and geographical perspectives. The authors come from and base their studies in Africa, Asia, Europe, North and South America. The book offers case studies describing the progress of people under the changes we call globalization. Several themes emerge indicating that from the household to regional levels, change is leading to new awareness and new survival strategies for both women and men.

For some, these strategies will bring wealth and prosperity and for others, an increase in suffering, confusion and poverty.

Background

Early research on economic development, a precursor of contemporary globalization studies, identified gendered trends within the practice and theory of development. For example, in order to open their economies to expanded trade in the 1980s, many countries set up export processing zones where imported raw materials were assembled using relatively cheaper labor resources. Firms in these export zones typically hired young, unmarried women to work in the factories. This phenomenon was called the feminization of the labor force (Catagay and Ozler 1995). Although these women often worked in rigorous conditions, they enjoyed the income, freedom, and access to city life that came with their jobs. The feminization of the labor force generated considerable debate as to whether or not these jobs would lead to long term improvements in well-being. Today, the jobs of the 1980s are moving to relatively lower-cost labor areas such as China, leaving the women workers behind while other women enjoy the benefits of a new job.

Other researchers found that under structural adjustment programs (SAPs), implemented in the 1980s in several countries, women were disproportionately affected if or when their husbands were retrenched. The retrenchment reduced the family income and forced the women into the informal sector to earn whatever they could (Benería and Feldman 1992; Tinker 1990). Measurement of the long-term effects of SAPs is now compounded by the influences of globalization. These influences put additional pressure on economies to become more efficient and competitive in export markets. What has emerged is a significant literature indicating that poverty is increasing in many countries in spite of attempts to restructure and create employment. Poverty alleviation, particularly for women and children, rather than efficiency currently motivates many calls for increased trade, development and employment generation. There is also a vigorous debate on the benefits of globalization (Perrons 2004; Stiglitz 2002, 2006).

Diane Elson (1991) and others established that economic development programs suffered from a gender bias when men both ran the programs and provided input to identify the needs for the programs. This research ultimately led to shifts in thinking about the implementation of economic development. Women in Development (WID) approaches evolved into Gender and Development (GAD) approaches. While WID was concerned with giving agency to women in the decisions and processes of economic development, GAD recognized that simply adding women, though an important step, may not be enough to fully empower the capabilities of women; and, that development processes and decisions need to take into account the constraints that gender relations put on achieving development outcomes (Bakker 1994). Much of this research on market, gender and work is reviewed and summarized in this volume in one or another of the chapters.

The challenge to these research streams is the integration into the analysis of the processes of globalization. Globalization involves opening borders and markets to new ideas, new products and new ways of communicating. Dynamic, competitive markets are enveloping more and more persons into their sphere of influence and creating pressures on time and energy. Although people are connected to larger worlds with global communications and technology, they remain deeply attached to the places where they work and live and to the rituals associated with those places. Maintaining these connections results in predictable time pressures where caring activities may be squeezed out by market activity. These responses may not be gender neutral. Women typically bear the burden of the double job, one in the field and one in the home. Feminist economists have done the critical research evaluating the trade offs to society of women carrying a disproportionate amount of the workload (e.g. Agarwal 1994; Albelda 1997; Folbre 1994, 2000).

The attention to gender equity is characteristic of the latest scholarship on gender, globalization, markets and work. This scholarship integrates issues from the past (impacts of national economic policies, poverty, gender inequalities) with the consequences of the globally integrated market (wealth creation, erosion of time for care work), recognizing that the market offers opportunities as well as challenges. The scholarship also recognizes that institutions as well as individual actors are powerful agents in globalization. This volume contributes to several levels of this established literature as it unpacks the gendered effects of globalization.

Unpacking Globalization

The first section of the book, *Gender Perspectives on Economics, Solidarity and Survival*, presents historical background and analysis of global changes from a variety of perspectives but with remarkably similar conclusions. Margaret Snyder and Saskia Sassen, in chapters 2 and 3, describe the state of the economic world in which women try to survive today. Snyder provides a history of the evolution of gender analysis through both activism and through scholarship. She explores the consequences for small producers, as the forces of globalization erode their capacity to compete with floods of imports into their domestic markets. She talks about victories such as convergence of the wage gap between women and men and some improvement in women's work benefits such as maternity leave. She offers solutions which promote economic justice at both the national and the global levels.

Saskia Sassen identifies the sites where international economic processes can be studied from a feminist perspective. She argues that globalization creates channels whereby profits can be made using "low valued" individuals. These individuals, such as migrant women, have traditionally been unaccounted for in discussions of globalization. Movement of these women around the globe, she says, has become a part of economic development strategy to earn income in the absence of other industries or as a complement to the entertainment or tourism industries.

Manisha Desai, in chapter 4, describes the evolution of women's international networking and the development of women's attempts to understand one another. She notes that networks provide multidirectional sites for action in response to global capital. Women have also used networks to seek agency and to confront one another's privilege. Ngila Mwase, in chapter 6, and Marta Chiappe and Emma Zapata Martelo in chapter 7, describe the wreckage in Africa and in Mexico, caused by economic policies which created dramatic impacts and disrupted the economic and social fabric in several countries. They show that the imposition of SAPs in both Africa and in Mexico led to seemingly intractable problems of creating jobs, of generating resources for development and of coping with complexities of trade. Chiappe and Martelo trace the conversion of peasant workers into cheap abundant labor for industry and show that women play a central role in this conversion. Kristen Timothy in chapter 5 sees the multiple openings of globalization as the opportune time to redefine the concept of human security away from narrow territoriality and discrete sovereign states to be more centered on people and their needs. The new definition she proposes would be engendered and would include economic security and freedoms from want as well as freedom from fear.

The second section of the book, *Shifting Realities: Women and Men Moving in the Economy,* offers ten case studies from six different countries: Burkino Faso, Canada, India, Malaysia, South Africa and Uganda. The cases show that women and men are moving within their economies in response to economic changes; but the evidence also shows that people have to cope with pressures they have not had before and in some cases are not doing well. The cases also explore the potential of government to support people in these changing environments.

Chapters 8 and 9 by Noor Rahamah and Linda E. Lucas, respectively, present very similar data from Malaysia and Uganda for about the same period in time (1980s–1990s). The data document the movement of women from the agricultural and unskilled sectors of the economy to the manufacturing and service sectors in response to radical economic restructuring policies. In both countries, more girls are being educated than in the past yet the structures of the economies are not yet fully friendly to women in the workforce. Mahua Mukherjee, in chapter 11 harks back to the debates around the export processing zones in a description of the nitty–gritty of rural women commuting to work in the urban districts around Calcutta. These women commute long hours, work physically exhausting jobs and still maintain a household. The women pay a cost but also appreciate the excitement and aspirations generated by the urban experience.

Several chapters explore linkages between family well–being and economic conditions. Claudia Roth, Fatoumata Badini-Kinda and Meg Luxton present studies of social security in Burkina Faso and in Canada in chapters 12 and 13. They show how, with the pressures of work and poverty, families are unable to maintain their social relationships. The relationships require resources that they no longer have. The elderly and their sons and daughters have to renegotiate family roles. Old age security is a topic also examined by Akello Zerupa, in chapter 10, where she presents the results of a study undertaken in rural areas of Uganda to identify the underlying values of well–being. She lets the poor tell their own stories. Her study reveals that women's well-being is closely associated with property ownership in a positive way and that marital relationships, if good, predicted high levels of well-being. Old age, little control over resources and weak kinship networks contributed to lower levels of well-being along with poor health and inability to educate one's children.

Ramesh Chand Swarankar, in chapter 14, describes the transformation of little girls into commercial sex objects and the economic role of these girls and women in their culture. Traditionally, the women in the Nat community in India have worked in traveling entertainment troupes (acting, circus, acrobatics) and cultural forms. Changes under globalization result in these cultural practices being replaced by sex work and auxiliary services. HIV/AIDS threatens the Nat with extinction as they pursue their limited economic options.

Several of the cases speculate on the future for women and the poor. Vannie Naidoo, in chapter 17, describes the current legal environment and enforcement profile for affirmative action in South Africa. She points out the historical tension between goals of pursuing equality of race and of sex. White women, Naidoo argues, benefited more than black women under apartheid and should therefore not benefit disproportionately under current affirmative action enforcement. Margaret Kigozi, in chapter 16, offers an encouraging vision that Africa with its plentiful resources and workforce is ready for development and market expansion when it arrives. She cites the accomplishments of women in Uganda as wealth creators and managers. Sakuntala Narasimhan, describing the conditions of women in India in chapter 15, asks whether political power can be translated into economic power and suggests that women remain socially marginalized in spite of some achievements in the political arena. She concludes that social-cultural perceptions of women and their capabilities are more detrimental than economic issues such as poverty.

The third section of the book entitled, *Engendering the World of Commerce*, describes research using a feminist lens to analyze theory and programs which are potential vehicles of globalization and gendered structures of work. There are several examples of implementation of gender training and knowledge. Ronit Kark, in chapter 18, reviews the feminist literature on job evaluation, leadership models, motivation, rationality and emotionality in organizations, and organizational collaborations. The review powerfully shows the gendered nature of leadership and charisma; concepts founded on the masculine heroic of what is good. Julius Kikooma, in chapter 22, takes a feminist perspective on the gendered context of the meaning of entrepreneurship. He argues that because the language and discourse of entrepreneurial practice are imported from the west, it does not reflect African culture and leads to reinforcement of gender stereotypes. Elsje Dijkgraaff, in chapter 23, reviews the challenges of being a woman entrepreneur in an economy which is gendered. She makes the case that training can enable women to overcome some of the bias of the business system and move ahead in a globalized world.

Lena Sawyer, in chapter 19, asks, "How is the discourse of empowerment, as a process of emancipation, used in specific contexts to translate rather than transform power relations?" Her analysis situated at the margins of paid work in Sweden shows how women become integrated into the larger social context through the discourse of empowerment. She criticizes the programs that simply remap the existing social structure into the culture of the new entrants. In chapter 20, Esperanza Tuñon, Carmen Osorio and Mariá Luisa Martínez describe consciousness-raising in the GID tradition in a rural Latin American village. They argue that a GID approach empowers women and creates the opportunity for them to assume responsibilities beyond traditional roles. Patricia Daniel, in chapter 21, describes a similar approach to the work of mainstreaming the "personal dimensions of social change" into the activities of a national training provider in Nigeria. This chapter is rich in quotes from participants and honest in reporting the mistakes made in implementation.

The final section of the book entitled, *Out of the House: Entrepreneurship, Savings and Networking as Empowerment,* details the experiences of current or future women entrepreneurs. The analysis shows that gender is a key issue in both the women's sense of their own abilities to meet the competition and their husband's willingness to participate in their empowerment.

Catherine KomugishaTindiwensi, in chapter 24, points out that women who own firms may not take advantage of the benefits of belonging to a business organization because it may be too costly in terms of their domestic responsibilities or the network may fail because of inability to provide desired outcomes for the female members. Angela Beigaruraho Bazarre and Juliet Nazziwa Musoke, in chapter 25, describe the successes and challenges of women-owned business in Uganda and conclude that university level training can enable students to broaden their visions from being employees to being cognizant of management responsibilities and themselves as contributors to decision-making and innovation.

Harriet Muwanika Kiwemba, in chapter 26, reports on the results of a study of a savings and credit facility program for women in Uganda. The chapter offers abundant evidence of changed attitudes toward saving, uses of loans, power sharing with their husbands, and acquisition of different types of property. Signe Ekenberg, in chapter 27, echoes some of the success in the other studies when she reports on a long term analysis of women in a Bangalore slum. Ekenberg argues that gender stereotypes (hard-programmed ideas) actually define the space women are allowed to occupy and that NGO attempts to engage women in micro-credit projects have to overcome patriarchal opposition. In the final chapter, Aurelia Kamuzora and Faustin Kamuzora identify the factors that determine longevity of Women's Economic Groups in Tanzania. They conclude that the major factors are: institutional framework (credit policies, group cohesion, social capital), business skills (innovation, presence of business skills, outsider interference), and culture (gender balance).

Conclusion

These chapters show that while the consequences of globalization may be dire in many cases, there are opportunities opening up for the empowerment of women and expansion of their sphere of activity. The authors identify new and creative strategies for coping with economic changes both at the micro and international levels. Older women, women without property and in many situations, women who own firms and are subject to gender stereotyping still are vulnerable in the face of these economic changes. Women and men are responding to and often resisting these forces of globalization. Documenting this response is the major contribution of this volume.

Notes

1. Structural adjustment programs refer to a series of the conditions imposed on countries under IMF loan agreements particularly during the 1980s. In order to restructure the economy, governments were required, for example, to reduce public sector employment, open their markets to imports, eliminate subsidies to domestic producers and sell off government owned businesses.

References

Agarwal, Bina. 1994. *A Field of One's Own: Gender and Land Rights in South Asia.* Cambridge: Cambridge University Press.

Albelda, Randy. 2001. "Welfare to Work, Farewell to Families? U.S. Welfare Reform and Work/Family Debates." *Feminist Economics* 7(1):119–36.

Benería, Lourdes and Shelley Feldman. eds. 1992. *Unequal Burden: Economic Crises, Persistent Poverty and Women's Work.* Boulder: Westview Press.

Benería, Lourdes. 2003. *Gender, Development and Globalization: Economics as if All People Mattered.* New York: Routledge.

Catagay, Nilufer and Sule Ozler. 1995. "Feminization Of The Labor Force: The Effects Of Long-Term Development And Structural Adjustment." *World Development* 23(11): 1883–1894.

Elson, Diane. 1991. *Male Bias in Development,* 2nd ed. Manchester: Manchester University Press.

Friedman, Thomas L. 1999. *The Lexus and The Olive Tree: Understanding Globalization.* New York: Farrar, Straus & Giroux.

———. 2005. *The World is Flat: A Brief History of the Twenty-first Century.* New York: Farrar, Straus & Giroux.

Folbre, Nancy. 1994. *Who Pays for the Kids? Gender and the Structures of Constraint.* New York: Routledge.

———. 1995. "Economic Restructuring, Gender and the Allocation of Time." *World Development* 23(11): 913–30.

Mittelman, James H. 2000. *The Globalization Syndrome: Transformation and Resistance.* Princeton: Princeton University Press.

Perrons, Diane. 2004. *Globalization and Social Change: People and Places in a Divided World.* New York: Routledge.

Sassen, Saskia. 1998. *Globalization and Its Discontents: Essays on the New Mobility of People and Money.* New York: New Press.

Stiglitz, Joseph E. 2002. *Globalization and its Discontents.* New York: W.W. Norton.

———. 2006. *Making Globalization Work.* New York: W. W. Norton.

Tinker, Irene. ed. 1990. *Persistent Inequalities: Women and Development.* New York: Oxford University Press.

Tripp, Aili Mari. 2002. "Deindustrialization and the Growth of Women's Economic Associations and Networks in Urban Tanzania." In Visvanathan, Nalini, Lynn Duggan, Laurie Nisonoff and Nan Wiegersma. eds. *The Women, Gender and Development Reader.* London: Zed Books.

Young, Kate. 2002. "Planning from a Gender Perspective: Making a World of Difference." In Visvanathan, Nalini, Lynn Duggan, Laurie Nisonoff and Nan Wiegersma. eds. *The Women, Gender and Development Reader.* London: Zed Books. p. 366–74.

Visvanathan, Nalini, Lynn Duggan, Laurie Nisonoff and Nan Wiegersma. eds. 2002. *The Women, Gender and Development Reader.* London: Zed Books.

Chapter 2

Gender, the Economy and the Workplace: Issues for the Women's Movement

Margaret Snyder

"To fail to pay attention to women's economic activities is both morally indefensible and economically absurd." —Bradford Morse, UNDP

Not many years ago, to speak of women and work was to focus almost exclusively on the workplace—be it an office, hospital, farm, or home. Today we consider ourselves negligent and our study incomplete if we do not also situate the workplace in the larger national or global economy.

How did this radical change come about? Its roots can be found in the first international women's conference a generation ago at Mexico City. The United Nations declared 1975 as International Women's Year and the conference was held to celebrate it. I attended as a representative of the UN Economic Commission for Africa (ECA), where I worked at the time. Women from the global South and the global North, from governments and civil society, came together for the first time to share their concerns about equality, about development and about peace. North and South brought very different understandings of women's issues!

At the time, the "women's liberation" movement was flourishing in North America and Europe. Its most extreme groups made newspaper headlines worldwide when they confronted men. The dominant thrust of "women's lib" was equality between men and women—between the sexes, we said then, but now we say "gender." The main focus was the workplace and the home.

At the same time in the global South, recent independence movements had forged a different approach to women's issues. Women of the South placed primary emphasis on development—on justice for all people, men and women. "How can women advance" they said, "if the whole society suffers under apartheid?" "Yes, we have political independence, but how can women advance when we are not yet economically independent of the industrial countries?" In other words, structural concerns had to be women's issues, too. There could be only limited opportunity for women to advance when all of a nation's people, women and men both, were constrained by dominant groups because of their race, ethnic origin or religion, or by unfree and unfair global trade. Former colonies still exported raw materials whose value-added through processing was profit to countries of the North. To correct such economic injustice, nations of the South at the Mexico Conference called for a New International Economic Order (NIEO).

The clash of those different perspectives at Mexico City set in motion a profound transformation in the definition of "women's issues" as well as the beginning of large-scale global cooperation among women. Ten years later, in East Africa at the Nairobi world conference the two poles converged: Northern and Southern women had adopted one another's positions and the two converged into one comprehensive view.

Today, we see "the economy" and "the workplace" as parts of a whole. "Women's issues" embrace gender equality between women and men, and also the well being of whole societies—a point that got only minor attention from the dominant stream of the Northern women's movement in 1975.

Today, thirty years and three world conferences after Mexico City, globalization has sped around the world. Thanks to fast-paced technological changes, particularly in communications, we can talk person to person or through our networks on email. We can meet face to face at meetings. But the relentless advance of globalization has negatives too. The rich and powerful increasingly dominate poor people and poor nations, just as the advocates of the NIEO predicted. "Globalization itself is neither good nor bad," says Nobel economist Joseph Stiglitz. "It has the power to do enormous good, and for the countries of East Asia who have embraced globalization under their own terms, at their own pace, it has been an enormous benefit" (Stiglitz 2002: 20).

It is the position of this paper that capturing the potential for "enormous good" in globalization through intensified co-operation among women globally (with a focus on the world and national economies) deserves our highest priority, so that women's—and men's—enterprises, jobs and other ways of earning money can survive and thrive in a world of economic and social justice.

Our subject is critical for reasons that all of us know: because women support future generations, the future labor force. They invest their earnings in their families—food, health services, and education. In the age of AIDS, their families often include AIDS orphans. Not least, they make substantial contributions to their countries' economic growth and create economic democracy.

Definition of Work

The World's Women 2000: Trends and Statistics refers to work as "the participation of individuals in productive activities for which they either receive remuneration (in cash or kind) for their participation or are unpaid because they are contributors to a family business enterprise. It also includes subsistence production of goods for their own households and non-economic activities such as domestic work, family and elder care, construction or repair of owner-occupied buildings and volunteer work for which individuals receive no remuneration" (UN 2000: 109).

I adopt this same broad definition because it includes key unpaid activities that have long been neglected when "women's work" is discussed. A global look at women's work shows that "Women now comprise at least one-third of the world's labor force—in all regions except Northern Africa and Western Asia and those proportions are increasing" (UN 2000: 109). We find women in four areas of the economy: rural, informal, small-scale business, and wage work. I shall not discuss household economic work here.

Women are the "backbone of the rural economy" in much of the developing world. Agriculture is the main occupation of the majority of working women in sub-Saharan Africa (SSA) (75%), in Southern Asia (55%), and significant percentages of women work on farms in other parts of the world (Southeast Asia 42%; North Africa 25%, South America and the Caribbean 10-11%; Central Asia 33%; Western Asia 23%).

Three of the cutting-edge issues in the workplace and the economy for many farm women in periods of rapid change are, first, their access to land and other factors of production; second, introduction of non-traditional agricultural exports (NTAEs); and third, imports of subsidized crops from rich countries.

"As land is increasingly a commodity bought and sold, farm women's inability to hold title to it puts them in a vulnerable position and also destabilizes the community food supply" (Snyder 2000: 104). Often, rural women must have a link to a man to gain access to land, and men fear that if women get land they will become economically independent and will cease to marry!

Sometimes, too, there are simply not enough hands to keep up with the work or expand it. Women working in the rural economy have so many tasks—weeding, harvesting, winnowing, care of small animals—and such little access to paid labor to assist them, that they face the problem of inelasticity of their labor—they have no more time. If productivity is to increase, more male labor is necessary, or crops must be switched to less labor-intensive ones.

Women's access to capital increased with the amazing appearance of micro-credit programs. But it is easier for entrepreneurs than for farmwomen to access financial capital—a reason why rural business and trade can be more profitable than agriculture.

Another issue for many farm women is their governments' promotion of non-traditional agricultural exports (NTAEs). "NTAEs" is a fancy phrase for what are mostly family food crops such as beans and maize, rather than coffee and tea—the "cash crops" of earlier years. An NTAE impact in Latin America is peasant farmers losing their land to large corporations such as Dole, and paid work on NTAE farms means for women long hours, low pay, and the presence of pesticides.

In Uganda, women's labor produces 80 percent of NTAE's (Snyder 2000: 10). Researchers find that family food security can be jeopardized, as can women's access to food and cash when income from traditional cash crops shrinks, so men take over NTAE production—women's source of both food and small cash income from sale of excess. It is wise to watch how the gender division of labor and power shifts when the market economy rewards different crops.

Globalization brings an additional cutting-edge issue to the rural economy of developing countries: competition from government-subsidized food imports from rich areas such as the USA and the EU. Rich countries pay their farmers in order to keep market prices low. How can a small farmer—man or woman—in a developing country compete with cheap, subsidized maize or wheat imports?

Developing country representatives spoke bluntly to the rich at an FAO conference on hunger in Rome in June 2002. They "pointed to the huge new subsidies to American farmers as one of the biggest obstacles to creating vital opportunities for their own farmers and enabling them to climb out of poverty" (Becker 2002). Development experts agreed, stating that the subsidies "drive down prices paid to local farmers, reduce rural family income around the world and push farmers off the land and into overcrowded cities" (Becker 2002).

The second large workplace—especially for the poor and women—is the informal economy. It is called "the people's economy" because it includes over 80 percent of workers in developing countries, 40 percent in middle-income countries, and 15 percent and growing in high-income countries (WIEGO 2001). Informal workers are found everywhere, from Kampala to New York. They are the "footloose" vendors, candlelight marketers, coffee pickers, home seamstresses, sweatshop workers, shoe-shiners, and domestic workers. They may be self-employed micro-entrepreneurs (those with less than five workers), unpaid family workers, temporary or part-time workers.

In Africa over the past decade, the informal economy absorbed a whopping 90 percent of new workers, and produced some 40 percent of countries' Gross Domestic Product (GDP). Even in industrial countries the informal sector is growing with globalization and the information economy as technologies make it possible for companies to shrink their work forces and globalization lets them wander the world in search of ever cheaper labor, using more part time or home workers.

Globalization also makes it possible for capital to alight in a country and to depart just as quickly. Partly for that reason, informal workers worldwide share insecurity. "They are not recognized or protected under the legal and regulatory frameworks" (ILO 2001: 3). They and their jobs are vulnerable, and they have no recourse to social protection from their employer or their government. They have no common voice because it is hard to organize them. While not all informal economy workers are poor, a much higher percentage of them than of formal economy workers are poor, and "A larger share of women relative to men working in the informal economy are poor" (ILO 2001:2).

The popularity of micro-credit in the last decade or two has had a spectacular but mixed influence on the informal economy. In Uganda, for example, one hundred NGOs offer micro-credit. But rotating savings and credit associations (ROSCAs) are the capital creating mechanism of choice for millions of women worldwide who do not wish to be indebted or have their husbands make use of their loans. Evolving systems of using ROSCA capital as collateral for larger bank credit are worthy of further study.

Some women micro-entrepreneurs who start in the informal economy find it possible to expand their businesses, hire more workers, and create "small-scale enterprises." In low-income countries they are the exceptions. The fact is that most women who own small to medium-size enterprises had start-up capital or land to offer as collateral, and business knowledge because of their education.

With the steady advance of economic globalization, business development has become chancy for many fledgling small entrepreneurs, both women and men. Countries subject to the structural adjustment programs (SAPs) of the International Monetary Fund (IMF) and World Bank make indigenous businesses highly vulnerable when they open the nation's doors to trade competition by eliminating tariffs on imports. Textiles—a field of choice for women—is an example: What Ugandan entrepreneur can compete with the cheap imported new and used clothing that floods Kampala's markets or with the newly introduced large-scale textile factory?

Nobel prize-winning economist Joseph Stiglitz describes the situation succinctly: The advanced industrial countries, such as the U.S. and Japan, "built up their economies by wisely and selectively protecting some of their industries until they were strong enough to compete with foreign companies." However, developing countries have been forced to open themselves to imported products, with "disastrous consequences" (2000: 16). Jobs are destroyed, small businesses go under, and farmers' crops don't sell because they are subject to competition from government subsidized crops from rich countries.

The third and final area where millions of women are found is the wage economy. "More than 50 percent of women are in paid employment" in all regions of the world except in SSA (excluding southern Africa) where about a third of economically active women have paid jobs (UN 2000: 115).

But women's work for wages continues to be stereotyped by sex, as evident from the fact that nursing and teaching are still the dominant professions for women. A recent ILO study (Anker 1998) concludes that there is "great similarity around the world in types of occupations that are female," adding "this strong world-wide pattern is consistent with typical gender stereotypes." Of course occupations vary widely by region of the world and individual country, but in recent decades (1970s and 1980s) occupational segregation has decreased (Anker 1998: 390–1).

Everywhere women are the large majority of part-time workers, and women's wages lag men's (UN 2000: 131). In no country where data are available do women earn as much as men, even though most have adopted "equal pay for equal work." Yet the wage gap has narrowed in the past decade in three-quarters of the countries having data available (UN 2000: 132). Progress has been made with benefits as well: 119 countries mandate maternity leave of twelve weeks or more, and 31 countries less than twelve. Most guarantee full payment or close to it during leave—but many provide no cash benefits at all (UN 2000: 133). Sexual harassment is another obstacle.

Employment of young women in export industries such as textiles and electronics began in Asia, where they have played an "important role in successful growth," according to a recent study (Horton 1996: 3). This fact must be qualified by many studies which show that mostly young, relatively unskilled women workers labor long hours for low pay and under poor working conditions in what are often dead-end jobs.

A very significant sign is that educated Asian women are increasingly found in the urban market economy, both in production-related work and in professional and administrative jobs. This increase is simultaneous with women's increase in education and women's earnings rising accordingly when compared to those of men.

The Asian experience may be useful to Latin American, Caribbean and African countries, where young women find employment in export industries. Within Africa, Lesotho and Uganda are both investing in textile production, with the goal of exporting to the United States under the African Growth and Opportunity Act (AGOA). In both countries, factories hire young, unmarried, secondary educated girls, and expatriates, despite the numbers of women owning small-scale textile businesses, own the factories.

Conclusion

We have examined four areas of women's work and some key issues arising as a result of gender inequality and globalization. We now turn to some conclusions: issues and priorities for individual or cooperative efforts between national and global women's movements.

Three areas for action that we have learned from women in many countries of both the South and the North are: (1) strengthen the women's movement worldwide; (2) strengthen the human right to personal empowerment; and (3) promote economic justice at national and global levels.

"Organization is key in the twenty first century," says trade union leader Ella Bhatt, leader of 250,000 mostly illiterate or lowly educated members of the Self Employed Women's Association (SEWA). These women roll cigarettes, carry head loads, and pick papers for recycling. They have a bank of their own. They approached Ella years ago to explain why such a bank was needed. She commented: "How can we have a bank when we are so poor?" And they replied,

"Because we are so many!" What a lesson for all of us in the women's movement—who are so many—about what we can do together!

SEWA members know that the united voices of thousands of concerned and committed seekers of social and economic justice cannot easily be ignored. SEWA has influenced national and local legislation and censuses; they moved the world's governments to set out a Convention of the ILO for all governments to sign on the informal economy and home workers. They helped organize two global trade unions: Streetnet for vendors and Homenet for home-based workers. Their mostly illiterate members make use of new ways to join hands and voices through information and communication technology (ICT) and the Internet.

SEWA is uniquely strong as are some other women's organizations around the world, for example in Peru and in Uganda. But on the whole, our NGOs and Community Based Organizations (CBOs) are "relatively weak" as the Association for Women in Development (AWID) says (Kerr 2001). The dominant urge for "mainstreaming" may have distracted us from women-specific groups in the 1990's. We neglected the need for solidarity among women and those men who are concerned that women constitute 70 percent of the world's poor but are a miserable 2.2 percent of the IMF Board of Governors and 5.5 percent of that in the World Bank. We neglected the fact that poor women often have to earn a living for themselves and their families in agriculture or the informal sector. To work with them we have to heighten the impact and sustainability of our organizations.

New types of organizations are being created to meet new challenges: the Council for the Economic Empowerment of Women in Africa (CEEWA) is one such. In Australia, S. Africa, Canada, the Philippines, Sweden, France, and in Uganda, among fifty-one countries, women's organizations support "gender budgets" which reveal inequities in the national budget. To unite us worldwide there is the Women's International Coalition for Economic Justice and innumerable cyber networks.

NGOs can assist removal of bureaucratic blockages and design legal and policy frameworks for workers and entrepreneurs. There are special measures needed for women, such as equal pay for equal work, maternity benefits and control of sexual harassment. Our global women's movement is an extraordinary vehicle to design and press for change in the economy and the workplace. We can do more.

A second issue is the human right to empowerment. When we think about women's greater poverty than men in the informal economy, or about women wage workers' lesser positions and smaller incomes, we recall another Nobel laureate, Amartya Sen, who sees "systemic barriers in the freedoms men and women enjoy—such as severe disadvantages in access to education, training, financial services and knowledge of legal rights" (1992: 122).

Empowering women points first of all to investing in education: formal schooling, literacy and basic education, training and skills development, both before and during employment. Secondly, empowerment comes through access to the factors of production—land, labor and capital—and today's technological tools.

We saw the key relationship of the education factor to women's work progress in Asia. My own study in Uganda, *Women in African Economies, from Burning Sun to Boardroom* (2000), is based on seventy-two interviews with women in all types of self-employment, from the informal sector to big business. Along the continuum from the roadside market to an international airfreight business, the single most empowering variable is education.

Not surprisingly, the single most important factor for women to access and find employment in the emerging field of information and communications technologies (ICTs) is also education, from literacy through science and technology.

Computer magnate Bill Gates says "poor women need good health, not computers," but women computer and development experts Nancy Hafkin and Nancy Taggert say there is "no choice between basic needs and IT for women. IT can be an important tool in meeting women's basic needs" (2001: 90). They insist that farmers can learn new productivity techniques, and learn about weather conditions and markets. In India, a milk cooperative weighs and pays for women's buffalo milk by computer, as I saw in 2002. Entrepreneurs can access market information and disseminate information on their products via the Internet. For example, The International Women's Tribune Centre (IWTC) has a CD-Rom, Rural Women in Africa: Ideas for Earning Money that is available in the Lugandan language and in English. It is an experiment in the use of ICT—in this case the computer—by illiterate women.

After education, a critical asset for women's economic empowerment is land ownership or permanent use. Four of every five of the large-scale entrepreneurs I interviewed own sizeable acreages of land, which many of them use as collateral to get bank loans to expand their businesses. Land ownership is the most highly politicized issue in many countries: women's legal organizations and coalitions of NGOs can be key—as Uganda's have.

On the legal side, too, it is my hope that women's law and development organizations will turn their attention to the laws that affect business, entrepreneurship and trade, areas where laws can be an entangled mass that strangles credit opportunities, imports and exports as well as production for local use.

Start-up and expansion capital of an appropriate size demands more than micro-credit organizations, whose loans are limited and often bear high interest for short-term use. ROSCAs and commercial banks are involved here.

Our third and final issue is economic justice at the national and global level. We move from gender equality to the broader issue of economic justice at national and global level—drawing again on the Mexico City 1975 origins of "women's issues." All of the empowering micro-credit in the world will not keep a micro-entrepreneur or farmer competitive with cheap imports that bring on the "disastrous consequences" that "small businesses go under and farmers' crops don't sell" because of competition from rich countries (Stiglitz 2002: 16).

We have seen the South/North poverty gap widen and deepen as Northern countries—through the IMF—insist that borrowing countries cancel all tariffs on imports from grains to textiles. Then they, the rich, subsidize their own industries so that they can outsell local produce in poor countries. We have seen the result: the death of fledgling industries.

This is where our global women's movement can be powerful. Members of it who come from the industrial countries that control the World Bank, IMF, and WTO can be—and many are—active in their own countries, joining others who protest policies that impact negatively on micro and small businesses in developing countries. At the same time, business women's organizations and their supporters in developing countries can bolster their governments' efforts to make appropriate agreements with international lending agencies such as the World Bank, IMF and bilaterals, so that their fledgling businesses will not be wiped out, farmers will not be pushed off the land into over-crowded cities, and family income will not be reduced.

The need exists for us to promote the potential for enormous good that globalization offers, and engender our national budgets to benefit the poor and women. Through cooperation between national and global organizations we can make women's contributions to their economies more visible, their voices heard.

In conclusion, "It will not be easy to democratize the economy and create economic justice through women, because their massive contributions to their countries' and the global economy and society are not yet fully understood. No matter in which area women work, they invest their earnings in the well being of their families—the future labor force. It will take a huge educational effort by women and men leaders and voluntary organizations. It will take the political will of national leaders" (Snyder 2002: 88).

Today we can bring together the two Mexico City approaches once again, the gender equity approach in the workplace and justice in the economy strategies. We can put the interests of the poorest at the center and help give them visibility and voice. Yes, as Dean Joy Kwesiga of Makerere University and the Department of Women's and Gender Studies says, we have "a gigantic job ahead" (Snyder 2000: 31). After all, the women's movement is a social revolution. Each of us must be prepared to spend a lifetime on it. Having done just that myself, I can assure you that the rewards are great!

Notes

1. On the subject of land ownership, several of the small-scale entrepreneurs I interviewed in Uganda were given land by their fathers and became highly productive farmers or businesswomen.

2. Imagine every girl in our world getting through secondary school! Imagine them getting science and technology education! Women of the North can contribute to scholarship funds to Keep Girls in School, especially through the critical years of secondary schooling. The contact for this fund is Marion Doro (email: medor@conncoll.edu).

3. Common use ICT facilities for communities are found in the Technology Information Centers of SEWA in India and in village telecenters in several African

countries: Uganda, Kenya, Senegal, South Africa and Mozambique, sponsored by International Development Research Centre (IDRC) of Canada.

References

Anker, Richard. 1998. *Gender & Jobs: Sex Segregation of Occupations in the World.* Geneva: International Labor Organization.

Becker, Elizabeth. 2002. "Raising Farm Subsidies, U.S. Widens International Rift." *The New York Times.* 15 June.

International Labour Organization (ILO). 2001. *Decent Work and the Informal Economy.* Geneva: International Labor Organization.

Hafkin, Nancy and Nancy Taggert. 2001. *Gender, Information Technology and Developing Countries: An Analytic Study.* Washington, DC: Academy for Educational Development.

Horton, Susan. ed. 1996. *Women and Industrialization in Asia.* London: Routledge.

Kerr, Joanna. 2001. "International Trends in Gender Equality Work." Toronto: AWID Occasional Paper No. 1.

Women's Edge. *Notes from the Edge.* vol. 5 no. 3, May/June 2002. Washington, D. C. Available at www.womensedge.org.

Sen, Amartya. 1999. *Development as Freedom.* New York: Knopf.

Snyder, Margaret. 1995. *Women in African Economies: From Burning Sun to Boardroom.* Kampala: Fountain Publishers.

Snyder, Margaret. 2000. "Women and African Development." *CHOICE: Current Reviews for Academic Libraries.* February.

Stiglitz, Joseph E. 2002. *Globalization and its Discontents.* New York: Norton.

Tripp, A. M. and J. C. Kwesiga. eds. 2002. *The Women's Movement in Uganda: History, Challenges and Prospects.* Kampala: Fountain Publishers.

United Nations. 2000. *The World's Women 2000.* New York: United Nations.

WEIGO. 2001. "Fact Sheets: the Informal Economy." Available at www.wiego.org/main/fact1.html.

Chapter 3

Countergeographies of Globalization: The Feminization of Survival

Saskia Sassen

The last decade has seen a growing presence of women in a variety of cross-border circuits.[1] These circuits are enormously diverse but share one feature: they are profit or revenue making circuits developed on the backs of the truly disadvantaged. They include the illegal trafficking in people for the sex industry and for various types of formal and informal labor markets. And they include cross-border migrations, both documented and not, which have become an important source of hard currency for governments in home countries. The formation and strengthening of these circuits is in good part a consequence of broader structural conditions. Among the key actors emerging out of these broader conditions to give shape to these particular circuits are the women themselves in search of work, but also, and increasingly so, illegal traffickers and contractors as well as governments of home countries.

I conceptualize these circuits as countergeographies of globalization. They are deeply imbricated with some of the major dynamics constitutive of globalization: the formation of global markets, the intensifying of transnational and trans-local networks, the development of communication technologies that easily escape conventional surveillance practices. The strengthening and, in some of these cases, the formation of new global circuits is embedded or made possible by the existence of a global economic system and its associated development of various institutional supports for cross-border money flows and markets. These countergeographies are dynamic and changing in their locational features: to some extent they are part of the shadow economy, but it is also clear that they use some of the institutional infrastructure of the regular economy.[2]

This chapter maps some of the key features of these countergeographies, particularly as they involve foreign-born women. The logic organizing this mapping is the possibility of systemic links between the growth of these alternative circuits for survival, for profit-making and for hard-currency earning, on the one hand, and major conditions in developing countries that are associated with economic globalization, on the other. Among these conditions are a growth in unemployment, the closure of a large number of typically small and medium-sized enterprises oriented to national rather than export markets, and large, often increasing government debt. While these economies are frequently grouped under the label developing, they are in some cases struggling or stagnant and even shrinking. For the sake of briefness I will use developing as shorthand for this variety of situations.

Mapping a New Conceptual Landscape

The variety of global circuits that are incorporating growing numbers of women has strengthened at a time when major dynamics linked to economic globalization have had significant impacts on developing economies. These countries had to implement a bundle of new policies and accommodate new conditions associated with globalization: structural adjustment programs, the opening up of these economies to foreign firms, the elimination of multiple state subsidies, and, it would seem almost inevitably, financial crises and the prevailing types of programmatic solutions put forth by the IMF. It is now clear that in most of the countries involved, whether Mexico or South Korea, these conditions have created enormous costs for certain sectors of the economy and of the population and have not fundamentally reduced government debt.

Among these costs are, prominently, the growth in unemployment, the closure of a large number of firms in often fairly traditional sectors oriented to the local or national market, the promotion of export-oriented cash crops which have increasingly replaced survival agriculture and food production for local or national markets, and, finally, the ongoing and mostly heavy burden of government debt in most of these economies.

Are there systemic links between these two sets of developments—the growing presence of women from developing economies in the variety of global circuits described above and the rise in unemployment and debt in those same economies? One way of articulating this in substantive terms is to posit that a) the shrinking opportunities for male employment in many of these countries, b) the shrinking opportunities for more traditional forms of profit-making in these same countries as they increasingly accept foreign firms in a widening range of economic sectors and are pressured to develop export industries, and c) the fall in revenues for the governments in many of these countries, partly linked to these conditions and to the burden of debt servicing, have d) all contributed to raise the importance of alternative ways of making a living, making a profit, and securing government revenue.

The evidence for any of these conditions is incomplete and partial, yet there is a growing consensus among experts about the first three listed above. I will go further and posit that these three conditions are expanding into a new politico economic reality for a growing number of developing, typically struggling economies, and that it is in this context that the fourth dynamic listed above emerges. It is also in this context that I posit that all of these conditions have emerged as factors in the lives of a growing number of women from developing or struggling economies, even when the articulations are often not self-evident or visible—a fact that has marked much of the difficulty of understanding the role of women in development generally, as I discuss in the next section. These are, in many ways, old conditions. What is different today is their rapid internationalization and considerable institutionalization.

My main effort, analytically, is to uncover the systemic connections between, on the one hand, what are considered as poor, low-earning and in that regard low value-added individuals, often represented as a burden rather than a resource, and on the other hand, what are emerging as significant sources for profit-making, especially in the shadow economy, and for government revenue enhancement. Prostitution and labor migration are growing in importance as ways of making a living; illegal trafficking in women and children for the sex industry and in laborers are growing in importance as ways of making a profit; and the remittances sent by emigrants, as well as the organized export of workers are increasingly important sources of revenues for some of these governments. Women are by far the majority group in prostitution and in trafficking for the sex industry, and they are becoming a majority group in migration for labor. The employment and/or use of foreign-born women cover an increasingly broad range of economic sectors, some illegal and illicit, such as prostitution, and some in highly regulated industries, such as nursing.

These circuits can be thought of as indicating the, albeit partial, feminization of survival, because it is increasingly on the backs of women that these forms of making a living, making a profit and securing government revenue are realized. Thus in using the notion of feminization of survival I am not only referring to the fact that households and indeed whole communities are increasingly dependent on women for their survival. I want to emphasize the fact that also governments are dependent on women's earnings in these various circuits, and so are types of enterprises whose ways of profit-making exist at the margins of the "licit" economy. Finally, in using the term circuits, I want to underline the fact that there is a degree of institutionalization in these dynamics—they are not simply aggregates of individual actions.

What I have described above is indeed a conceptual landscape. The data are inadequate to prove the argument as such. There are, however, partial bodies of data to document some of these developments. Further, it is possible to juxtapose several data sets, albeit each gathered autonomously from the other, to document some of the interconnections presented above. There is, also, an older literature on women and the debt, focused on the implementation of a first generation of Structural Adjustment Programs in several developing countries linked to the growing debt of governments in the 1980s; this literature has documented the disproportionate burden these Programs put on women (Ward 1991; Ward and Pyle 1995; Bose and Acosta-Belen 1995; Benería and Feldman 1992; Bradshaw et al. 1993; Tinker 1990; Moser 1989). And now there is a new literature on a second generation of such programs, one more directly linked to the implementation of the global economy in the 1990s (UNDP 2005; Pyle and Ward 2003; Khotari 2006).

Strategic Instantiations of Gendering in the Global Economy

There is by now a fairly long-standing research and theorization effort engaged in recovering the role of women in international economic processes. The central effort in much of this earlier research literature was to balance the excessive focus, typically unexplicated, on men in international economic development research. In the mainstream development literature, these processes have often, perhaps unwittingly, been represented as neutral when it comes to gender.

In my reading, globalization has produced yet another set of dynamics in which women are playing a critical role. And, once again, the new economic literature on current globalization processes proceeds as if this new economic phase is gender-neutral. These gender dynamics have been rendered invisible in terms of their articulation with the mainstream global economy. This set of dynamics can be found in the alternative cross-border circuits described above in which the role of women, and especially the condition of being a migrant woman, is crucial. These gender dynamics can also be found in key features of the mainstream global economy, but this is not the place to discuss these. I think we need to see these current developments as part of this longer standing history that has made visible women's role in crucial economic processes.

We can identify two older phases in the study of gendering in the recent history of economic internationalization, both concerned with processes that continue today, and a third phase focused on more recent transformations, often involving an elaboration of the categories and findings of the previous two phases.

A first phase is the development literature about the implantation of cash crops and wage labor generally, typically by foreign firms, and its partial dependence on a dynamic whereby women subsidized the waged labor of men through their household production and subsistence farming. Boserup, Deere, and many others produced an enormously rich and nuanced literature showing the variants of this dynamic (Boserup 1970; Deere 1976). Far from being unconnected, the subsistence sector and the modern capitalist enterprise were shown to be articulated through a gender dynamic; this gender dynamic, furthermore, veiled this articulation. It was the "invisible" work of women producing food and other necessities in the subsistence economy that contributed to maintain extremely low wages on commercial plantations and mines, mostly geared to export markets. Women in the so-called subsistence sector thereby contributed to the financing of the "modernized" sector through their largely unmonetized subsistence production. But the standard development literature represented the subsistence sector, if at all, as a drag on the modern sector and as an indicator of backwardness. It was not measured in standard economic analyses. Feminist analyses showed the actual dynamics of this process of modernization and its dependence on the subsistence sector.

A second phase was the scholarship on the internationalization of manufacturing production and the feminization of the proletariat that came with it (Lim 1980; Enloe 1988; Nash and Fernandez Kelly 1982; Safa 1995; Sassen 1988; Ward 1991; Chant 1992; Bonacich et al. 1994; Castro 1986). The key analytic element in this scholarship was that off-shoring manufacturing jobs under pressure of low-cost imports mobilized a disproportionately female workforce in poorer countries that had hitherto largely remained outside the industrial economy. In this regard it is an analysis that also intersected with national issues, such as why women predominate in certain industries, notably garment and electronics assembly, no matter what the level of development of a country (Milkman 1980; Benería and Feldman 1992). From the perspective of the world economy, the formation of a feminized offshore proletariat facilitated firms' avoidance of increasingly strong unions in the countries where the capital originated and securing competitive prices for the re-imported goods assembled offshore.

A third phase of scholarship on women and the global economy is emerging around processes that underline transformations in gendering (Buchler 2007; Chant and Kraske 2002; Ribas 2005; Yamamoto 2006). These represent many different literatures. Among the richest, and most pertinent to the subjects discussed in this chapter, is the new feminist scholarship on women immigrants which examines, for example, how international migration alters gender patterns and how the formation of transnational households can empower women (Hondagneu-Sotelo 2003; Mahler and Pessar and Mahler 2003). There is also an important scholarship which focuses on new forms of cross-border solidarity (Nash 2005; Naples and Desai 2002) and experiences of membership and identity formation that represent new subjectivities, including feminist subjectivities (Eisenstein 1996; Moghadam 2005).

One important methodological question concerns the strategic sites where international economic processes can be studied from a feminist perspective. In the case of export-oriented agriculture, this strategic site is the nexus between subsistence economies and capitalist enterprise. And in the case of the internationalization of manufacturing production, it is the nexus between the dismantling of an established, largely male "labor aristocracy" in major industries whose gains spread to a large share of the workforce in developed economies, and the formation of a low-wage off-shore, largely female proletariat in new and old growth sectors. Off-shoring and feminizing this proletariat (which is, after all, employed in what are growth industries) has kept it from becoming an empowered "labor aristocracy" with actual union power, and prevents existing largely male "labor aristocracies" from becoming stronger.

Introducing a gendered understanding of economic processes lays bare these connections—the existence of the nexus as an operational reality and an analytic strategy.

What are the strategic sites in today's leading processes of globalization? Elsewhere I have examined this issue from the perspective of key features of the current global economic system (Sassen 2006a). There I emphasized global cities—strategic sites for the specialized servicing, financing and management of global economic processes. These cities are also a site for the incorporation of large numbers of women and immigrants in activities that service the strategic sectors; but this is a mode of incorporation that makes invisible the fact that these workers are part of the global information economy, therewith breaking the nexus between being workers in leading industries and the opportunity to become—as had been historically the case in industrialized economies—a "labor aristocracy" or its contemporary equivalent. In this sense "women and immigrants" emerge as the systemic equivalent of the offshore proletariat. Further, the demands placed on the top-level professional and managerial workforce in global cities are such that the usual modes of handling household tasks and lifestyle are inadequate. As a consequence we are seeing the return of the so-called "serving classes" in all the global cities around the world, made up largely of immigrant and migrant women (Sassen 2006b).

The alternative global circuits that concern me here are yet another instantiation of these dynamics of globalization, but from the perspective of developing economies rather than from the perspective of global cities. Economic globalization needs to be understood in its multiple localizations, many of which do not generally get coded as having anything to do with the global economy. In the next section I give a first empirical specification of some of the localizations of these alternative global circuits, these countergeographies of globalization. Because the data are inadequate, this is a partial specification. Yet it should serve to illustrate some of the key dimensions.

Government Debt

Debt and debt servicing problems are systemic features of the developing world since the 1980s. They are, in my reading, also a systemic feature inducing the formation of the new countergeographies of globalization. The impact on women and on the feminization of survival is mediated through the particular features of this debt rather than the fact of debt per se. It is with this logic in mind that this section examines various features of government debt in developing economies.

There is considerable research showing the detrimental effects of such debt on government programs for women and children, notably education and health care—clearly investments necessary to ensure a better future. Further, the increased unemployment typically associated with the austerity and adjustment programs implemented by international agencies to address government debt have also been found to have adverse effects on women (Pyle and Ward 2003;

Chossudovsky 1997; Standing 1999; Rahman 1999). Unemployment, both of women themselves but also more generally of the men in their households, has added to the pressure on women to find ways to ensure household survival. Subsistence food productions, informal work, emigration, prostitution, have all grown as survival options for women.

Heavy government debt and high unemployment have brought with them the need to search for survival alternatives; and a shrinking of regular economic opportunities has brought with it a widened use of illegal profit making by enterprises and organizations. In this regard, heavy debt burdens play an important role in the formation of countergeographies of survival, of profit making and of government revenue enhancement. Economic globalization has to some extent added to the rapid increase in certain components of this debt and it has provided an institutional infrastructure for cross-border flows and global markets. We can see economic globalization as facilitating the operation of these countergeographies at a global scale.

Generally, most countries which became deeply indebted in the 1980s have not been able to solve this problem. And in the 1990s we have seen a whole new set of countries become deeply indebted. The IMF and the World Bank, specifically through their Structural Adjustment Programs (SAP) and Structural Adjustment Loans, respectively, emerged as critical actors in the handling (and I argue sharp growth) of the debt. The purpose of such programs is to make states more "competitive," which typically means sharp cuts in various social programs.

IMF program countries have paid significant shares of their total revenues to service their debt. Thirty-three of the forty-one Highly Indebted Countries paid US\$3 in debt service payments to the North for every US\$1 in development assistance. The IMF asks HIPCs to pay 20 to 25 percent of their export earnings toward debt service. In contrast, in 1953 the Allies cancelled 80 percent of Germany's war debt and only insisted on 3 to 5 percent of export earnings debt service. And the Central European countries were asked 8 percent after the fall of Communism. Ratios of debt service to gross national product in many of the HIPC countries exceed sustainable limits; many are far more extreme than what were considered unmanageable levels in the Latin American debt crisis of the 1980s (OXFAM 1999a). Debt to GNP ratios are especially high in Africa, at 123 percent, compared with 42 percent in Latin America and 28 percent in Asia (Cheru 1999). The rich countries finally acknowledged the failure of these programs in January 2006, and cancelled the debt of the eighteen poorest HIPCs.

Alternative Circuits for Survival

High unemployment, poverty, bankruptcies of large numbers of firms and shrinking resources in the state to meet social needs, all contribute to a need for alternative circuits of survival emerge. Immigration has emerged as one key such alternative circuit, as has the illegal trafficking of people, including of women for the sex industry.

Women, and migrants generally, enter the macro-level of development strategies through the sending of remittances, a major source of foreign exchange reserves for the governments of poor countries. While the flows of remittances may be minor compared to the massive daily capital flows in various financial markets, they are often very significant for developing or struggling economies. Worldwide immigrant remittances reached US$230 billion in 2005 (World Bank 2006).

Trafficking in Women

Trafficking in women for the sex industry is highly profitable for those running the trade (IOM 2006). The UN estimates that four million people were trafficked in 1998 and seven million in 2004, producing a profit of US$7 billion for criminal groups. These funds include remittances from prostitutes' earnings and payments to organizers and facilitators in these countries.

Trafficking is today a global industry, taking place worldwide. It is estimated that in recent years several million women and girls are trafficked within and out of Asia and the former Soviet Union, two major trafficking areas. Increases in trafficking in both these areas can be linked to women being pushed into poverty or sold to brokers due to the poverty of their households or parents. High unemployment in the former Soviet republics has been one factor promoting growth of criminal gangs as well as growth of trafficking in women. Unemployment rates among women in Armenia, Russia, Bulgaria, and Croatia reached 70 percent and in Ukraine 80 percent with the implementation of market policies. There is some research indicating that economic need is the bottom line for entry into prostitution.

The entry of organized crime is a recent development in the case of migrant trafficking; in the past it was mostly petty criminals who engaged in this type of trafficking. There are also reports that organized crime groups are creating intercontinental strategic alliances through networks of co-ethnics throughout several countries; this facilitates transport, local contact and distribution as well as provision of false documents. The Global Survival Network reported on these practices after a two-year investigation using the establishment of a dummy company to enter the illegal trade (Global Survival Network 1997). Such networks also facilitate the organized circulation of trafficked women among third countries—not only from sending to receiving countries. Traffickers may move women from Burma, Laos, Vietnam, and China to Thailand, while Thai women may have been moved to Japan and the US.

Further, in many countries prostitution is forbidden for foreign women, which further enhances the role of criminal gangs in prostitution. It also diminishes one of the survival options of foreign women who may have limited access to jobs generally. Prostitution is tolerated for foreign women in many countries while regular labor market jobs are less so—this is the case for instance in the Netherlands and in Switzerland. According to IOM data, the number of migrant women prostitutes in many European Union countries is far higher than that for nationals: 75 percent in Germany, 80 percent in the case of Milan in Italy.

As tourism has grown sharply over the last decade and become a major development strategy for cities, regions and whole countries, the entertainment sector has seen a parallel growth and recognition as a key development strategy (Judd and Fainstein 1999). In many places, the sex trade is part of the entertainment industry and has similarly grown (Bishop and Robinson 1998; Booth 1999). At some point it becomes clear that the sex trade itself can become a development strategy in areas with high unemployment and poverty and governments desperate for revenue and foreign exchange reserves. When local manufacturing and agriculture can no longer function as sources of employment, of profits and of government revenue, what was once a marginal source of earnings, profits and revenues, now becomes a far more important one. The increased importance of these sectors in development generates growing tie-ins. For instance, when the IMF and the World Bank see tourism as a solution to some of the growth challenges in many poor countries and provide loans for its development or expansion, they may well be contributing to develop a broader institutional setting for the expansion of the entertainment industry and indirectly of the sex trade. This tie-in with development strategies signals that trafficking in women may well see a sharp expansion.

The entry of organized crime in the sex trades, the formation of cross-border ethnic networks, and the growing transnationalization in so many aspects of tourism, suggests that we are likely to see a further development of a global sex industry. This could mean greater attempts to enter into more and more "markets" and a general expansion of the industry. It is a worrisome possibility especially in the context of growing numbers of women with few if any employment options. And such growing numbers are to be expected given high unemployment and poverty, the shrinking of a world of work opportunities that were embedded in the more traditional sectors of these economies, and the growing debt burden of governments rendering them incapable of providing social services and support to the poor.

Women in the sex industry become—in certain kinds of economies—a crucial link supporting the expansion of the entertainment industry and thereby of tourism as a development strategy, which in turn becomes a source of government revenue. These tie-ins are structural, not a function of conspiracies. Their weight in an economy will be raised by the absence or limitations of other sources for securing a livelihood, profits and revenues for respectively workers, enterprises, and governments.

Conclusion

We are seeing the growth of a variety of alternative global circuits for making a living, making profit, and securing government revenue. These circuits incorporate increasing numbers of women. Among the most important of these global circuits are the illegal trafficking in women for prostitution as well as for regular work, organized exports of women as brides, nurses and domestic servants, and the remittances sent back to their home countries by an increasingly female emigrant workforce. Some of these circuits operate partly or wholly in the shadow economy.

The chapter mapped some of the main features of these circuits and argued that their emergence and/or strengthening is linked to major dynamics of economic globalization which have had significant impacts on developing economies. Key indicators of such impacts are the heavy and rising burden of government debt, the growth in unemployment, sharp cuts in government social expenditures, the closure of a large number of firms in often fairly traditional sectors oriented to the local or national market, and the promotion of export-oriented growth.

I call these circuits countergeographies of globalization because they are i) directly or indirectly associated with some of the key programs and conditions that are at the heart of the global economy, but ii) are circuits not typically represented or seen as connected to globalization, and often actually operate outside and in violation of laws and treaties, yet are not exclusively embedded in criminal operations as is the case with the illegal drug trade. Further, the growth of a global economy has brought with it an institutional infrastructure that facilitates cross-border flows and represents, in that regard, an enabling environment for these alternative circuits.

It is increasingly on the backs of women that these forms of survival, profit-making and government revenue enhancement operate. To this we can add the additional government revenue through savings due to severe cuts in health care and education. These cuts are often part of the effort of making the state more competitive as demanded by Structural Adjustment Programs and other policies linked to the current phase of globalization. These types of cuts are generally recognized as hitting women particularly hard insofar as women are responsible for the health and education of household members.

These countergeographies lay bare the systemic connections between, on the one hand, the mostly poor and low-wage women often represented as a burden rather than a resource, and, on the other hand, what are emerging as significant sources for illegal profit-making and as an important source of hard currency for governments. Linking these countergeographies to programs and conditions at the heart of the global economy also helps us understand how gendering enters into their formation and viability.

Notes

1. This is an abridged version of the original publication in Lucas (2005). It is part of the author's larger multi-year project recently published as *Territory, Authority, Rights: From Medieval to Global Assemblages*, Princeton University Press 2006.

2. For instance, the Coalition Against Trafficking in Women has centers and representatives in Australia, Bangladesh, Europe, Latin America, North America, Africa, and Asia Pacific. The Women's Rights Advocacy Program has established the Initiative

Against Trafficking in Persons to combat the global trade in persons. Other organizations are referred to throughout this article.

References

Alarcon-Gonzalez, Diana and Terry McKinley. 1999. "The Adverse Effects Of Structural Adjustment On Working Women In Mexico." *Latin American Perspectives* 26(3): 103–117.

Altink, Sietske. 1995. *Stolen Lives: Trading Women into Sex and Slavery*. London: Scarlet Press.

Ambroggi, Thomas. 1999. "Jubilee 2000 And The Campaign For Debt Cancellation." *National Catholic Reporter* (July).

Anon. u.d. "Brides From the Philippines." Available at www.geocities.co.jp/Milkyway-Kaigan/5501/ph7.html.

Bandarage, Asoka. 1997. *Women, Population, and Crisis*. London: Zed.

Bello, Walden. 1998. *A Siamese Tragedy: Development and Disintegration in Modern Thailand*. London: Zed.

Benería, Lourdes and Shelley Feldman. eds. 1992. *Unequal Burden: Economic Crises, Persistent Poverty, and Women's Work*. Boulder CO: Westview.

Bonacich, Edna, Lucie Cheng, Norma Chinchilla, Nora Hamilton, and Paul Ong. eds. 1994. *Global Production: The Apparel Industry in the Pacific Rim*. Philadelphia: Temple University Press.

Bonilla, Frank, Melendez, Edwin, Morales, Rebecca, and Torres, Maria de los Angeles. eds. 1998. *Borderless Borders*. Philadelphia: Temple University Press.

Booth, William. 1999. "Thirteen Charged In Gang Importing Prostitutes." *Washington Post* August 21.

Bose, Christine E. and Edna Acosta-Belen. eds. *Women in the Latin American Development Process: From Structural Subordination to Empowerment*. Philadelphia: Temple University Press.

Boserup, E. 1970. *Woman's Role in Economic Development*. New York: St. Martin's Press.

Bradshaw, York, Rita Noonan, Laura Gash, and Claudia Buchmann. 1993. "Borrowing Against The Future: Children And Third World Indebtedness." *Social Forces* 71 (3): 629–656.

Buchler, Simone. 2007. "Women in the informal economy of Sao Paulo." In Saskia Sassen. ed. *Deciphering Globalization*. New York and London: Routledge.

Buchmann, Claudia. 1996. "The Debt Crisis, Structural Adjustment And Women's Education." *International Journal of Comparative Studies* 37 (1–2): 5–30.

Castles, Stephen and Mark J. Miller. 1998. *The Age of Migration: International Population Movements in the Modern World*. 2nd ed. New York: Macmillan.

Castro, Max. ed. 1999. *Free Markets, Open Societies, Closed Borders?* Miami: University of Miami—North-South Center Press.

Catagay, Nilufer and Sule Ozler. 1995. "Feminisation Of The Labour Force: The Effects Of Long-Term Development And Structural Adjustment." *World Development* 23(11): 1883–1894.

Chant, Sylvia. ed. 1992. *Gender and Migration in Developing Countries*. London and New York: Belhaven Press.

Chant, Sylvia and Nikki Kraske. 2002. "Gender in Latin America." Rutgers, NJ: Rutgers University Press.

Chossudovsky, Michel. 1997. *The Globalisation of Poverty*. London: Zed/TWN.

Chin, Christine. 1997. "Walls Of Silence And Late 20th Century Representations Of Foreign Female Domestic Workers: The Case Of Filipina And Indonesian House Servants In Malaysia." *International Migration Review* 31(1): 353–385.

Chuang, Janie. 1998. "Redirecting the Debate over Trafficking in Women: Definitions, Paradigms, and Contexts." *Harvard Human Rights Journal* 11:65–107.

Coalition to Abolish Slavery and Trafficking. *Annual Factsheet. Available at* www.traffickedwomen.org/fact.html.

Coalition Against Trafficking in Women. *Annual Reports.* Various Years.

Copjec, Joan, and Michael Sorkin. eds. 1999. *Giving Ground.* London: Verso.

David, Natacha. 1999. "Migrants Made The Scapegoats Of The Crisis." *ICFTU Online.* International Confederation of Free Trade Unions. Available at www.hartford-hwp.com/archives/50/012.html.

Deere, C. D. 1976."Rural Women's Subsistence Production In The Capitalist Periphery." *Review of Radical Political Economy* 8 (1): 9–17.

Elson, Diane. 1995. *Male Bias in Development.* 2nd ed. Manchester: University of Manchester Press.

Enloe, Cynthia. 1988. *Bananas, Beaches, and Bases.* California: University of California Press.

Eisenstein, Zillah. 1996. "Stop Stomping On The Rest Of Us: Retrieving Public-ness From The Privatisation Of The Globe." In *Special Symposium on Feminism and Globalization: The Impact of The Global Economy on Women and Feminist Theory,* Indiana *Journal of Global Legal Studies* vol. 1: 59–95.

Global Survival Network. 1997. "Crime and Servitude: An Expose of the Traffic in Women for Prostitution from the Newly Independent States." Available at *www.globalsurvival.net/femaletrade.html* (November).

Heyzer, Noeleen. 1994. *The Trade in Domestic Workers.* London: Zed.

Hondagneu-Sotelo, Pierrette. 1994. *Gendered Transitions.* Berkeley: University of California Press.

Hondagneu-Sotelo, Pierrette. ed. 2003. "Gender and U.S. Immigration: Contemporary Trends." Los Angeles: University of California Press.

Indiana Journal of Global Legal Studies. *Special Symposium on Feminism and Globalisation: The Impact of The Global Economy on Women and Feminist Theory* 4 (1). Fall

IOM (International Migration Office). Annual Quarterly, Various Years. *Trafficking in Migrants.* (Quarterly Bulletin). Geneva: IOM.

Ismi, Asad. 1998. "Plunder with a Human Face." *Z Magazine* (February).

Jones, Erika. 1999. "The Gendered Toll Of Global Debt Crisis." *Sojourner* 25(3): 20–38.

Judd, Dennis and Susan Fainstein. 1999. *The Tourist City.* New Haven, CT: Yale University Press.

Kabria, Nazli. 1993. *Family Tightrope.* Princeton: Princeton University Press.

Kempadoo, Kamala and Jo Doezema. 1998. *Global Sex Workers: Rights, Resistance, and Redefinition.* London: Routledge.

Knop, Karen. 1993. "Re/Statements: Feminism and State Sovereignty in International Law." *Transnational Law and Contemporary Problems.* vol 3 p. 293–344.

Khotari, Uma. 2006. *A Radical History of Development Studies: Individuals, Institutions and Ideologies.* London: Zed Books.

Lim, Lin. 1998. *The Sex Sector: The Economic and Social Bases of Prostitution in Southeast Asia.* Geneva: International Labour Office.

Lin, Lap-Chew and Marjan Wijerns. 1997. *Trafficking In Women, Forced Labour And Slavery-Like Practices In Marriage, Domestic Labour And Prostitution.* Utrecht: Foundation Against Trafficking in Women (STV), and Bangkok: Global Alliance Against Traffic in Women (GAATW).

Lucas, Linda E. ed. 2005. *Unpacking Globalization: Markets, Gender, and Work.* Kampala, Uganda: Gendered World Series.

Mahler, Sarah. 1995. *American Dreaming: Immigrant Life on the Margins.* Princeton, NJ: Princeton University Press.

Malkki, Liisa H. 1995. "Refugees and Exile: From 'Refugee Studies' to the National Order of Things" *Annual Review of Anthropology* 24: 495–523.

Mehra, Rekha. 1997. "Women, Empowerment And Economic Development." *Annals of the American Academy of Political and Social Science,* (November): 136–149.

Moghadam, Valentine M. 2005. *Globalizing Women: Transnational Feminist Networks.* Baltimore: The Johns Hopkins University Press.

Morokvasic, Mirjana. 1984. Special Issue on Women Immigrants, *International Migration Review* 18 (4).

Moser, Carolyn. 1989. "The Impact Of Recession And Structural Adjustment Policies At The Micro-Level: Low Income Women And Their Households in Guayaquil, Ecuador." *Invisible Adjustment* vol. 2. UNICEF.

Naples, Nancy A. and Manisha Desai. eds. 2002. *Women's Activism and Globalization: Linking Local Struggles and Transnational Politics.* New York and London: Routledge.

Nash, June. 2005. *Social Movements: An Anthropological Reader.* Malden, MA: Blackwell.

Olds, Kris, Peter Dicken, Phillip F. Kelly, Lilly Kong, and Henry Wai-Chung Yeung eds. 1999. *Globalization and the Asian Pacific: Contested Territories.* London: Routledge.

Ong, Aihwa. 1996. "Globalisation and Women's Rights: The Asian Debate on Citizenship and Communitarianism." In *Special Symposium on Feminism and Globalisation: The Impact of The Global Economy on Women and Feminist Theory, Indiana Journal of Global Legal Studies.* vol. 4, no. 1.

OXFAM. 1999. *"International Submission to the HIPC Debt Review."* April. Available at www.caa.org/au/oxfam/advocacy/debt/hipcreview.html.

Parrenas, Rhacel Salazar. ed. 2001. *Servants of Globalization: Women, Migration and Domestic Workers.* Stanford, CA: Stanford University Press.

Pessar, P. R. and S. J. Mahler. 2003. "Transnational Migration: Bringing Gender In." *International Migration Review.* vol. 37 no 3: 812–846.

Peterson, V. Spike. ed. 1992. *Gendered States: Feminist (Re)Visions of International Relations Theory.* Boulder CO: Lynne Reinner Publishers.

Pyle, Jean L. and Kathryn Ward. 2003. "Recasting our Understanding of Gender and Work During Global Restructuring." *International Sociology* 18(3): 461–89.

Rahman, Aminur. 1999. "Micro-Credit Initiatives For Equitable And Sustainable Development: Who Pays?" *World Development* 27(1): 67–82.

Ribas-Mateos, Natalia. 2005. *The Mediterranean In The Age Of Globalization: Migration, Welfare, And Borders.* Somerset, NJ: Transaction.

Safa, Helen. 1995. *The Myth of the Male Breadwinner: Women and Industrialization in the Caribbean.* Boulder CO: Westview.

Sassen, Saskia. 2006a. *Territory, Authority, Rights: From Medieval to Global Assemblages.* Princeton, NJ: Princeton University Press.

———. 2006b. *Cities in a World Economy.* 3rd ed. Thousand Oaks, CA: Sage/Pine Forge.

———. 2001. *The Global City: New York, London, Tokyo.* (New Updated ed.). Princeton, NJ: Princeton University Press.

———. 1999. *Guests and Aliens.* New York: New Press.

———. 1998. *Globalization and its Discontents: Essays on the Mobility of People and Money.* New York: New Press.

————. 1988 *The Mobility of Labor and Capital*. Cambridge: Cambridge University Press.

Shannon, Susan. 1999. "The Global Sex Trade: Humans as the Ultimate Commodity." *Crime and Justice International*, p. 5–25. May

Smith, Joan and Immanuel Wallerstein. eds. 1992. *Creating And Transforming Housholds, The Constraints Of The World-Economy*. Cambridge and Paris: Cambridge University Press and Maison des Sciences de l'Homme.

Standing, Guy. 1999. "Global Feminization Through Flexible Labor: A Theme Revisited." *World Development* 27(3): 583–602.

Tinker, Irene. ed. 1990. *Persistent Inequalities: Women and World Development*. New York: Oxford University Press.

Toussaint, Eric. 1999. "Poor Countries Pay More Under Debt Reduction Scheme?" July, Available at www.twnside.org.sg/souths/twn/title/1921-cn.htm.

United Nations Development Programme (UNDP). 2005. "A Time For Bold Ambition: Together We Can Cut Poverty in Half." In *UNDP Annual Report 2005*. Geneva: United Nations.

Ward, Kathryn. 1991. *Women Workers and Global Restructuring*. Ithaca, NY: Cornell University Press.

————. 1999. "Women and The Debt." Paper presented at the Colloquium on Globalization and the Debt. Emory University (Atlanta).

Ward, Kathryn and Jean Pyle. 1995. "Gender, Industrialization and Development." In *Global Economic Prospects: Economic Implications of Remittances and Migration*. Washington, D. C.: The World Bank.

Yamamoto, Satomi. 2006. "Habituating Migration: The Role of Intermediary in the Case of Filipina Nurses' Migration to the U.S." Urbana-Champaign, IL: University of Illinois. Unpublished Manuscript.

Yeoh, Brenda, Shirlena Huang, and Joaquin Gonzalez III. 1999. "Migrant Female Domestic Workers: Debating The Economic, Social And Political Impacts In Singapore." *International Migration Review* 33(1): 114–136.

Chapter 4

Globalization, Structural Adjustment and Women's Transnational Solidarities

Manisha Desai

In this chapter, I examine how global capital, structural adjustment programs (SAPs) and international institutions such as the United Nations (UN) have shaped women's agency around the world. I begin with the gendered effects of SAPs and then discuss women's transnational organizing around economic and health issues raised by SAPs and around UN conferences.

The Gendered Effects of Structural Adjustment Politics

SAPs are the primary mechanism through which globalization has impacted women's daily lives in the South. In the North, similar effects resulted from economic restructuring of manufacturing and neoliberal policies that emphasize privatization in all aspects of the political economy. SAPs were first engineered by the International Monetary Fund (IMF) and the World Bank. Sean Riain (2000) argues that globalization has imposed the dominant Anglo-American neoliberal model of the relationship between state and transnational capital, on-neoliberal, socialist, and postcolonial states. Hence, most states have adopted a package that shares some variant of the following features:

1) cutbacks in public spending to balance government budgets and service debts; 2) monetary policies designed to fight inflation by restricting the money

supply (and incomes); 3) the selling of government enterprises (privatization) in an attempt to balance government budgets and improve business production efficiency; and, 4) the shift of manufacturing and agricultural sectors toward production for export instead of the domestic market, in order to improve international balances (Wiegersma 1997: 258).

The basic argument scholars have made about the impact of SAPs on women worldwide is that "adjustment intensifies the trade-off between women's producer and non-producer roles, or, in stronger terms, that the 'crisis of social disinvestment (under adjustment) is financed from a "social fund" provided by the superhuman efforts of poor women'" (Baden 1997: 38).

These policies have had three major effects on women. First, there has been a contradictory impact on women's paid work. There has been a feminization of the global labor force and an increase in women's employment in the low paid service sector (Fuentes and Ehrenreich 1983; Nash and Fernandez-Kelly 1983; Ward 1990). This is evident in the increasing rate of women's share of paid economic activity all over the South and the North. In 2000, women comprised 36percent of the total global work force. Second, there has been an increase in women's employment in the informal sector where workers receive no protections from unemployment, no benefits and below poverty wages. Third, women's share of unpaid labor in the home has increased as public funding for health, education and other social services has declined. Women in the North and South have responded to each of these impacts in multiple ways leading to what are best called scattered resistance.

Women's Organizing Against SAPs

In this section, I discuss some examples of women's organizing around economic and health issues. While overt unionizing was, and still remains, difficult in the Export Processing Zones (EPZs), transnational solidarity networks have grown to post a significant challenge to SAPs and other neo-liberal policies. These networks include unions, movements and non-governmental organizations (NGOs) of local women working in the EPZs as well as middle class activists. Activist networks are often supported by public consciousness-raising efforts that are mainly located in the Northern countries and whose focus is educating Northern consumers. Many NGOs include consumer education as part of their advocacy work on behalf of maquiladora workers and other low waged workers in the "global assembly line." For example, Women Working Worldwide in the United Kingdom is an international coalition that highlights the impact of trade liberalization on women workers in Bangladesh, India, Korea, Mexico, Peru, South Korea, Thailand and the U.K. through networking and public education. The Clean Clothes Campaign based in the Netherlands supports the struggles of women workers in garment producing units, sweatshops, factories and home-based industry for improved working conditions in the South and North by making the European public aware of the situation. Label Behind the

Label is a similar effort based in the U.K. to promote the rights and working conditions of women workers in the garment industries around the world.

In addition to activist networks, many academic and policy-oriented international groups work together with NGOs around the world to contextualize the oppressive features of global economic restructuring. Groups like DAWN (Development Alternatives With Women for a New Era) and Women's Alternative Economic Summit focus on research and policy through developing regional centers in Latin America, Asia and Africa. While the local and transnational networks focus on women in the global economy, most women find themselves in the so-called informal sector where the struggle is to assert a right to work.

Over the globe, 71 percent of women's work is in the less visible informal sector where they prepare products for sale in the market, domestic service and work in their homes to produce goods for sub-contractors (Benería and Feldman 1992; SEWA 1998; Ward 1990). Although such work is unregulated, poorly paid and involves long hours, it plays a crucial role in maintaining a modicum of livelihood for most poor women in a post-structural adjustment world. In fact, the World Bank and other development agencies like the U.S. Agency for International Development (USAID) have celebrated and supported the micro-credit movement.

Women have been at the forefront of showing the relationship of their informal work and unpaid household labor to the formal economy. The Self Employed Women's Association (SEWA) in India was one of the first organizations that defined the various informal activities such as vegetable vending, rag picking and producing goods at home for sale as work. Established in 1972, SEWA successfully unionized informal women workers who had been prevented from organizing unions because trade union laws in India did not recognize them as workers. In addition to unionizing, women in India have formed cooperatives based on their various economic activities in order to market effectively, share resources and form support networks. Most importantly, SEWA has trained community health workers and set up a SEWA university to train women not just in production and managerial skills but to be leaders and organizers who can participate in decisions that impact their lives. SEWA now has close to two million members in cities throughout India as well as rural areas in Gujarat. The focus of women in SEWA is to develop a critical understanding of the economy, gender and social relations and use that knowledge to address social inequalities and their effects such as religious violence among Hindus and Muslims.

Similarly women working in the informal economies in Tanzania, Ghana, Zimbabwe, Ecuador and Peru, among other countries, have formed networks to pool resources, start savings and credit associations and form solidarities for survival (Bose and Acosta-Belen 1995; Osirim 1996; Rowbotham and Mitter 1994). In addition to local networks, self-employed women, like their counterparts in the EPZs, have also formed transnational networks such as GROOTS (Grassroots Organizations Operating Together in Sisterhood) International, primarily to learn new ideas, share best practices and influence local and international policy making around informal sector issues.

The absence of women's unpaid work and informal labor from national statistics continues to be a concern for feminist activists. The Beijing Declaration and Platform For Action generated in the context of the World Women's Conference in 1995 affirmed the need to count women's work in the home and remunerate women for that work, but most countries have not taken any serious steps in that direction. To highlight this non-compliance, women in Ireland called a Women's Strike on March 8, 1999, demanding an end to the devaluation of women's waged and unwaged labor. Since then the strike has become global as women from sixty-four countries observed it in 2000. It has also been taken up by the International Wages for Housework Campaign and International Women Count Network.

Other women's groups have organized in urban and rural areas to provide and demand health services from the state. However, many of these services are being dismantled or privatized. Women and children are the main users of health services and women are the primary providers of health care. If health is taken to mean, in accordance with the World Health Organization (WHO), a "state of complete physical, mental, and social well-being," then women's health has deteriorated in all respects in the contemporary era of global trade.

Starting in the early 1980s, the World Bank promoted a series of health-related initiatives to pressure Third World governments to control population growth. The Bank recommended universal measures for reform that did not take into consideration Third World women's economic, social or cultural realities. These initiatives emphasized privatization of health care to be understood as: introduction of user charges in state health facilities, especially for consumer drugs and curative care (the rationale was that the rich of a particular country would be made to pay, thus leaving the government free to pay for community services and public health for the poor); promotion of third party insurance such as sickness funds and social security; promotion of private facilities and clinics; and decentralization of planning, budgeting and purchasing for government health services (Turshen 1994). Such privatization recommendations are especially problematic in countries where the people already assume a greater share of health care burden than in First World countries. In the latter, especially Scandinavian countries, governments assume over 90 percent of health expenditure. By contrast, in Sub-Saharan Africa and Asia, governments only contribute about 52–57 percent towards the total health budget (Turshen 1994).

Women responded to declining health services by developing community-based health projects, making demands on the state to be more accountable and linking with groups around the country and the world to influence national and international policies. In India, groups like the Centre for Enquiry Into Health and Allied Themes (CEHAT) are at the forefront of providing services to women and also researching and providing critiques of the impact of SAPs on women's health. The acronym CEHAT also means health in several Indian languages. Studies by CEHAT reveal that the state has never committed more than 3.5percent of its GNP to the health sector (CEHAT 1995). This small percentage has further eroded since the 1970s and reached a low of 2.6 percent in 1994–1995, at the peak of the liberalization effort. The public health expenditure's share in the national income since SAPs is only 0.95 percent. Most of the health budget comes from the state and not the national government. At the individual level, the studies found that given the paucity of public health availability, 80 percent of health care costs come out of people's own pockets.

In addition to research, CEHAT's service strategy is based on activists living in urban and rural poor communities and developing health education and primary health care projects alongside the people in the communities. Many CEHAT members are founders of the second wave of the women's movement in India. Through their effort, they have incorporated a feminist perspective into the health debates and have added a concern for health to the women's movement agenda. CEHAT's assumption is that health care can only be possible in a context of economic and social equality and justice. Hence, CEHAT has worked with local women to form village level women's health teams, to establish a bank run by women and to provide training for health work.

In addition to community-based work, CEHAT has formed a national level network called HealthWatch: A Network for Action and Research on Women's Health. Its major objective is to increase the attention paid to women's health needs and concerns in public debates and national policy. HealthWatch has begun a dialogue with the government at various levels. For example, in 1998 it brought together activists from the western region of India to discuss a new government initiative known as a "target-free" approach to population policy. This initiative provides for a more woman-centered approach to reproduction, and quotas that the local health practitioners had to meet for population control have been eliminated. In the CEHAT-sponsored regional meeting, activists critically analyzed the new initiative and worked out ways possibly to link to primary care activities at the community level.

CEHAT is also part of international networks such as the International Network of Health and Human Rights Organizations, ISIS International, the Women's Global Network on Reproductive Rights and the International Women's Tribune Centre. It was the mobilizing efforts initiated by such international networks that led to the presence of many women's health NGOs like CEHAT at the Cairo Population Conference in 1994. The declaration from the population conference in Cairo, which emphasized the need to empower women and protect their human rights as the best strategy for population control, was an important victory for the international women's movement. It affirmed women's right to determine their reproductive rights despite the efforts of the Vatican and other religious fundamentalist organizations to reverse women's reproductive rights.

Women's Transnational Organizing Around the UN

International women's networks and transnational organizing date back to the middle of the nineteenth century when women from the U.S. and Europe came together around anti-slavery efforts (Rupp 1997). At the turn of the twentieth century women from Europe, the U.S. and India joined to fight colonization. In the early part of the twentieth century women from Europe and the U.S. lobbied the newly formed League of Nations and the Pan American Organization to lay the groundwork for what was to become the UN Charter and the Universal Declaration of Human Rights. One of the major differences between earlier transnational activism and current efforts is the scope and the variety of actors engaged in it.

The U.N. declared International Women's Year in 1975, with a focus on equality, development and peace. The last focus was added by the delegations of Greece and Guatemala who felt that women's role in peace and disarmament should be recognized and furthered. The Year was highlighted by the First Women's World Conference in Mexico City in 1975. Two thousand delegates from 133 countries, of which women headed 113, attended the conference. Around six thousand women and men from NGOs attended the parallel International Women's Year Tribune, which had been organized following similar gatherings of NGOs at the 1972 World Conference on the Human Environment and the 1974 Bucharest Population Conference. The Mexico City Tribune was unique in its scope and intensity. It was dubbed history's largest consciousness-raising session (UN 1997). Women gathered from around the world to share experiences. For many, it was a transforming experience as they interacted and engaged women in dialogue—around common and divergent issues. This level of engagement was possible because of the emergence of the second wave of women's movements in many countries of the North and South.

Not only did this focus the world's attention on women, but it also enabled women from around the world to come together. The conference adopted a World Plan of Action on the Equality of Women and their Contribution to Development and Peace. There were regional follow-up meetings held throughout Africa, Asia, and the Pacific regions. The UN subsequently declared 1975–1985 the International Women's Decade, with international conferences to be held in 1980 in Copenhagen and in 1985 in Nairobi. The International Women's Decade marked the third phase of the UN's efforts for women. The decade promoted and legitimized the already growing international women's movement and really marked the beginning of the transnational feminist solidarities that have come to characterize women's agency in the global era.

The most enduring impact and contribution of the decade was its facilitation of transnational solidarities. Prior to each world conference there were local, national, and regional-level meetings that led to the formation of many local and national grassroots groups as well as international NGOs that wanted to participate in the process. While the world conferences were limited to formal governmental delegations from each country, the NGO Fora, which were organized parallel to each World Conference, provided the opportunity for women from around the world to meet and discuss women's issues. Approximately six thousand women met at the Mexico City Tribune in 1975, fifteen thousand women attended the Nairobi Conference in 1985, and at least thirty thousand women convened in Beijing in 1995.

These world conferences and their accompanying NGO Fora, however, were highly contentious occasions (Desai 1996). For example, most Third World women's groups and governments were still influenced by the nationalist rhetoric that had informed their freedom struggles. The decolonization of most countries in Africa and Asia following the end of WWII, together with the Cold War between the U.S. and the USSR, shaped the sensibilities of governments as well as women's groups. The postcolonial states were defined in opposition to the Western colonial empire. In this context, women were constituted as the bearers of tradition and posed against the modernizing influence of the colonial powers. Such self-understanding was further consolidated as Western women cast Third World women as the oppressed "other" of their more liberated selves (Mohanty 1991; Spivak 1987; Trinh 1989). Therefore, early encounters between so-called First World and Third World women were strained.

The conferences in Mexico City and Copenhagen were particularly volatile (Basu 2000; Desai 1995; Peters and Wolpert 1995). Women from India, Brazil, Palestine and other Third World countries, based on their own anti-colonial struggles and assumptions of the role of the West, challenged First World feminists' claims that women were universally oppressed due to their gender and that "sisterhood was global." They countered that for women in the Third World, class, nationality, race/ethnicity and religion intersected with gender in both oppressing them and providing spaces for liberation. Some of the differences among women at these world conferences also reflected the geopolitical tensions of the time. For example, two of the most heated issues were, first, whether Israel was racist in its relationship to Palestinians, and second, the role of the West in perpetuating neo-colonial strategies.

Such critical confrontations were resolved not by the force of the better argument but by the reciprocal recognition of the validity of various claims. This recognition, in turn, was fuelled by women's grassroots organizing around the various issues. The breakthrough for transnational solidarities came at the Nairobi conference in 1985, where because of its location, there was a real presence of women from Africa and Asia. The timing of the conference, at the end of the International Decade, when women from all parts of the world had a chance to interact for a decade contributed to the recognition that women's issues are manifest differently in different societies and require varied and multiple strategies of liberation. In addition, Third World women were able to show First World women their own privilege and complicity in the oppression of women in the Third World. Learning about the common goals of freedom, justice and equality variously defined, and of apparently different women's movements around the world inspired "reflective solidarity" among women who otherwise were on different sides of the north/south, left/liberal, white/black, lesbian/straight, feminist/non-feminist divide.

The breakthrough in women's transnational solidarities at Nairobi, and later in Beijing, was also a result of other social forces playing out in their respective locales (Desai 1996). For example, in the U.S. and United Kingdom, women of color were challenging the white feminist understanding of the category "women" and introducing race, class and sexuality as among the factors destabilizing "sisterhood." In the Third World countries, the postcolonial governments based on constitutional equality for women were still defining women in circumscribed roles in nation building. The rise of religious fundamentalisms, which defined women only as culture bearers, further sharpened women's feminist consciousness. Such larger social forces as well as the ongoing encounters among women enabled them to create solidarities based not on preconceived identities but on historically specific circumstances of the global economy that were constraining the lives of women around the world. This mutual understanding was further consolidated in Beijing in 1995 where the collapse of the Soviet Union and the consolidation of the global economy had enabled a framing of issues in terms other than the nationalist, First World/Third World terms of earlier decades. It was at this conference that human rights discourse became the language for demanding women's rights. Thus, the third phase of the UN's efforts helped catapult transnational women's networks and brought women into the center stage of world politics. The networks established during the decade became the basis for solidarity and action in the current phase of the UN's work, from 1986 to present. It was very clear to everyone at the end of the Decade that despite the energy and optimism the Decade had failed to achieve the goals of sustained progress for a majority of women. The 1990s posed a further challenge to women's equality as capitalist expansion and political displacement further interfered with women's social, economic and political empowerment. In response, the UN declared a series of world conferences in the 1990s that were to measure the success of its various efforts in the previous decades, particularly around issues of women's rights, human rights, population, development and the environment.

This last phase demonstrates the power of women's transnational solidarities. The World Environmental Conference in 1992 in Rio, the World Human Rights Conference in 1993, the Population Conference in Cairo in 1994, the World Summit for Social Development in 1995 and the World Women's Conference in Beijing in 1995 all capitalized on the networks women had established during the previous decades. Women's NGOs were at the forefront of these world conferences. For example, in preparation for Vienna in 1993, the Center for Women's Global Leadership, based at Rutgers University in the U.S., helped to coordinate a Global Campaign For Women's Human Rights. In 1991, the Center organized a leadership institute where women from all over the world explored linkages between human rights, women's rights and violence against women. Women organized on both Human Rights Day and the International Day Against Violence Against Women to generate a petition drive calling on the World Human Rights Conference to "comprehensively address women's human rights at every level of its proceedings" and to recognize gender-based violence as a "violation of human rights requiring immediate action" (Bunch and Reilly 1994). The petition received three hundred thousand signatures from fifty countries and was signed by eight hundred organizations when it was delivered to the World Conference.

At the World Human Rights Conference, women's groups were the most organized and vocal. They held over sixty workshops, seminars and lectures at the fora specifically on women's human rights. They held over the Conference and coined the now famous slogan: "Human Rights are Women's Rights and Women's Rights are Human Rights," popularized by Hillary Rodham Clinton at

Beijing in 1995. Similarly, the international conferences at Rio, Copenhagen and Cairo were occasions for women's transnational networks to influence the agenda and policies of the UN and its member states. They also provided additional opportunities for women's groups from around the world to network and forge more strategies for action. According to Alvarez (2000), this activism embodies the "transnational IGO (Intergovernmental Organizations)-advocacy logic" which is focused on influencing the policy arena. Since these transnational IGOs are dominated by northern feminist non-government organizations, they have a contradictory impact at the local level (Friedberg 1999; Sandberg 1998). However, most women who participated at the NGO Forums of these conferences were more interested in what Alvarez (2000) has described as "international identity-solidarity logic." Women's NGOs at the world conferences adopted two different strategies (Clark, Freidman, and Hochstetler 1998). The more prominent national and international groups tended to caucus to influence the agenda setting of the world conferences and the UN bodies, while the vast majority of the NGOs focused on sharing information and experiences and networking for collaborative action in the future.

It is this last phase of the UN's efforts for women which helped cement the nature of women's agency in the global era. Women's networks have now taken over the review processes following the world conferences, namely the Beijing Plus 5, Copenhagen Plus 5, and Cairo Plus 5, to assess what has been achieved and to make their governments accountable for their international agreements. Women's groups have learned to negotiate the national and international arenas. However, as Basu (2000) argues, transnational activism around women's political and civil rights is much more likely to succeed than similar activism around economic rights. This stems in great measure from the dominance of these forms of rights claims in the West as opposed to the second generation of rights.

While transnational solidarities among women have grown, they are not without problems. These solidarities often reproduce existing inequalities. For example, women from the North and educated women from the South are more dominant in the international networks and NGOs than grassroots women. Of the thirty thousand women present at Beijing over eight thousand women were from the U.S. alone. Furthermore, as Basu (2000) argues, transnational activism creates divisions at the national level between the elites who belong to such networks and the vast majority of grassroots women who don't.

Another problematic aspect of the transnational solidarities is the continuing reliance of women and NGOs of the South on Northern donors and funders. The Ford Foundation, in particular, has been responsible for supporting a great deal of such transactional activism (Alvarez 1999; Basu 2000). Many Northern groups are aware of this and have made attempts to make their Southern partners more independent by enabling them to look for sustainable alternatives. In addition, other Northern NGOs are actively engaged in understanding and publicizing the ways in which Northern women's consumerism implicates them in global inequalities, for example, Label Behind the Label and Clean Clothes Campaign.

Alvarez (2000: 33) has identified yet another problem with transnational solidarities, namely the contradictions between the two different kinds of transnational logics, the internationalist identity-solidarity logic, and the transnational IGO-advocacy logic. According to her, the former logic is guided by identity, reciprocity, affinity, complementarily and substitutionism and has a very benign impact on local progressive politics. Transnational IGO advocacy, by contrast, is guided by experts with special skills shaping international gender policy. While Alvarez acknowledges that these two logics can work in tandem, she is concerned about the contradictions. I think that as with all binaries, this one, too, overstates the differences and selectively highlights contradictions of one logic while understating those of the other logic.

Conclusion

Research by academics, policymakers and various UN agencies overwhelmingly shows that women and children have suffered disproportionately as a result of global economic restructuring (e.g., Afshar and Dennis 1992; Blank 1997; Naples 1998; Visvanathan et. al. 1997). Policies associated with economic restructuring use existing patriarchal assumptions such as the definition of women's labor and women's endurance abilities, and therefore reproduce inequalities. Furthermore, women are considered only as economic agents rather than central political actors on the global stage. Globalization has reduced women's enjoyment of livelihoods with security and dignity around the world. The U.N.'s perspective is that the negative impacts of the policies are short-term. There is in addition a gendered division in the implementation policies of international institutions. The IMF and the World Bank institute structural adjustment policies while UN agencies facilitate legal and cultural changes that would allow women access to the new market forces. The flaw in this analysis is that it misses the gendered nature of most economic policies.

Women have organized in response to the hegemonies of global capital. Their new political presence has been defined alternatively as "global civil society" (Waterman 1998) or globalization from below (Falk 1999). While some analysts see these scattered counter hegemonies as ineffective against the hegemonizing presence of global capital (Sklair 1991) others celebrate the new global solidarities (Brecher et. al. 2000). As I have shown, however, the important point is that global capital is not unchallenged. Many resistance strategies embody a radical critique not just of global capital but also of pre-existing social inequalities based on race, class, gender, sexuality and nationality among others. Many activist women's efforts focus, to varying degrees and in various ways, on developing concrete economic alternatives based on sustainable development, social equality and participatory processes though such economic initiatives have not been as successful at the transnational level (Basu 2000). These "counter hegemonies" have succeeded in transforming the daily lives of many women at the local level. This, in my view, is what gives women's agency immense potential. Similarly, the transnational feminist solidarities, while they reproduce existing inequalities, are forged not on preconceived identities and experiences but in the context of struggle and as such are more reflexive about these inequalities. To what extent can these fluid, multiple, reflexive transnational feminist solidarities change the shape of the global political economy? As noted above in various works, there are both possibilities and limitations to these solidarities.

References

Afshar, Hale and Carline Dennis. 1992. *Women and Adjustment Policies in the Third World.* New York: St. Martins.

Alvarez, S. 1999. "Advocating Feminism: The Latin American Feminist NGO Boom." *International Feminist Journal of Politics* 1(2): 181–209.

———. 2000 "Translating the Global: Effects of Transnational Organizing on Local Feminist Discourses and Practices in Latin America." *Meridians* 1(1): 29–67.

Baden, Sally. 1997. "Recession and Structural Adjustment's Impact on Women's Work in Selected Developing Regions." In *Promoting Gender Equality At Work: Turning Vision Into Reality,* E. Dat-Bh. ed. London: Zed Books/ILO.

Basu, A. 2000. "Globalization of the Local/Localization of the Global: Mapping Transnational Women's Movements." *Meridians* 1(1): 68–84.

Benería, L. and S. Feldman. 1992. *Unequal Burdens: Economic Crises, Persistent Poverty, and Women's Work.* Boulder: Westview.

Blank, R. 1997. *It Takes A Nation.* Princeton: Princeton University Press.

Bose, C. E. and E. Acosta-Belen. eds. 1995. *Women in the Latin American Development Process.* Philadelphia: Temple University Press.

Brecher Jeremy, Tim Costello, and Brendan Smith. 2000. *Globalization From Below: The Power of Solidarity.* Boston: South End Press.

Bunch, C. and N. Reilly. 1994. *Demanding Accountability: The Global Campaign and Vienna Tribunal For Women's Rights.* New York: UNDP.

CEHAT. 1995. *Five Years of CEHAT 1991–1995.* Mumbai: CEHAT

Clark, A. E. Friedman, and K. Hochstetler. 1998. "The Sovereign Limits of Global Civil Society: A Comparison of NGO Participation in UN World Conferences on the Environment, Human Rights, and Women." *World Politics* 51(Oct.): 1–35.

Desai, M. 1995. "If Peasants Build Dams What Will the State Have Left to Do? Practices of New Social Movements in India." *Research in Social Movements, Conflict and Change* 19:203–218.

———. 1996. "From Vienna To Beijing: The International Women's Human Rights Movement." *New Political Science* 35 (spring): 107–119.

Falk, Richard. 1999. *Predatory Globalization: A Critique.* London: Blackwell.

Freidberg, Elizabeth. 1999. "The Effects of 'Transnationalism Reversed' in Venezuela: Assessing the Impact of UN Global Conferences on the Women's Movement." *International Journal of Politics* 1(3): 357–81.

Fuentes, A. and B. Ehrenreich.1983. *Women in the Global Factory.* INC Pamphlet No. 2. Boston: South End Press.

Mohanty, Chandra. 1991. "Under Western Eyes: Feminist Scholarship and Colonial Discourses." In *Third World Women and the Politics of Feminism*, C. Mohanty, A. Russo, and L. Torres. eds. Bloomington: Indiana University Press, p. 1–47.

Naples, Nancy. 1998. *Grassroots Warriors: Activist Mothering, Community Work, and the War on Poverty.* New York: Routledge.

Nash, June and M. P. Fernandez-Kelly. eds. 1983. *Women, Men, and The International Division of Labor.* Albany, NY: SUNY Press.

Osirim, M. 1996. "The Dilemmas of Modern Development: Structural Adjustment and Women Micro Entrepreneurs in Nigeria and Zimbabwe." In J. Turpin and L. Lorentzen eds. *The Gendered New World Order: Militarism, Development, and the Environment.* New York: Routledge.

Peters, J. and A. Wolper. Eds. 1995. *Women's Rights Human Rights: International Feminist Perspectives.* New York: Routledge.

Rowbotham, S. and S. Mitter. eds. 1994. *Dignity and Daily Bread.* London: Routledge.

Rupp, Leila J. 1997. *Worlds of Women: The Making of an International Women's Movement.* Princeton: Princeton University Press.

Sandberg, Eve. 1998. "Multilateral Women's Conferences: The Domestic Political Organization of Zambian Women." *Contemporary Politics* 4(3): 271–83.

SEWA. 1998. *Annual Report.* Ahmedabad, India.

Sklair, L. 1991. *Sociology of the Global System.* Baltimore, MD: Johns Hopkins University Press.

Smith Jackie, Charles Chatfield and Ron Pagnucco. eds. 1997. *Transnational Social Movements and Global Politics: Solidarity Beyond the State.* NYC: Syracuse Univ. Press.

Spivak, G. 1987. *In Other Worlds: Essays in Cultural Politics.* New York: Meuthen.

Trinh, T. Minh-ha.1989. *Woman Native Other: Writing Postcoloniality and Feminism.* Bloomington: Indiana University Press.

Turshen, Meredeth. 1994. "The Impact of Economic Reforms on Women's Health and Health Care in Sub-Saharan Africa." In *Women in the Age of Economic Transformation,* Nahid Aslanbeigui, S. Pressman, and Gale Summerfield (eds.). London: Routledge. p. 77–95

U.N. 1997. *The United Nations and the Advancement of Women 1945–1996.* New York: UN Press.

Visvanathan, N., L. Duggan, L. Nisonoff, and N. Wiegersma. eds. 1997. *The Women, Gender, and Development Reader.* London: Zed Books.

Wachtel, Howard. 2001. "Tax Distortion in the Global Economy." Paper presented at the Global Tensions Conference. Ithaca: Cornell University: March 10, 2001.

Ward, Kathy. ed 1990. *Women Workers and Global Restructuring.* Ithaca, NY: Cornell University Press.

Waterman, Peter. 1998. *Globalization, Social Movements, and the New Internationalisms.* London: Mansell.

Westra, L., and P. Wenz. eds. 1995. *Faces of Environmental Racism: Confronting Issues of Global Justice.* London: Rowman & Littlefield.

Wiegersma, Nan. 1997. "A Introduction to Part 4." In *The Women, Gender, and Development Reader,* N. Visvanathan, L. Duggan, L. Nisonoff, and N. Wiegersma. eds. London: Zed Books.

Chapter 5

Engendering Human Security: Intersections of Security, Globalization and Gender

Kristen Timothy

Since the global Beijing women's conference in 1995, interest has been growing in a concept of security that broadens the focus from the traditional definition centered solely on protecting nations from aggression and on military might, to one that emphasizes safety and security in terms of daily human life and dignity. This broad approach to security encompasses safety from chronic threats such as hunger, disease, crime and repression. It also looks at protection from sudden hurtful disruptions of daily life including domestic violence. It links to traditional development concepts focused on basic needs in terms of whether people enjoy adequate food, appropriate health care, access to resources such as water and land, physical safety and economic security. It takes into account that loss of human security can be slow or abrupt, as in an emergency. Or, it can be both—as in the case of environmental degradation.

The new security paradigm explores questions of risk reduction in relation to chronic threats and threats of everyday violence. Advocates for this broader security discourse depart from orthodox security analysis in which the state is the primary referent object and give primacy instead to individuals and groups. Thomas and Wilkin, for example, argue that changing the primary referent object of security helps in understanding the sources of threats to security and in elucidating strategies to increase security particularly under the conditions created by the global capitalist economy (1999). Rather than focusing on the experiences of territorially discrete sovereign states operating in an international system composed of similar units, they argue for a security discourse focused on understanding security in terms of the real-life everyday experience of people embedded within global social, economic and political structures.

The new thinking about security is a response in large part to the forces of rapid globalization[1] that have created both new risks and new sources of wealth and that are being felt around the world. While not a new phenomenon, globalization is changing relations between individuals and nation states, the private and public and the local and global. It is generating new markets, new tools, new actors and new rules. At the same time, it is attributed with creating instability and new vulnerabilities for certain societies and population groups. Notably, pressures of globalization have led governments, especially in poor countries, to reduce health, education and social budgets to be competitive. This has slowed down development and stimulated emigration. As policies for redistribution, safety nets and universal provision of social services have been neglected, chances for security in every day life for a large share of the population have also been reduced. Ethnic differences and shifting political alliances have also led to uncertainty and conflict. Many of the negative effects of globalization have fallen disproportionately on women and girls, creating new forms of insecurity and reviving old forms.

Central to the discourse of human security are forms of violence or threats that have not generally been viewed as linked or as being forms of violence. These "soft" security threats pose, in the words of the *New York Times*, a "greater worldwide danger than anything that comes out of the barrel of a gun" (*New York Times* 2001). Globally they include: unchecked population growth; disparities in economic opportunities; excessive international migration (trafficking in persons); environmental degradation; drug production and trafficking; and international terrorism.

Recent terrorist attacks have reinforced awareness of global threats and their impact on ordinary citizens. These events, according to one analyst have offered an "opportunity to see more clearly the quiet violence that is the daily dread of countless lives around the world" (AWID 2001). Now more than ever before there is need to strive for globalization with human security, not with additional forms of insecurity and to better understand how this can be accomplished without violating basic human rights. In the words of an editorial that appeared in *The Nation* after the attacks of 9/11: "We have now entered a new era—one without battlefields and borders, in which old ideas about national security are obsolete. In this new era, Richard Falk argues that the only viable security is what is being called these days "human security" in the form of economic and social well being for all people (Falk 2001: 4). What is not yet clear is how such security can be achieved without seriously compromising freedom and dignity for individuals and groups and how principles of equality can be applied in the process of ensuring human security, including equality for both women and men.

As noted earlier, definitions of human security encompass both basic needs and human dignity and differentiate "human" security from "state" security:

> At one level it (human security) is about the fulfillment of basic material needs and at another it is about the achievement of human dignity, which incorporates personal autonomy, control over one's life and unhindered participation in the life of the community.... Under study is the search by human beings to make daily life more stable, predictable and autonomous. The immediate medium through which that search is conducted will vary; for example, it may be the household, a grassroots organization, an ethnic network or a combination of these. The state will also play a role that can vary along the spectrum from facilitating to obstructive. Human security therefore requires a starting point and cognitive map that are different from those of orthodox security (Thomas and Wilkin 1999: 3).

This paper asks the question of how a human security discourse that incorporates human rights might be employed by women activists in their struggles for gender justice. The paper argues for a discourse on human security that integrates feminist discourse with discourses of development, human rights and citizenship. To be useful for women's activism, the human security paradigm needs to encompass equity objectives in relation to women's as well as men's daily economic and social security and identify sites of accountability—public and private, for safety and dignity throughout the life cycle. The paper begins to examine ways in which the human security paradigm might offer strategic opportunities for ending violence against women in all its forms, keeping in mind the potential for abusing security in the name, for instance, of state power, cultural and or ethnic identity.

Emergence of a Human Security Paradigm

In 1982, the Palme Commission (Independent Commission on Disarmament and Security Issues) advocated for a more holistic approach to security including factoring in economics, politics and culture for joint survival. It did so in its influential report entitled *Common Security: A Blueprint for Survival* (Independent Commission on Disarmament and Security Issues 1982). A decade later, the MacArthur Foundation initiated the Common Security Forum to facilitate international dialogue among decision-makers and scholars on the nature of security in a changing world. Until recently, advocates for an alternative conception of security have remained largely outside the mainstream security discourse (Falk 1971; Mendlovitz 1975; Thomas 1987; Tickner 1992).

At the end of the Cold War, the widespread application of structural adjustment policies in developed and developing countries alike has led to a decline in the role that individual governments are playing in meeting the everyday basic needs of people, e.g. healthcare, education, security in old age. Moreover, there has been a gradual shifting of power from individual states to multinational corporations and international financial institutions like the World Bank and the

International Monetary Fund (IMF) where women have little voice. At the same time, long time critics of militarization and of huge levels of defense spending hoped that reductions in East West tensions would redirect resources into peaceful uses lending support to a broader definition of security than had been acceptable during the Cold War. (This hope is increasingly being compromised by ethnic conflicts and a rising tide of discontent in many parts of the world.)

By the mid-1990s, there seemed to be growing interest in viewing security in terms of risks and opportunities attributed to intensified forces of globalization, particularly as some of the emerging risks or "forms of violence" transcend national boundaries and are therefore outside the traditional role of the State. Many activists, including women, see globalization as creating both opportunities as well as new forms of instability and vulnerability. After years of looking to State governments to address social and economic needs, the women's movement has been confronted with a weakening of the State in the face of global capital. This has contributed to the growing inability of States to respond to the needs of their populations placing women even lower on the list of priorities despite their importance for the well being of societies as a whole.

In the run up to the World Social Summit at Copenhagen in 1994, the concept of human security was featured in the 1994 *United Nations Human Development Report* (HDR). The HDR noted that the idea of human security had not yet been incorporated into global policy debates. It argued that where there is a low degree of human security, people worry about their very survival with very little scope for improving their lives in a sustainable way. Feelings of insecurity arise more from worries about daily life than from the dread of cataclysmic world events. Job security, income security, health security, environmental security, security from crime (and violence)—all constitute the common concerns of human security (United Nations Development Program (UNDP) 1994). The HDR also emphasized that human security means being able to exercise choices freely and safely.

In many ways, the UNDP human security framework mirrored provisions of the UN Convention on Economic, Social and Cultural Rights, one of the more controversial of the UN human rights treaties. Issues of accountability in ensuring economic, social and cultural rights and of their indivisibility are being hotly debated in the human rights arena. Feminists and others are engaged in debates on the legitimacy of framing human rights as universally applicable and on who is accountable for protecting these rights particularly as some of the violations are perpetrated in the name of culture and religion, or are considered to be in the private rather than the public domain. In the light of the obstacles encountered, some analysts have voiced doubts about the ability of the human rights framework to address social, cultural and economic violence experienced by women in their daily lives (Grewal 1999).

On the other hand, Nobel Prize winner Amartya Sen has long been an advocate of human security. Sen argues that there is a fundamental connection between democracy and security. In *Development and Freedom*, he sees freedom (including freedom from fear and from want) not only as the main objective of development, but also as a means to development (Sen 1999). He expands on his earlier argument that famine (i.e. food insecurity) occurs mainly in military dictatorships or colonial regimes or in one party regimes where people are not encouraged to express their needs (Sen 1982). Sen is a strong advocate of the crucial role women play in societies and of the need to consider issues of their security.

The report of UN Secretary General Kofi Annan to the UN Millennium Summit in 2000 argued for "freedom from fear" and "freedom from want" as key components of a sustainable and secure future. These twin goals were subsequently embraced by the leaders at the Summit and reflected in the Millennium Development Goals that they endorsed. The eight goals include one addressed specifically to gender, but clearly all of the goals have important gender dimensions and clear potential for targeting women as a way to expedite progress toward goal achievement and contribute to "human security."

In 2000, a Global Commission on Human Security was set up under the co-chairmanship of Sadako Ogata, former UN High Commissioner for Refugees and Professor Amartya Sen with funding from the Japanese Government. (The Japanese Government has incorporated human security as an important pillar of its foreign policy and has established a UN Trust Fund for human Security to support projects aimed at attaining a "human centered twenty-first century" (Koizumi 2001). The Commission held its first meeting in June 2001 and prepared a report for issuance in early 2003.[2] Several other governments, including Canada and Austria, have featured the concept of human security as a key element in their humanitarian assistance programs (MacRae and Hubert 2001).

There have also been recent efforts to study the concept of human security. The Fletcher School of Law and Diplomacy in the United States established an Institute for Human Security offering a certificate in Human Security and the University of British Colombia initiated a program in Human Security.

While the Global Commission on Security noted at its first meeting that gender issues should receive special attention, cutting across all areas related to human security, for the most part gender has been given little more than lip service in various efforts to interrogate human security. This was pointed out at a joint meeting in December 1999, of the OECD/DAC Working Party on Gender Equality and the UN Interagency Committee on Women and Gender Equality on "Women's Empowerment in the Context of Human Security." The meeting concluded that: "One missing element . . . in human security discussions has been an understanding of the fundamental differences and inequalities between women's and men's security" (United Nations 1999: 5).

Recognizing the failure to incorporate gender into the debates on human security, the National Council for Research on Women and the Center for the Study of Women and Society at the City University of New York Graduate School in 2001 pioneered with support from the Rockefeller Foundation, a humanities fellowship program to investigate human security from a gender perspective. The three year fellowship program, Facing Global Capital, Finding Human Security: A Gendered Critique examines research and writing by scholars in a number of disciplines, including feminist scholars, to shed light on the relevance and value of a human security discourse and its usefulness in identifying accountability for security of women and girls under conditions of rapid globalization.

At the same time, there are those who question the usefulness of the concept of human security in view of what they see as its potential for abuse. They cite, for example, the extension of the traditional security agenda in the context of justifying military interventions in the Gulf War in 1991 and in Timor in 1999 in the name of protecting human rights (Edson 2001). Critics also argue that the attention to human security "is a retreat from the more ambitious human development goals of the 1960s and 1970s, i.e. an assertion of neo-realism" (Woodward 1999: 272–281). Others question whether human security is "just an extension of the development agenda or alternatively of the security agenda? Or is it a hybrid of the two? And if so, does the new terminology serve a purpose?" (Edson 2001).

Still others have expressed concern that the human security discourse if it fails to adequately encompass human rights may serve to divert attention from human rights without offering another internationally agreed framework in exchange. Moreover, while it may have seemed as if various soft threats to the economic and social well-being of people would move to center stage in the post cold war era, recent events have thrown this assumption into question making advocacy for human security even more challenging.

Gender and Human Security

Research has shown that while women and girls face security threats similar to those faced by men and boys, they also confront threats that derive specifically from their identities as women and their often subordinate and low status in society. For women and girls, security includes protection from domestic and other forms of violence, the chance for an adequate living in old age and the absence of various forms of oppression and injustice based on their sex. Security entails protection of political and civil as well as economic, social and cultural rights and the empowerment to exercise rights.

Perhaps the most pervasive threat to the human security of women and girls is violence in its various forms including incest and rape, wife battery, dowry deaths, genital mutilation and female sexual slavery. Statistics reveal the staggering extent of violence against women globally: one in four women experience domestic violence. The threat and practice of violence against women is a restriction on their dignity, liberty and movement. At the same time, it is a direct violation of their security. "These abuses occur in every country and are found in the home and in the workplace, on streets, on campuses and in prisons and refugee camps. They cross class, race, age and national lines; and at the same time, the forms this violence takes often reinforce other oppressions such as racism, "able-bodyism," and "imperialism" (Bunch 1990: 489). Nevertheless, as a number of feminists have pointed out, violence against the female sex, on a scale that "far exceeds the list of Amnesty International victims, is tolerated publicly. Indeed, some acts of violence are not crimes in law, others are legitimized in custom or court opinion and most are blamed on the victims themselves" (Ashworth 1986).

In many countries, states fail to ensure human security for women by sanctioning customs that increase women's vulnerability and dependence on men. Many condone violence against women, by remaining silent on issues such as property rights, forced marriage, rights of widows and of minority groups and by condoning extremist conduct, behavior and social norms by militant religious groups (Jahangir 1999). Violence against women is an issue of both women's rights and of security. It is also an area where States are reluctant to be held accountable if it requires interference in "private" matters despite on-going debates on this question. For example, "the issue is what types of private acts are and are not protected by the right to privacy and/or the principle of family autonomy." Even more specifically, "the issue is whether violations of human rights within the family such as genital mutilation, wife beating and other forms of violence designed to maintain patriarchal control should be within the purview of human rights theory and action" (Eisler 1987: 297). When placed in a security context, violence against women and girls may seem more compelling than when it is framed merely in terms of human rights. Violence against women, both domestic and in situations of conflict is the most obvious example of a violation of both the security and rights of women and girls.

Failure to meet the development needs of women is linked to failure to protect their human rights. While efforts to protect women's human rights have enjoyed some success since the Beijing Conference, the application of human rights norms and standards has encountered serious resistance in some countries from governments and increasingly from conservative religious groups. The lack of accountability by governments for women's rights has been attributed, *inter alia* to the particular reluctance to address women's economic, social and cultural rights. Feminist activists have therefore advocated transformative development that engages women's political, economic and cultural empowerment, shifting from a focus on welfare to emphasis on empowerment and from dependency and subordination to autonomy.

Providing security for women is an important component of any effective development process. That being the case, failure to meet women's needs for safety and security is generally an indicator of underdevelopment. There is therefore a need for new strategies to achieve gender equality and women's empowerment in part by removing obstacles. Use of a human security paradigm that addresses the risks faced by women and girls as well as men and boys may help to focus action and identify those accountable for reducing risks in daily life and in relation to long-term threats. Dismantling institutions of social protection often as a result of economic restructuring, has multiplied women's unpaid work in the home and their role as providers of social services. Mounting competition from imported food is forcing subsistence farmers, many of whom are women, out of business. As one observer has stated: "Governments cannot be allowed to abandon their citizens to the uncertainties and perils of globalization" (El-Lakhany 1999: 1, 20). In the current manifestations of globalization, women in some parts of the developing world, Africa in particular, have recognized the vulnerability of the state that makes it difficult for states to address women's needs. Women's response has been to participate in political processes that result in dialogue and in 'more assertive and positive actions' essential for their survival and for effective democratic politics (Mikell 1997: 32).

Feminist human rights advocate, Charlotte Bunch, points out that "the inclusion of 'second generation' or socioeconomic human rights to food, shelter and work—which are clearly delineated as part of the Universal Declaration of Human Rights—is vital to addressing women's concerns fully" (Bunch 1990: 488). In Bunch's words: "Sex discrimination kills women daily. When combined with race, class and other forms of oppression, it constitutes a deadly denial of women's right to life and liberty on a large scale throughout the world" (Bunch: 489). Bunch essentially embeds basic components of human security for women in the framework of human rights and thereby makes a link between security and rights. She stresses that "few governments exhibit more than token commitment to women's equality as a basic human right in domestic or foreign policy," (Bunch: 487) and few accept responsibility for violations of women's rights:

> The assumption that states are not responsible for most violations of women's rights ignores the fact that such abuses, although committed perhaps by private citizens, are often condoned or even sanctioned by states.... Feminists have shown how the distinction between private and public abuse is a dichotomy often used to justify female subordination in the home. Governments regulate many matters in the family and individual spheres. For example, human rights activists pressure states to prevent slavery or racial discrimination and segregation even when these are conducted by non governmental forces in private or proclaimed as cultural traditions... (Bunch: 488, 491).

Economic insecurity is also a phenomenon that is impacting women increasingly under conditions of globalization. A symposium on "Risks and Rights in the 21st Century" held at the University of Illinois at Urbana-Champaign in October 2000, concluded that the accelerating reconfiguration of the global economy in recent years has produced especially complex consequences for women posing unprecedented risks as well as opportunities for the acquisition of rights. The consequences of globalization have increased "women's risks from violence and sexual assault within the home, on the street and in war. The consequences of financial and economic crisis are even more widespread than the effects of poverty. Since they are distributed across class, age, education and other lines of demarcation, they affect more people directly, including the wealthy and educated" (Anon 2001: 5).

Women are extremely vulnerable to risk in this rapidly globalizing world, despite the opportunities created. The United Nations Fourth World Conference on Women held in Beijing in 1995 moved the international discourse on equality away from the idea of women's vulnerability and women as victims and emphasized instead women's rights, empowerment and women as just recipients of development benefits. The human security discourse, if infused with a gender perspective, may enable us to both examine womens' and girls' vulnerability as an issue deserving renewed attention, as well as continuing to strengthen the focus on protection of women's human rights—particularly their economic, social and cultural rights under conditions of rapid globalization.

Challenges Ahead

It is important to lay down some markers for investigating the uses of a human security framework in relation to the human security of women and girls. For example, there is need to:

- elaborate further the human security paradigm with a view in broad terms to determining its uses as a framework for socio-economic analysis and policy making and as a rationale for resource allocation and budgeting at national and international levels;
- gather more data on the different ways men and women experience insecurity in diverse societies, often as a result of entrenched customs and rising militancy among religious groups and clarify the factors that differentiate women and cause discrimination based on gender;
- identify sites of accountability—both public and private (especially in family situations where women have no independent means and are rendered insecure and vulnerable)—for women's security, taking into consideration the various costs and benefits;
- examine the role women should play in power and decision making to authenticate their own needs, acquire equitable access to resources and have a voice in policy making and ways to promote greater empowerment;
- at the national level, as proposed by Kabeer and Subrahamian (1996), build objectives of security and agency into project frameworks and develop methods for monitoring the human security impact of projects using indicators of survival, security and autonomy.

Notes

1. Globalization as used here is "the revolution in transport and communication technology, the collapse of barriers to world trade that followed the collapse of the Soviet Empire, the interpenetrating of domestic and international markets and the universalization and integration of commodity, financial and labour markets." See *International Journal of Politics, Culture and Society*, Vol. 15. Number 1, Fall, 2001.
2. Co-chairs: Sadako Ogata, Former UN High Commissioner for Refugees; Amartya Sen, Master, Trinity College, Cambridge University.

References

Anon. 2001a. "Risks and Rights in the 21st Century": Papers from the Women and Gender in Global Perspectives Program Symposium, *International Journal of Politics, Culture and Society*, Special Issue, volume 15, no. 1, Fall.

Anon. 2001b. *New York Times*. 2001. January 29, p. A22. New York City.

Ashworth, Georgina. 1986. "Of Violence and Violation, Women and Human Rights. *Change Thinkbook II*. London: Change

Bunch, Charlotte. 1990. "Women's Rights as Human Rights: Toward a Re-vision of Human Rights." *Human Rights Quarterly*, vol. 12 no.4.

Edson, Sharon. 2001. "Human Security: An Extended and Annotated International Bibl. raphy." Cambridge UK: Kings College Press.

Eisler, Riane. 1987. "Human Rights: Toward an Integrated Theory for Action." *Hu Rights Quarterly* 9.

El-Lakany, Riham 1999. "Agreements Leave Women Worldwide At A Disadvantage i. This Age Of Globalization." *WEDO News and Views*, November, nos. 2 & 3.

Falk, Richard. 1971. *This Endangered Planet*. New York: Random House.

———. 1975. *A Study of Future Worlds*. New York: Free Press.

———. 2001. "A Just Response." *The Nation* October 8 p.11–15.

Grewal, Inderpal. 1999. "'Women's Rights as Human Rights': Feminist Practices, Global Feminism, and Human Rights Regimes in Transnationality" *Citizenship Studies* vol. 3, no. 3.

Independent Commission on Disarmament and Security Issues. 1982. *Common Security: A Blueprint for Survival*, New York: Simon and Schuster.

Jahangir, Asma. 1999. Statement on "Human Security and Social Protection" by the Special Rapporteur on Extrajudicial, Summary or Arbitrary Execution at the Commission on the Status of Women. New York 15 March.

Kabeer, N. and R. Subrahamian. 1996. *Institutions, Relations and Outcomes: Concepts and Methods of Gender Aware Planning*, IDS Discussion Paper. Sussex: University of Sussex.

Koizumi, Junichiro. 2001. Message from the Prime Minister on the Occasion of the First Meeting of the Commission on Human Security, 9 June. See www.mofa.go.jp/policy.

McRae, R. and D. Hubert. eds. 2001. *Human Security and the New Diplomacy: Protecting People, Promoting Peace*. Montreal: McGill-Queen's University Press. See also www.dfait-maeci.gc.ca/foreignp/humansecurity

Mendlovitz, S. ed. 1975. *On the Creation of a Just World Order*. New York: Free Press.

Mikell, Gwendolyn. 1997. *African Feminism: The Politics of Survival in Sub-Saharan Africa*. Philadelphia: University of Pennsylvania Press.

Sen, Amartya K. 1982. *Poverty and Famines, An Essay on Entitlement and Deprivation*. London: Oxford University Press.

———. 1999. *Development as Freedom*. Oxford: Oxford University Press.

Shohat, Ella. ed. 2000. *Talking Visions, Multicultural Feminism in a Transnational Age*. Cambridge. MA: MIT Press.

Summerfield, Gail. 2001. "Introduction to the Symposium." Papers from the Women and Gender in Global Perspectives Program Symposium, *International Journal of Politics, Culture and Society*, Special Issue, vol 15, no. 1, Fall.

Thomas, Caroline. 1987. *In Search of Security: The Third World in International Relations*. Boulder CO: Harvester Wheatsheaf Brighton and Lynne Rienner.

Thomas, Caroline and Peter Wilkin. eds. 1999. *Globalization, Human Security, and the African Experience*. Boulder: Lynne Rienner Publishers.

Tickner, J. A. 1992. *Gender in International Relations: Feminist Perspectives on Achieving Global Security.* New York: Colombia University Press.

The Nation. 2001. "*Justice, Not Vengeance.*" editorial, October 8, p. 3–4.

United Nations Development Program. 1994. *Human Development Report.* New York and London: Oxford University Press.

United Nations. 1999. *Women's Empowerment in the Context of Human Security,* Report of the Joint Meeting of the OECD/DAC Working Party on Gender Equality and the UN ACC Interagency Committee on Women and Gender Equality, held on 7–8 December, 1999, Bangkok, Thailand. New York: United Nations.

Woodward, Susan. 1999. "Should We Think Before We Leap: A Rejoinder." *Security Dialogue,* vol. 30(X)

Chapter 6

Sub-Saharan Africa: Globalization, Trade Liberalization and Impact on the Lives of the Poor

Ngila Mwase

The world and especially Sub-Saharan Africa (SSA) has been grappling with the forces of globalization, economic trade and financial liberalization and the impact that this has on society, especially its poor segments. We discuss in this paper changes in development paradigms including economic, political and administrative governance and the role of the civil society. We discuss the liberalization of national economies, relations with the WTO multilateral trade negotiations and systems and the need for enhanced capacity to negotiate.

Rapid and far-reaching changes have occurred in the development paradigm and in the functioning of national economies since Gorbachev's *Perestroika* and *Glasnost* revolution. Recent political, economic, social, environmental and technological changes have created an entirely new context for SSA economies and prospects for their integration.

These changes include: a) Economic liberalization, deregulation, commercialization, privatization of national economies and the drive towards free market economies, coupled with marginalization of central planning and planned approaches to economic integration. The International Monetary Fund (IMF) and the World Bank structural adjustment programs (SAPs) have fostered liberalization through tariff reductions and various initiatives to establish a regime of trade liberalization and cross-border investment in SSA and its sub-regions; b) Rapid technological advancement and increased importance of "high-tech" products, information and communication technology (ICT) in international trade. Sub-Saharan Africa (SSA), save for the Republic of South Africa (RSA), lags far behind; c) The new WTO trade regime, with extensive opening up of trade including in the service sector; d) Increased efforts for greater South-South "collective self-reliance" especially through the Non-Aligned Movement (NAM). The South Commission chaired by the late Tanzanian President Julius Nyerere in this regard addressed these challenges. The Commission's 1990 Report showed how the existing global trade, financial and technological regimes handicap the South. The Commission left behind a Geneva-based South Centre, which continues to analyze the problems of less developed country (LDC) and joint efforts in addressing some of them; e) Renewed efforts for (sub) regional cooperation and integration and the proliferation of Regional Economic Communities (RECs) with economic integration as their *raison d'etre*. The RECs, with more or less similar objectives, projects and programs cause duplication, wasteful competition and the determination of member states to rationalize their activities; f) Recognition of poverty eradication and sustainable human development as the overarching objective of all development efforts. Substantial donor assistance is now premised on a clear national vision that prioritizes poverty eradication; g) Continued donor community/development partner interest, especially in infrastructure provision and maintenance, which is underlined in the New Partnership for Africa's Development (NEPAD). However, this is limited by donor fatigue, changing global priorities, including diversion of resources to the ex-Soviet Union republics and the war on terror, increased aid conditionalities and despite NEPAD, declining interest in and reduced inflows of concessional development aid to Africa; h) A new political environment calling for democratic, decentralized governance and the increased importance of civil society including Non-governmental organizations (NGOs), community based organizations (CBOs) and the private sector in the development process.

Of late these changes have been influenced by, or have had to respond to the challenges and implications of managing national economies in the era of the Highly Indebted Poor Countries (HIPC) debt relief initiative, the Poverty Reduction Strategy Papers (PRSPs), the Millennium Development Goals (MDGs) and NEPAD.

Civil society involvement in the development process is a new phenomenon and increasingly a benchmark for sustainable good governance. Incorporating as it does the mass media, it is in effect the "fourth estate." With a few exceptions one cannot talk of a "fourth estate" in SSA, unless one sees it in the context of the overall civil society. The civil society can take development partners to task for bottlenecks in development cooperation; it can enhance transparency and accountability and reinforce monitoring and evaluation of Poverty Reduction Strategies especially the proposed African peer review mechanism.

The civil society as a key government partner is engaged in policy dialogue on emerging development concerns. In much of SSA the civil society usually deals with political issues. However, in some countries such as Uganda, civil society organizations (CSOs) are ever present in the economic development arena. CSOs are increasingly active in program design and implementation, especially in service delivery, monitoring and evaluation. Poverty monitoring by CSOs at district and sub-district levels is a practical expression of what the civil society can do. Local and international NGOs are addressing development and humanitarian concerns, some of which are beyond the capacities of the state, including maintaining dialogue in difficult or hostile environments, such as intermediation between government and rebels. This has been the case with the church in northern Uganda. The civil society has also made important contributions to the Consultative Group (CG) mechanism, the budgetary process and sensitization work such as the Jubilee 2000 Debt relief campaigns. The civil society has undertaken impressive work, including taking stock of progress towards the attainment of commitments made at major global conferences such as the World Summit on Social Development. In this regard, it is important for CSOs to ensure that through their legitimizing role they do not endorse policies or programs inimical to the welfare of the poor.

In the past, for various reasons and to varying degrees, governments of all political persuasions intervened in the economy by actual takeover or by lesser forms of control such as influencing the pricing system, at least for public utilities such as water and electricity. By definition, the market does not produce fairness or justice and in order to promote these values for society, we need to regulate either through mechanisms of self-regulation of business or governance structures. As Milton Friedman argued, "there is one and only one social responsibility of business, to use its resources and engage in activities designed to increase its profits" (1982). Although there are reservations over the *modus operandi* of the private sector, there is general consensus that if regulated, the private sector can be an engine of development as well as be profitable. Despite past reservations about transnational corporations, improvement in corporate governance enhances their performance for their benefit and that of society at large.

Most Sub-Saharan African countries started with or inherited free market economies before opting for African socialism, central planning and a predominance of parastatals, state owned business. The results of these public sector expenditures were mixed. Although the basic needs of the poor were addressed through egalitarianism and increased social sector spending (e.g., in Tanzania, Zambia and Sri Lanka), with low economic growth rates meeting these basic needs was unsustainable.

Economic liberalization has now reduced the public sector through the sale of state-owned enterprises and the shifting of activities from the public to the private sector, thereby ending costly state financing of loss-making enterprises. The removal of controls (physical and monetary) allowing the free flow of goods, services, capital and hopefully labor can lead to increased trade, incomes and employment. The Asian "Tigers," for instance, benefited from greater economic space and free movement of factor inputs. Malaysia and Singapore, for example, were among the poorest countries in the world in the 1960s, with a per capita income of less than $US200, which was comparable to per capita incomes of several SSA countries including Ghana, Uganda and Zambia. Malaysia has managed to increase its annual per capita income to over $US4,000 and has a national vision with a target year of 2020 to attain First World status. Thus current efforts at developing common labor laws in East Africa will hasten the establishment of an East African Community investment area. With trade and other barriers removed, with central planning marginalized and with investment left essentially to the private sector and especially foreign big business, it is likely that investment will be concentrated in certain countries and locations. In East Africa it may be in Kenya—and Mombasa (especially for import-export industries) or Nairobi for products whose inputs rely on local raw materials and/or whose outputs rely on a large domestic market provided by the capital city.

There has been an outcry that economic liberalization has led to the loss of jobs. This is yet to be ascertained through full-fledged labor surveys. However the current private sector survey may throw light on the performance of the privatized firms and allow comparisons among Uganda, Tanzania and Kenya. The challenge of employment creation cannot be overemphasized. As Ugandan President Museveni told the 2000 Consultative Group, "the most pressing challenge is to deliver employment. Uganda's labor force is expanding by 300,000 persons a year. The public sector clearly cannot and should not absorb the increase in the labor force. Yet the private sector is not delivering the increase in employment opportunities at anything like the rate to absorb the increase in the labor force" (Museveni 2000).

This statement is loaded, for there are those who feel parastatals should have remained even if they were loss making. This would have been unsustainable. On the other hand the economic reform package for Uganda including parastatal divestiture and overall privatization policies was expected to deliver jobs. If they are not delivering, it is a serious issue. In the advanced countries, more particularly in the UK and USA, the unemployment level is both a key test of economic performance and an influential factor in electoral voting patterns. In poor countries the choice might be between a job and starvation; unemployment is not a mere statistical head count. Policy reforms must deliver on employment. As Stiglitz has noted, in the LDCs "the unemployed are people, with families, whose lives are affected—sometimes devastated—by the economic policies that outsiders recommend and, in the case of the IMF, effectively impose" (2002: 24).

Most SSA exports are agricultural commodities, which support and are produced by millions of poor rural households. Therefore, a competitive exchange rate provides incentives and encourages exports, increases payment in local currency and also helps to distribute incomes to the poor. An overvalued exchange rate would make exports less competitive and therefore incomes of smallholder producers would fall.

Economic and financial liberalization was expected to result in positive real interest rates, increased domestic savings and efficient allocation of financial resources. With increased monetization and a more competitive financial market, the cost of financial intermediation and borrowing was expected to go down. In many SSA countries this has not happened. This has hardened the *modus operandi* of small-scale producers and entrepreneurs and inflicted hardships on vulnerable groups, for whom some limited safety nets have been instituted.

Lack of cooperation and of good governance have made intra and inter-state trade, transport, communications and investment flows low. Transport and trade routes are few and often underlying the colonial pattern of export/import trade and traffic flows. Despite the sub-regional initiatives on the abolition of visas, especially under the Common Market of Eastern and Southern Africa (COMESA) and Economic Community of West African States, movement of (African) peoples and rights of residence are still restricted, not least by insecurity, political squabbles and police checkpoints. This has contributed to the overall outward orientation of the economy, people's values, consumption patterns and tastes (including of political systems) now exacerbated by globalization. Uganda's landlockedness has made transport costs of exports exorbitantly high and depressed the country's export competitiveness. Likewise the costs of imports are excessively high due to exorbitant transport costs.

The liberalization and privatization of agricultural marketing streamlined crop procurement, processing and export. This streamlining allowed private entrepreneurs to purchase agricultural produce in the villages. The ensuing competition has been more rewarding to smallholder producers. The end of single channel marketing of major agricultural commodities—coffee in Uganda, coffee in Rwanda and coffee, cotton, tobacco, tea and sisal in Tanzania—has had a positive impact. A clear example is the end in the early 1990s of the monopoly of the Uganda Coffee Marketing Board, which entailed not only inputs supply but also crop procurement, processing and transportation to markets. The challenge is to develop a liberal, privatized and sustainable marketing system that is responsible to producer needs and expectations.

A major reason for underdevelopment, small size and fundamental structural dependency relationships is the creation of symmetry between the structures of production and consumption such that most LDC economies produce what they do not consume and consume what they do not produce. This is unlike the United States, for example, where production is first and foremost for the internal market, with the surplus for exports. Thus the Caribbean economist Clive Thomas, in a Tanzania-based study on dependency and transformation, argued for a "convergence of domestic resource use and domestic production" (1974). In this regard the development of the domestic market and internal trade ranging from food crops such as bananas, to services such as tourism, cannot be overemphasized.

Most SSA countries have neither the resources nor capacity to excel in trade infrastructure and services provision. As Keynes noted, "the important thing for government is not to do things which individuals are doing already and to do them a little better or a little worse; but to do those things which at present are not done at all" (1926).

There is now a general consensus that the role of government should be to develop a framework and an enabling environment for economic activity to flourish. In other words, government should steer the boat, but not row it. In exceptional circumstances governments can intervene in strategic activities, or address special development needs, including those in marginalized or economically depressed areas. Encouraging private traders and taxing their profits is more economical and perhaps more equitable than inefficient, loss making, state-owned, controlled and subsidized commercial firms. Ensuring that private traders are aware of and are responsive to societal concerns may moderate the crude pursuit of profits – what Edward Heath called the "unacceptable face of capitalism" (1985).[1] The then British Prime Minister's comments came in the course of the work of an international panel of experts that studied the functioning of transnational corporations, which left much to be desired.

The Challenge of Globalization

In its most general terms globalization refers to increasing interdependence of the world's economies, exemplified by rapid and easy communication, due to technological advancement and independence fostered by the ICT revolution; rapid growth of world trade partly due to extensive trade liberalization; the internationalization of production spread by large corporations operating in many countries; huge capital movements; and an overwhelming return to liberalized and market-led economies including by countries which had ditched the system with the 1917 Bolshevik Revolution.

Sub-Saharan Africa is facing a new world order. This is neither the New International Economic Order (NIEO) spearheaded by late Algerian President Houari Boumedianne, first proposed at the 1969 NAM Summit in Algiers in 1969, nor the NIEO that the LDCs strived for through the NAM and other fora three decades ago. The economic and political powerhouses of the world did not accept the clamor for an NIEO. Addressing the United Nations Conference on Trade and Development (UNCTAD) in Nairobi in 1975, the then US Secretary of State Henry Kissinger, said that, "the United States takes no responsibility that the world is now on a course called New International Economic Order." He added, "The present world order has served us very well" (1975).

Kissinger's world order is increasingly skewed in favor of the rich and the powerful, now strengthened by the forces of globalization. This is a new world order of rapid technological changes, of free market systems, of economic blocks, of massive political and economic changes, of economic and financial liberalization and above all, globalization. The latter, whose conveyor belt is ICT, is a dramatic development with far-reaching effects on the development process. It in essence entails bringing down the barriers to free trade and closer integration of national economies. While there seems to be no obvious insulation from the adverse forces of globalization, developing countries can come to terms with globalization by marshalling the capacity to redirect it to maximize its benefits and minimize its adverse impacts, especially on the poor. While it has innovative and dynamic attributes, excessive market and profit-driven globalization harbors negative, disruptive and marginalizing effects, including: the erosion of state control and sovereignty especially over international capital and trade as TNCs increase their ownership and control of national economies or key and strategic industries and as they spearhead "business without borders"; increased cross-border labor migration, crime, drug trafficking, money laundering and infectious diseases; increased extra-territorial scrutiny over the conduct of public affairs, especially cross-border trade, investment and payment systems; and increased economic, political and social exclusion and inequity, which is one of the root causes of poverty.

As Tanzanian President and co-Chairperson of the World Commission on the Social Dimensions of Globalization, Benjamin Mkapa has noted, "As production and exchange increasingly move to global proportions, there is concern that the social dimension has not been an integral part of the process of globalization. Addressing the social dimension is critical, for there is a widespread perception that globalization exacerbates inequalities, raises uncertainty and insecurity, that it may erode basic rights, that the risks for people and enterprises are distributed unevenly or unfairly. There is a growing sense that to sustain the process of globalization, it is necessary to deal with the problems of insecurity, equity and exclusion associated with it, whatever their origin" (2002: 2).

There has for a number of years been a lot of excitement about the effects of rapid developments in information and communications technology (ICT), which brings peoples of all nationalities and cultural backgrounds together. This was underlined by the notion of the world moving towards a "global village."

However, in arguing for "globalization with a human face" [2] the 2000 UNDP *Human Development Report* noted, "the collapse of space, time and borders may be creating a global village, but not everyone can be a citizen." The challenge, as ILO Director General Juan Somaia has said, is to "work together for a new social contract based on decent work for all and a globalization that leaves no one behind" (2003: 14). There has been a surge of ratifications of international labor standards, especially those dealing with the worst abuses of labor and especially child labor. As UN Secretary General Kofi Annan said at the UNDP Millennium Ministerial meeting in September 2000, "globalization is like an express train. It only stops at those stations where the platform is high enough for passengers to get on. The platform consists of education, technology and especially, today, information technology; infrastructure; and governance, which is the necessary condition of all those things" (2000).

The evolution of globalization and the way it is being managed, including some of the international trade agreements, are at best not beneficial and at worst can hurt the LDCs, especially poor segments of the population. Joseph Stiglitz, the 2001 Nobel laureate in economics and significantly hitherto a pillar of the "Washington consensus," having served as World Bank Senior Vice President and Chief Economist and before that as Chairman of the U.S. President Clinton's Council of Economic Advisors, provides an excellent illustration in his book, *Globalization and its Discontents* (2002). The book's publication brought a hysterical reaction from the IMF. It was as hysterical as the US's reaction to the publication of Ghanaian President Came Nkrumah's book, *Neo-colonialism: The Last Stage of Imperialism* (1965) or indeed the Bowie's reaction to UNICEF's annual *State of the World's Children* (1996) and its references to the adverse impact of SAP policies on the urban poor and especially on children in Zimbabwe. Both the President of the World Bank and the Managing Editor of the IMF issued separate statements on the same day questioning the accuracy of the data and information in UNICEF's book and its supposedly negative impact on policy-making and they called on UNICEF to retract it. The UNICEF Executive Director, Ms. Caroline Bellany, despite her being relatively new in the job, stuck to her organization's side of the story. Unlike political liberalization, differences over the impact of economic and financial liberalization and application of ensuing instruments and tools has caused some cracks or more precisely "inter-family differences" in the "Washington consensus" and to some extent in trans-Atlantic alliances.

And yet globalization, whatever its drawbacks, cannot be wished away! Unless SSA comes to grips with it, much of the continent is in danger of being by-passed by Kofi Annan's "express train" de-linked and marginalized, with attendant adverse consequences on the productive economic sectors, employment generation and eradication of mass poverty and hunger.

With respect to globalization's impact on the poor, there are, as Professor Tony Killick noted in the ninth Joseph Mubiru Memorial Lecture (2000) entitled "Globalization: Is It Good for the poor?' divergent views are aggravated by a "shortage of hard evidence." This is partly because of difficulties in tracing the causal effects between the macro policies of globalization and trade liberalization and the micro impacts on poverty, especially on rural households and individuals.

Sub-Saharan Africa complained of an unfair global trading system and practices: that it sells primary commodities cheaply and buys manufactured goods dearly, resulting in unfavorable terms of trade and balance of payment deficits; that the world market is "imperfect" and not really free and fair. These complaints have characterized the trade discourse for decades, especially since Raul Prebisch's exposition of unequal trade at the inaugural UNCTAD in Geneva in 1964. Multilateral trade negotiations under the General Agreement on Tariffs and Trade (GATT) and its successor, the World Trade Organization (WTO), have overseen phased trade liberalization. However, of late excessive and speedy liberalization amidst somewhat selective application of GATT/WTO rules and regulations in the developed world has sometimes unduly opened up LDC markets. This is being resisted by LDCs. The Uruguay Round provisions, for example, while opening up LDC markets, were very protective of the OECD interests, especially in the agricultural sector where the US, for example, had a phased approach to opening up markets for agricultural products and heavily subsidized agricultural production. This distorts market prices, rendering LDC agricultural exports uncompetitive.

Under WTO, despite reservations from LDCs, the crusade for liberalization and especially of the services sector has been expedited. Unlike GATT, the WTO decision-making process is swift and by and large skewed in favor of the rich and powerful OECD countries, especially the US, Japan and the EU. The LDCs' representation in the WTO and its Committees leaves much to be desired. The somewhat rigid WTO trade regime, its rules, regulations and appeals procedures have been resented and partly contributed to the civil-society-led protestations and stand-off at Seattle and subsequent protests at Prague and Doha. In Seattle, the civil society and LDC government delegations flatly rejected the draft trade liberalization proposals. The LDCs' rebellion in Seattle, spearheaded by the civil society both from the South and the North and its aftermath, especially the "Doha consensus," has not satisfied the aspirations of the LDCs but it has set people thinking! However, the easing of restrictions on LDC exports through the US's African Growth and Opportunities Act (AGOA), the EU's "all but arms" scheme, the EU-ACP Cotonou Agreement and somewhat similar trade liberalization efforts by Japan and to some extent Canada, while appreciated may be undermined by difficulties of meeting regulations and "process standards" such as on labor, the environment and animal welfare.

After a trying episode at Seattle and costly LDC compromises or consensus at Doha, the stage was set, for better or worse, for the negotiations to go forward.   The Multilateral Investment Agreement targeted the wholesale opening up of the investment area to outside investment without any ability to reserve particular strategic industries to national ownership and/or control through either the public or private sector. Both the UK and USA have been uncomfortable about outside purchase of strategic industries, such as, British Extelcoms.

President Nyerere and his government successfully challenged international capital and power brokers in Tanzania and Southern Africa respectively. In Tanzania, following the Arusha Declaration in 1967, massive nationalization of private enterprises was done and the "commanding heights" of the economy put under public ownership and control. In Southern Africa, through Tanzanians' support for the armed liberation struggle and the ensuing left wing regimes, international capital was challenged. But times have changed and the CSOs have a heavy responsibility to reverse things. Addressing the Association of Commonwealth Universities in Ottawa in 1998, Dr. Nyerere said, "There was a time when a developing country leader could say 'No' to the IMF or World Bank. But no leader of a highly indebted poor country, or a financially troubled Indonesia or South Korea, can with impunity say 'No' today. His country will be crucified! So a time comes when the leader is forced to accept a neo-colonial status for his country in return for a financial bail out from its international creditors. This is the case today in many countries in Africa" (1999: 81). The civil society is in a better position to endeavor to restore Africa's credibility and honor in this regard.

Capacity Building for Sustainable Trade and Poverty Eradication

To increase its clout in trade negotiations, Africa has to first and foremost reverse its declining share of world trade, which stands at less than two percent of global trade. SSA's share is dismally small, especially if the Republic of South Africa share is not taken into account. SSA has to reinforce its negotiating capacity in trade and other areas by appointing officers with technical competence and related credentials, undertaking staff retooling and strengthening its overseas missions, especially in Geneva. This would entail conceiving them as "cost centers" whose benefits (trade and investment flows) should surpass (operational) costs. It is not cost-effective to have a multiplicity of high commissions and embassies if there are no resources to run them, let alone to go beyond meeting operational costs to program development and implementation.

A number of African countries including Mobutu's Zaire (now Democratic Republic Congo) and Chiluba's Zambia have suffered the indignity of host countries' threats or action to close embassies for non-payment of staff. In this regard Uganda, whose missions, especially in Geneva, are better staffed, has tried to measure up to expectations, especially in linking the work of the mission to developments at home.

Uganda has come closest to proper conceptualization of the application of the principle of cost-benefit analysis in the running of foreign missions. Trade benefits are at the core of the rationale of the existence of foreign diplomatic missions. Thus in the year 2000-01 Ugandan President Yoweri Museveni closed some embassies that did not meet this test including those in important donor countries such as France, Germany, Japan and China arguing that he was not interested in embassies "for decoration or drinking wine." The re-opening of some of them; such as, Beijing's, was tied in with trade prospects. Beijing allowed Kampala to open shops for selling coffee. In this regard the importance of very knowledgeable, experienced and enthusiastic Trade Commissioners at home and Trade Attaches and other diplomats at foreign missions cannot be overemphasized. In the latter case we can learn from the Japanese who appoint trade attaches from the private sector to serve on contract basis in their overseas missions. The pace of trade negotiations is demanding, calling for well-trained and informed negotiators. The cream are those who have learned, first hand and through the mill, how to do it. The plethora of bilateral and multilateral trade agreements that guide and regulate the global trading system underlines the critical place and role of the trade negotiator. The tact, skill, resources, staff preparedness and hands on approach of the trade negotiator and negotiating teams are crucial.

There is a need to strengthen the technical capacities in LDCs' Ministries of Trade and other economic line ministries, taking advantage of various capacity-building programs including the ITC/WTO/UNCTAD and Joint Integrated Technical Assistance Program (JITAP). JITAP has assisted countries in preparing export development strategies that inter alia take into account the development of small and medium scale enterprises (SMEs). Trade negotiators and officials should be very conversant with internal and external trade policy and practices. Their familiarity with multilateral trade regimes and interface with (sub) regional trade arrangements such as COMESA and ECOWAS cannot be over-emphasized

Sub-Saharan Africa and its regions can through regional economic groupings benefit from economies of scale and strengthen their bargaining power especially vis-à-vis the WTO by taking on the WTO as regional blocks. This is the best way to minimize the negative aspects of Africa's balkanization and fragmented markets. In this regard, COMESA has followed-up the technical discussions in multilateral trade negotiations. Likewise, the EAC countries have adopted the same commodity standards for WTO purposes, hence the importance of strengthening national Bureaus of Standards.

Conclusion

To break the vicious cycle of poverty, we argue for enhanced broad-based growth and development, increased opportunities for inclusion in the development process, regional economic cooperation and integration and improved governance and security. Goods and services cannot be produced, let alone traded at competitive prices in an unstable, war-ravaged and insecure region. In this regard the civil society can play a significant role in enhancing social cohesion and in advocacy for debt relief, fair and equitable international trade and above all prioritization of trade over development aid.

Regional cooperation and integration provide an opportunity to address growth, investment, export promotion and trade-related national and cross-border challenges. Key areas in this regard include: trade, transport and communication systems; sustainable exploitation of natural resources; social and economic interaction; information and communication technology; the external environment, including new modalities for technical cooperation; political instability, insecurity and war; and sustainable and good political, economic and administrative governance.

The World Bank's words of caution in a 1989 report entitled *Sub-Saharan Africa: From Crisis to Sustainable Growth* are still valid:

> It is not sufficient for African governments merely to consolidate the progress made in their adjustment programs. They need to go beyond the issues of public finance, monetary policy, prices and markets to address fundamental questions relating to human capacities, institutions, governance....Changes in perceptions and priorities as well as incentives, will be required to bring about improvements. Above all, ordinary people should participate more in designing and implementing development programs. Much of this will take time. But the call is to take action now to bring about long run changes that will promote growth and reduce poverty.

Notes

1. The former British Premier was in 1973/74, referring to the behavior of the UK based London-Rhodesia corporation (Lonrho) which had substantial investments in Africa.

2. This was to some extent inspired by the work of Richard Jolly through UNICEF's pioneering work on "adjustment with a human face" (1987); or in a way Alexander Dubceck's "Socialism with a Human Face" Czech experiment, which was put down by force by the Soviet-led Warsaw Pact in 1968.

References

Achebe, Chinua. 1958. *Things Fall Apart*. New York: Anchor Books.

Annan, Kofi. 2000. *Statement at the UNDP Millennium Ministerial Meeting*. New York. September.

Clive, Thomas. 1974. *Dependency and Transformation: The Economics of The Transition to Socialism*. New York: Monthly Review Press.

Cornia, G. Andrea, Richard Jolly, and Frances Stewart. 1987. *Adjustment with a Human Face*, vol. 1. New York: Oxford University Press (for UNICEF).

Heath, Edward. 1985. quoted in Mwaanga, Vernon. 1985. *An Extraordinary Life*. Lusaka: Multimedia. Zambia.

Friedman, Milton. 1982. *Capitalism and Freedom*. Chicago: University of Chicago Press.

Keynes, John Maynard. 1926. *The End of Laissez-Faire*. London: Hogarth Press.

Killick, Tony. 2000. "Globalisation: Is it Good for the Poor?" 9th ed. Joseph Mubiru Memorial Lecture. Kampala.

Kissinger, Henry. 1975. *Statement at the UNCTAD Conference*, Nairobi.

Mkapa, Benjamin. *2002 Keynote Address at the UNDP Africa Regional Symposium on the Human Development Report*. Dar-es-Salaam: Government Printer. 11 October.

Mwase, Ngila. 1998. *Economic Liberalization and Privatisation of Agricultural Marketing and Input Supply in Tanzania: A Case Study of Cashew Nuts*. Nairobi: African Eco-nomic Research Foundation (AERC). Research Paper PR 86. 30 p.

Museveni, Yoweri. 2000. *Address at the Consultative Group Meeting*, Kampala Uganda 22 March quoted in UNDP (2002:32), *Uganda Human Development Report*. Kampala: UNDP.

Nkrumah, Kwame. 1965. *Neo Colonialism: The Last Stage of Imperialism*. London: PANAF Books.

Nyerere, Julius. 2002. "Money and Politics." *Africa Today and Tomorrow*, no. 4, p.85.

———. 1999. "Managing our Own Democratic Development and Change in the South." in UNDP (2002), *Cooperation and Change*. no. 2. New York.

Somaia, Juan. 2003. *Financial Times*, 28 March, p.14.

South Commission. 1990. *The Challenge of the South*. London: Oxford University Press.

Stiglitz, Joseph. 2002. *Globalization and Its Discontents*. London: Penguin Books.

United Nations. 1996. *State of the World's Children*. Geneva: UNICEF.

United Nations Development Programme. (UNDP). 2002. *Human Development Report: Globalisation with a Human Face*. New York: Oxford University Press.

World Bank.1989. *Sub-Saharan Africa: From Crises to Sustainable Development, A Long Term Perspective Study*. Washington D.C.: The World Bank.

Chapter 7

Sustainability of Rural Communities in a Global Perspective: Limitations and Opportunities

Marta B. Chiappe and Emma Zapata Martelo
Translated by Jennifer Terrett

The study presented here examines the social effects of globalization and the role of mediating mechanisms (such as industrialization, government policies and actions related to human capital development) on the social and economic situation of families and rural communities of Mexico. The intent is to deepen our understanding of the intersection of macro socio-economic change and the relative success of local adaptive strategies from different types of communities.

This study was carried out in the state of Tlaxcala, Mexico. This area was chosen firstly because it has been one of the most dynamic states in recent years, as regards the installation of industries from abroad, and secondly because the personnel contracted by these industries come, by and large, from communities undergoing a process of transition but which also have a rural base.

The state of Tlaxcala is situated in the southeast central area of the Mexican Republic. It has a surface area of 4,060.9 squared kilometers (the smallest state in Mexico), and an economically active population (EAP) of 405,008 inhabitants (40% of the state's total population), of whom 68 percent are men and 32 percent are women. The employed population (the EAP minus the population seeking work) totals 394,888, which is constituted in the following manner: 18 percent in the primary sector, 51 percent in the secondary sector and 30.5 percent in the tertiary sector (0.2% is not specified). In the primary sector, the percentage of the working population according to gender, is made up of 22.6 percent men and 8 percent women; in the secondary sector, 51.5 percent are men and 51.2 percent are women; and in the tertiary sector, 25.8 percent are men and 40.7 percent are women (INEGI 1999).

Since the 1970s, when the establishment of *maquila[1]* industries was authorized for the whole country, rural manufacturing has acquired a certain importance in the form of different productive modes—from sub-contracting to home-based workers (cottage industries), to the installation of small and medium-sized workshops that employ the rural population. Tlaxcala was not exempted from this industrialization process, which, added to the incipient industry set up in 1840, began to gain force starting in the 1960s. This has meant that the state of Tlaxcala has gone from having a predominantly rural population, devoted to agricultural activity, to having a population diversified among the three productive sectors (Barrientos 2000).

Since the 1960s, the development of the industrial sector in Tlaxcala was supported by different factors: the availability of means of communication and services, an official policy of industrialization and a geographical location which places the state on the Federal District (Mexico City)-Puebla-Tlaxcala-Veracruz commercial route, connecting the state with the country's main consumer center. In this scenario, the establishment of manufacturing centers began to take root in the southern part of the state of Tlaxcala (where the greater part of the state's industry is currently concentrated). It was only in 1978 that, for the first time, an industrial center (Ciudad Industrial Xicohténcatl) was installed in the northern part of the state, with the objectives of generating jobs and taking advantage of the raw materials naturally found in the region. The location of Tlaxcala in a strategic zone within Mexico and the existing infrastructure make this region attractive to capital from the United States and Canada in the context of the North American Free Trade Agreement (NAFTA).

In the 1980s, the productive structure in Tlaxcala included two main activities: agriculture and industry. During the same period, the state of the agricultural activity implied a high rate of unemployment, misery and uncertainty. One of the options open to the peasant sector was migration to the towns where they could market their labor in Tlaxcala's industries (Leñero Franco 1984). Added to this, new ways of being contracted to work at home came into operation, a tendency appearing first in the 1970s, only to increase during the 1980s (Alonso 1991).

Given the precarious living conditions of the peasant workers, both men and women, and the process of industrialization in the State, the agricultural population has been converted into a sizeable source of cheap, abundant labor for industry, which in turn has transformed the productive structure. In other words, from being a zone that was eminently rural and with a population linked fundamentally to agricultural activities, the state of Tlaxcala has turned into a mainly industrial area.

Although the state of Tlaxcala is the smallest in area in the Mexican Republic, it has played a very important role in the process of industrialization. Its peasant communities have been adapting themselves to the combination of agricultural and manufacturing activities, with the result that the old stereotype of the self-sufficient peasant worker disappeared long ago. Because of high costs of production, lack of subsidies, high interest rates and scarcity of land (2.7 ha of crop land per peasant worker), rural families are no longer able to satisfy their needs regarding maize and beans (staple foods), and thus the peasants find themselves forced either to take up paying jobs in local businesses or to migrate. Worse yet, the income earned from the paid employment has become indispensable for the investment and productivity of the fields (Calva 1994; 1998; Wilson, cited by Barrientos 2000). As pointed out by Lara (1996), many communities currently combine agrarian and extra-agrarian activities, which are both formal and informal, within the same physical space, becoming a population which is ever more diversified, and in which women play a central role.

However, whilst these communities are in the process of generating new forms of organization, they can no longer be defined in their most simple forms as either rural or urban. By the year 2000, the State had 313 industries (including small, medium and large) dedicated to the manufacture of food products, drinks, footwear, electrical and electronic goods, chemical substances, products derived from petroleum, carbon, rubber, plastics, textiles, clothing, wood products, basic metals industries and non-metallic mineral products. Most of these industries were oriented to exports. The main destinies were the United States, Australia, Guatemala, Venezuela, Italy, Canada, Ecuador, Chile, Korea and the Philippines (Gobierno del Estado de Tlaxcala 1998, cited by Barrientos 2000).

Ciudad Industrial Xicohténcatl (Industrial City Xicohténcatl) is the most extensive of the new industrial cities now in Tlaxcala. The first is located in an isolated rural area approximately twenty minutes from the city of Apizaco, which provides most of the labor for Ciudad Industrial I (hereinafter referred to as CIXI). The second (hereinafter referred to as CIXII) is located about ten minutes from the city of Huamantla, and very near the community of Benito Juárez, the community analyzed in this study. Currently, Ciudad Industrial Xicohténcatl is made up of forty industries (thirty-four in the first section and six in the second), thus making it one of the manufacturing centers that has generated the most jobs in recent years.

The main industries include chemical production and the manufacture of clothing, together with the traditional textile industry. The chemical industry has a different pattern of employment than the textile and clothing industries. The chemical industry tends to offer employment to men, both adults and young men, whereas the textile industry mainly employs young women. The companies originate from various countries. Considering both sections of Ciudad Industrial together, twenty-one of the companies are Mexican, eight are German, six are from the United States, three from France, one from Holland, and one from Italy. The branches of activity include: the motor industry (7), chemical industries, pharmaceuticals and agri-chemicals (6), *maquila* clothing and textile industries (5), plastics (4), non-metallic minerals (3), metal (2), mechanical metal (2), manufacturing (2), electronics (2), paper and cellulose (1), industrial fabrics (1), wood (1), fiber glass (1), agricultural machinery (1), metal wood (1) and food (1). According to data provided by the Ciudad Industrial Trust (Pers. Com, CIXI Trust March 2001), in January 2001 both sections together employed a total of 9,635 workers in the different companies, even though only three of the companies (Linda Vista, Vista of Huamantla, and Olivetti) accounted for 55 percent of these workers. Taking only Linda Vista and Vista of Huamantla (which are both part of the same US company), the number of workers employed in January 2001 was 3,881 (40 percent of the total). It is worth mentioning that women are mainly employed in the *maquila* clothing industries and in industries assembling typewriters (Linda Vista, Vista of Huamantla and Olivetti respectively) or for cleaning in other types of factories (Pers. Com. CIXI Trust March 2001). This demonstrates a selective preference for either men or women for given activities. Nevertheless, the lack of employment in the economy has resulted in qualified workers joining *maquila* companies, thereby creating inequitable competition for the women laborers. The women, because they have fewer opportunities for training than men, are thus displaced and have to relocate in places where the working conditions are outside the law: in other words, in workshops or doing piecework at home, these being the only other options open to women (UNIFEM 1999).

The Principal Characteristics of the Communities

The information presented in this paper was gathered in three different communities in the state of Tlaxcala: Emiliano Zapata, Lázaro Cárdenas and Benito Juárez. The first two are municipal capitals, and the third forms part of the municipality of Huamantla. These three communities are close to Ciudad Industrial. They have a similar number of inhabitants, and are fundamentally agricultural in nature.

Moreover, as CIXII was more recently founded than CIXI, it is logical to assume that the effects observed in communities located in the zones of respective influence will be different. In other words, the community of Benito Juárez, which is near CIXII, can be considered a community in transition where the changes are still in an early phase. Emiliano Zapata and Lázaro Cárdenas, on the other hand, as they are near CIXI, can be expected to demonstrate more consolidated changes. Thus, on comparing the results, it will be possible to see the differences between these three communities, all of which have an agricultural base but which are passing through different stages of industrialization. Set out below are the principal characteristics of each of these communities, in relation to their existing natural resources, population, productive activities and services.

The municipality of Emiliano Zapata is located in the east of the state, some twenty-three kilometers from Ciudad Industrial Xicohténcat. It extends over a large area of fertile land and forest. Emiliano Zapata comprises a total of 1,864 hectares of *ejido* land (plots of land owned individually but administrated collectively) and approximately two hundred hectares of cultivated land and forest. The Municipality has public education services: primary, tele-secondary and preparatory schools and there are roads in good condition linking Emiliano Zapata with nearby villages. The community has running water and electricity available, although the water only arrives every three or four days, and therefore has to be stored in household tanks in the interim (Paz Arriaga 2000).

The lands are fundamentally used for maize, frijol beans, potatoes, oats and other cereals. These are mainly for the population's own consumption, except for the potatoes which are usually taken to market. The lands are economically productive between the months of June and August. After that, the local people devote their time to harvesting, gathering seeds for the following year, leaving some land lying fallow and preparing other areas for the following crop. This municipality has no irrigation that would allow year-round cultivation of all the lands. The wage-laborers (19% of the total adult population) go off to work in Ciudad Industrial Xicohténcatl in the different companies, or they are employed by the local *maquila* workshops. About thirty to forty small dressmaking workshops operate here, distributed throughout the community, as well as a small timber industry directed by the community on *ejido* land. Four of these workshops are large (employing about fifty people), and the others are family workshops (each providing employment for four to ten members of a family). In both categories, young men and women predominate. The existence of jobs in the dressmaking workshops offers an alternative to Ciudad Industrial Xicohténcatl. At a very early age (between eleven and sixteen), the women of this community begin working in the *maquila* businesses. The family workshops are where the women start their apprenticeship, and they are later employed in the bigger workshops or in the companies (Barrientos 2000; Nelson 1999).

As regards health services, Emiliano Zapata has a Health Center staffed by a senior student of medicine (a year's service in an outlying community is a requirement for graduation). There is a municipal Presidency, an auditorium and a Roman Catholic Church (99% of the population is Roman Catholic, and 1% are Jehovah's Witnesses). There are also basketball and football fields where the young people (mostly the young men) gather at weekends; this being the only recreation facility in this community. There is a telephone booth with two lines, a messenger service and a postal service, although this is unreliable. Emiliano Zapata also has a group of shops selling food and other products, some diners, butcher shops, bakeries, stationery shops, sandwich bars and a pharmacy. The presence of these businesses, which provide the majority of the services, makes it unnecessary for the local people to go into Apizaco or other places (Nelson 1999).

Lázaro Cárdenas is located to the southeast of Emiliano Zapata and was founded in 1938. In September 1995, it was declared an independent municipality (Serrano Camacho 2001; Nelson 1999; Macías Lima 2000). The education services include a pre-primary, primary and a tele-secondary school, as well as a distance learning center for a first degree in education. The Health Center also provides medical attention to ten neighboring communities that lack that service. Lázaro Cárdenas has five grocery shops, bakeries, clothing shops, *tortilla* shops, restaurants and other businesses such as a stationery shop, an ironmonger, a tinsmith and a paint shop. All of these together mean that most of the basic necessities can be acquired within the community itself. There is also a private medical practice and a dental practice. However, as there is no pharmacy, medicines have to be obtained either from the Health Center or in Apizaco. Lázaro Cárdenas has a drinking-water system, drainage, sewage system, street lighting and a paved road that goes to Ciudad Industrial Xicohténcatl and to the city of Apizaco. In addition, there are also warehouses to store fertilizers, a public telephone booth, two recreational areas and a municipal cemetery. There are three public transport lines that pass through every fifteen minutes and cover three different routes.

The agricultural surface area of the community is 1,108 hectares, of which 503 hectares are under irrigation. The irrigation is supplied by a system of gravity from two dams, one located at either end of the community. The main crops are maize, wheat (produced fundamentally on non-irrigated seasonal lands) and vegetables cultivated under irrigation, such as lettuce (the most widely grown in terms of surface area), broccoli, carrots, beetroot, cauliflower, potatoes, white beans and others. Other agricultural activities include the production of dairy herds, both cattle and goat and some pig farms.

Benito Juárez is closest to Ciudad Industrial Xicohténcatl II, linked by a paved motorway that continues on to the city of Huamantla. Benito Juárez was founded in 1935, but it was not until 1970 that this community was declared a separate village (Chávez Márquez 2000). The education services include one preschool, one morning school and one evening school for primary level and one tele-secondary school. The local agriculture is fundamentally seasonal, the main crops being maize, wheat and barley, given that the irrigation available is scanty. The *ejido* land covers about 1,360 hectares, with a further 500 hectares under irrigation, and a surface area of 300 hectares of *ejido* land devoted to cattle grazing. Some members of the community also work in the production of milk and dairy derivatives. The main destination of the products is for local consumption. Dressmaking workshops are also growing in number, and these form the principal source of work for the young women. Table 7.1 shows some demographic characteristics for the three communities.

Community surveys were directed as much to both men and women. Twenty surveys were carried out in each community, selecting one home per block. The information was collected through both closed and open questions on the following themes: composition and characteristics of the domestic/family unit; educational levels; infrastructure of the homes; paid and unpaid working practices; distribution of work and its rationality; migration patterns; perceptions of the changes in family and community relations.

The surveys were administered to fifteen men and forty-five women, distributed in the following manner: In Benito Juárez eleven women and nine men; in Lázaro Cárdenas, eighteen women and two men; and in Emiliano Zapata, sixteen women and four men. Even though efforts were made to include a similar number of men and women, the unequal distribution was due mainly to the fact that, at the time when the surveys were carried out, it was the women who were at home. However, as a large part of the information collected referred to the family group, both women and men were represented in similar proportions.

Of the interviewees, forty-three (71.6%) were born in the same community where they currently reside, whilst the rest had moved from nearby places to live in the respective communities. Of the remaining seventeen, fourteen were women who had moved into the communities because they had married residents of those communities, and the other three had moved together with their respective families for reasons of work. The ages of those interviewed ranged from fifteen to seventy-five years old, the greatest number (sixteen) being in the forty to forty-nine range and the second and third groups (twelve in each) being between twenty and twenty-nine and thirty and thirty-nine respectively. The majority (forty-four) were married, eight were single, three were unmarried but living with a partner, three were single mothers and two were widowed.

Table 7.1 Demographic Characteristics by Community

	Benito Juárez	*Lázaro Cárdenas*	*Emiliano Zapata*
Total Population	4542	2638	2512
Men	2241 (49.3%)	1334 (50.6%)	1236 (49.2%)
Women	2301 (50.7%)	1304 (49.4%)	1276 (50.8%)
Predominant age group	5–9	10–14	5–9
Primary school	70%	35%	65%
Illiterate population	7%	4.8%	6.9%
Number of families	971	556	543
Type of families			
Nuclear*	54%	69%	80%
Extended**	36%	15%	13%
Compound Extended***	10%	16%	7%

Source: Chávez Márquez, 2000; Paz Arriaga, 2000; Serrano Camacho, 2001.
Note: *Nuclear family: father, mother, children; **Extended family: father, mother, children, and father and mother of either one of the couple; ***Compound extended family: all of the above, and brothers and/or sisters-in-law, nieces and nephews and others.

Six of those interviewed had no schooling at all, nineteen had not completed primary school, eighteen had finished primary school, three had done a year or two of secondary school, eleven had finished secondary school and three had done a year or two of preparatory school. Nuclear type families (father, mother, children) predominated, there being forty-three; compound extended families were next (more than one family on the same dwelling site) with a total of twelve, and lastly there were the extended families, numbering five.

The number of children per family ranges from one to fourteen, the mean per family in Benito Juárez being 4.6, in Lázaro Cárdenas 4.9, and in Emiliano Zapata 3.8. In Benito Juárez five families had children living away from home, in Lázaro Cárdenas the number of families with children living away from home was seven, and in Emiliano Zapata it was also seven.

The majority of the families interviewed had access to *ejido* lands. In effect, of the sixty families, fifty owned a plot of *ejido* land and one family in Lázaro Cárdenas leases one hectare. In some cases, those interviewed worked together with their parents or parents-in-law. The surface area of the plots ranged from one to eight hectares, the average among those interviewed in Benito Juárez being four hectares, in Lázaro Cárdenas 2.5 hectares, and in Emiliano Zapata 1.8 hectares. The main crops grown in Benito Juárez are maize and frijol beans, in Emiliano Zapata there is also a potato crop which was common until 2000 (the fall in prices, rise in production costs and the diminishing yields determined that the sowing also reduced considerably), whilst in Lázaro Cárdenas it is common to combine the maize crop with vegetables (lettuce, carrots, beetroot, broccoli) because of the existence of irrigation. In general, the production of maize and frijol beans is destined for family consumption, and when the production exceeds the consumption needs, the surplus is sold in the nearby cities. In Lázaro Cárdenas the vegetables are sold through an intermediary who transports them to Guanajuato to be exported. Some families also have animals (cattle, sheep, birds), the production of which is in general destined also for the family's consumption. Eight families have dairy cattle. The production is mainly for their own consumption, but any surplus is sold to local merchants.

Of the men interviewed and the partners of the women interviewed, thirty-nine had as their main occupation that of peasant worker. Even though the greater responsibility for work in the fields falls on the men, the women and children also perform tasks in the fields, on the weekend and fundamentally during the periods when the work is heaviest, which is at the time of sowing or harvesting. During the rest of the year, it is fairly usual for the men to take temporary work as builders, either in their own communities or in nearby cities (Tlaxcala, Puebla, Mexico DF), and/or as day workers in neighboring fields. This is also a common occurrence among the oldest sons of those interviewed. According to many, these activities are essential for complementing the family income, and for the family to be able to subsist during the year. The *ejido* administrator of one of the communities said in this context: "I work as a builder and I get paid $100 a day if I go to Puebla to work. I earn more as a builder than as a peasant worker." The low prices the peasant workers receive for their production, and the difficulty of competing with products from the other countries in NAFTA, are made clear in the following comments:

NAFTA affects us because they have brought lots of products in and those of the community don't move. A year ago the maize crop froze. I took it to Huamantla to sell, they rejected it and I had to sell at $1.00 to be able to sell it. There [in the USA] they grow 10 tons per hectare and here we only raise three tons per hectare; there they use a lot of chemicals and here it is only produced in the traditional way; for big industry, NAFTA it's worth it, but for the peasant worker sector it's a disadvantage.

—man, ejido administrator, Benito Juárez

I'm still stuck with the countryside . . . according to policy the countryside comes first, but we don't make anything. You put in money but the maize isn't worth anything, they are paying $1. You hoe, you plough, you clean, you harvest, you stack the corn and who pays you?

—man, aged 63, Benito Juárez

Some of the men interviewed or the partners of women interviewed performed other types of activity. In some cases these were part-time and in others, full-time. These activities included electrician (1), carpenter (1), company driver (1), shop owner (1), transport inspector (1), family dressmaking workshop (3) and employees in Ciudad Industrial Xicohténcatl (5). As opposed to those who worked for themselves, those who were employed on contract had social security, an annual holiday with holiday pay and a Christmas bonus.

According to one of the young people interviewed who used to work in one of the factories in Ciudad Industrial Xicohténcatl, there are about twenty young people in Benito Juárez under the age of twenty-five who work in these industries. The requisite to have finished secondary school is an obstacle to entry, and because of this condition the greater part of the population is ineligible.

The women mainly devote themselves to duties in the home. That is what thirty-two of the women interviewed said, as did ten of the men interviewed when they spoke about the main activity of their partners. Several of the women mentioned having worked at various activities which they gave up when they married.These occupations varied: looking after children, housemaids and employees in the factories in Ciudad Industrial or in dressmaking workshops. The main reason they gave for leaving their jobs was that their husbands did not want them to continue working at these occupations but wanted them to devote themselves to the home. This is a very deeply ingrained tradition in the communities and represents, in some cases, a cause of frustration. The raising of small children also means that the women are limited in their possibilities as regards working outside the home. The following are some of the comments the women made about their situation:

Men say that the woman who marries is for the house. I think they ought to help each other.

—woman, aged nineteen, Emiliano Zapata

If I could, I would work outside the house, but my husband won't let me. I'd like to have work in my house which would allow me to watch my children, because I can't leave them alone because when I come who knows what they have done. But I really would like to have something to do in my house to have money, to be able to help my husband a little.

—woman, aged 33, Lázaro Cárdenas

The truth is that I really like working. I have always been restless, you notice that you are needed, and I feel that I develop more, that I learn new things... Where I have been [factory Lindavista] they have given me a lot of confidence, lots of help to learn things that you don't learn at home . . . I had to leave. My husband didn't want me to go on working.

—woman, aged 39, Lázaro Cárdenas

Regarding the remaining thirteen women interviewed who did not have the home as their only occupation, one is a student, another is a peasant worker (widow), and the other eleven have paying jobs. Thus, five women iron or take washing into their homes, either from other families or for the dressmaking workshops of their communities, two have dressmaking workshops (in which case it is seen as a family activity), two work in dressmaking workshops in the community, another works in a shop, and the last one works in a factory in Ciudad Industrial Xicohténcatl. These women considered it very necessary to be generating some extra income for the family, or for their personal spending.

In general there is a positive evaluation regarding the existence of other work opportunities, such as the dressmaking workshops and the factories in Ciudad Industrial, given that these represent the possibility of remaining in the community. Nevertheless, some comments were critical about the factories.

There was an advance of the dressmaking workshops; they [owners] bring their dressmaking from Mexico (City). Before it was hard work trying to earn money, the children went around barefoot before. The families don't leave so often for other places.

—woman, aged 59, Emiliano Zapata

I say it's better, before there wasn't anywhere to work, now there are workshops it's better.

—woman, aged 19, Emiliano Zapata

The factories have helped a lot; this was a really poor colony. At least the girls have begun to look and dress better.

—woman, aged 62, Emiliano Zapata

Since my daughters work [in the workshops] we don't suffer like before. Before we never had any money.

—woman, aged 55, Emiliano Zapata

The factories have brought improvements but not for the workers, for the owners. The workers don't get better, don't make any progress. We prefer working at home because in the factories you still get tired, you get bored.

—woman, aged 23, Emiliano Zapata

When they started installing these factories four years ago you saw more support for the people, for the young people, but from then until now... Almost only young people get in, older people no. But for the young people it has helped somewhat. Many people have avoided going to the cities, to Puebla, to Mexico (City). You don't earn much. The wages are low. What they buy is more expensive, but it's a relief, at least so that they can buy clothes and shoes. I see that even the villages look as if they're expanding more, because people go and work in the industries, they come back, they meet someone there among the young people, they marry, and make their own homes, people no longer leave.

—man, aged 59, Lázaro Cárdenas

In some cases there is a preference for working in the workshops, and not in the factories, because it is more convenient and requires less effort:

It takes up a lot of time going to the factories, with the workshop you are your own boss.

—man, aged 29, Emiliano Zapata

However, emigration to other cities and abroad is still frequent:

Many people emigrate, leaving the land rented.

—*ejido* administrator, Benito Juárez

In some cases, emigration is only for a few months a year, returning to the community once the activity for which they were contracted has terminated.

Through the office of the Tlaxcala State Employment Service, a federal program is also administered for the placement of agricultural workers abroad (Canada), a programme that has been in operation since 1996. Through this program peasant workers between the ages of twenty-two and forty-five, who have economic dependents, can put their names forward for seasonal work in Canada, doing agricultural work. The result is that, each month, sixty people are sent from different parts of the state (Pers.Com. Tlaxcala State Employment Service, April 2001).

Conclusion

The signing of NAFTA, in the context of the application of neo-liberal economic policies, has provoked enormous social and economic changes in rural communities, but the effects cannot be said to be entirely favorable. On the one hand, the importing of basic grains from the United States, with the consequent decrease in the price of the products, has affected peasant families, forcing their members to seek productive alternatives in order to be able to subsist. Amongst these alternatives is the use of irrigation in crop production. The crops then sell for higher prices and may even enter foreign markets. This is a means of alleviating in part the economic deficiencies generated by the fall in the price of maize and of other basic grains. However, this situation does not apply to all the communities, because the required agricultural, ecological and economic conditions do not always exist. One important restriction is that irrigation is very costly, and subsidies have been reduced with the liberalization of the economy. Of the three communities studied, only one (Lázaro Cárdenas) had adopted the irrigation production strategy with subsidies from the government and farmers' economic contribution.

On the other hand, the implantation of industries in rural areas—a process that has been accentuated since the implementation of NAFTA—has altered the rural landscape. However, according to this study, the profile of the occupation of the residents has not been greatly affected. Even though the impact of these industries on the communities studied has been favorable from the point of view of the creation of new jobs, this has been limited to the young population and to those with a better level of education, benefiting thus only a small part of the population. The creation of home-based or community *maquila* workshops has constituted an alternative strategy which has, in part, made up for the lack of job opportunities in industry. The weight of the gender division of work, where the women—once they form their own home—carry out duties linked essentially to the domestic sphere, adds to the paltry incidence of industry in the occupational patterns of the inhabitants of these communities. This tendency can be reverted to the extent that the economic benefits obtained through employment in industry, are sufficiently attractive to engage the better educated male population as much as the female population.

Notes

1. *Maquila or Maquiladora,* also known as twin plant, in bond plant, offshore production plant or runaway plant. Article 321 of the Mexican Customs Code defines a Maquiladora as an industrial enterprise with: (1) temporarily imported machinery, whatever the manufacturing costs, exports its total production, or (2) a permanent industrial plant originally installed to supply the domestic market, now directs part or all of its production for exportation, and the direct manufacturing cost of its product at the time of exportation does not reach 40 percent (Fernández-Kelly 1983, p. 221).

References

Alonso, José A. 1991. *Mujeres, Maquiladoras Y Microindustria Doméstica.* México: Fontamara.
Barrientos, María del Socorro. 2000. *Género Y Maquila. Situación Laboral E Identidad De Género De Mujeres Trabajadoras De Tres Comunidades De Tlaxcala.* Tesis De

Maestra En Ciencias. Departamento de Desarrollo Rural. Colegio de Postgraduados. Montecillo. México.

Calva, José Luis. 1994. *Probables Efectos De Un Tratado De Libre Comercio En El Campo Mexicano.* México Fontamara.

———. 1998. "La Economía Nacional Y La Agricultura De México a Tres Años De Operación Del TLCAN." In Rita Schwentesius Rindermann, Manuel Angel Gómez Cruz and Gary W. Williams. coords. *TLC y agricultura: ¿Funciona el experimento?* p. 85–110. CIESTAAM, Universidad Autónoma de Chapingo, México.

Chávez Márquez, Eduardo. 2000. *Diagnóstico De Salud / Estudio De Comunidad. Pueblo De Benito Juárez, Municipio De Huamantla. Jurisdicción Sanitaria II. 1o. Febrero 1999–31 Enero 2000.* UNAM-Facultad de Medicina, Organismo Público D scentralizado de Salud de Tlaxcala (inédito).

INEGI. 1999. *Encuesta Nacional de Empleo. 1998.* Tlaxcala. Aguascalientes:Instituto Nacional de Estadística, Geografía e Informática.

Lara Flores, Sara M. 1996. "El Papel De Las Mujeres En La Nueva Estructura De Los Mercados De Trabajo Rural-Urbanos." In Hubert C. de Grammont and Hector Tejeda Gaona. coords. *La Sociedad Rural Mexicana Frente Al Nuevo Milenio.* vol. II. México: INAH, UNAM, Plaza de Valdés Editores, p. 145–76.

Leñero Franco, Estela. 1984. *El Heno Y El Sexo (La Mujer Obrera En Dos Industrias D Tlaxcala).* México Centro de Investigaciones y Estudios Superiores en Antropología Social. Cuadernos de la Casa Chata Hidalgo y Matamoros.

Macías Lima, Fortunato. 2000. "Diagnóstico de Lázaro Cárdenas." unpublished.

Nelson, Becky M. 1999. *Economic And Social Impacts Of The North American Free Trade Agreement in Tlaxcala, México.* Masters Thesis. Stillwater: Oklahoma State University

Paz Arriaga, Donaciano F. 2000. *Diagnóstico de Salud: Emiliano Zapata 2000.* Tlaxcala: UNAM-Facultad de Medicina. Secretaría de Salud. O. P. D. Salud de Tlaxcala. unpublished.

Pers. Com. 2001. March. CIXI Trust. Fideicomiso de Ciudad Industrial Xicohténcatl I.

Pers. Com. 2001. April. Tlaxcala State Employment Service.

Serrano Camacho, Vicente. 2001. *Estudio de Comunidad. U.A.S. Lázaro Cárdenas.* Secretaría de Salud del Estado de Tlaxcala. UNAM-Facultad de Medicina (unpublished).

UNIFEM (United Nations Development Fund for Women). 1999. *El Impacto Del TLC En La Mano De Obra Femenina En México.* México: UNIFEM.

Part II

Shifting Realities: Women and Men Moving in the Economy

Chapter 8

Gender and Work in Malaysia: Forces behind the Work Patterns

Noor Rahamah Hj. Abu Bakar

There have been some changes in the distribution of employment by gender in Malaysia, where women account for about 40 percent of all employed workers. Women find their labor in high demand at a time when it is becoming increasingly acceptable for them to participate in paid employment. Women and men seem to be involved in different types of industries doing different kinds of work. They are also found at different levels of the organizational hierarchy. Why has the number of women in certain industries risen since 1991? This question is the central concern of this chapter. We propose that the answer is related to the different forces behind the work patterns of women and men in the Malaysian situation.

The analysis of trends in occupation shows some changes in the detailed occupational structure, involving a shift of the women and men's labor force into different industrial and occupational categories. Secondary and primary data clearly show that the factors that influence the changes in the employment structure are the changing structure of the economy, the level of formal education received, the division of domestic labor and societal attitudes. The discussion in this chapter is presented in three sections. The first section reviews the trends in labor force participation by age group, level of education, industrial sector, occupational group and employment status, followed by a section which discusses the forces behind the work patterns, and the conclusion follows.

To know the factors influencing changes in the employment structure by gender, we need to first analyze the occupational gender structure of the Malaysian labor force. Direct comparisons are possible using secondary data from the Population and Housing Census published by the Malaysia Department of Statistics for the years 1970, 1980 and 1991. Population censuses are the only source of data covering a long enough time-span to allow the measurement of change in employment. To obtain primary data for the attitudinal section of this study, a survey was carried out using purposive sampling. A sample of 12 families, each containing three generations, was selected. An in-depth interview was used to gather information regarding individuals' attitude toward work. These results are presented in the last section of the chapter in support of the census data.[1]

The labor force participation rates of men have always been relatively high and remained steady at around 83.8 percent in 1991. The work rates for women were also fairly stable, at about 41.9 percent in the same year (table 8.1).

Table 8.1 Labor Force Participation Rates, Malaysia

Year	Total	Female	Male
1970	60.2	38.9	81.6
1980	63.3	42.2	84.4
1991	62.9	41.9	83.8

Source: Population and Housing Census, Malaysia Department of Statistics, 1970, 1980 and 1991.

The beginning working age in Malaysia has shifted to the age group of 20–24 years because more children are receiving formal education. The percentage of those involved in the labor force beyond the retirement age of about 55 years has decreased for both women and men (table 8.2). The participation pattern for women influenced by the women's life-cycle is different from that of men. The trend for men is one of an increase and later a decrease in labor force participation, in an inverse U-shaped curve. Participation of men in 1991 increases from the age of fifteen years peaking at almost 100 percent for the most productive age of 35–39 years. The drop from 1970 to 1991 of men in the labor force at the younger age (15–19 years) was due to the rise in men's educational attainment.

Women enter the labor force at a younger age (15–19 years), 34.6 percent of women in this group were in the labor force. Their participation rates before 1991 are highest in the age group of 20–24 years, start to decrease in the age group of 25–29 years, but increase again in the age group of 30–34 and decline again in the age group of 50–54 years. The situation is a bit different for 1991, whereby the participation rate increase is at its highest in the age group of 20–24 years, an average of 59.6 percent. Work rates drop again to 50.1 percent in the age group of 25–29 years and continue to decrease until the age of retirement. Statistics also show that the rate of economic activity among the women in the age group of 40–49 years is higher compared to the age group of 15–19 years.

The participation trends of women in the labor force have been termed the "two-phase" working life, or the bimodal pattern of female employment. In 1970 we see the emergence of the bimodal pattern. After a drop in the economic

Table 8.2 Labor Force Participation Rates by Age Group and Gender, Malaysia

Age	1970		1980		1991	
	Male	Female	Male	Female	Male	Female
15–19	53.0	34.6	48.9	34.6	43.1	32.9
20–24	87.3	43.1	91.5	53.5	88.1	59.6
25–29	93.4	40.0	97.3	44.7	96.6	50.1
30–34	94.1	40.5	97.9	41.5	97.4	45.1
35–39	93.9	41.8	98.0	43.7	97.7	42.2
40–44	92.9	41.9	97.6	44.8	97.2	39.7
45–49	91.3	42.5	96.4	42.9	95.9	37.7
50–54	86.9	38.4	92.7	38.3	90.6	31.5
55–59	76.6	30.9	78.8	33.1	68.3	22.4
60–64	66.4	28.1	70.1	27.2	56.1	16.3
Average	81.6	38.9	84.8	42.2	83.8	41.9

Source: Population and Housing Census, Malaysia Department of Statistics, 1970, 1980 and 1991.

Figure 8.1 Labor Force Participation Rates

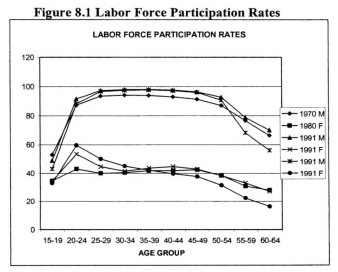

activity rate in the 25–29 age group, there is a slight increase in the rate of women's participation for ages 35–39 years. The age group in which peak work rates occur changed from 20–24 years and 45–49 years in 1970 to 20–24 years in 1991 (figure 8.1). In 1991, changes can be seen when the participation rate of women by age group is similar to that of a unimodal curve. The emergence of

**Table 8.3 Distribution of Population Age Six and Above by
Educational Attainment and Gender, Malaysia**

	Never Attended School (Percent)	Attended School (Percent)	Total (Percent)	Number (000s)
	Total Population			
1970	43	57	100	10,319.3
1980	23	77	100	10,932.6
1991	16*	84	100	14,705.3
	Male			
1970	36	64	100	5,198.4
1980	16	84	100	5,441.8
1991	12*	88	100	7,390.4
	Female			
1970	51	49	100	5,120.9
1980	29	71	100	5,490.8
1991	20*	80	100	7,314.9

Source: Population and Housing Census, Malaysia Department of Statistics, 1970,
1980 and 1991;
Note: *includes pre-school.

Changes can also be seen in the level of education received among the labor
force. Table 8.3 shows that the total percent of the labor force never attending
school decreased from 43.0 percent in 1970 to 16.0 percent in 1991. The increase in the percentage of the female population attending school is very encouraging. There was an increase from 49 percent in 1970 to 80 percent in 1991.

Educational opportunity for women has increased, as seen from the participation rate that is almost the same for female and male students at the primary
and secondary level. The total number of women having secondary and tertiary
education increased between 1970 and 1990 (table 8.4). Female students at the
upper secondary level are about 59.3 percent of the total enrolment in 1990. The
intake of female students at university level is about 44.3 percent of the total
intake for 1990. The intake of female students is increasing in fields such as
medicine, dentistry, engineering, architecture and accounting (Malaysia 1991a).
However, in terms of the discipline chosen by the students, there still exist differences by gender whereby female students are keener to enter the art stream.
An interesting trend is that the number of female students in the technical stream
had increased from 4.3 percent in 1970 to 35.9 percent in 1990. Male students
seem to be more interested in vocational disciplines (table 8.5).

Women and men seem to do different kinds of work in the labor market.
According to Hartmann (1976), Walby (1986, 1988), and Reskin and Roos

(1990), women are concentrated in certain types of industries and occupations. Changes in the gender composition can be seen from the changes that take

Table 8.4 Female Population by Educational Attainment, Malaysia, 1991

Educational Attainment	1970 Number (000s)	1970 percent	1991 Number (000s)	1991 percent
Primary				
(7–12 yrs.)	4,570.5	89.25	5,621.4	64.84
Some Primary	1,957.3	38.20	2,772.2	31.98
No School	2,613.1	51.00	2,559.3	29.52
Pre-School	na	na	220.7	2.54
Unknown	na	na	69.0	0.80
Secondary			2,619.1	30.21
(13–17 yrs.)	525.1			
Tertiary				
(18–22 yrs.)	25.1	0.49	428.8	4.95
Total	5,120.9	100.00	8,669.5	100.00

Source: Population and Housing Census, Malaysia Department of Statistics, 1970, 1980 and 1991
Note: na-data not available

Table 8.5 Female Student Enrollments as Percentage of Total Enrollment by Educational Level and Stream, Malaysia

	1970 percent	1980 percent	1990 percent
Educational Level			
Primary	46.8	48.6	48.6
Secondary	40.6	47.6	50.6
Upper Secondary	42.6	45.5	59.3
University	29.1	35.5	44.3
College (3 years)			
Polytechnic	13.2	21.5	25.2
Teachers Training Institute	41.9	48.3	56.1
Universiti Teknologi MARA (formerly Institute)	32.4	42.9	45.8
Tunku Abdul Rahman College	23.5	33.9	37.2
Stream			
Arts	47.4	61.0	64.8
Science	24.5	36.3	44.7
Vocational	24.2	30.4	22.0
Technical	4.3	27.1	35.9

Source: Population and Housing Census, Malaysia Department of Statistics, 1970, 1980 and 1991.

place in the type of industry, occupation category and employment status (table 8.6).

To what extent are the changes discussed earlier for the total population reflected in gender differences among the employed during 1970–1991? In table 8.6, the industrial groupings that had the highest percentage of women in 1970 were agriculture, forestry, hunting and fishing (38.0%), community, social and personal services (28.9%) and manufacturing (28.1%). Women's percentage in agriculture increased slightly between 1970 and 1980, but by 1991 their proportionate role in agriculture had declined.

Table 8.6 Percent Distribution of Employed Persons by Gender and Major Industry Group, Malaysia

Industry	1970		1980		1991	
	Male	Female	Male	Female	Male	Female
1.	62.0	38.0	61.0	39.0	71.7	28.3
2.	87.5	12.5	89.6	10.4	88.9	11.1
3.	71.9	28.1	59.9	40.1	54.6	45.4
4.	93.2	6.8	92.9	7.1	91.1	8.9
5.	94.6	5.4	93.0	7.0	95.3	4.7
6.	81.8	18.2	70.7	29.3	65.6	34.4
7.	95.7	4.3	93.7	6.3	91.3	8.7
8.	na	na	70.5	29.5	60.8	39.2
9.	71.1	28.9	70.6	29.4	64.8	35.2

Source: Population and Housing Census, Malaysia Department of Statistics, 1970, 1980 and 1991
Note: na-not available; Industry: 1. Agriculture, forestry, hunting and fishing; 2. Mining and quarrying; 3. Manufacturing; 4. Electricity, gas and water; 5. Construction; 6. Wholesale, retail trade, restaurants, hotels; 7. Transport, storage and communication; 8. Financing, insurance, real estate, and business services; 9. Community, social and personal services.

An interesting scenario happened in the manufacturing industry. In 1970, the statistics show that about three-quarters of the workers in manufacturing electrical machinery, appliances and supplies were male (71.9%) as compared to only 28.1 percent female workers. However, data for 1991 shows an entirely a different picture. The percentage distribution was almost the same between the male and female workers, 54.6 percent and 45.4 percent respectively. The large majority of women in manufacturing in 1970 were producing footwear, except rubber or plastic footwear (62.1%). By 1991 women's involvement moved to other sub-sectors, especially the manufacture of electrical machinery, appliances and supplies and the manufacture of apparel (except footwear) (table 8.7).

There has been considerable growth in recent decades in such capital-intensive industries as the manufacturing of machinery and transport equipment, miscellaneous products of petroleum and coal, and the manufacturing of

Table 8.7 Distribution of Employed Persons by Gender in the Manufacturing Sector, Malaysia (percents)

Industry	1970		1980		1991	
	Male	Female	Male	Female	Male	Female
Food Manufacturing	68.9	31.1	66.9	31.1	67.1	32.9
Beverage industries	78.1	21.9	72.6	27.4	71	29
Tobacco manufacturing	43.9	56.1	47.8	52.2	55	45
Manufacture of textiles	42.5	57.5	37.8	62.2	46.6	53.4
Manufacture of wearing apparel (except footwear)	na	na	20.5	79.5	17.8	82.2
Manufacture of leather, leather products, leather substitutes and fur (not footwear or wearing apparel)	55.1	44.9	49.2	50.8	43.9	56.1
Manufacture of footwear (except vulcanized or molded rubber or plastic footwear)	37.9	62.1	50.7	49.3	46.9	53.1
Manufacture of wood/cork products (except furniture)	75.7	24.3	79.5	20.5	77.2	22.7
Manufacture of furniture and fixtures (except primarily of metal)	95	5	84.8	15.2	81.7	18.3
Manufacture of paper and paper products	55.2	44.8	59.6	40.4	67.1	32.9
Printing, publishing and allied industries	74.7	25.3	62.8	37.2	61.4	8.6
Manufacture of industrial chemicals	69.3	30.7	81.8	18.2	83.5	16.5
Manufacture of other chemicals	na	na	57.4	42.6	58.9	41.1
Petroleum refineries	na	na	89.3	10.7	83.4	16.6
Products of petroleum and coal	95.2	4.8	80.6	19.4	83.7	16.3
Manufacture of rubber products	61.8	38.2	62.6	37.4	54.5	45.5
Manufacture of plastic products	na	na	46.4	53.6	52.3	47.7
Manufacture of pottery, china, and earthware	na	na	62.1	37.9	50.9	49.1
Manufacture of glass and glass products	na	na	77.7	22.3	76.8	23.2
Manufacture of non-metallic products	80.7	19.3	78.2	21.8	82	18
Iron and steel basic industries	94.7	5.3	89.1	10.9	89.2	10.8
Non-ferrous metal basic industries	na	na	88.1	11.9	87	13
Manufacture of fabricated metal products (except machinery and equipment)	85.7	14.3	79.6	20.4	79.2	20.8
Manufacture of machinery (except electrical)	93.4	6.6	88	12	72.2	27.8
Manufacture of electrical machinery, appliances, and supplies	85.6	14.4	26.8	73.2	31.4	68.6
Manufacture of transport equipment	97.8	2.2	88.9	11.1	83.9	16.1
Manufacture of professional and scientific measuring equipment	na	na	40.5	59.5	34.4	65.6
Other industries	78.4	21.6	74.6	25.4	52.3	47.7
Total manufacturing	71.9	28.1	59.9	40.1	54.6	45.4

Source: Population and Housing Census, Malaysia Department of Statistics, 1970, 1980 and 1991.
Note: na-not available; *working population age 10 years and above.

furniture and fixtures. Although these industries are predominantly male, the female share in the manufacturing of machinery in 1991 was a substantial 27.8 percent and 16.1 percent in the manufacturing of transport equipment (table 8.7). The growth in women's share of the labor force at a time when their overall share in agriculture was declining can be explained largely by women's increasing share in the manufacturing and the service sectors.

Table 8.8 Percent of All Employed Persons by Gender and Major Occupational Group, Malaysia

	1970		1980		1991	
Occupations	Male	Female	Male	Female	Male	Female
1.	66.1	33.9	57.8	42.2	56.5	43.5
2.	96.9	3.1	90.3	9.7	81.4	18.6
3.	74.7	25.3	50.3	49.7	47.5	52.5
4.	81.8	18.2	68.8	31.2	71.3	28.7
5.	68.2	31.8	60.0	40.0	63.8	36.2
6.	61.5	38.5	61.9	38.1	72.3	27.7
7.	83.4	16.6	76.2	23.8	73.7	26.3

Source: Population and Housing Census, Malaysia Department of Statistics, 1970, 1980 & 1991.
Note: Occupations: 1. Professional, technical and related workers; 2. Administrative and managerial workers; 3. Clerical and related workers; 4. Sales workers; 5. Service workers; 6. Agricultural, animal husbandry and forestry workers, fishermen and hunters; 7. Production and related workers, transport equipment operators and laborers.

While there have been dramatic changes in the female-male ratios in particular sectors and industries in Malaysia, there have been dramatic changes across occupations as well. Table 8.8 shows the percentage distribution of employed persons by gender. In 1970, a high percentage of male workers were seen in all types of occupations. However, by 1991 the percentage of male workers decreased in all types of occupation except in agriculture. The decreases are drastic in the clerical-type work: 47 percent male in 1991 compared to 74.7 percent male in 1970. The opposite happened with female workers. In 1991, the percentage of female workers increased in all types of occupations except agriculture. They represented about half of those in the clerical occupations in 1991. Concurrently, women increased their share in professional, technical and related fields, from 33.9 percent in 1970 to 43 percent in 1991. Other notable increases include among the administrative and managerial workers, from 3.1 percent in 1970 to 18.6 percent in 1991 and in production and related workers as well as transport equipment operators and laborers, from 16.6 percent to 26.3 percent in the same time frame. A notable decline occurred in the proportion of females who were agricultural, animal husbandry and forestry workers, fishermen and hunters, from 38.5 percent in 1970 to 27.7 percent in 1991.

The analysis thus far understates the occupational differences between women and men, since it is based on broad occupational groupings that do not reveal more detailed occupational differences. For example, although almost half of all those with professional and technical occupations were females, most of these women were teachers and nurses. Professional men were in a much wider range of occupations that included, along with teachers, substantial proportions that were architects, engineers, scientists, accountants, and lawyers.

The large concentration of women in relatively few occupations is characteristic of all employed women in Malaysia, not just professionals. Table 8.9a shows the top five detailed occupations for women from a total of 80 subcategories. Women are still seen working in the same categories between 1970 and 1991. However, their involvement as electrical fitters and related electrical and electronic workers increased. Although their participation in the agricultural industry is the highest among other sub-categories, the percentage declined. The total number working as teachers increased in 1991. It should be noted that the top five occupations in 1970 as compared with 1991 show a pattern of a slight shift in the employment of women from the informal sector to the formal sector of the economy. The focus of government towards industrialization and the opening of more factories provided opportunities for women to be involved in paid employment.

These data show that women still remain in the traditionally female jobs that are associated with light industry and the service sector. This shift in the leading occupations of employed women from one set of traditionally female jobs to another provides a view of the trend in the occupations by sex. The same applies to male workers. They still work in the agricultural industry, but the percentage of involvement had decreased in 1991. In 1970, the males worked as salesmen and shop assistants. However, the number had decreased by 1991 and this type of job was taken over by females. The employed males are now more likely to work as bricklayers and carpenters. This scenario is directly related to the rapid development of the construction industry (table 8.9b).

Table 8.9a The Five Most Prevalent Occupations Among Employed Females in Malaysia, 1970, 1991

1970	Total Number in Occupation	Percent in Occupation
Agricultural or animal husbandry	509,810	53.0
Planters and farmers	130,760	13.6
Maids and housekeeping services	46,272	4.8
Teachers	33,125	3.4
Salesmen and shop assistants	32,214	3.3
Top Five Total	962,217	78.2
1991		
Agricultural or animal husbandry	272,172	4.3
Planters and farmers	152,738	8.0
Maids and housekeeping services	151,556	8.0
Teachers	140,407	7.4
Salesmen and shop assistants	112,335	5.9
Top Five Total	1,902,369	33.6

Source: Population and Housing Census, Malaysia Department of Statistics, 1970, 1980 and 1991

Employment data at the industry level did not include employment status. To explain whether women are found in a less satisfactory work environment than men, work pattern by employment status should be examined. Employment status is classified into four categories, defined by the statistics department: employer, employee, own account worker and unpaid family worker. Economic

Table 8.9b The Five Most Prevalent Occupations Among Employed Males, Malaysia, 1970, 1991

	1970	Total Number in Occupation	Percent in Occupation
	Planters and farmers	483,143	22.4
	Agricultural and animal husbandry	429,221	19.9
	Salesmen and shop assistants	112,158	5.2
	Protective service workers	94,903	4.4
	Transport equipment operation	86,275	4.0
Top Five Total		1,119,427	52.0
	1991		
	Planters and farmers	459,608	11.4
2.	Agricultural and animal husbandry	427,355	10.6
3.	Salesmen and shop assistants	258,026	6.4
4.	Protective service workers	237,867	5.9
5.	Transport equipment operation	221,741	5.5
Top Five Total		1,604,597	40.0

Source: Population and Housing Census, Malaysia Department of Statistics, 1970, 1980 and 1991.

development in Malaysia has resulted in an increase of both males and females in the employee category and a decrease in unpaid family worker categories.

As shown in table 8.10, the employee category for male workers increased from 49.3 percent in 1970 to 64.1 percent in 1991. For female employees, the percentage distribution was 36.9 percent in 1970 and 70.8 percent in 1991.

The rate for own account worker and employer categories for both males and females decreased (Population and Housing Census, Malaysia Department of Statistics, 1970, 1980 and 1991(a)).

Forces behind the Changing Work Patterns

Secondary data show that women's involvement in the labor force increased slightly in 1991 as compared to 1970, concurrent with a slight decrease for males. Women are now participating in all types of jobs. There are four factors that can be considered to influence this change: (1) the changing structure of the economy; (2) level of formal education received; (3) the attitude of the society; and (4) the division of domestic labor.

Table 8.10 Percentage Distribution of Working Population by Gender and Employment Status, Malaysia, 1970, 1991

	1970		1991	
	Male	Female	Male	Female
Employer	4.2	2.3	3.6	2.0
Employee	49.3	36.9	64.1	70.8
Own account worker	31.9	18.0	28.3	16.7
Unpaid family worker	10.9	37.7	2.4	8.1
Looking for first job	3.7	5.1	na	na
Status not known	na	na	1.6	2.4
Total	100	100	100	100

Source: Population and Housing Census, Malaysia Department of Statistics, 1970, 1980 and 1991

The economic policy environment of Malaysia begins with the import-substitution type of approach from 1958 to 1968. The import-oriented industrialization strategy focused on the usage of local raw materials and did not require a high level of technology or skill in the workforce. Therefore, women had easy access to sectors such as agriculture, where they became farmers. In agriculture, the working hours are flexible and workers can bring their children to the field. The work they do does not require any training nor do they handle any heavy machinery. With the increase in the labor force, the import-substitution industry did not provide jobs for everyone. Therefore, high unemployment problems encouraged the government to introduce export-oriented industrialization in the early 1970s, which focused on labor-intensive industries. This encouraged multinational companies to invest in Malaysia, which offered cheap labor and financial incentives. The inflow of foreign investment was largely in the manufacturing sector. Both the electronics and textile/garment industries relied heavily on female workers because they could be paid lower wages and were deemed dexterous and obedient to the employer. In the 1980s the heavy industry strategy was implemented, whereby high levels of capital and technology were required. In the 1990s, the industrialization strategy of Malaysia was based on high technology and capital-intensive types of industry. These various processes of industrialization led to changes in women's role in the economy. Women have increased their presence in the workforce since 1970. They play an important role in the success of Malaysia's economy (Malaysia 1986).

Education is an important determinant of employment in the formal sector. Secondary education is very important for entry into the modern sector. The low achievement rate of women in education in 1970 is related to the domestic division of labor. According to human capital theory (Walby 1988), daughters are needed to look after their younger sisters and brothers and to help with the housework. Only 49.0 percent of women attended school in 1970, compared to 80.0 percent in 1991. The proportion that achieved the secondary level of schooling in 1970 was only 40.6 percent. However, the rate who received tertiary education increased from 29.1 percent in 1970 to 44.3 percent in 1990. The stream of education influenced women to choose work suitable for their skills.

The number of female students in the science and technical stream is very encouraging. In 1970, only 24.5 percent chose to be in the science stream as compared to 44.7 percent in 1990. The rate in technical schools also increased from 4.3 percent in 1970 to 35.9 percent in 1990.

Another factor that influenced the changing pattern of women's employment was the attitude of society. In order to establish any change in attitude, a sample of three generational families was selected and interviewed. The average age of respondents from first generation was 73, second generation 49 and 26 years old for the third generation. The average age at the time of first marriage for the first, second and third generation is seventeen, twenty-two and twenty-three years old. The difference in age at the time of first marriage among the three generations is related to the level of education received. The first generation married at an early age and they either did not go to school or received only primary education. The second generation married after high school whilst the third generation married after attending college or tertiary education.

In the sample, seven respondents received no formal education, twelve received primary education, eight secondary, four college and four university level education. Average family size is four but when looking by generation the picture is a bit different. The average size for first, second and third generation is six, four and one respectively. According to the economic status, sixteen respondents are not working, that is, eleven from the first generation and five from the second generation. Seven respondents had been working previously and nine are still working.

Respondents from the first generation said that they were not working because their husband and parents had not allowed them to do so. According to one respondent from the first generation, " ... auntie get objection from husband and mother-in-law when working as a production operator. Due to this objection, I was able to work for only two months. Well, at least I got the feeling of being a working woman." Respondents from the first generation married at an early age and had to be a full-time housewife looking after the children and the needs of their husbands. The narrow perception of the society towards work influenced the type of work women chose to do in 1970. Society had set a standard for the type of work suitable for women. Analysis shows the type of work suitable for women was as teachers, doctors, clerks and nurses. As one respondent said, "...working as a teacher is suitable for women. We need to work only half of the day; at 2:00 in the afternoon we are already at home. In the afternoon we can take care of the children and do the housework such as cleaning the house and cooking." However, with education the attitude of the society towards work changed. They ceased to categorize certain work as "women's work" and "men's work." Today, there are a number of women working as engineers, architects and lawyers.

The work carried out in the private sphere also influenced the type of work carried out by women in the 1990s. There was no longer a strict division of domestic labor such as existed in the 1970s. Members of the family do not make any specific rule as to who should do the housework such as cooking, cleaning, sending the children to school and attending to the children when they are ill.

The housework is not the sole responsibility of the women but also of members of the family including males. Empirical data show that the husbands do give a hand with the housework such as washing the clothes and cleaning the house. The help given by other family members enables women to be involved in the labor force.

Conclusion

This paper reviewed the detailed occupational structure of the Malaysia labor force. It examined policy changes instituted by the government; that is, from import-substitution industrialization to the adoption of an export-promotion strategy based upon foreign direct investment for continued growth rates. It has shown that economic development in Malaysia has depended heavily on the role of women to provide the supply of labor necessary for export-led development. This has indirectly influenced and changed the structure of employment.

Notes

1. Macro and micro analyses were used to obtain data. At the macro level, library research is carried out while a sampled survey is used to get primary data. Purposive sampling was used. Sampling unit of twelve families are chosen from families that have three female generations whether they are in the nucleus or extended family unit. The second generation is set as the main sample according to the highest level of education received. The families are chosen using the snowball technique. Data of the twelve families (thirty-six respondents) are gathered using the "life history method." An in-depth interview was carried out to gather information regarding individual's attitude towards work.

References

Beechey, V. 1983. *The Changing Experience of Women*. Milton Keynes: The Open University Press.

Hartmann, H. 1976. "Capitalism, Patriarchy and Job Segregation by Sex." In Beechey, V. *The Changing Experience Of Women*. Milton Keynes: The Open University Press.

Government of Malaysia. 1970. *Population and Housing Census*, vol. 1. Kuala Lumpur.

———. 1980. *Population and Housing Census*, vol. 1 and 2. Kuala Lumpur.

———. 1986. *Fifth Malaysia Plan, 1986–1990*. Kuala Lumpur.

———. 1991. *Population and Housing Census*. vol. 1 and 2. Kuala Lumpur.

———. 1991a. *Sixth Malaysia Plan 1991–1995*. Malaysia. 1995 *Seventh Malaysia Plan 1996–2000*. Kuala Lumpur.

Reskin, B. F. and Roos, P. A. 1990. *Job Queues, Gender Queues: Women's Inroad Into Male Occupations*. Philadelphia: Temple University Press.

Walby, S. 1986. *Patriarchy at Work: Patriarchal and Capitalist Relations in Employment*. Cambridge UK: Polity Press.

———. ed. 1988. *Gender Segregation at Work*. Milton Keynes: The Open University Press.

Chapter 9

Locating Women: Structure and Work in the Ugandan Macroeconomy

Linda E. Lucas

Women are working in Uganda as farmers in subsistence agriculture providing food and some income for their families; in the formal and informal marketplace selling and trading; in government service as teachers, nurses and administrators; in the professional arena as physicians, administrators, artists and professors; and in the private sector as clerks, managers, midwives, coffee bean sorters, entrepreneurs and typists. Although women are present across the occupational distribution in Uganda, their numbers outside agriculture and at paid levels in the private sector are relatively small.

The Government of Uganda is committed to public policy articulated through a gender lens. For this purpose, there is a mandate to collect gender specific data. There has thus far been little research on labor markets that considers the gendered distribution of labor. This chapter begins that research by documenting the location of women's work in the Ugandan macroeconomy by physical area of the country, by sector and by paid or unpaid status. This information is important in order to guide economic policy particularly with respect to initiatives on poverty reduction and inequality.

This research locates the place(s) of women in the Ugandan macroeconomy and discusses their opportunities within this context. "A place-based strategy for women recognizes that political change can only come about by changes in power relations . . ." and that these power relations occur in a place (Harcourt

2002: 292). Policy is often directed not only at an industry but also to a particular location within the country. This research enables gender policy to be targeted at the most disadvantaged groups. The next section offers background on current law that governs gender and economic policy analysis in Uganda; this is followed by a gender sensitive structural analysis of the labor force in Uganda; the last two sections contrast the labor force structure with the structure of the macroeconomy and provide conclusions and recommendations for policy and future research.

Economic Background and Legislative Framework

In 1987, the Government of Uganda embarked on a rigorous program of structural adjustment and economic reform, which included liberalization and privatization. Since then Uganda has achieved high rates of economic growth along with reductions in inflation and increases in per capita gross domestic product (GDP).[1]

In spite of these advances, poverty rates of over 40 percent have persisted. Currently, more than 50 percent of the Ugandan population is female and at least one-third of these live in absolute poverty, defined as being unable to meet basic needs (Government of Uganda 2001b). Women comprise between 70 and 80 percent of the agricultural labor force in Uganda producing most of the food crops and yet owning only about 7 percent of the land. Of all agricultural workers, about 70 percent are unpaid, typically working and living on family land titled to a male, perhaps a husband.[2] Few women have access to capital or collateral and little control over the proceeds from their agricultural productivity. More boys than girls are enrolled at all levels of education in Uganda although enrollments of girls at all levels, including university, are increasing (Butegwa et al. 2000; Elson and Evers 1996; Government of Uganda (GOU) 1997, 2002; Karuhanga-Beraho 2002; Kwagala et al. 2000; Kwagala 1999; Kwesiga 2002).

The Poverty Eradication Action Plan (PEAP), Uganda's national planning framework for development, proposes a vision for poverty reduction to less than 10 percent of the population by 2017. The PEAP explicitly acknowledges gender differentials in the development process. This attention to gender is also codified in the National Gender Policy and in the Constitution that was developed though a participatory process in 1995. The National Gender Policy identifies the problems of women in Uganda quite frankly: "Uganda is a patriarchal society where men are the dominant players in decision making, although women shoulder most reproductive, productive and community management responsibilities many of which are not remunerated or reflected in national statistics" (GOU 1997: 1). This Gender Policy authorizes the Ministry of Gender, Labor, and Community Development to ensure "that all policies, both macro and micro are gender responsive. Programs and projects shall include strategies to address gender concerns" (GOU 1997: 1). The Policy specifically directs that gender disaggregated data be collected and analyzed; that other ministries cooperate in sensitizing policy and staff to gender; and that the economic development of the country be articulated through a gender lens. Although these official policy documents of Uganda reflect knowledge of the literature identifying the differential effects of economic development on women relative to men, there is little analysis of women and work in Uganda.

Labor Force in Uganda

There are approximately nine million persons of the fourteen million in the working-age population in Uganda who are counted as being in the Labor force while the rest are not engaged in economic activity as of the 1991 census. Of the economically active, about 4.8 million are women and 4.3 million are men. Of the economically inactive most are in school with smaller numbers identified as homemakers (GOU 1995a; 1998a; 2001c).

Table 9.1 Labor Force Participation Rates by Sex and Year in Uganda, 1980–2010

Year	Male	Female
1980	93.4	83.3
1995	92.0	82.2
2000	91.3	81.5
2010*	90.0	80.2

Source: ILO 2000:285, Table 7
Note: * projected

The labor force participation rate of women in Uganda is the highest in sub-Saharan Africa at over 80 percent (International Labour Organization (ILO) 2000). The historical labor force participation rates (LFPR) for Uganda are given in tables 9.1–9.3. LFPR represents the numbers of working age, able-bodied persons engaged in economic activity. Table 9.1 shows current and projected labor force participation rates by sex and year in Uganda for 1980–2010 developed by the ILO and published in 2000. In every year, women have high rates of participation, which includes both the formal and the informal sectors.

Table 9.2 Labor Force Participation Rates for Uganda by Location and Sex, 1992–1993

	Male	Female	Average
Urban Total	93.4	80.0	86.7
Urban informal	67.6*	80.6*	83.7*
Rural total	91.6	59.4	75.5

Source: Government of Uganda (GOU) 1994b: 9, 285. Note: these data include waged workers and self-employed (casual workers), but exclude housekeepers in their own homes.
Note: * percentage of urban total

Data in table 9.2 were collected by the Government of Uganda and published in 1994 and show that at that time there was a wide difference between male and female participation rates in urban and rural settings as well as between urban formal and informal sectors. Participation rates of female workers are higher than males in the urban informal sector with 80.6 percent and 67.6 percent, respectively, while men are documented with higher participation rates in the rural area at 91.6 percent compared to female participation at 59.4 percent. This differential in the rural areas may reflect undercounting or non-counting of unpaid family workers or women engaged in activity not considered economic such as attending the sick, pregnancy, childcare, or housekeeping. Because of this lower female participation rate in the rural area, the overall LFPR is higher in the urban formal and informal sectors than in the rural sector. Table 9.3, compiled by the Uganda Bureau of Statistics (1998), a government agency formed in the late 1990s, shows more disaggregation of the labor force data by sex, type of residence and status of employment. These data are based on the 1991 census figures and show the differential between urban and rural unemployment rates. Rural unemployment rates are at 5.1 percent. Kampala, the capital city and major urban settlement has 31.1 percent unemployment while other urban areas have 21.7 percent unemployment rates. Both men and women in urban and rural settings have high LFPRs and relatively low unemployment rates except for Kampala.

Table 9.3 Working Age Population, Total Labor Force, Labor Force Participation Rate and Unemployment Rate, Uganda, 1997

	Working Age Population (thousands)	Total Labor Force (thousands)	Labor Force Participation Rate	Unemployment Rate
Uganda	14,005	9,050	64.6	7.4
Female	7,222	4,780	66.2	8.0
Male	6,783	4,269	62.2	6.7
Rural	12,056	7,818	64.9	5.1
Urban	1,950	1,231	63.2	21.7
Kampala	851	571	67.1	31.1

Source: Government of Uganda 1998.

The data in table 9.4 shows comparative rates of women's percentage of total labor force by several countries both developed and developing. As of 1995, Uganda, with 52 percent women as percentage of the labor force, is higher than all these countries: Australia, People's Republic of China, Mexico, Singapore, and the United States. The next closest is China with 45 percent of its total labor force that are women. Table 9.5 presents data on the labor force participation rates of women in selected countries. This gives an idea of the numbers of women available to work that actually are participating in the labor force and counted as economically active. Again, Uganda is high in relative numbers of women who are economically active.

Women's work in the Ugandan economy has seen little structural variation over time. Most women work in subsistence agriculture provisioning their families or in the informal sector with small enterprises. Structural adjustment programs implemented in the 1990s resulted in retrenchment in the public sector, pushing men out of jobs and women into income generating activities in the informal sector in both urban and rural settings. When the public sector later grew, there was expansion in the teaching and nursing professions, typically female dominated work. The data for these professions are given in a following section.

Table 9.4 Women's Percentage of Total Labor Force
by Selected Country and Year, 1980 and 1995

Country	1980	1995
Australia	37	43
People's Rep of China	43	45
Mexico	27	31
Singapore	35	38
Uganda	n/a	52
United States	42	46

Source: Corner 1998: Annex 1:31; ILO 2000; GOU 1998b.

The majority of women in agriculture are employed in an unpaid status, on family farms. Since most women own no land, they face severe constraints in credit markets, which rarely make loans on collateral other than land. These

Table 9.5 Women's Labor Force Participation Rates by Selected
Country and Year, 1975 and 1994

Country	1975	1994
People's Rep. Of China	53	73
Singapore	30	51
Uganda	83*	66–80**
United States	46	58

Source: Corner 1998: Annex 2:32; ILO 2000; GOU 1998;
Note: *Data for 1980; ** data for 1993 and 1997.

ownership conditions result in women being marginalized from credit markets and unable to take advantage of government initiatives such as the Plan for Modernization of Agriculture (PMA), a program that might present opportunities for capital mobilization or expansion of production. Women in the formal agricultural sector may be casual workers (self-employed) in the coffee or tea industries or in unpaid status. Women are typically laboring to provide food for their family's consumption. In the agricultural sector, 68 percent of women workers are laborers who grow food crops while 53 percent labor for cash crops often from the same plot. Women farmers sell 30 percent of all the food crops sold (maize, beans) and 9 percent of cash crops sold. The standard cash crops in Uganda are coffee, cotton, sesame, tobacco, maize, and beans (ILO 1995). The ILO says of women's family labor in Uganda, "their labor inputs are perceived as a property of the family under the control of the male head of household" (ILO 1995: 241). The women regularly report that although they grow the crops and provide labor, their husband takes the crop to market and does not share the proceeds of whatever is sold.

Employment data on the formal agricultural sector by sex is given in table 9.6. These data are presented by the ILO and derived from the 1991 Uganda census. Self-employed workers are employed typically as casual independent workers, perhaps on tea plantations, while unpaid workers work on small farms.

Table 9.6 Percentage Distribution of Agricultural Workers in Uganda by Sex and Status, 1991

	Female	Male
Employee	0.2	1.1
Self-Employed (casual)	26.6	69.1
Unpaid	73.2	29.8

Source: ILO 1995:241, derived from 1991 Uganda Census data.

Locating Women in the Structure of the Economy: 1988–2000

Only about one percent of Ugandan workers are engaged in the formal manufacturing sector and those predominantly in the apparel industry for export (ILO 1995: 245). Available research on women and industrial development for other countries indicates that women are often constrained to certain occupations or industries thereby limiting their lifetime earning power and increasing their possibility of remaining in poverty (Kim 1997). Education and lack of aggregate demand have probably been the major limiting factors in terms of women's movement from agriculture into the formal or manufacturing sector in Uganda. Women may also be constrained within their company or industry by the "Glass Ceiling" which refers to the presence of invisible restrictions which delay or prohibit promotion (Benería and Feldman 1992; Benería and Roldán 1987; Corner 1998; Elson 1995; Snyder 1995; Tinker 1990). The data presented in tables 9.7, 9.8, and 9.9 differentiate female and male workers by skill level when possible and provide some means to assess whether or not women are moving up within the structure of the economy in terms of higher paid or skilled positions in the formal sector.

Table 9.8 shows the subtle shifts of the structure of the economy since 1988 when the adjustment program was implemented. This table shows available data on employment and contribution to GDP by industry categories for the two periods: 1988 and 1995–2000. Women are clustered in agriculture relative to men in the overall economy. The contribution of the agricultural sector to GDP is relatively large at 41 percent but absorbs over 70 percent of the labor. Women typi cally capture large numbers of jobs in the service sector. The one area where female and male workers are about the same percentage of the workforce is in Wholesale, Retail, Hotels and Restaurants in the service sector. Manufacturing, as a percent of GDP, increased by about two percent between the periods and construction increased by about 0.5 percent. The current monthly survey of establishments identifies the following products produced in the manufacturing sector: beer, cement, cigarettes, edible oils, electricity, soap, soft drinks, sugar, and textiles. Between 1999 and 2000 the wage bill in the manufacturing sector increased 3.5 percent mainly in firms producing sugar, paper, and paper products, soft drinks, edible oil, soap, pharmaceuticals, and cigarettes (GOU 2002b). This may reflect in a small way, growth of these sectors and an increase in domestic demand.

In 1988, the total number for formal sector employment in Uganda was 378,000, of which about 165,000 were skilled and about two-thirds were employed by government (table 9.8). Over 75 percent of the skilled women workers in government service included those in the medical (nurses and midwives) and teaching fields. Men outnumbered women by three to one overall in the formal sector at that time, before the structural adjustment policies were implemented. Average monthly earnings in the non-governmental formal sector were double that relative to the governmental sector in 1988.

The historical data in tables 9.7 and 9.8 are derived from the 1988 Uganda National Manpower Survey and were dramatically affected by the structural adjustment policies (SAPs) imposed on the Ugandan economy during the 1990s. A part of the SAPs was retrenchment in the civil service, which reduced the overall numbers to less than 150,000 from the 1988 total of 239,528 (Baguma and Matagi 2002: 2–4; Nankunda 2002). By the year 2000, the Uganda civil service totaled 178,080 with ten thousand in the civil service proper, plus 106,000 teachers, 18,000 police and prison employees, five thousand in university employment and 33,000 employed in the local government district governmental offices (GOU 2002b: 36).

Table 9.7 Distribution of Workers in the Formal Sector by Government and Non-Government (private) Employment and by Sex, Uganda, 1988

Sector	Female %	Male %	Number of employees
Total Formal Sector	20	80	378,277
Skilled Workers	26	74	164,868
Government	76	24	239,528
Non-Government	24	76	138,749

Source: ILO 1995:244; GOU 1989:36, 38.

Recent analysis of the impact of the structural adjustment program (SAP) indicates that women bore the brunt of the adjustment process in their working lives. The documented impacts of SAPs on Ugandan women are that women's hours of work and workload in general increased with the demands to produce for export; cuts in government social spending in health and education transferred the social burden to women; devaluation and de-subsidization policies increased the cost of education and health care; and women's health as well as low education levels became worse in rural areas (Busingye 2002:14; Mugyenyi 1992).

Table 9.8 Distribution of Employees by Industry and Sex, Number of Employees by Industry, 1988; Industry Contribution to GDP 1996–2000 Uganda

Industry	Formal Sector 1988 Employees (000s)	1999–2000 Percent of Working Population ***		Industry Percent Contribution to GDP 1996–2000			
		Female	Male	96–97	97–98	98–99	99–00
Agriculture	8.1	86.1	66.2	44.2	42.7	42.5	41.6
Mining	0.4	0.4	0.4				
Manufacturing	14.2	1.8	3.5	8.6	9.3	9.7	10.0
Electricity, Water, Gas	1.2	0	0.3				
Construction	4.5	0	2.2	7.7	7.9	7.9	8.1
Wholesale, Retail, Hotel, Restaurants	6.1	7.5	8.6				
Transportation Storage	3.1	0.1	3.0	5.0	5.2	5.2	5.4
Finance, Real Estate, Insurance	3.0						
Communication							
Social and Personal Services				15.4	15.5	15.2	15.2
Public Administration	31.1**						
Educational Services	11.3**						
Medical	11.9**						
Other Services	5.1	4	9.8				
Total formal employment (skilled) 000s	378.2 (164.9)	1,040	793				

Source: GOU (1989: 36, 38); Uganda Investment Authority 2001a: 4; GOU 2002b, Table 4.9 p 31.
Note: *Calculated in constant 1991 prices; **Government employment; ***Includes unpaid family workers

Contemporary Structure and Work Status

Some movement in the agricultural labor force from unpaid status to self-employed or from unpaid to employee status between 1995 and 1999–00 is shown in the data in table 9.9. Females in the unpaid status went from 73 percent of all female workers to 55.5 percent of all female workers while males in the unpaid status went from 29.8 percent in 1995 to 15.6 percent of all male workers in 1999–2000.

There are increases for females in self-employed and employee categories while for males the increase is in the employee category. Recent research on the characteristics of the chronically poor between the years 1992–1996 indicates that of the poor in both time periods, 70 percent were in households headed by persons whose main economic activity was self-employed in agriculture (Okidi and McKay 2003). This implies that movement into self-employed for women may not be an improvement in well-being. This movement may also indicate stress on food growing capacity and an increased need for cash generating employment.

The data in table 9.10 give an overview of the distribution of jobs in the private sector by category in 2000. Over 64 percent of all workers in the private sector job categories are classified as casual workers. That is, those without job security or income security. Twenty-three percent are classified as skilled/technical.

Table 9.9 Employment Status of All Female and Male Workers by Percent, Both Agricultural and Non-Agricultural, Uganda, 1995 and 1999–2000

Year	Female		Male	
Employment Category	1995	1999–2000	1995	1999–2000
Employee	0.2	5.9	1.1	20.7
Self Employed	26.6	38.2	69.1	63.7
Unpaid	73.0	55.5	29.8	15.6

Source: ILO 1995: 241; GOU 2001c: 26, table 4.1; table 4.5.

Kabuye (2002) offers additional detail to these data with a breakdown of private sector employment by nationality, sex, and firm size. Kabuye's data are for a sample of firms, which includes manufacturing, construction, metal work, textiles, and a number of other activities. Almost half (48%) of private sector female employees are grouped in smaller firms with less than ten employees while male employees are located both in smaller and somewhat larger firms with between eleven and fifty employees. There are no female employees or non-Ugandan employees found in firms with above fifty employees. Given the structure of the Ugandan economy, there are relatively few firms with large permanent employee bases in the formal sector. Although this is a small sample of firms, it does give an indication of where female employees are located relative to males in the private sector.

Kabonesa (2001) analyzed the structural arrangement of jobs within companies in the private sector in Uganda. The research sample included highly educated men and women (those with secondary and university level education). Her results from establishments in the industrial, services, non-governmental, government, and educational sectors showed that male employees outnumbered female employees in every sector except services.

Women were concentrated in clerical and support positions within firms and agencies. Men were grouped in administrator and director positions. The overall terms of employment favored male employees among permanent workers.

Table 9.10 Private Sector Job Categories and Numbers Employed, Uganda, 2000

Job category	Number of employees	Percent of total
Management/Supervisor	4,992	5.6
Administrative/Account	4,799	5.5
Skilled/Technical	19,499	22.3
Casual/Unskilled	55,894	64.0
Not Stated	2,264	2.6
Total	87,448	100

Source: GOU 2001a, table 2.3.2.

50 percent of female workers were permanent while 60 percent of male workers were permanent. Female employees predominated in part-time conditions (21% female employees had part-time work and 12% male employees had part-time work). Her data indicate that women may be moving into the private sector but face relatively higher rates of impermanence in their work environment as well as occupational segregation in lower paid positions.

Kabonesa also measured perceptions of employees with respect to gender roles of jobs within their firms. Most of the men who were interviewed perceived women to be better suited for work in the service sector (banks, hotels, interactive and communication technology, clearing and forwarding activities, and government office cleaning) and in agriculture and food processing (food packaging, coffee processing). Other research examining work within a firm in Uganda indicates that women in the private sector in Uganda may be subject to the same pressures in the workplace as women are in more developed economies. The pressures come from sexual harassment, low wages, occupational segregation, and stereotypical attitudes in the workplace. In addition, Ugandan women entrepreneurs face barriers with credit accessibility and collateral for loans (Kiiza et al 2000; Snyder 2000).

The gender wage gap, the percentage of average female wages relative to average male wages, in both the agricultural and the non-agricultural sectors is given in table 9.11. The gap is worst in the Central district, which includes Kampala the most industrialized area. In non-agricultural activities, women lag behind men in wages in every region of the country. The worst is in the eastern region where women make only 55 percent of what men make for one days work. The wage gap in non-agricultural work in the Central district worsened between 1992–1993 and 1995–96 going from 80 percent to 63 percent. Only in the north do the data show an improvement between the years of the household survey. Unfortunately, those data are perhaps the least reliable in terms of coverage because of the conflict situation there. Wages in the agricultural sector during the 1990s increased slightly and relatively more for men than women (GOU 1998b: 66). In agriculture in 1995, women only earned 68 percent of men's earnings. This gap closed two percentage points between 1992–1993 and 1995–1996. In the east and in the west of the country, the agricultural wages for women and men are the same. In the west, the gender wage gap closed almost six percentage points between 1992–1993 and 1995–1996. It clearly makes a difference with respect to the gender wage gap where women are located.

When we consider the impact of education on wages and skilled job availability, even with a secondary or greater level of education, there is no guarantee that a skilled job will be available or that wages will reflect a reasonable return to education. Of those women with a secondary or greater education, 24 percent are working on family land while over 40 percent are working in the sales, professional/technical, and management fields predominantly in urban areas.

Snyder (2002) finds that women traders and marketers in the informal sector in Uganda have educational levels ranging from illiterate up to some secondary education. They have financed their business ventures from private savings while women with small to medium scale business (five to fifty employees) have some post-secondary education and have financed their enterprises with their own savings from prior salaried employment as well as with land, used as collateral. (GOU 1998b: 32).

The links between education, work that permits savings, and access to credit markets for investment savings are critical to women's future in Uganda. The location of the workforce, both inside and outside of agriculture, reflects the overall conditions in the economy with respect to aggregate demand, export opportunities, availability of markets, and access to educational opportunities, which might lead to skilled jobs. Most women working in Uganda are in unpaid agricultural labor, secondly in government, and thirdly located in the private sector. More people are self-employed today than in the past, having moved from the unpaid employment status but there are little data to indicate if this

Table 9.11 Average Daily Wages to Agricultural and Non-Agricultural Labor by Region and Sex, 1992–93 and 1995–96 (Uganda Shillings)

Region	Central		Eastern		Northern		Western	
Year	1992–1993	1995–1996	1992–1993	1995–1996	1992–1993	1995–1996	1992–1993	1995–1996
Agriculture								
Women	600	1100	400	700	500	500	400	600
Men	900	1600	500	700	500	500	500	700
Non-Agriculture								
Women	800	1200	600	500	600	500	500	600
Men	1000	1900	600	900	800	600	500	800

Source: GOU 1998b: 66, table 7.3.15.

move reflected an improved livelihood situation. There is a gender wage gap in the paid agricultural sector, which varies by region where in some cases women make as little as 68 percent of men's wages. In the private sector, most jobs are in the casual and unskilled categories where women are concentrated and there are large percentages of women and men working in impermanent circumstances. Few women are at the top levels of the private sector.

Conclusion and the Way Forward

The macroeconomy in Uganda, although growing, is still weak with respect to job/employment/income generation. The economy is currently reliant on the agricultural sector to produce work and jobs. Without growth in domestic demand or increases in exports, agriculture will not be able to absorb more workers into paid employment. Uganda's exports are competing with many other countries in markets for coffee, tea, cotton, and vanilla and so face uncertain revenue streams. As Uganda moves forward with gender sensitized policy to reduce poverty, which is actually increasing according to official estimates, there will be obstacles to the general expansion of the macroeconomy. Reinikka and Collier (2001) characterize the way forward as narrow. They suggest that Uganda is unlikely to increase its exposure in world markets beyond what it already has; that Uganda may be non-competitive in regional manufacturing but may be able to gain from trade with the Democratic Republic of Congo and Rwanda; that Uganda's agricultural practices may benefit from investment of knowledge in order to increase productivity; and that Uganda may develop comparative advantage in tertiary education and telecommunications.

The current investment picture given in table 9.13 shows that the tourism sector had the largest number of investment projects licensed by the Uganda Investment Authority in the year 2000. Tourism was followed by agriculture and property services. Between 1991–2000, foreign investments have come from, in order of size of investments: 1. United Kingdom, 2. Canada, 3. Kenya, 4. South Africa, 5. USA, 6. Switzerland, 7. Sudan, 8 India, 9. Sweden, and 10. Germany (GOU 2001).

Table 9.12 Investment Projects Licensed and in Operation
Uganda, 2000

Sector	Number of Licensed Projects
Tourism	77
Agriculture	57
Property Services	55

Source: GOU 2001/02.

The conversion rate of these investment projects into actual producing firms was only 54.6 percent in 2000 with an average capacity utilization rate of 41.7 percent. When investors are interviewed about low conversion and capacity utilization rates, they indicate the causes to be 1) weakness in Ugandan domestic aggregate demand for their products, 2) management skills, and 3) other issues (GOU, 2001–2002).

General growth and development of the Ugandan economy has potential to enhance women's position in spite of their current relatively low status. It is crucial to identify areas for growth of industry and employment, both agriculturally and non-agriculturally based, and link them to women's employment and economic activity (Sonko 2002). This research is a first attempt to map the location of the labor force in Uganda. The locations of workers, physically as well as occupationally, enable policymakers to target policy more effectively.

Notes

1. Between 1988 and 2002 per capita GDP increased from 334,700 Ush to 365,200 Ush (at 1800 Ush per US$ this would be $185–$202). There has also been a relatively high birth rate during this period.

2. Recent data indicate a movement of people out of the unpaid category into the self-employed and employee categories.

References

Baguma, Peter and Leon Matagi. 2002. *The Effects of the Retrenchment Exercise on Organisational Performance and Quality of Work Life Among Public Servants in Uganda*, Working Paper #7. Kampala: NURRU Publications.

Benería, Lourdes and Shelley Feldman. 1992. *Unequal Burden: Economic Crises, Persistent Poverty and Women's Work*. Boulder, CO: Westview Press.

Benería, Lourdes and Martha Roldán. 1987. *The Crossroads of Class and Gender: Industrial Homework, Subcontracting, and Household Dynamics in Mexico City*. Chicago: University of Chicago Press.

Busingye, Winnie. 2002. *The Impact of Structural Adjustment Programs on Women and Gender Relations in the Household: The Case of Kabale District*. Working Paper #11, Kampala: NURRU Publications.

Butegwa, Florence, Taaka Awori, and Stella Mukasa. 2000. "Private Sector Development in Uganda: Making Room for Gender on the Economic Reform Agenda." In Tsikata, Dzodi and Joanna Kerr with Cathy Blacklock and Jocelyne Laforce. eds. *Demanding Dignity: Women Confronting Economic Reforms in Africa*. Ottawa: The North-South Institute and Third World Network-Africa.

Corner, Lorraine. 1998. *Women and Economic Development and Cooperation in Asia Pacific Economic Cooperation (APEP)*. Bangkok: Economic Empowerment Series, UNIFEM East and Southeast Asia Regional Office.

Council for the Economic Empowerment for Women in Africa (CEEWA-U). 1999. *Gender Analysis for Economic Decision Making in Selected Government Departments*. Kampala: CEEWA-U, P.O. Box 10968.

Elson, Diane. 1995. "Gender Awareness in Modelling Structural Adjustment." *World Development* vol. 23, no. 11, p. 237–47.

Elson, Diane and Barbara Evers. 1996. *Gender Aware Country Economic Reports*, Working Paper Number 2 Uganda. The Netherlands: University of Manchester Graduate School of Social Sciences, Genecon Unit.

Government of Uganda (GOU). 1989. *Manpower and Employment in Uganda. Report of the National Manpower Survey. 1989.* Kampala: Ministry of Planning and Economic Development. Entebbe.

———. 1994. *Report on Uganda National Integrated Household Survey, 1992–93. Vol. II.* Entebbe: Statistics Department, Ministry of Finance, Planning and Economic Development.

———. 1995. *Labour Statistics: A National Programme, 1995–2000.* Addis Ababa: Eastern Africa Multi-disciplinary Advisory Team Paper.

———. 1997. *The National Gender Policy.* Kampala: Ministry of Gender and Community Development and Ministry of Planning and Economic Development.

———. 1998a. *Women and Men in Uganda: Facts and Figures, 1998.* Kampala: Ministry of Gender and Community Development and Ministry of Planning and Economic Development.

———. 1998b. *Uganda National Household Survey, 1995/96. Vol. 2: Summary Analytical Report.* Entebbe: Statistics Department, Ministry of Finance, Planning and Economic Development.

———. 2001a. *Final Report on The Investor Survey 2001.* Kampala: Uganda Investment Authority. (UIA), Submitted by Merit Management Consulting and Training. Kampala, Uganda.

———. 2001b. *National Program for Good Governance in the Context of the PEAP,* Kampala: Ministry of Finance, Planning and Economic Development.

———. 2001c. *Background to the Budget 2001/02. Enhancing Economic Growth and Structural Transformation,* Kampala: Ministry of Finance, Planning and Economic Development.

———. 2001–2002. *The Investor* (various issues). Kampala: Uganda Investment Authority.

———. 2002a. *Uganda Demographic and Health Survey 2000–2001: Statistics on Characteristics of Households and Household Educational Levels, Occupation, Earnings, Employer and Continuity of Employment.* Calverton, MD: Uganda Bureau of Statistics (UBOS) and ORC Macro.

———. 2002b. *Statistical Abstract 2001* Entebbe: Uganda Bureau of Statistics.

Harcourt, Wendy. 2002. "Body Politics: Revisiting the Population Question." In Kriemild Saunders. ed. *Feminist Post Development Thought.* London: Zed.

International Labour Organization. 1995. *Employment Generation and Poverty Reduction in Uganda: Towards a National Programme of Action.* Addis Ababa: Eastern Africa Multidisciplinary Advisory Team.

International Labour Organization. 2000. *World Labour Report 2000: Income Security and Social Protection in a Changing World.* Geneva: ILO Office.

Kabonesa, Consolata. 2001. *Women and Employment in Industry, Services, NGOs, Government and Educational Organizations in Uganda.* unpublished. Presented at conference on Women and Employment sponsored by International Labor Organization, Kampala, November.

Kiiza, Enid, Winifred Rwe-Beyanga and Agnes Kamya. 2000. "Accounting for Gender: Improving Ugandan Credit Policies, Processes, and Programs." In Tsikata, Dzodi and Joanna Kerr with Cathy Blacklock and Jocelyne Laforce. eds. *Demanding Dignity: Women Confronting Economic Reforms in Africa.* Ottawa: The North-South Institute and Third World Network-Africa.

Kim, Marlene. 1997. "Poor Women Survey Poor Women: Feminist Perspectives in Survey Research." *Feminist Economics* vol. 3, no. 2, p. 99–117.

Kabuye, Matia Kagimu. 2002. *The Impact of SAPs on Private Sector Employment in Uganda: A Case Study of Kampala District.* Working Paper No. 19. Kampala: NURRU Publications.

Kwagala, Betty. 1999. "Integrating Women's Reproductive Roles with Productive Activities in Commerce: The Case of Businesswomen in Kampala, Uganda." *Urban Studies.* vol. 36, no. 9, p 1535–1550.

Kwagala, Betty and Hope Kabuchu, Lydia Kapiriri with special input by Rebecca Wasswa. 2000. "Health and the Economic Empowerment of Women: Life in a Kampala Unplanned Settlement." In Tsikata, Dzodi and Joanna Kerr with Cathy Blacklock and Jocelyne Laforce. eds. *Demanding Dignity: Women Confronting Economic Reforms in Africa.* Ottawa: The North-South Institute and Third World Network-Africa.

Kwesiga, Joy C. 2002. *Women's Access to Higher Education in Africa: Uganda's Experience.* Kampala: Fountain Publishers.

Mugyeni, Mary. 1992. *Structural Adjustment Program on Uganda Rural Women in the 1980s: Prospects for Empowerment in the New Decade.* Ottawa: A Research Report Sponsored by the Canadian Bureau for International Education.

Nankunda, Hilda. 2002. *Civil Service Reforms and the Living Standards of Retrenched Civil Servants: A Case Study of Kampala District,* Working Paper No. 18. Kampala: NURRU Publications.

Okidi, John and Andrew McKay. 2003. *Poverty Dynamics in Uganda: 1992–2000. Research Series No. 32.* Kampala: Economic Policy Research Centre.

Reinikka, Ritva and Paul Collier. eds. 2001. *Uganda's Recovery: The Role of Farms, Firms, and Government. International Bank for Reconstruction and Development.* Washington D.C.: The World Bank.

Snyder, Margaret. 1995. *Transforming Development: Women, Poverty and Politics.* London: Intermediate Technology Publications.

Snyder, Margaret 2000. *Women in African Economies: From Burning Sun to Boardroom, Business Ventures and Investment Patterns of 74 Ugandan Women.* Kampala: Fountain Press.

Snyder, Margaret. 2002. "Women's Agency in the Economy: Business and Investment Patterns." In Aili Mari Tripp and Joy C. Kwesiga. eds. *The Women's Movement in Uganda: A History, Challenges and Prospects.* Kampala: Fountain Publishers.

Sonko, Mary. 2002. *Action Aid: Lessons from Elsewhere.* Unpublished. Presented at the Women's Worlds Congress, July 25–30. Kampala, Uganda.

Tinker, Irene. ed. 1990. *Persistent Inequalities: Women and World Development.* New York: Oxford University Press.

Tripp, Aili Mari and Joy C. Kwesiga. eds. 2002. *The Women's Movement in Uganda: A History, Challenges and Prospects.* Kampala: Fountain Publishers.

Tsikata, Dzodi and Joanna Kerr with Cathy Blacklock and Jocelyne Laforce. eds. 2000. *Demanding Dignity: Women Confronting Economic Reforms in Africa.* Ottawa: The North-South Institute and Third World Network-Africa.

Chapter 10

Inquiries into Women's Perceptions of What Constitutes Their Well-Being

Akello Zerupa

There is clear evidence that human well-being is the overall goal of many development policies. However, the notion of well-being does not have a uniform meaning for all individuals (Kabeer and Subrahmanian 1996). This means that steps taken to bring about the enhancement of well-being must take into consideration the definition of well-being as defined by those for whom policies are being made. Considerable research suggests that as far as the poor are concerned, well-being consists of goals of survival: security and self-esteem (Chambers 1989). It is also evident that most studies regarding the well-being of households assume that a household is a homogeneous unit and therefore the well-being of women, children and men can clearly be read from that of the household to which they belong. Other studies done on the links between gender and poverty through gender disaggregating of well-being indicators have shown that females have a significant disadvantage under these measurement systems (UNDP 1995). Given this state of difference between women and men, there is a great need to take into account the perceptions of both sexes on poverty and well-being if poverty is to be reduced.

This chapter draws from a study carried out in five selected districts in Uganda under the Gender and Poverty Impact Monitoring of the Agriculture Sector Programme Support. The Department of Agricultural Economics, Makerere University, in collaboration with the Center for Development Research, Co-

117

penhagen, is conducting the long term monitoring of the impact of the Agriculture Sector Programme Support activities with respect to poverty alleviation and reduction of gender based inequalities. A three-pronged monitoring methodology is being used along the dimensions of (a) socio-economic and policy context; (b) district-level gender and poverty profiling; and (c) impact processes. This particular analysis is under the district gender and poverty-profiling dimension.

Poverty affects men, women and children differently because of differences in opportunities and needs. Therefore, their definitions of poverty and well-being are also different and this warrants specific studies so as to capture all the variations.

Not many studies on well-being and poverty have put emphasis on the well-being of individual members of households; this can possibly be explained by the view many people hold that children's, women's and men's needs and priorities can be automatically read from those of the households to which they belong. This view is still very strong: it influences the design of methodologies as well as the planning of project interventions. The myth of the household as a homogeneous unit needs to be critically analyzed for proper planning, especially for policy makers, project designers and implementers. This will ensure that the needs of women, children and men are recognized and where possible, appropriate interventions are put in place to meet their needs.

Methodology and Data

The methodology used for this study was derived from *Developing Regional Poverty Profiles Based on Local Perceptions* by Helle Munk Ravnborg, 1999. The methodology allows for the exploration of the extent to which women's well-being is different from household well-being and the extent to which it overlaps household well-being. A total of 180 persons in five districts (Tororo, Masaka, Rakai, Pallisa and Kabarole) were randomly selected and interviewed. There were three household heads and three women per village (six per district) selected so at least one-half of the sample was women. The districts were chosen to evaluate the impact of the agricultural sector support program. The key informants were asked to evaluate their own well-being and that of their neighbors within a particular village.

The rankings were based on the informant's subjective ranking of themselves and their neighbors in terms of poverty or well-being status. Most of the previous studies ranked only households. This approach is unique in that it gives room for the development of well-being indices based on local perceptions of individuals. Through the systematic sampling of communities and individuals and careful analysis of data on poverty, the methodology allows qualitative poverty perceptions to be turned into quantitative and absolute poverty indices. The combination of quantitative and qualitative methods and comparison of the different perceptions from the different areas is a complex approach, which has been a challenge to poverty analysis and monitoring.

Findings

The study revealed that the description of women's well-being includes more than just the wealth of the women. There is clear evidence of other measures of well-being such as social, health, emotional and physical. Indicators such as decision making, women's sources of income, women's access to land, women's animal ownership, husbands' contribution towards meeting basic household expenditures, polygamy, social assets such as kinship networks, health and education were clearly described by the respondents as key issues that pertain to female well-being.

The extent to which a woman has a say over the spending of income earned, either by herself, by her husband, or by the household has a great effect on her well-being. The findings from this study indicate that within the five selected districts in Uganda, about 60 percent of the married women have a say in how proceeds from crop or animal sales are spent. With the exception of one of the districts (Tororo), the degree to which women have influence on decision making regarding spending of income was found to not be significantly associated with poverty level.

The extent to which husbands contribute towards basic household expenditures was another key feature of female well-being. Women who carry the sole responsibility in this respect due to failure of their husbands to assist them were regarded as having a lower well-being level than those who could count on the cooperation of their husbands. A thirty-year-old farmer in Agule Pallisa had this to say about husbands' support: "Some of the women in this lowest group have husbands who are irresponsible and drunkards; they do not assist them in any way."

Women in a third of the households in Rakai and Pallisa have husbands who contribute meeting basic household expenditures as compared to less than 20 percent of the households in the other districts. In a quarter of the households in Kabarole and Tororo, husbands do not contribute towards meeting any of the basic household needs. In Rakai, Masaka and Pallisa, husbands from the poorest households are just as likely to contribute towards meeting basic household needs, as are husbands from the less-poor and the better-off households.

In all the districts, the likelihood of a married woman having her own sources of income is associated with increasing levels of well-being. Thus, women from better off households are more likely to have independent sources of income than those in the poorest households. Significant differences exist regarding women who have independent sources of income, with Tororo and Rakai representing the extremes. In Tororo, 55 percent of the women in the households have their own sources of income, whereas in Rakai the percentage of women with their own sources of income is 82 percent. With respect to women in the less-poor households, between 59 percent and 83 percent have independent sources of income, while among women in the poorest households, between 37 percent and 71 percent have independent sources of income.

Women who have access to land were regarded as having a higher well-being level than those with no access. Women's access to land is most restricted in Pallisa and Tororo districts and yet land appears to be more abundant in these two districts. Women less than half of the households in Pallisa and Tororo have access to land, whereas in the remaining districts between 59 percent of women in Kabarole and 66 percent of women in Rakai have access to land. In Tororo, Pallisa and Masaka women's likelihood of having access to land increases with decreasing levels of poverty. In Kabarole and Rakai, no significant correlation was found between poverty level and women's access to land.

Owning animals was yet another indicator of women's well-being. A woman who owns a cow or any other smaller animals is regarded as having a higher well-being than one who does not own even a hen. A twenty-six-year-old woman from Masaka described women in the lowest level of well-being as: "they have no animals, not even hens." Households in Tororo have the highest number of animals and yet women in Tororo and Kabarole are least likely to own animals. Married women in Masaka on the other hand are most likely to own animals, with about two-thirds owning some type of animal.

The issue of polygamy had an effect on the well-being of the women. Women in polygamous marriages did not have the same well-being level; the first wives were said to have the lowest level of well-being because in most cases their husbands did not favor them. The last women to be married are the favorites. This can be seen from these quotations:

> Some of the women in the lowest well-being level are first wives who have been abandoned by their husbands. These women who have been abandoned are worse than widows.
>
> —A fifty-six-year-old farmer in Kwapa Tororo

> Most of the women in this group are married in polygamous homes and are suffering because of discrimination by their husbands, who in most cases prefer the second, third, or fourth wives to the first ones. Their husbands do not give them assistance—most of them are shouldering all the home responsibilities on their own.
>
> —A fifty-five-year-old woman in Kabarole

Polygamy was said to reduce resources for the women because the polygamous men must divide the little they have among all the women; some were looking after only the newly married women. Gender relations in polygamous relationships deteriorate, resulting in desertion and discrimination. Polygamy is associated with a deprivation trap characterized by a cycle of poverty, poor education, or no education at all.

Marital status was found to affect well-being. Twelve communities regarded it as one of the main indicators of well-being. Those who are widows and widowers were ranked in the lowest well-being level. A twenty-two-year-old woman from Iyolwa Tororo had this to say:

> The widows have many dependents who are orphans. The orphans use up all their income and yet the widows have very low income. Some of them use old

clothes for bed sheets, they do not have home utensils, some of them do not have people to build for them.

Another respondent from Rakai, when asked to describe women in the lowest well-being level, had this to say:

> The women in the lowest group are widows who did not inherit anything or whose land was grabbed by the husband's relatives.
> —A forty-five-year-old businesswoman in Kalisizo Rakai.

This is partly due to cultural practices of inheritance and lack of appropriate laws to protect widows and their property. Many widows have suffered due to this type of cultural practice regarding inheritance where a male relative is given the responsibility to be in charge of the property of the deceased. These results by marital status are reported in table 10.1.

Single and newly married women were among those who were said to be in the lowest level of well-being; this is similar to the findings of a study done by the World Bank in 1990, where female-headed households in Uganda and Zambia were found to be poorer than male headed ones (World Bank 1990).

Table 10.1 Distribution of Levels of Well-Being by Marital Status, Uganda

	Respondents in Each Category			
	Communities Sampled	Low Level of Well-Being	Middle Level of Well-Being	High Level of Well-Being
Newly married	6	0	1	7
Married	6	3	3	3
Widows	28	6	13	40
Singles	12	3	3	8

Source: Author interviews.

A thirty-year-old farmer in Kasule Kabarole had this to say about women in the lowest level of well-being:

> Some of the women in the lowest group are single women with no husbands to help them earn a living.
> —A woman in Rakai

The length of time one had spent in marriage was yet another factor that determined one's well-being: the newly married couples were said to be in the lowest level of well-being due to the fact that they are not well established as shown in the quotation below:

Some of the women in the lowest well-being category are newly married; their husbands are not yet established.
—A twenty-seven-year-old teacher in Kyanamukkaka Masaka

The newly married couples normally have a humble beginning, especially if both of them are young; some of the newly married men are still on their parent's land and are therefore not independent. The well-being of the newly married women depends on the well-being of their husbands.

Marital relationships were yet another indicator that was found to highly correlate with well-being. Women who had good marital relationships with their husbands were said to be in the highest level of well-being and those who did not have good marital relationships were said to be in the lowest level of well-being. Some women said that their well-being was poor because of their husband's behaviour and lack of support; the women's effort to improve on their well-being was being frustrated by their husbands as shown in this quotation:

The women in the lowest category suffer because their husbands take away all that they earn, if they resist they are beaten.
—A twenty-seven-year-old farmer in Kasule Kabarole

Inequality in consumption of household resources had an influence on the women's well-being status. Women who did not have control over their resources were said to be in the lowest well-being level. Lack of control over resources renders the women powerless with respect to decision making. The patriarchal attitude of the men towards their wives has contributed towards some women's low well-being status.

Control over women's labor had an effect on women's well-being; women who were restricted by husbands from engaging in income generating activities were said to have a low well-being status. On the other hand, the women in the highest level of well-being were said to have no interference from their husbands regarding their involvement in income generating activities, as shown by the quotation below:

The husbands of the women in the highest level of well-being allow them to carry out income-generating activities and most of them do not interfere with their wives' money.
—A nineteen-year-old farmer in Busolwe Tororo

Women in unstable marital relationships are more likely to be poor due to restrictions they face from their partners.

Age was yet another issue that was mentioned as affecting the well-being of the women; it was mostly used to indicate women and households in the lowest level of well-being. Those who are old were unable to utilize the resources at their disposal, such as land, to improve their well-being, as seen from:

The old men and women do not have strength to dig and yet some of them have enough land. Some of them are helpless and yet they have many orphans to look after.

—A forty-year-old farmer in Kyamulibwa Masaka

The physical assets that determined one's high well-being differed from place to place; however, some were common in all the places: land, business premises such as shops and bars, schools, brick-walled and iron-roofed houses with good furniture, goats, cars, motorcycles and bicycles. All were common indicators of high well-being in all the districts. Owning expensive shoes, watches, bags and clothes, especially Gomesi (the traditional gown), were of particular concern to the women.

In the districts of Rakai and Masaka the valued physical assets were: land, banana and coffee plantations, brick-walled and iron-roofed houses and some cattle as shown below:

Those in the high level of well-being have permanent houses made of bricks and iron roofs. They also have large coffee and banana and animals.
—A seventy-year-old female farmer in Kalisiso Rakai

In the district of Masaka the common physical assets were land and the possession of coffee and banana plantations and animals. As seen below:

They have coffee and banana plantations; some have cattle, goats, pigs and chickens.
—A farmer in Kitanda Masaka.

In Tororo and Pallisa valuable assets were mainly ownership of cattle, land and ox-ploughs. Lack of the above assets was a sign of poor well-being, as shown in the description below:

Those in the lower levels of well-being cannot afford to hire ox-ploughs or rent land. They depend on hiring out their labor in order to get some income.
—A sixty-year-old female farmer in Puti-Piti Pallisa

The kinship networks, neighbors and associations were very important in determining one's well-being especially for the old. Those who did not have any social attachment were regarded as being worse off than those who social net works.

Human assets such as education, health care, training and labor power were among the assets that were considered to be important in determining one's well-being level. Well-being level was determined by one's level of education and one's ability to educate his or her children.

Those in the first group have enough education; some have gone up to senior four. Those in the middle group have gone up to primary level and those in the lowest group have very low education—some are primary dropouts.
—A thirty-eight-year-old male teacher in Kalisizo, Rakai

The women in the first group can afford to educate their children; they can afford to buy for them necessities for school.

—A forty-six-year-old woman in Kitanda Masaka district

One's health status also determined one's well-being level as shown in the quotation below:

Those in the lower group are elderly and most of them are terminally ill.
—A thirty-four-year-old female farmer in Kirumba Rakai district

Support from children, from husbands and external support had influence on the well-being of the women and households. Those who had support were said to be in a higher level of well-being than those who did not have any help. Some of the respondents had this to say:

Some of the women in the highest level of well-being have husbands and some have grown-up children who give them assistance.
—A thirty-five-year-old woman in Asinge Tororo

The lowest group has widows who are the worst hit; some of them do not have children to help them with digging. They use clay pots for cooking and fetching water. Most of them sleep on polyethylene bags filled with grass. Some of them hire out their labor to survive.
—A thirty-year-old woman in Agule Pallisa

Women's well-being to some extent is dependent upon the well-being of their households. This is due to the fact that women's access to economically significant resources is through their husbands/fathers/brothers; that is, through their relationship with men. A thirty-two-year-old woman in Masaka described women in high levels of well-being in these words, "Their husbands have cattle, cars, their children are educated and they feed well in their homes. Their homes are okay; they have good houses, some have animals, land, businesses such as shops, coffee and banana plantations."

Conclusion

Some of the indicators mentioned by women as essential for their well-being show that women and their neighbors have perceptions about specific priorities with regard to their well-being. This makes women's needs unique; therefore, specific interventions may be used to improve women's well-being.

References

Chambers, Robert, Arnold Pacey and Lori Ann Thrupp. eds. 1989. *Farmer First: Farmer Innovation and Agricultural Research.* London: Intermediate Technology Publications.
Kabeer, N. and R. Subrahmanian. 1996. *Institutions, Relations and Outcomes: Framework and Tools for Gender Aware Planning.* London: IDS.

Ravnborg, Helle Munk with collaboration of R. M. Escolan, M .P. Guerrero, M. A. Mendez, F. Mendoza, E. M. de Paez and F. Motta. 1999. *Developing Regional Poverty Profiles Based on Local Perception.* CIAT Publication No. 291. Cali: Internacional de Agricultura Tropical.

United Nations Development Programme. 1995. *Human Development Report.* New York: Oxford University Press.

Whiteheard, A. and M. Lockwood. 1999. "Gender in the World Bank's Poverty Assessments: Six Case Studies from Sub-Saharan Africa." Discussion Paper 99. Geneva: UNRISD.

World Bank. 1990. *World Development Report.* Washington DC: Oxford University Press.

Zerupa, Akello. 2000. Field Notes On Well-being Ranking In Tororo, Masaka, Rakai, Pallisa and Kabarole, Uganda. unpublished.

Chapter 11

Urban Employment for Rural Women–Gains and Challenges

Mahua Mukherjee

The metropolises are magnetic fields that attract and refract the economic and socio-environmental lives of people living in the hinterlands. The Calcutta metropolitan area is surrounded by districts like Howrah, Hoogly and North & South 24 Parganas. As the South 24 Parganas district shares the longest border with Calcutta, it has maximum interactions with the metropolis. Calcutta offers a better quality of living and the districts supply many things, from vegetables to laborers. The strength of this relation lies in the system of exchange of necessary items. The city's support system is kept alive through communication networks with these districts. The poor economic conditions of the people of South 24 Parganas district also lead the womenfolk to commute to the city to earn money; but to do that they have to suffer and sacrifice a lot. These challenges and gains are depicted in Figure 11.1.

The South 24 Parganas district is primarily rural in nature but experiencing very rapid yet haphazard urbanization in the fringe areas where it is near the city. South 24 Parganas is one of the largest districts in West Bengal. It has an area of 9,962 squared kilometers and a population of around six million. Approximately 0.7 million people commute daily from the district to the city, out of which 5 percent are poor, rural women. The modes of transportation available include walking to the nearest road, and then using rickshaw, bus or van for travel along the roads, followed by walking at the end to the job location.

The women who commute to the city are mostly illiterate and predominantly engaged in the unorganized service sectors. Vending of vegetables, flowers and fish, domestic help, helpers to eateries and tea stalls, small-scale industries like leather, plastic, glass, garments and unskilled attendants to medical patients are the areas open for these women to join without any prior training. The jobs are temporary in nature. In contrast, organized private and public sectors' offices find a very low number of women commuting long distances from districts such as South 24 Parganas. As they are comparatively economically stronger, these women try to migrate from the city suburb/fringe areas.

Figure 11.1 Balancing Act between Gains and Challenges for Rural Women in India

transportation
workplace
family

money
food
clothing

CHALLENGES   **GAINS**

Urban employment offers certain things that are considered as advantages by the rural women, and they work unbelievably hard to meet these ends. The gains can be listed in the following order according to rural women's preferences: Money is the primary factor that attracts and motivates poor rural women to undertake all the trouble related to their jobs. In the unorganized sector the money they receive against their hard work is marginal, something around $US 40 to $US 100 per month.

In the case of domestic helpers or helpers in eateries, food comes as a part of their contract. They get breakfast and lunch for themselves and are also able to pack something for their children. But others, like vendors, have to buy their own food. Some good employers arrange for medical facilities when they are required.

Similar to food, clothing also comes as part of the pay contract. In general workers get new clothing once a year, and from time to time they get a variety of different, used things from clothing to household items.

Rural women become exposed to the urban standard of living. The ideas of cleanliness, health and hygiene, and literacy programs are the brighter side of urban life, which they try to imitate in the domain of their own households. But at the same time, the difference between their needs and wants becomes blurred. TV, music systems, and lipsticks become priorities over basic food, clothing, and shelter. Urban employment for rural women comes at a heavy cost, and it is neither an easy decision for them to make nor a smooth process to continue with. The challenges come from transportation, the workplace, and their own families. Rural women experience both the non-availability of transportation in the rural sector and at the same time urban traffic congestion in the urban stretch of their journey. Their daily woes are related to mode of transportation, time, expenditure, climate and season, physical strain, and safety and security. Rural women use different modes of transportation, such as train, bus, auto, rickshaw, van, motorized and non-motorized boat, cycle, and carts. Both availability of different modes and the time required for the entire journey create lots of problems for the workers.

The gross journey time is much longer in comparison to the net journey time, as the women have to wait for a longer period in between changing modes of transportation. The women commuters stay away from home on an average of about twelve hours per day. Their journeys take about four and a half hours and they waste about fifty to sixty minutes while waiting between journeys. They start their commute early in the morning (sometimes around three o'clock) and reach home late in the evenings (around seven p.m. or so). Trains run late or get cancelled without prior warnings.

Day travel is becoming expensive and fares are increasing, whereas an increase in pay structure is not increasing at that rate. Sometimes women walk, as they are unable to pay for travel by van or rickshaw. Other problems faced by women commuters are varied: it is too cold in the dawn during winter, and summer heats also have to be dealt with in the workplace. During the rainy season the kutcha village roads become muddy, and some natural calamities wreak havoc on them. These long journeys make the women exhausted. But they have to perform as per expectations of the employer or family members after such strenuous journeys. Young women feel unsafe if they have to travel alone. Elderly women also fear having their money snatched. Thus, women try to commute in groups. The problems related to the workplace are not confined to money only. There are other social aspects like job security, job respect, child labor, sexual harassment, and leave allowances. In most cases the rural women engaged in urban employment belong to the unorganized sector, so losing any job does not necessarily depend on some logical grounds. This also gets reflected in the job culture of these women.

As women are mostly engaged as domestic help, they rarely get due respect in their work place. Very few families treat them as equals.

Small children generally accompany their mothers, especially if they do not have any elderly person in their home to look after them. In some cases their parents engage children in some eateries/tea stalls where they have to work for long hours and very little pay. They do not have the opportunity for primary education.

The women are worried about sexual harassment in their workplaces. This comes easily, as they are both physically and economically vulnerable. Urban society is more aware of this and women's groups support harassed women to speak out against this oppression.

The unorganized sector does not formally allow leaves, and this becomes a dispute between the employer and employee. The employees avail their leaves as and when required without any prior information in the workplace. As these women are away from their home daily for most of the working hours it becomes very difficult to run the home smoothly. The problems are faced both by them and their family members. The children are neglected as their mothers are away from home for the maximum stretch of daytime. Health, education, and every basic necessity for the children at this tender age may be jeopardized during the daytime.

In many cases the women who are in urban employment have no other options to rear their families. Often their husbands have deserted them, or the husbands are too physically ill to earn money. Sometimes even the husbands have earnings, but these are too meager to support the entire family. In addition, some of the men are addicted to country liquors. In these cases the women bear the sole responsibilities of earning money and running the home.

Conclusion

These women from South 24 Parganas will find many persons who share their experiences. Any intervention for betterment of the quality of living of these women and their dependents has to be through a well planned out program. Improvement of communication networks and generation of local income are the two primary issues. These will directly and indirectly impact on health and education systems once the society can afford to think beyond the struggle for existence. Thus, the immediate emphasis must be on economic upliftment.

Chapter 12

Family Responsibilities: The Politics of Love and Care

Meg Luxton

At the 1995 Non-governmental Organization (NGO) conference associated with the United Nations Fourth International conference on women in Beijing, China, thirty thousand delegates from 186 countries took a position condemning the neoliberal economic policies that have come to dominate international political and economic life.[1] Women from country after country reported on the terrible consequences of neoliberalism on the lives of the majority of women in the world. They encouraged each other to fight both its pernicious effects and its predominance as a legitimate way of organizing. They urged each other, as part of that fight, to monitor the impacts of neoliberalism on the lives of people in their countries. This paper is a contribution to that effort.

At the various UN conferences on women, the official Canadian delegations have played leadership roles and have presented Canada as a country whose government is committed to gender equality (Status of Women Canada 1994). The Canadian government has prided itself on the fact that, since 1990 when the United Nations first began issuing its Human Development Index (which measures longevity, levels of education and standards of living), Canada has ranked among the top countries in the world.[2] But government affirmations and national averages easily obscure the grim reality that neoliberal policies since the 1980s have increased the numbers of people who live in poverty and rendered life more difficult for even more. For example, when looking specifically at poverty among children, Canada's U.N. rank drops.[3] The United Nations Children's Fund issued a report on child poverty in twenty-three industrialized countries ranking Canada in seventeenth place, below nations like Spain, Greece, Hungary and the Czech Republic and only five above the US which had a child poverty rate of 22.4 percent. The report noted that 15.5 percent of children in Canada live in poverty (UNICEF 2000a). Statistics Canada low-income cut-off figures indicate that child poverty is even higher—19.8 percent (The Vanier Institute 2000: 116–123; CCPA Monitor 2000: 23). And even for the average working person in Canada, whose standard of living is one of the most comfortable in the world, neoliberal policies have created new pressures. In this chapter I look at the dynamics of life in an advanced capitalist country to show that even in such economies, neoliberalism cannot live up to the claims that the full implementation of its policies will result in a better standard of living for a majority of people.

The Importance of Social Reproduction

A defining feature of capitalism is the separation of the production of commodities from the production and reproduction of people. Capitalist economics only recognizes activities of the market as economically valuable, taking for granted the existence of people available as workers and consumers. And while wages are recognized as a cost of production they are not directly tied to the costs of social reproduction—all the activities that ensure the day to day and generational survival of people: having babies, raising children, provisioning household members by cooking, cleaning, maintaining the home and caring for those who are ill or elderly (Fox and Luxton 2001: 26). Two spheres, the state and family households, act to mediate the gap between earnings and costs of living. The state through its regulations, by redistributing wealth and providing services, plays a role in ensuring certain standards of living (Ursel 1992). Families, and particularly women, through the unpaid work they do in their own homes, taking care of themselves and the people they love, make up the difference (Luxton and Corman 2001).

One of the major contributions of the women's movement has been its insistence that the care giving activities that go on in our homes are important, economically valuable work. Feminists have challenged prevailing economic theories and the policies informed by them, insisting that the labors of love central to domestic labor and care giving are necessary for capitalist economics and for the survival of all of us, as individuals and as a people or a species (Waring 1988). The women's movement also argues that the duty and self-sacrifice required by those providing care giving are often oppressive. Feminists call for a reorganization of society so that love and care can flourish as creative social forces. The on-going struggles of the women's movement have focused on efforts to win social recognition and support for interpersonal care giving (Luxton 1997). However, the neoliberal political agenda that has come to dominate international economics and governing practices opposes such initiatives and is creating a climate in which such demands seem, at best, outdated and impractical.

Neoliberalism and the Privatization of Caregiving

A neoliberal agenda has dominated policy making in Canada since the early 1980s. As these policies have been implemented, the central tenets of neoliberalism have become increasingly clear. Most obvious is its commitment to expanding the unfettered investment of capital and a growing reliance on markets and private profit making. Key to this is the emphasis on reducing the role of the state in providing services and protections for the population as a whole, while strengthening its activities in support of business interests and private profit making. One of the main assumptions motivating this agenda is that "private choice is better than public regulation as a mechanism for allocating resources and ordering social affairs" (Philipps 2000: 1). What neoliberalism attacks is not just the existing welfare state and the social security net already in place, but also what it might have become in response to the expansionist and transformative demands of what are called the "equity seeking groups."

That attack has had significant success. As Marjorie Cohen has argued, it was a shift from a period in which "the deep contradictions in capitalism were modified by a system of social welfare based on the assumption that the well-being of the economy depended on the well-being of the people in it" to a situation in which "social and economic well-being for people is subordinate to the well-being of the corporate sector" (1997: 5). There has also been a strong move away from collective responsibility to individual initiative with a commitant acceptance of greater insecurity and inequality, as government's practice moves from a redistributive state to one that more openly justifies and reinforces market outcomes by rewarding those who place the least demand on public social programs and to cajoling the rest of us to follow their example.[4]

Central to this is a claim that individuals and their families should take more responsibility for their own care, that government provision of services is inefficient and costly, that reliance on state services weakens individual initiative and undermines family and community ties and that care giving is best arranged through voluntary familial and community networks. In almost all welfare economies, family care giving, and particularly women's unpaid labor, is a crucial but unrecognized part of welfare provision. State policies have assumed that families have always been the main provider of welfare: family members are left to work out their own solutions to the problems of combining paid employment and unpaid domestic labor, and women have typically had the primary responsibility for implementing those solutions (Luxton and Corman 2001). The women's movement has challenged such arrangements, calling for state support for women's economic independence (through equal work and pay legislation and the provision of child care services, maternity and parental leaves, for example), and for public recognition and valuing of the activities such as love, service, sacrifice, mutual aid and duty, that are so central to unpaid work in the home (Armstrong and Armstrong 1994; Maroney and Luxton 1997). Yet, the success of neoliberalism rests on widespread acceptance that households must absorb more of the work necessary to ensure their subsistence and the liveli-hoods of their members. In neoliberalist discourse, support for privatization car-ries a double meaning, implying both the private sector of the economy and the private realm of the family. A whole range of developments has reduced or eliminated government services, enforcing "self-reliance," that is, compelling people to rely on earnings, support from friends and family and voluntary orga-nizations and privatized services. This perspective was articulated quite explic-itly in Ontario by the Conservative Harris government (1995-2003) when they justified cuts to social services by arguing that family, friends, neighbors and communities should be more active in providing such care.[5]

Changing   government   policies,   especially   cuts   to   unemploy-ment/employment insurance, social services and welfare, have had a dispropor-tionately negative impact on women and the percentage of women in Canada living in poverty has steadily increased. In 1980, 1.8 million women had low incomes; by 2000, about 2.2 million adult women had low incomes. Almost 19 percent of adult women are poor. When women have low incomes, their chil-dren live in poverty too. About 20 percent of low-income women are mothers raising children on their own; another 51 percent are co-parents in low-income families (Townson 2000: 12). The National Council of Welfare estimates that the total welfare income for a single parent with one child ranged from a low of 50 percent of the poverty level in Alberta to a high of 69 percent in Newfound-land. For couples with two children, welfare incomes averaged around 50 to 55 percent of the poverty level (National Council of Welfare 1999).

While poverty rates and levels offer one measure of the impact of current policies on social life, we know less about the impact of the changing economic order on individual and family responsibility for care giving. Precisely because family life is private and individualized, what happens to individuals and in in-dividual family households is often difficult to assess. Motivated by the Harris government's assertion that people should rely less on government services and more on family, friends, neighbors and community, I did a study based on in-depth interviews with 117 people, of various class and ethnic backgrounds, liv-ing in the greater Toronto region.[6] The study asked, in the context of changing job markets and government cutbacks to social services, what care giving do people provide and accept from others in their households, extended family, friendship, or neighborhood networks or their communities? What prompts peo-ple to give support and aid? What reduces their sense of responsibility to each other? What strengthens it? How are care giving exchanges negotiated and what principles underlie such negotiations?

Here I want to report on two themes which shed light on the impact of neo-liberalism on the way love and care are practiced. One theme relates to the con-straints that force people to depend on others while making it difficult for people to provide the kind of care they value; and, two, the way people's tendency to contribute to care giving increases when these responsibilities are shared or sup-ported by government services, while the lack of other supporting services often causes people to withdraw from care giving, often at the expense of important personal relationships.

The majority of people I interviewed described how their ability to provide care was constrained by their material circumstances, many of which had become more limiting as a result of neoliberal policies. For example, in twenty-two out of twenty-five households where adult children were cohabiting with their parents, the two generations were living together only because at least one party could not afford an alternative, either because they had lost their job or their income was insufficient. Even those who willingly accepted the arrangement said there were problematic consequences for their relationships. A man explained that he had readily converted part of his house so his son, daughter-in-law and their two children could have an apartment. He enjoyed living with them and willingly watched the children after school each day, relishing his intimacy with the grandchildren. He described the costs of their arrangement:

> It seems like it's a success but it is actually not. We all know I am helping them out, because they can't manage on their own. We know we wouldn't live like this if we didn't have to, so every day we have to struggle with that knowledge. They feel inadequate and I feel noble. Neither is healthy. I catch myself watching how they spend their money and resenting it. I think I have the right to tell them how to live. After all, I'm making sacrifices for them. It is not good for my relationship with my son and his wife (M A #36).

Many people reported that cutbacks to social services had forced them to pick up more unpaid work or left them struggling to cope with new demands. A mother of two school-aged children described what she faced:

> My kids' school used to have a great after school program. For just a dollar per day per kid, there were things to do every afternoon—sports, chess club, drama, arts and crafts, you name it. Then it got cut. So now, for my youngest, I have this deal with three other parents. We hire a high school student who comes to the school everyday and picks the kids up. We arranged for a taxi to pick the student and the three kids up and drive them to the community center where there is a drop-in, but kids have to have their own babysitter or parent. Then we pick the kids up from there. It is endlessly complicated. If the student gets sick, or has exams or whatever, or just last week, one kid was sick for a week so her parents didn't want to pay the sitter or taxi, so my budget was shot. Sometimes things get very tense (F A #31).

A woman whose husband was hospitalized for three weeks said that her employer allowed her to have one week paid "emergency" leave and two weeks unpaid leave. She was grateful and made full use of both:

> It was so wonderful. I could just stay at the hospital and not have to even think about work. My company was really good to me (F M #21).

However, her husband's illness lasted longer than the time allowed her. She had to go back to work just when he was sent home, still too ill to care for himself. Like so many others in her situation, she found existing policies insufficient:

I was in a state of panic for weeks. It was so difficult. I went to work, but how could I concentrate? I was frantic with worry about what was happening at home (F M #21).

Another woman described the new responsibilities and new stress she acquired when her husband was injured:

So on top of my regular job I now have almost a second job, at home, looking after him. I have to get up with him at night, sometimes three or four times. I have to make sure he gets his medication at the right time. Sometimes if I get stuck in traffic on the way home I get so scared because he has to get his injections right on time and if I'm late, it's just so much a problem (F M #16).

New insecurities in the workplace created problems for many. People reported having difficulties finding satisfactory care, even when they could afford it. A highly paid lawyer described what happened when her mother required constant care after a serious illness:

For the first few days, she came to my home and I hired round the clock nursing care. But it was very unsatisfactory. I couldn't rely on them. They kept telephoning me to ask questions and I didn't really trust them around the house. So I contacted one of these services and got them to locate a good nursing home. It costs the earth, but I don't have to worry (F M #15).

However, while she was satisfied with the quality of care her mother received, she regretted her lack of personal involvement, a lack imposed by her need to work long hours in order to make enough money to pay for the care:

I could afford it. That wasn't the problem. However, I felt terrible. I want to be more involved, you know. If she could have stayed at home I could have seen her more often and been much more involved in her care every day. As it is, I go to visit early in the morning on the way to work and I pop in briefly at night. But it's not the same (F M #15).

She approached the senior partner in her firm to ask if she could cut back her hours for a few months:

I guess I was naive or something. A few years ago, it was nothing for people to get time off, or go part time. The firm was renowned for its flexibility and openness. Well, was I in for a shock. He didn't just say "no." He actually asked me if I were really cut out for this job! He said this is a new era. Things are more competitive now. Firms that want to survive have to be tough, and this firm, he said, expected everyone who works for it to be tough. He said he was sorry my mother was ill and he knew I would make the right decision (F M #15).

She recognized that if she stopped practicing law to care for her mother all her wealth and skills would be diminished and she could risk poverty.

Other people reported difficulties paid caregivers faced as their workplaces changed. A paid care provider reported that changes in the organization of her work undermined the quality of care she and her co-workers could offer:

> I used to work for a government agency as a home care provider. They privatized the agency, so I lost my job. Later I got another job in a private agency but it wasn't unionized and I make about half what I made before. In addition, all they care about is making their money so we actually don't provide care to people any more. We go in and get out as fast as we can. I feel terrible about it (F A #13).

These examples illustrate the way neoliberal economic policies reduce standards of living for many and impose even more unpaid work on private family households, relying on families, typically women, to absorb the social costs of care giving. But families' resources are not infinite and women's ability to increase their unpaid work can only stretch so far. While most people were loath to talk about their breaking points, a few described the devastating effects of overload. The lawyer, unable to get time off work to spend time with her mother, described her sense of loss:

> For a brief moment, my mother and I reached a new level of intimacy. We were the closest we've ever been, and we were starting to talk about our relationship, to heal old hurts. But then I wasn't there very much. She never said anything but I know she felt hurt. And I felt guilty and couldn't talk about it. So the barriers went back up (F M #15).

A mother described the difficult choices she made when restructuring at her factory meant her employer changed the time she had to start work:

> My shift used to start at 10 am. That was very good. I got the children up and took them to the day care. We had a lot of time. We could sing and tell stories and I didn't have to rush them. Mornings were a very good time. Now I have to be at work at 7 am. I let the children sleep until 5:30. Then I must wake them. It is very hard. They are so tired and do not want to get up and then I have to rush, rush, rush. My employer, he says if we are late three times we get fired so I am very mean to my children in the morning now. It makes me very sad (F A #28).

People were reluctant to talk about family situations that were not supportive but a few indicated some of the tensions and dangers they faced when forced to rely on families. A woman, aged thirty-four, described how she and her two young children had moved into her parents' home after her partner died. She had left that home at fifteen to escape her father's sexual abuse. She returned because the authorities had threatened to take her children away unless she found a home, something she had failed to do in the Toronto housing market on her income from welfare. Feeling trapped, she was frightened that her decision might put her children at risk:

> I told him not to go anywhere near my kids or I'll kill him. And I never leave them alone with him, ever. It's a hell of a life (F A#31).

She went on to offer a trenchant critique of neoliberalism, referring to the slogan of the Tory government, the "commonsense revolution":

> When I was a kid and ran away from home, the welfare at least kept me out of my dad's way and off the streets. I was on it about three years. I finished school, got a job and had a good life. That seems like a good return on the investment, I think. Then [my husband] gets killed, I apply but now it's not enough for me and my kids to live on. All we need is a bit of help for a couple of years until I can get on my feet—a place to live, day care, and a job I can support us on. Instead, we're here and trapped, just so someone can enjoy a nice tax cut, but there are big costs for me and my kids—some commonsense way to do things! (F A #31).

There was a clear relationship between the extent of the potential dependence of the care receiver and the willingness of potential caregivers to commit themselves. The more caregivers anticipated that once they expressed a willingness to provide care, they would be expected to take on full responsibility, the more hesitant they were to make the commitment. A recurring theme was that most professionals and officials associated with government institutions and agencies assumed that family members, and especially women, would provide care and exerted considerable pressure to force families to accept that decision regardless of their actual circumstances and ability to provide care. Such pressures easily evoked anguish or guilt for those who wanted to provide care but couldn't:

> My husband was injured at work. He was in hospital for weeks and we thought he was going to die. So I took time off work to stay with him. Then I had to go back to work. When he got out of hospital, he needed full time care. Everyone—the doctors, the social workers, the nurses—they all assumed I would take care of him. When I said I couldn't, they acted like I was a monster! Surely if I was a good wife I would do anything for him. Like who was going to pay the bills? I said, he needs care, he should get it. That's what health care is for. Or, he was injured at work, the company should pay someone to care for him. It was a big struggle. I spent hours fighting to get him the care he needed. They really tried to make me do everything but I said I can't, I have to work. I felt terrible, but he understood (F M #16).

Such decisions can have painful and disruptive effects on important relationships. A man had been actively involved in looking after his mother for several years. He visited her daily, ran errands for her, paid her bills, helped with household maintenance and offered her extensive emotional support. As her mobility decreased, it became clear she would need full time care. She described their negotiations:

He was stretched to the limit already. We both knew he could keep up what he was doing but he couldn't handle more. But we were all under such pressure for him to move me in with him. And we talked about it and finally we agreed he should take a job he was offered in another city. That way they couldn't force him to do more and he wouldn't feel totally guilty. It was so sad because if I could have got the support I get when he isn't around, he'd still be here. Instead he comes once a month but it's not the same (F M #28).

Official policies about limits to state support when family support is available, may act to block or reduce such support. A mother explained her hesitation about agreeing to have her son and his child move in with her:

You know, I feel like the wicked witch of the west, but I keep saying "No. You can't move in here." I am afraid that once they move in, they will lose their welfare benefits and the day care subsidy, and I will be expected to support them for the rest of my life. I just have my pension. It doesn't go far. If I could just have them move in here that would be very nice. I love my son. He is a lovely man to live with and my grandchild is a joy. I would be happy to help look after him. But I can't take on the whole responsibility. It is too much (F A #27).

Official assumptions that family members will provide care sometimes violate the recipient's desire for independence or evoke their fears of obligation to loved ones. A daughter described her father's position:

When my father was ready to leave hospital, everyone, his doctor, the social worker, they all assumed I would bring him home to my house. My father was very clear. He said "No. I do not live with my daughter. You have to get me help." It was quite a struggle because it was obvious I was a simple solution for them (F M #31).

Official assumptions that family should provide care sometimes created painful situations for those needing care:

There I was. They were ready to send me home and I couldn't even stand up by myself. The hospital social worker walked in all cheery to ask when my family was coming to get me. I had to say I had no one to come and get me. Do you have any idea how painful that was to say? Then, it was like I was a bad person because I didn't have someone to look after me and I was such a problem because they had to find services for me! (M M #32).

In contrast, when people had a sense that they could make a helpful contribution to someone's well being without getting overwhelmed by demands, they were often happy to volunteer.

When my daughter lost her day care subsidy, she was desperate for childcare and asked if I would do it. I wasn't sure at first but when I heard she had made an arrangement with another mother for two days a week, I agreed to take [the child] the other three. It works out really well (F A #32).

What emerged from these interviews most clearly is that these people are coping with the erosion of their standards of living, but at significant cost, both economic and interpersonal. They continue to provide care for each other but recognize the wear and tear that increased stress imposes on their relationships. As one man put it:

The bonds of love are strong so we use them to keep us afloat. But there's always the risk those same bonds may strangle us when we have to pull hard on them (M A#28).

Many of the people interviewed expressed a strong sense that the circumstances they found themselves in offered few choices. Repeatedly, stories about increased stress and interpersonal strain were concluded with a shrug and a resigned "but what can you do?" This response is perhaps not surprising in the face of widespread claims that neoliberal policies are the only option, that there is no alternative. One thing that came out in the interviews was that, while most people did not know how to make changes to improve their circumstances, they had clear ideas about what would improve their situations. What people identified most clearly will come as no surprise. They wanted a living income, decent housing, good health care, time freed from employment to provide care and access to quality care from reliable sources when they were unable to provide it themselves.

This is where historical memory is so important. For despite all the claims that this is a new world order and that globalization is new, as the term "neo" implies, these are actually a revival of old policies. The assumption that individuals and their families must be self-reliant, bearing as much of the cost of social reproduction as possible, is actually as old as eighteenth century liberalism itself, and has been central to the organization of capitalist economic relations since their inception (Picchio 1992). There has also been a long tradition of opposition with well-developed visions of alternatives: a living income, access to education, jobs and training, effective health and safety protections on the job, a safe environment, a shorter working day, week, and year, access to housing, health care, child care, elder care and support for people with disabilities. These are old demands, demands that the labor movement, the women's movement, the left and other progressive movements have put forward for decades (Heron 1996; Carroll 1997). They are demands that put a decent standard of living for everyone ahead of capitalist profit making, that refuse to subordinate love and care to economic factors. And, contrary to the assertions of neoliberal proponents, there is extensive historical evidence available to support claims that such alternatives are indeed viable and that the social world they produce is more equitable. That historical record fuels the current challenge to neoliberalism (Klein 2001: A15).

Another theme emerged less clearly from the interviews. Many of the people interviewed alluded to a critique of the way political decision-making excludes them. They expressed a wish for greater participation in the decisions that affect their lives. Precisely because we have all been involved in care giving relationships for significant periods of our lives, we all have a level of expertise to draw on when searching for alternatives. As one of the men interviewed said:

> I think about the kind of care I would like if I needed it. I want proof that they love me. I want everyone in my life to really want nothing more than to shower attention and love on me all day every day. But I want them to care for me the way I want; I want to say what happens (M A #26).

He identified several important points that need to be taken into account when developing effective care giving policies. First, such policies must make available to families, friends, neighbors and communities the resources necessary to permit them to provide top-quality care. Second, while most people probably yearn to be surrounded by people eager to demonstrate their love, effective social policy must ensure that all people receive the quality of care regardless of whether they have loving family, friends or neighbors willing to provide it. Finally, his assertion that he wants a say in what happens to him offers an important key to effective policy planning.

One of the arguments of neoliberalism that resonates with widespread experience is that governments are excessively bureaucratic and so provide inefficient and uncaring services. Big institutions, they argue, do not provide personalized and loving care as effectively as care at home. But the problem is not government or institutions per se. The best way to ensure quality care giving is not less government or privatized services, but more democratic government and institutions that involve both providers and users in genuine participatory planning and implementation, based on norms of self-determination, reciprocity and dignity. A solution is not tax cuts, but a democratic use of taxes to provide high quality care for everyone based on new democratic decision-making processes at all levels of society—in the home, the workplace, in all organizations and institutions, in government bureaucracies and parliaments and in all the international organizations that shape the global economy—so that people can participate, in informed ways, in making the decisions that affect their lives.

Notes

1. I would like to thank Professor Thelma McCormack and Jane Springer for their helpful comments. A longer version of this paper was published as the 32nd Annual Sorokin Lecture by the Department of Sociology of the University of Saskatchewan at Saskatoon.

2. See the United Nations *Human Development Report* for each year from 1990–2000. For definitions of the Human Development Index and the Human Poverty Index, see *Human Development Report* New York: Oxford University Press, 1998: 14–15. However, since 2001, Canada's rank has dropped to fourth or lower, largely because of growing poverty rates produced by current neoliberal policies.

3. On the Human Poverty Index (which measures the percentage of people expected to die before age sixty, the percentage of adults whose ability to read and write is inadequate and deprivation in overall economic provisioning reflected by access to health services, safe water and the percentages of children under five who are underweight), Canada consistently ranks lower, typically around tenth.

4. This description of neoliberal state orientation derives from Lisa Philips' important paper on tax law and social reproduction in which she documents the ways in which tax laws regulate social reproduction showing how the changes in the 1990s imposed more of "the costs of social reproduction on women, undermining women's economic security, autonomy and equality" (2000: 1).

5. For example, Premier Mike Harris said that poor families who can't feed their children should not rely on Ontario's welfare system but turn to "neighbors and churches" (Toughill 1995b). Community and Social Services Minister David Tsubouchi argued that families who can't afford childcare should "get a neighbor or relative to care for their children" (Toughill 1995c). He defended the Tory government workfare proposals by saying "We believe individuals, families and communities have a primary responsibility to provide for themselves."

6. This study was funded by a grant from the Social Sciences and Humanities Research Council of Canada. I thank that organization for its support and the people who participated in the study. I also thank Ann Eyerman who as the research associate on the project conducted many of the interviews and managed the project. For details of the study, see Appendix A.

Appendix A: Sample for Survey

Care Giving Among Family, Friends, Neighbors and Community
I. Interviews conducted in Toronto, Ontario January 19–January 2001: two samples: The Medical Emergency: sample of twenty-five individuals (eighteen years of age or older) who had experienced an unexpected medical emergency as a result of which they required short term help (such as getting around the house, shopping, cooking, errands, medical treatment). Adult Children and Parents Cohabiting (after time living separately): sample of twenty-five households (where the child was eighteen years of age or older).
II. Ethnicity of samples: Canadian (37), Eastern European (9), American (17), Vietnamese (8), Caribbean (16), Chinese (7), British or Irish (10), First Nations (3), Southern European (9), Philippines (1). Total: 117 interviews; seventy-seven women, forty men.

References

Armstrong, Pat and Hugh Armstrong. 1994. *The Double Ghetto: Canadian Women and Their Segregated Work.* 3rd edition. Toronto: McClelland and Stewart.

Barlow, Maude. 1998. *The Fight of My Life: Confessions of an Unrepentant Canadian.* Toronto: HarperCollins.

Brodie, Janine. 1995. *Politics on the Margins, Restructuring and the Canadian Women's Movement.* Halifax: Fernwood.

Brodie, Janine. 1996. "Canadian Women, Changing State Forms, and Public Policy." In Janine Brodie. ed. *Women and Canadian Public Policy.* Toronto: Harcourt Brace and Co.

Carroll, William. ed. 1997. *Organizing Dissent Contemporary Social Movements in Theory and Practice,* 2nd edition. Toronto: Garamond.

Che-Alford, Janet and Brian Hamm. 1999. "Under One Roof: Three Generations Living Together", *Social Trends,* Statistics Canada-Catalogue no. 11–008, Summer, 6–9.

Cohen, Marjorie. 1997. "What Women Should Know About Economic Fundamentalism." *Atlantis: A Women's Studies Journal.* vol. 21.2 Spring/Summer.

Day, Shelagh and Gwen Brodsky. 1998. *Women and the Equality Deficit: The Impact of Restructuring Canada's Social Programs.* Ottawa: Status of Women.

Drolet, Marie. 1999. *The Persistent Gap: New Evidence on the Canadian Gender Wage Gap.* Income Statistics Division, Statistics Canada, Catalogue No. 75F0002MIE 99008. Ottawa: Minister of Industry.

Finch, Janet. 1989. *Family Obligations and Social Change.* Cambridge: Polity Press.

——— and Jennifer Mason. 1993. *Negotiating Family Responsibilities.* London: Routledge.

Finestone, Sheila.1992–95. *Message from the Secretary of State: Women's Equality in Canada, Progress in Implementing the Nairobi Forward-Looking Strategies for the Advancement of Women Status of Women.* Ottawa: Secretary of State, Government of Canada.

Fischer, Charles. 1994. "The Valuation of Household Production: Divorce, Wrongful Injury and Death Litigation." *American Journal of Economics and Sociology,* vol. 53, No. 2 April, p. 187–201.

Fox, Bonnie and Meg Luxton. 2001. "Conceptualizing Family." In Bonnie Fox. ed. *Family Patterns Gender Relations.* Toronto: Oxford University Press.

Hansard, Ontario. 1998. "Throne Speech Debate." Thursday 30 April www.ontla.on.ca/hansard/36–parl/session/L005a–3.htm–101K.

Harvey, David. 2000. *Spaces of Hope.* Berkeley, Los Angeles: The University of California Press.

Heron, Craig. 1996. *The Canadian Labour Movement A Short History.* Toronto: Lorimer and Company.

Janigan, Mary. 2000. "Towards a Two-Tier System" *Maclean's Canada's Weekly News Magazine.* November 13, p. 22.

Klein, Naomi. 2001. "The Battle Of The Global Gatherings." *The Globe and Mail.* January 24, p. A15

Leblanc, Daniel. 2000. "UI Fraud Suspected As Sickness Claims Soar." *The Globe and Mail,* March 23, p. A1, A6.

Luxton, Meg. ed. 1997. *Feminism and Families Critical Policies and Changing Practices.* Halifax: Fernwood.

——— and June Corman. 2001. *Getting By In Hard Times: Gendered Labour at Home and on the Job.* Toronto: University of Toronto Press.

——— and Ester Reiter. 1997. "Double, Double, Toil and Trouble . . . Women's Experience of Work and Family 1980–1995." in Patricia Evans and Gerda Wekerle. eds.*Women and the Canadian Welfare State Challenges and Change.* Toronto: University of Toronto Press. p.197–221.

Maroney, Heather Jon and Meg Luxton. 1997. "Gender at Work: Canadian Feminist Political Economy since 1988." In Wallace Clement. ed. *Understanding Canada Building on the New Canadian Political Economy.* Montreal and Kingston: McGill Queen's University Press, p. 85–117.

National Council of Welfare. 1997. *Poverty Profile: a Report by the National Council of Welfare 1995.* Ottawa: National Council of Welfare.

―――. 1999. *Poverty Profile: a Report by the National Council of Welfare 1997.* Ottawa: National Council of Welfare.

Orwen, Patricia and Laurie Mousebraaten. 1998. "Pregnant Women Lose Benefit." *The Toronto Star.* 16 April, p. A2.

Philipps, Lisa. 2000. "Tax Law and Social Reproduction: The Gender of Fiscal Policy in an Age of Privatization." unpublished. Paper from the SSHRC-funded project on "Feminism, Law and the Challenge of Privatization" Osgoode Hall Law School York University, July.

Picchio, Antonella. 1992. *Social Reproduction: The Political Economy Of The Labour Market.* Cambridge: Cambridge University Press.

Rebick, Judy. 2000. *Imagine Democracy.* Toronto: Stoddart.

Scoffield, Heather. 2001. "Wealth Gap Grew Wiser, Statscan Study Finds." *The Globe and Mail.* March 16, p. A3.

Shillington, Richard and Clare Lochead. 1997. "National Council of Welfare." *Poverty Profile 1995.* Ottawa.

Sorokin, Pitrim. 2000. *Fads and Foibles in Modern Sociology.* Chicago: Henry Regnery.

Statistics Canada. 2000. *Women In Canada 2000 A Gender-Based Statistical Report.* Ottawa: Minister of Industry.

Status of Women Canada. 1994. *Canada's National Report to the United Nations for the Fourth World Conference on Women.* Ottawa: Status of Women Canada

Toughill, Kelly. 1995a. "Find Job To Feed Kids, Tsubouchi Urges." *The Toronto Star*, 27 September.

―――. 1995b. "Welfare Not Set Up To Feed Kids: Harris." *The Toronto Star*, 28 September, p. A14.

―――. 1995c. " Find Your Own Sitters Working Moms Told." *The Toronto Star,* 8 September:A20.

Townson, Monica. 2000. "Women In Canada Remain Among "Poorest Of The Poor." *The CCPA Monitor*, Vol.7 No.1, The Canadian Centre for Policy Alternatives, May.

UNICEF. 2000a. "A League Table of Child Poverty in Rich Nations." *Innocenti Report Card 1, United Nations' Children's Fund.* Florence: Innocenti Research Centre.

Ursel, Jane. 1992. *Private Lives, Public Policy One Hundred Years of State Intervention in the Family.* Toronto: The Women's Press.

Vanier Institute of the Family. 2000. *Profiling Canada's Families II.* Ottawa: Vanier Institute.

Vosko, Leah. 2000. *Temporary Work: The Gendered Rise of Contingent Work.* Toronto: University of Toronto Press.

Waring, Marilyn. 1988. *If Women Counted: A New Feminist Economics.* New York: Harper and Row.

Yalnizyan, Armine. 1998. *The Growing Gap: A Report On Growing Inequality Between The Rich and the Poor in Canada. Toronto: The Centre for Social Justice.*

Chapter 13

Social Security of Elderly Women and Men in Burkina Faso

Claudia Roth and Fatoumata Badini-Kinda

Social security is nowadays a much-debated issue in the North and in the South. On the one hand, the welfare state is disputed in the North, and on the other hand, impoverishment related to economic developments of the global market threatens large parts of the population in the South. In the South, questions are being raised about how people organize their social security locally and how existing social security arrangements are changing. Research about these issues is still rare.

After two years of research, we are presenting the main lines of our field study—a work in progress—on social security, old age and gender in urban and rural Burkina Faso, West Africa. In 2001, we did three months of field research in Bobo-Dioulasso, the second-largest town in Burkina Faso, and in Kuila, a village near the capital Ouagadougou, after having studied the general situation of local social security in these locations during the first phase of our research in 2000.[1]

The elderly form about 9 percent of the total population in Burkina Faso, and this number is expected to increase (Ministère de l'Action Sociale et de la Solidarité Nationale 2001). Though Burkina Faso is an "aging society," government and society are not prepared to tackle the problems related to the aging population (Ministère de l'Action Sociale et de la Solidarité Nationale 2001; Besana 2001). Concerning this issue, Schoumaker notes: "In a context of rapid urbanization and social changes, the elderly face the risk of finding themselves between traditional family solidarities which are decreasing and a public assistance which is inadequate.... The current problems of Africa, and especially AIDS, also modify inter-generational relations and traditional social care and support of the elderly" (2000: 379, translated by the authors).[2]

In our research, we are asking how the elderly women and men in Burkina Faso are organizing their social security, which is covered in the North by the welfare state and all kinds of insurance and pensions. We want to understand which relations and resources can provide social security, and are following the definition of social security of Keebet and Franz von Benda-Beckmann:

We talk about social security as the dimension of social organization dealing with the provision of security not considered to be an exclusive matter of individual responsibility. Empirically, social security refers to the social phenomena with which the abstract domain of social security is filled: efforts of individuals, groups of individuals and organizations to overcome insecurities related to their existence. That is, concerning food and water, shelter, care and physical and mental health, education and income, to the extent that the contingencies are not considered a purely individual responsibility, as well as the intended and unintended consequences of these efforts (2000: 14).

The perspective of the individuals and their ways of converting their resources (economic, social, and cultural) into actual social security provisions are at the center of our attention. We look at gender as a structuring principle related to social exclusion in the distribution of education, labor, property and other valued resources of the individuals (Kabeer 2000). Our results are based on qualitative research, and we are working with an actor-oriented and holistic approach, i.e. elderly studied as active agents with their cultural notions and social practices in contexts of structural constraints and historical developments (Yanagisako and Collier 1987).

Methodology

Our research questions are: 1. What kind of insecurities do the elderly perceive and experience in urban and rural Burkina Faso? 2. What kinds of resources, social relationships, and institutions are the elderly able to mobilize in coping with old age insecurities? What are the limits of old age support by the family? 3. To what extent is old age gendered (gender as a structuring principle in the (re) distribution of resources and social positions, and as a cultural construct)?

With four hundred thousand inhabitants, Bobo-Dioulasso is the second-largest city in Burkina Faso. The urban district of Koko is located next to the heart of the town. Koko, with about ten thousand inhabitants, is one of the smallest districts of the town, and surveyed by the French in 1929, it is one of the oldest neighborhoods of the city. The social life in Koko is historically marked by two important lineages from various ethnic groups living there, and migrants who moved in the fifties and sixties from villages outside Bobo-Dioulasso and other regions of the country to this neighborhood, where they built up extended families. Koko is a socially-balanced and constant neighborhood: many of the family courtyards have remained in the hands of the initial family, which means that sons, fathers, and grandfathers have had the same neighbors over time (patrilineal, patrilocal societies). Economically, Koko is a modest district.

The research in Koko is based on twenty-two individual interviews with women and men of the middle and lower class, three group interviews (with elderly women, elderly men, and young men), eight interviews with key persons of the district and of the town (e.g. the chief of a lineage, the general secretary of a women's association, a muezzin, the deputy director of an elderly people's association, an economist, representatives of urban social services and a Catholic organization), and participatory observation (Roth 1996).[3]

Kuila is a rural Moose[4] village located thirty-five kilometers from the capital, Ouagadougou. In 1996, its population was estimated at 1,357 inhabitants, with a predominance of women: 51.85 percent vis-à-vis 48.2 percent men. As a Moose village, Kuila has a highly patriarchal social structure in which the chief and the elderly play an important role in the organization of social life. All the families are related by kinship, as they all originate from the same lineage. This reinforces kinship and neighborhood relations and maintains a communal type of life in the village. Kuila faces an adverse natural environment: soils are poor and rain is scarce. The bulk of the population lives on subsistence agriculture.

The research in Kuila is based on twenty individual interviews with women and men of the middle and the lower class, two group interviews with elderly women and men, eight interviews with key persons (e.g. administrative officials, leaders of three health structures and the chief of the village), and participatory observation.[5]

Insecurity—Living Standard in Old Age

In the urban situation in Koko in Bobo-Dioulasso, old age is for everyone potentially a phase of impoverishment. The women and men of the middle class prepare for old age as long as they work (buying land, building houses, saving) and can face potential impoverishment, whereas the lower class faces a certain decrease of its living standard. Both women and men of the lower class live in insecurity. All elderly men and women work and make money as long as their physical conditions allow it. This actual material necessity reflects the cultural conception of old age.

In the rural situation in Kuila, living standard is synonymous with vulnerability, destitution, and dependence, especially among the lower class. Agricultural activity requires much physical strength, which the elderly lose as years go by. The level of resources is generally low, and village people face numerous natural contingencies. Opportunities for resource accumulation are limited. In Kuila, most elderly live in insecurity and destitution. The few people living in security are those with a high social position in the village (the village chief, the religious chief, the retired civil servant) or those who receive assistance from well-off children.

In urban contexts, we tend to have a reversed contract between generations: according to the concept, which is still valuable today, children are the social security of the elderly. In practice, parents are children's unemployment insurance and grandchildren's orphan insurance. An increasing number of elderly parents take care of their adult children (married sons with their wife and children and unmarried daughters with their children) and their orphan grandchildren. High unemployment and the death rate caused by AIDS among the younger generation cause this situation. The reversed contract between generations increases the impoverishment of the lower class in old age: the physical strength of the elderly dwindles and they are less able to work, but expenses remain the same or increase.

In the village, the social contract between generations is more or less well maintained. According to traditional concepts, a child represents a source of security—a social insurance. In return, the elderly provide moral and spiritual security, "medicine" for the younger generation. In Kuila, the elderly interviewed said that their children took care of them, with the exception of some unfortunate cases and circumstances outside of their control (the death or migration of young people, abandoning their spouses and children in the care of the family). The reversed contract between generations is exceptional in Kuila. Agricultural labor and the Moose social organization, which confers very early responsibility to the youth, lend a special twist to youth unemployment in the village. In Kuila, the intergenerational contact is still respected, but due to rural poverty, it does not cover all the needs of the elderly.

According to the concept that children are the social security of the elderly, the sons take care of their elderly parents; in practice daughters' support is more important—an indicator for women's strategies. Married daughters support their own kin with their income and the fruits of their labor (gender separation of property). Because of the numerous cases of separations and divorces, marriage relations are not reliable anymore, and run contrary to descent relationships that are determined by birth. Women's own interests also benefit the elderly; through the strategy of supporting and caring for their parents, women maintain a place to which they can return in times of distress, thereby providing for their own future social security, as well as for the actual social security of their parents. Sons evolve in a varied field of expectations shaped by their own interests and wishes for a certain autonomy, the interests of their spouses and family in-law, and the interests of their own parents.

In the village, sons are supposed to take care of their elderly parents. Sons work in the field of their elderly parents, provide them with food and healthcare, redo the roofs of their huts every season, and give them clothing. They also provide for them in terms of some vices such as kola nut eating, tobacco chewing, and dolo (local beer) drinking. They run errands for their parents, especially during social events. Daughters-in-law replace their mothers-in-law in terms of domestic chores. This confers prestige and privilege upon the mothers-in-law who benefit from such services. The support of sons to their elderly parents is thus made visible. It is noteworthy that in villages, sons' own interests are less visible than in towns.

For their part, daughters marry outside their own village and return to it only occasionally. Their support to their elderly parents is considered less visible because it is occasional. But in practice, more and more elderly acknowledge the importance of their daughters' contribution to their social security. Some daughters send their parents food, money, and various gifts (Cattell 1997). The daughters support their elderly parents through assisting their husbands. Because marriages are arranged, in villages sons-in-law tend to take better care of their parents-in-law than in towns. With reference to sons-in-law, the Moose have a saying: "You bring a daughter to life to exchange her against a son."

Kinship in the urban situation still remains the main point of reference, but it finds expression through individuals, not through the community and without working principles, which operate automatically. The production and reproduction of kinship relations depend on individual efforts and investments, good social behavior and the personal material situation. It is the individual's responsibility to try to implement reciprocity, which is the foundation of social life. As with all relationships, kinship relations are in jeopardy when material resources are not available to allow for participation in reciprocal exchanges. In urban contexts, social class and kinship relations are interdependent variables: the more an individual is well off, the more his or her kinship relations are important and substantial—or conversely, the more a person is needy, the more his or her kinship relations are precarious and may even disappear.

In the rural situation, kinship relations are a support for elderly persons; kin staying with them improve their living conditions in terms of food, lodging, health, and clothing. In villages, elderly parents without offspring rely on the extended family to survive. In Kuila, kinship networks are large, and combined with physical proximity, they tend to nurture kinship. The reciprocity-based social rules provide support through the kinship network as long as the principle is followed. The most destitute, who can't follow it, tend to be marginalized. Elderly persons enjoying economic or symbolic power are those with the most important kinship networks. The emergence of individual interests is a new but still rare phenomena in Kuila.

For urban dwellers, social life is based on generalized reciprocity, on a triple commitment: to give, to receive, and to render (Mauss 1968). Credits are made through giving, thus generating a continuous circuit of gifts and countergifts, which correspond to rights and duties and represent social security. In distress, one may resort to people whom one helped in the past. To participate in this reciprocal exchange, women and men must have a minimum of resources. If not, they are socially marginalized (Marie 1997; Vuarin 2000).

In rural areas, reciprocity exists between generations at the community level through regular exchanges of goods and services practiced daily and during social events. Failure to observe this pillar and integrating principle of social organization exposes the individual to marginality. In the village, the individual tends to confirm his marginality by withdrawing himself.

Because of historical reasons, neighborhood, kinship relations, and religious community relations overlap and reinforce one another. In old neighborhoods like Koko, relations have a "generational depth" (Vuarin 2000), which constitutes social protection and slows down the process of social marginalization initiated by poverty. At the same time, Koko seems to impoverish. Persons of the young generation, earning a good income, often move to other districts or even to other towns. Left behind are the elderly women and men with their unemployed children and their grandchildren – the part of the population with little or no income. Many ethnic associations in Koko serve in the first place to guarantee and to perform under the conditions of poverty the most important kinship ceremony, the funerals. Additionally, in Bobo-Dioulasso, some old lineages have recently started to organize themselves to face their precarious socioeconomic situation and to develop lineage-based alternatives to generating income.

In Kuila, kinship relations are predominant and constitute the base of all other forms of neighborhood relations and community life. The community has mechanisms to support the elderly through gifts and services (e.g. sisoaga or collective fieldwork sessions). These traditional security nets limit and even push back the threat of marginalization of the elderly. However, more and more this type of service requires important investment in terms of food, beer, kola nut, tobacco, and even money, which the most destitute cannot afford. This means that the most needy are deprived of this kind of support.

Local groups consist of customary and religious associations which, depending on circumstances, provide support and succor to needy persons, including elderly persons. Actually, one development association, called Nebgninga, is being set up to provide support to the elderly persons of Kuila.

The State's role in relation to the social security of the elderly is insignificant; support targeting elderly people is absent both at the state level and the private level, which also reflects the situation of the country. The role of the State concerning the social security of elderly persons is not clearly perceived in Kuila. Besides episodic gifts of food to the needy (which often benefit elderly persons), there is hardly any action of the State towards the elderly in Kuila.

Mobilizing social support is based on reciprocal exchange. With impoverishment, the circle of social relations shrinks, including kinship relations. Due to its material resources, the middle class interacts over a wide social network within and beyond kinship relations, and therefore lives independently. Lower-class women and men have to struggle in their daily lives to acquire the resources necessary to maintain their position in the reciprocal exchanges. They face the danger of resorting to relations of dependency, like in the patron-client relationship, and of being marginalized.

In Kuila, most elderly survive thanks to their offspring and/or their kinship relations. Everybody is considered a parent, but the level of operation of this network in terms of support is more and more determined by the individual's power and wealth. The powerful and wealthy generally belong to the middle class, and they are the ones who enjoy the most important and diversified relation networks. The most destitute can barely rely on the friendship and kinship relationships. This situation is akin to a vicious circle, and it is aggravated in the village by a new phenomena, the emergence of individual interests, and the middle class placing social distance toward their poor kin.

In day to day life, elderly women in Koko have as much influence on family and community life as elderly men, but they do not show it. It remains "a secret" between men and women; it is part of the secret of marriage (furugundo)[6], where men and women realize their relationship. The social position of women and men is adjusted to each other in old age. However, the importance of resources and the density of an individual's social network are decisive for social security, which means that money, resources and time must be available. The gender division of labor, differences of income (labor market is gender structured) and the subordinate position of women make it more difficult for women than for men to provide for their own social security.[7] Women's duties, as a result of the gender division of labor, have consequences for them in old age; they are responsible for food, health care for the sick, and their dependents. This explains why more wives take care of their elderly husbands than the reverse, why more mothers than fathers support their unemployed adult children, why more grandmothers than grandfathers raise their orphan grandchildren, and why the women provide health care to the sick. Because women's resources are generally less substantial than men's, women take care of their husbands, children, and grandchildren in often precarious material conditions.

In old age, women in Kuila acquire a new social position that gives them some power over younger women and moves them closer to men in stature. They take part in some decision-making and some rituals. Equal position beside men is not valid in the case of Moose society. In old age, women are more exposed to insecurity and social exclusion. They age more rapidly than men as a result of numerous childbearings and heavy household chores. The gender division of labor also operates against women. More elderly women than men live in destitution because their capacity to accumulate wealth is traditionally low. They have no access to animal breeding, which is the main source of investment in the village. Jewelry, silver necklaces, bracelets, and woven loincloths, which constitute the hidden treasure of elderly women in villages, have now lost value in modern markets.

Social exclusion is the most discriminating situation with respect to gender. In villages, witchcraft remains a current phenomenon in the third millennium, and more elderly women than men are accused of witchcraft. Most often, this accusation is lodged against destitute elderly women who have no support. They are feared, publicly laughed at, beaten up, and chased out of the village with sticks and stones. They are called "soul-eaters." Women accused of witchcraft in Kuila have found refuge in the center of Tanghin, Ouagadougou, a center for excluded women. In the course of this investigation, cases of witchcraft were pending trial at the chief's compound.

In old age, marriage is an important social protection in urban areas for both men and women. On the one hand, it is the base of all other social protection strategies by reason of respect derived from being married, and on the other hand, it allows the spouses to insure themselves in a mutual way (Leliveld 1994). But marriage becomes a source of insecurity for women when, in the case of distress, the wife has to take over the additional responsibilities and tasks that her husband doesn't fulfill anymore and leaves up to her. This makes it difficult or even impossible for the wife to maintain her social network. To live singly—as a result of separation, divorce, or death of the partner – means a loss of security for both men and women. However, in such a situation women are more vulnerable than men for the reasons given above.

For most villagers, the duties and obligations related to marriage, as well as its effects, constitute a source of security in old age. Spouses mutually support each other and enjoy social consideration, which is a guarantee for integration into community life and for a secure life.

In practice, marriage becomes a source of insecurity when it generates numerous conflicts between spouses and between spouses and their in-laws. The case of widows who refuse the levirate system[8] is indicative. Living outside the marriage circuit as a result of separation, divorce or widowhood is, however, a gateway to numerous insecurities to which women are again more exposed than men.

The main aim of the strategies of women and men is to avoid exclusion from the reciprocal exchange and therefore to avoid being socially marginalized. This requires the ability to convert material and symbolic resources into social relations (von Benda-Beckmann 2000; Vuarin 1994). Women's strategies are characterized by the fact that they do not overtly compete with men; they remain in the background and make use of all the good opportunities that come up (Hainard andVerschuur 2001, 2002).

Conclusion

Our preliminary results enable us to conclude the following: in the research context of Burkina Faso, marriage and family are perceived as havens of security. In reality, however, they are ambivalent institutions as far as the social support of its members is concerned, particularly among the poor population. The reasons are, on the one hand, an accumulation of critical events in later phases of the developmental cycle of the domestic group (e.g. marriage ceremonies of children and illness of parents), and on the other hand, a drain of household resources or no contribution by members who neglect the norms of familial responsibility and solidarity, often males.

In Burkina Faso there is a clear notion of "African solidarity," but the scale of the available resources determines whether social security is guaranteed or whether marginalization is at stake. Kinship is most important for social support. Provisions by local organizations and the state can hardly be claimed, because they exist only to a minimal extent.

Middle class individuals can often make provisions for old age, but lower class individuals are completely dependent on their children. Because of economic conditions, in the rural context children are barely able to support their parents, and in the urban context, in many cases not at all. In town, we find more and more the reversed contract between the generations, e.g. elderly parents who care for their children and orphan grandchildren. Poor elderly are in danger of being socially marginalized; generally, elderly females are more often in precarious material conditions than males. This is attenuated in the village by kin relationships and in the city by the longstanding networks of kinship, neighborhood, and religious community. Potentially, old age is a phase of impoverishment for all. In old age, women and men of the lower class have to make a daily effort to survive —they can't sit down and take a rest.

Notes

1. Research in Bobo-Dioulasso: Claudia Roth, social anthropologist, University of Zurich; research in Kuila: Fatoumata Kinda, sociologist, University of Ouagadougou.
2. See also contributions in Attias-Donfut and Rosenmayr 1994.
3. Research in 2000 on the general situation of local social security: thirty individual interviews with women and men of the middle and the lower class of the older and the younger generation, two group interviews (elderly women and widows), seven interviews with key persons of the district and of the town.
4. The Moose (Mossi) are the major ethnic group of Burkina Faso.
5. Research in 2000: thirty-one individual interviews with women and men of the middle and the lower class of the older and the younger generation, four group interviews (elderly women, elderly men, widows and young men), and several interviews with key persons.
6. Dioula expression for the concept "secret of marriage."
7. Concerning the gendered labor market and the gender division of labor see also Baerends 1998, Lachaud 1997, Schoumaker 2000.
8. Levirate system: marriage between a widow and a brother of her deceased husband, a traditional form of social security for widows. The levirate system also allows for the continued maintainse of alliances between lineages or clans.

References

Attias-Donfut, Claudine and Léopold Rosenmayr. eds. 1994. "Changing Kinship. Family and Gender Relations in Sub-Saharan Africa." *Vieillir en Afrique*. Paris: PUF.
Baerends, Elsa. 1998. "Changing Kinship. Family and Gender Relations in Sub-Saharan Africa." In: C. Risseeuw, K. Ganesh. eds. *Negotiation and Social Space: A Gendered Analysis of Changing Kin and Security Networks in South Asia and Sub-Saharan Africa*. New Delhi, London: Sage Publications. p. 47–86.
Benda-Beckmann, Franz and Keebet von. 2000. "Coping with Insecurity." In F. K. von Benda-Beckmann, H. Marks. eds. *Coping with Insecurity. An Underall Perspective on Social Security In The Third World. Special Issue Focal*, 22–23: 7–31.
Besana, Laura. 2001. *Les Personnes Âgées Au Burkina Faso. Rapport De Recherche*. Berne: Secrétariat Suisse de la FAO.
Cattell, Maria. 1997. "The Discourse of Neglect: Family Support for the Elderly in Samia." In Th. Weisner et al. eds. *African Families and the Crisis of Social Change*. London: Begin & Garvey. p. 157–183.
Hainard, François et Christine Verschuur. 2001. *Femmes Dans Les Crises Urbaines. Relations De Genre Et Environnements Précaires*. Paris: Karthala.
Hainard, François und Christine Verschuur. 2002. "Städte, Lebensumfeld Und Geschlechterrollen. Ein Forschungsprojekt In Sieben Ländern Des Südens Und Des Ostens." *Neue Zürcher Zeitung* 15 (19–20 Jan.): 91.

Kabeer, Naila. 2000. "Social Exclusion, Poverty and Discrimination. Towards an Analytical Framework." *IDS Bulletin* 31: 83–97.

Kinda, Fatoumata. 1998. *La Pauvreté Des Femmes Au Burkina Faso.* Ouagadougou: Ministère de l'Economie et des Finances du Burkina Faso, Direction de l'Orientation Economique et de la Prospective. UNICEF.

Lachaud, Jean-Pierre. 1997. *Les Femmes Et Le Marché Du Travail Urbain En Afrique Subsaharienne.* Paris: L'Harmattan.

Leliveld, André. 1994. *Social Security in Developing Countries. Operation and Dyna mics of Social Security Mechanisms in Rural Swaziland.* Amsterdam: Thesis Publishers.

Marie, Alain. 1997. "Conclusion. Individualisation: Entre Communauté Et Société, L'avènement Du Sujet." In A. Marie. ed. *L'Afrique des Individus.* Paris: Karthala. p. 407–436.

Mauss, Marcel. 1968. *Die Gabe.* Frankfurt: Suhrkamp.

Ministère de l'Action Sociale et de la Solidarité Nationale. 2001. *Plan D'action National En Faveur Des Personnes Âgées Au Burkina Faso.* Ouagadougou.

Roth, Claudia. 1996. *La Séparation Des Sexes Chez Les Zara Au Burkina Faso.* Paris: L'Harmattan.

Schoumaker, Bruno. 2000. "Le Vieillissement En Afrique Subsaharienne." *Espace, Papulations, Sociétés.* no. 3: 379–390.

Vuarin, Robert. 2000. *"Un Système Africain De Protection Sociale Au Temps De La Mondialisation Ou 'Venez M'aider À Tuer Mon Lion' . . . "* Paris: L'Harmattan.

Yanagisako, Sylvia J. and Jane F. Collier. 1987. "Toward a Unified Analysis of Gender and Kinship." In Collier, Jane F. and Sylvia Yanagisako. eds. *Gender and Kinship: Essays Toward a Unified Analysis.* Stanford: Stanford University Press. p. 14–50.

Chapter 14

Traditional Female Sex Workers of Rajasthan, India: An Ethnographic Study of the Nat Community

Ramesh Chand Swarankar

The Nat have been referred to as a vagrant gypsy tribe, which led a nomadic life for much of their history. They were traditionally engaged in the occupations of rope dancing, acrobatics (*kalabazi*) jugglery, traditional plays (*kartab*), and shows (*nautanki*) in which women called natani played a major role (Crooke 1975). They have been the traditional entertainers to rulers, feudal lords (*zagirdar*), and people in rural areas. Nat women coming to the zagirdars to perform dance and music on social occasions were used for sensuous and sexual pleasure as well. In the 19th century, Britishers ruling the *Rajputana* were invited to festive ceremonies for marriages and births at which Nat women performed singing and dancing. *Rajwada* or *Rajputana* were the terms used for the state of Rajasthan (Tod 1829). Nat were gifted with cash and in-kind for their traditional skills demonstrated in the form of dance and song. They were part of the traditional system of extending services among castes (*jajmani*) and had a relationship of patron and performer (*jajman-jachak*) in the traditional social structure of Rajasthan. Women and thus the community were paid in cash and kind for their services under the *jajmani* system. After the decline of feudalism, patronage extended to the Nat community came to an end. The local people no longer appreciated traditional plays performed by their women, as alternate modern sources of entertainment became popular with the pace of time.

Nat, classified as *Karnat* and *Rajnat,* claim themselves to be the descendents of *Rajput* rulers. They practice polytheism and worship deities and gods like Hindus do. The members of a family *(dera)* and the group of three to four families *(tola)* of close kin lived in the temporary hutments of bamboo sticks *(sirki).* A donkey for transport, a dog for security, and a hen to provide eggs had functional importance for the Nat.

The family was the occupational unit as young women danced on rope while the men played drums and supported them morally and physically. The viewers provided these women with cereals and other consumable items. Particularly, landlords gave them gifts, clothes, goats, and cattle. They were known for their beauty, bodily charms, and acrobatic feats with sensual and sexual appeal. The practice of *paasvan* (keeping a mistress) in some situations permitted the dominant persons to keep *natani* for sexual pleasure.

The Nat, a nomadic community, unskilled and not prepared for any other occupation, could not adapt themselves in changing situations. The misfit Nat population without any land and its own place for shelter found it difficult to survive. Nat, losing their functional utility in the weakened *jajmani* system of rural social structure, had to change from nomadic to sedentary life in the vicinity or at a distance from the village. It was easier for them to settle down and erect temporary hutments in *benami* land (unused land not owned by any individual in revenue records) outside the village. The land awarded to a few *natani* (Nat women) dancers by feudal lords was also used for this purpose. Such land was used for living temporarily on the outskirts of and at a distance from the villages, still in a type of *dera*, inhabited by two or three families of *Nat* in close kinship.

Population

Nat are distributed in almost all the districts of Rajasthan. They are also found in Madhya Pradesh, Bihar, West Bengal, Haryana, Punjab, and Himachal Pradesh states. Their total population in Rajasthan, according to the 1981 census, was 23,225. The Nat speak Hindi or the dialect locally known as *bagri,* and they use the *devnagari* script. They are non-vegetarians and *roti*, prepared of wheat or *bajra* (millet), is their staple food. Alcoholic drink is an integral part of their social life. After the settling of disputes and on social and ceremonial occasions and festivities, drinks are served by the host. The Nat living in Madhya Pradesh are believed to have migrated from Uttar Pradesh. They use *Prasad* as their surname, but a separate population figure is not available. Their total population including the *Kalbelia*, and *Sapera* (ethnic groups like Nat community) was 44,127. They are predominantly returned from rural areas. The Nat of Bihar has three synonyms, namely *Bazigar, Sapera,* and *Gulgulia.* Their population in Bihar was 24,897. In West Bengal, the Nat are also known as the *natta*, which means those who are proficient in dance and music. They migrated to West Bengal in the remote past, and their total population there is 3,376. They speak Bengali and the Bengali script is used at all levels of communication. The Nat sporadically distributed in the Ferozpur and Patiala districts of Punjab and their population was 466 (245 males and 221 females). The Nat are also noted as a scheduled caste in Chandigarh and Himachal Pradesh, where their populations were only 21 and 232 respectively (Census of India 1981). The Nat, an ethnic group numerically in the minority is thus spread throughout Rajasthan and other states in India.

According to the 1981 census, 25.67 percent of them were classified as workers (42.16% of males and 8.97% of females). Of those, 41.82 percent were cultivators, 22.01 percent worked as agricultural laborers, 3.97 percent were engaged in rearing livestock, and forestry, and 4.04 percent in trade and commerce. The remaining 28.34 percent of the workers were engaged in various other services. The total literacy rate was only 8.14 percent consisting of 14.89 percent for males and only 1.31 percent for females (Singh 1993). Traditionally, about half of the Nat women practice prostitution; usually the unmarried girls are allowed to do so. Besides prostitution, theft and begging have been reported among the Nat (Raghav 1993).

Study Hamlets

This chapter is based on an ethnographic study of the hamlets of the 'Nat' community in the state of Rajasthan in northwestern India. The Nat hamlets (*bustee* or *dhani*) of a revenue village of different sizes, namely Bandar Sindari (large), Dantari, Teelawala (medium) and Chamand-ka-Mand (small), were covered under the present study carried out in 2000. The first two hamlets on national highway 8 are situated at a distance of seventy-five to eighty-five kilometers southeast of Jaipur, the capital of Rajasthan. Teelawala and Chamand-ka-Mand hamlets are located at distances of about thirty and twenty-one kilometers, south and northwest respectively, from Jaipur. These started taking the shape of settlements about four decades ago, except Chamand-ka-Mand, a new habitat of Nat community that came into being in 1997.

A total population of 514 Nats was unequally distributed into thirty-five, thirty-two, ten and four households in Bandar Sindari, Dantari, Teelawala, and Chamand-ka-Mand hamlets respectively. A maximum 91.6 percent and 75 percent of the houses were of the pucca type (concrete and cement) in Teelawala and Chamand-ka-Mand, while 90.6 percent and 60 percent were mud and thatched (*kutcha)* houses in Dantari and Bandar Sindari hamlets, respectively. Families taken together were almost equally divided into nuclear family (49.3%) and joint family (50.7%) structures. A nuclear family may also be formed by the female sex worker and her children without a sociological husband, or an FSW (with or without children) and partner contracted temporarily like a husband living *(ghar janwai)* with the parents or brother's joint family. Of a total of seventy-nine respondents interviewed, only seven married women and twenty-five FSWs (fourteen working FSWs and eleven retired FSWs) could finally provide qualitative data related to the study. Of working FSWs, half in Chamand-ka-Mand, one-third in Bandar Sindari and one-fourth in Teelawala had *ghar janwai* as their family members. Many of them were mothers whose children were fathered by clients or *ghar janwai*. Commercial sex is the major source of income, practiced by as much as 62.3 percent of Nat women, while 37.7 percent of women lead a married life in the study hamlets. Nat women working as commercial sex workers were in the age group of 16 to 35 years. A few FSWs (7.1%) below 16 years of age were engaged in child prostitution. All of them from all four hamlets were illiterate, except five or six who studied up to the primary level. NGOs and parents themselves in the changing situation are persuading children, including females, to enter into elementary education.

At Bandar Sindari and Teelawala, telephone connections were found in one or two Nat households. There was no school for the Nat children within these hamlets. A few children have to walk one to three kilometres for primary education, to the school located in the main village. Electricity was available in all four hamlets except Chamand-ka-Mand, the interior one, which is without any approach, connectivity and other facilities. In Chamdn-ka-Mand the scarcity of drinking water was more acute compared to the other three hamlets. Even health and medical facilities were not available in all the Nat hamlets except Bandar Sindari, where private medical practitioners are available nearby on Highway 8.

Female Sex Workers

Women occupy a lower status in the patrilineal, male-dominated social order of the Nat community; the status of an unmarried female sex worker is still lower than that of the married Nat woman, despite the FSW's position as an earning member for the family. Married women receive respect, while FSWs are neither recognized much in the family nor in society. FSWs are not encouraged to participate in any ritual associated with the social ceremonies considered auspicious, which the married women perform. A married woman observes all restrictions like wearing the veil (*purdah*), distance from elder males of family and outsiders, sexual relations strictly within wedlock, and taboo on premarital and post-marital sex with any one except the husband, while such rules are not applied to women pursuing commercial sex.

In Rajasthan, traditionally the women, especially the unmarried girls belonging to Nat, Rajnat, Bedia, and Kanjar communities practice commercial sex (*dhandha*). Over five thousand female sex workers belonging to these communities were estimated in Rajasthan (Swarankar 2000). About 10 percent of the total sex workers in Delhi are from villages primarily inhabited by Bedias, Nat, and Kanjar, the castes that have traditionally accepted prostitution as their primary occupation (Mukherjee 1989).

The induction into *dhandha* and its continuation depends on the economic condition of the family and the health of the women. Nat women are vulnerable due to commercial sex practiced for the family's livelihood. FSWs, especially the young girls, are deprived of all opportunities for personal development; they are denied the rights to education, health care and other opportunities for empowerment. In many cases, FSWs after retirement in old age are left with no option but to lead a lonely life in the absence of family. Socially, they are not permitted to marry within the caste. Complicating the situation, modernization has affected the lives of Nat and rendered, particularly the families without girl(s) for commercial sex, poverty stricken.

An FSW bears the expenses of a brothers' marriage, for which a heavy amount is spent. A brother's marriage is considered essential to sustaining the lineage amongst the Nat. Being earning members; many of the FSWs are involved in the decision making for family affairs with financial implications.

According to the norms of the Nat caste *Panchayat* (traditional council governing their social political affairs), a retired FSW has to be looked after by her brother's children. She and her children usually have a share in the parental property, though in practice this does not happen. FSWs usually do not take part in adult franchise despite the fact that they are voters. No FSW has contested an election, though as an exception a retired FSW from a *Panchayat samiti* (block level council) of Jaipur district was elected as *Pradhan* (block level leader) of *Panchayatraj* institution under democratic decentralization in 1998 on a seat reserved to a woman of other backward classes (OBC).

Socialization for Commercial Sex

A girl in a Nat family is distinguished from an early age. Initially during socialization, a girl who is to lead a married life is prepared for domestic chores. She is made to observe social restrictions like high Hindu castes, while a girl who is to be inducted into prostitution is trained by a retired FSW (*patelan*) about the *dhandha* and its secrets. Such a girl comes in closer contact with retired FSWs and eventually with the clients and their activities. The environment and 'demonstration effect' mentally prepare these immature girls. These girls either willingly accept *dhandha* or are brainwashed by retired FSWs to accept the same for the economic and perceived traditional reasons.

Nath Utrai has been a prominent ritual in the Nat community and is celebrated as a custom. *Nath* is the nose ring a Nat girl wears, which is removed symbolically by her first client. Amongst the clients, one who pays the highest amount performs the custom of *Nath Utrai*. The needy parents' or guardians' first priority is to procure the maximum possible amount for *Nath Utrai*. This amount usually ranges from Rs 10,000 to Rs 25,000 or even more depending upon the age and beauty of the girl. The client gets the right to initiate sex with the virgin girl, who is dressed up like a Hindu high-caste bride. He is considered her husband and is given priority over other clients on future visits. Once the deal has been struck, offerings are made to a deity, followed by a feast for kith, kin, and the community. After such a ritual, a girl is inducted and the community socially permits her to pursue *dhandha*. *Dhandha*, therefore, has a community sanction, and the control of Nat caste *Panchayat*. The norms of *dhandha*, amongst others, include sex as an occupation, in which a minimum time essential for intercourse should be spent with clients, sentimental attachment with clients is forbidden and no Nat male can be the client of a Nat FSW. These are part of the induction process.

The Nat perceive a girl to be sexually mature soon after the onset of menstruation. Tradition, economic, and family structure are the factors responsible for induction of a girl child into prostitution. Clients' preference for sex with a girl child for sexual pleasure, and curing a sexually transmitted disease via sex with a virgin are the other reasons child prostitution is practiced in the villages in this study.

Occupational Structure

There is a popular saying among villagers about the Nat, that plenty of money without labor (*andhi kamai*) is earned by their women through prostitution. Commercial sex practiced by the unmarried women is the major source of income of the Nat. A girl child prostitute preferred by many clients earns more than others. Nat neither practice agriculture, nor do they take interest in pursuing any other economic activity. A few Nat families own agricultural land, which they cultivate on the basis of sharecropping. Some run kiosks and small shops. At the two hamlets on highways, two Nat youth and one retired FSW work to implement an NGO's AIDS awareness project in the community. Males mostly remain idle except for a few engaged in transport activity as drivers or helpers in the private jeeps owned by them or others. Most of them solicit clients for their sisters and other FSWs in the family and kinship. Invariably, Nat males assist in the occupation of commercial sex carried on by their women. They not only solicit clients but also deal with them if they create a nuisance. They also handle the police. Males escort the FSWs to Mumbai, hotels and other places. In Mumbai, some males reportedly work at telephone booths, while the females work as bar dancers and sex workers there. Catering to an increasing number of clients has enhanced the income of FSWs. An FSW can earn much more in Mumbai than in a native hamlet in Rajasthan, for obvious reasons.

In-depth studies revealed the exploitation of FSWs by retired FSWs (*patelan*), pimps, middlemen, and others involved in the occupation, who pocket one-fourth to one-third of a FSWs' earnings. A commission is paid to the persons in the sex trade network, hoteliers, transporters and others in Mumbai. A substantial amount is also spent when the police catch FSWs. A small proportion of income is utilized by the FSW for meeting her necessities, while the rest is sent for the livelihood of dependents and accomplishing family affairs like the marriage of a brother (s). A heavy amount of money is spent on the marriage of a brother, considered a matter of social prestige. The amount of dowry as well as bride price paid has increased over the years. Food, clothes, cosmetics, medical treatment, and delivery of the FSW to private clinics are other major expenses. The expenditure on education is minimal, as only a very small number of Nat children attend and private schools are preferred. They often turn out to be drop-outs in the primary and post-primary levels. Discrimination as such was not re-ported, but the children of Nat were not encouraged to attend school.

Migration Pattern

Nat FSWs migrate outside as well as locally within their hamlets. Permanent and casual types of migration of FSWs have been reported from the hamlets in this study. Their migration has increased and emerged as a trend over the years. It was difficult to measure the migration due to the fluctuating number of mi-grating sex workers. However, over two-thirds of total sex workers were esti-mated to have migrated mainly to Mumbai city. Nat kin and community youth already living there arrange for accommodation for them. They are involved in the sex trade network, which arranges for their occupation as bar dancers and sex workers. Male family members from native hamlets accompany the migrat-ing girls. They may travel with community youth and other peer women for se-curity reasons. The major reasons for migration of FSWs are income, lack of opportunities in the native place, social stigma, and police harassment.

The improvement in access to highways and railways has facilitated the mi-gration of sex workers. The mobility of local as well as outside clients of FSWs has increased over the decades. Truckers, transporters, youths, laborers, immi-grants, and students are seen in and around FSW hamlets. Most of them who can afford to visit such women are young (twenty to forty years old), who need to be educated about the transmission of HIV/AIDS and the use of condom for safe sex. In hamlets, an FSW charges Rs50-100 for each client. FSWs are arranged to visit the clients in hotels in some situations. The nexus of middlemen and FSWs joined by hoteliers/transporters for commercial sex has been thus facilitated by transport, communication, and infrastructure development.

Women affected by HIV/AIDS are out of the reach of doctors because they cannot afford to go due to both social and economic factors. The precariousness of women's families, their personal status, the disadvantaged state of the female population, and biological vulnerability lead to the rapid spread of the epidemic. Similarly, infected women face greater risks of rejection, ostracism, and neglect, making them even more vulnerable. Where women participate in earning for the household, lost labor due to HIV may well affect the ability of women to feed their households (Reid and Bailey 1993).

In India, the most common route for HIV transmission is through hetero-sexual sex (NACO 1995). Despite some recent studies, very little is known about sexual behaviour (Mane and Maitra 1992; Nag 1994; and Pauchary 1994).

More than 50 percent of the HIV infections in Asia, the region exhibiting the fastest growth of the epidemic, are in India (WHO 1997). As sexual behaviour is the largest single factor (70%-80%) of the transmission, behavioral intervention may affect results of singular benefit.

In the geographical area of this study, despite numerous attempts by the Government of Rajasthan, the unprotected commercial sex practiced by FSWs— including those from the Nat community—has been compounding the existing situation of AIDS. The perception of Nat FSWs as not being infected because of commercial sex practiced for generations by their caste women has resulted in an indifferent attitude towards safe sex. FSWs neither go for blood tests and other routine medical check ups, nor are they motivated to do so by officials and NGOs. However, in-depth case studies with FSWs have inferred that condoms were used invariably during intercourse with clients. It was also revealed by a few FSWs that the condom was not used with those willing to pay extra for sex, viz. permanent clients, clients of choice, and *ghar janwai* (the temporary husband) so that the client may attain greater sexual pleasure and the FSW may conceive a child from him. It is different with a casual client with whom the sex is exclusively penetration sex, preferably with a condom and for money alone (Swarankar 2002).

Ethnic Identity Crisis

Nat communities claiming to be the descendents of *Rajputs,* the rulers of *Rajputana,* may face a crisis related to their ethnic identity. This is because almost half of their women are sex workers who cannot marry within the Nat caste, and they are culturally permitted to have children without marriage from non-Nat clients, lovers, and *ghar janwai,* with whom the symbolic marriage or court marriage is solemnized. The institution of a *ghar janwai* socially permits a male of any caste or religion not only to be the client but also to establish a relationship with an FSW for a long duration, like a husband. During this period she remains as the wife of a *ghar janwai* and is supposed to confine her sexual contact to him alone. He is expected to meet the economic needs of a Nat FSW-turned-wife and her family members. The presence of a biological father scores over the sociological father, though both roles are substituted by the maternal uncle of children born from the Nat female sex worker and male non-Nat belonging to other castes and religions. As the Nat females in *dhandha* do not marry, ultimately Nat boys accept girls for their marriage from an analogous Kanjar community. With the matrimonial alliances of the Nat and Kanjar castes, an increasing number of Kanjar women, mostly other than those married to Nat, are becoming FSWs and migrating to pursue *dhandha* on the highway hamlets, namely Bandar Sindari and Dantari. Kanjar girls are accepted as daughters-in-law, but Nat do not marry off their daughters to boys of the Kanjar caste because it is considered lower in the social hierarchy. The caste endogamy in the Nat is disappearing. The clan remains an exogamous group, and surprisingly the dowry as well as the bride price is practiced among the Nat. In addition to births from FSWs, children born through nuptial ties of Nat males with Kanjar females have been outnumbering those born from the *asal* Nat (where both husband and wife are Nat). Thus, there is an increasing number of births from non-Nat fathers and Nat FSW mothers, as well as from Nat fathers and Kanjar mothers; a decreasing number of children born from real (*asal*) Nat husbands with Nat wives is leading to an ethnic identity crisis of the Nat caste.

Conclusion

Briefly, it could be stated that the habitat pattern of the Nat has changed from *dera* (one family) and *tola* (three to four families) to *bustee* (hamlet comprising a few or more families), preferably along the highways. The traditional occupation of rope dancing and acrobatics has been replaced by commercial sex. Traditional Nat plays are almost extinct and rarely visible in modified forms in the shows and circuses organized by professionals.

The impact of globalization is visible in fashions and the comforts of life; the majority of Nat youths utilize electric appliances and costly household articles in their *pucca* (brick or stone) houses. Modern names emulated from the cinema by the FSWs serve the purpose of maintaining anonymity to escape from police and society, which is required for *dhandha*. Crimes of various types, including crimes against women, are on rise. Dislocation of the Nat community in general and FSWs in particular has brought constant fear of police raids and harsh treatment. Such matters are also taken to courts of law. Attempts by local police and others to force the Nat to give up the traditional *dhandha* pursued by the women have failed for a variety of reasons and forces them to operate within and outside the Nat community.

Commercial sex, perceived to be an age-old occupation, continues to be practiced by approximately half of Nat women for economic reasons. It is accepted and institutionalized in the culture evolved by the community over decades. Poverty is perceived to be the dominant cause for commercial sex, for which long term and holistic approaches need to be adopted by the state and citizens. To ameliorate the culture of poverty, it is imperative to provide economic activities for Nat males who are dependent on the earnings of their female sex workers, making the males more economically responsible to fulfill family and social liabilities. Youth should be provided with education and vocational training with an emphasis on generating employment through small-scale industry and other suitable economic activities. Loans from banks and other financial institutions in easy payments could be arranged for this purpose. Education, particularly the female education is the need of the hour for the Nat caste. Parents desiring to marry their daughters, instead of becoming sex workers, need to be encouraged by their *Panchayat*. Retired FSWs and working FSWs willing to withdraw from the current occupation require alternative employment and security for old age under a pension and other schemes of the government of Rajasthan. They can be oriented to take up the task to foster participation and women empowerment in the community.

Sex traders like female managers, often retired FSWs (*patelan*), pimps (community youth), and middlemen associated with the transport and bar/hotel industries in the urban areas, including Mumbai, are the real challenge. They are the beneficiaries who make the lion's share from the income of FSWs whom they exploit. Nat caste youth assisting female sex workers for *dhandha* need to be provided alternate employment for their livelihood. In due course of time empowerment and a rise in the status of Nat women may not enable outside sex traders to exploit them for commercial sex.

Police and administration ought to be clear in their task and role towards commercial sex activities. The dislocation and involuntary displacement of local Nat FSWs has been sporadically undertaken by the establishment of a sub-police station, and by frequent police raids on the grounds of illegal acts of *dhandha* under prevention of immoral trafficking Act (PITA, amended in 1986). As a result, FSWs are forced to migrate for their livelihood, with or without family, from their hamlets to Mumbai and elsewhere. The complaints and offensive cases registered against them at a police station and court of law may not be a viable step. This is not the solution to this social problem. Instead, the coordinated and concentrated efforts of police officials, NGOs, and representatives of the Nat caste may help attain the desired goals. A FSW is a person with all rights like other citizens of the country. She needs to be dealt with using a humanistic approach.

The caste *Panchayat,* the strong and effective political institution, governs the socio-sexual behaviour of the Nat population, including women sex workers. It has accorded social sanctions for commercial sex (*dhandha*) practiced by Nat women, which is now perceived as normative in the community. The fact remains that the on-going practice of *dhandha* may lead to a crisis of ethnic identity. An increasing number of children born from non-Nat partners may genetically replace the Nat in successive generations. This requires a rethinking of the changing scenario by the caste *Panchayat* members and *Panchs*, the Nat social elite. A dialogue among them is indispensable for any welfare and reform of the community.

Acknowledgement

Fieldwork amongst the traditional female sex workers (including Nat community) in the rural areas of Rajasthan and Mumbai was supported by the Ford Foundation and ICHAP. I am grateful to Professors R. K. Mutatkar, Preeti Pelto and John O'Neil for their input during the study and later to analyze and conceptualize the issues of sex work and sex workers in the cultural context.

References

Crooke W. 1975. *The Tribes and Castes of North Western India.* vol IV. Delhi: Cosmo Publications.

Mane, Purnima and Maitra Shubhada A. 1992. *AIDS Prevention: The Socio-Cultural Context in India.* Mumbai: TISS.

Mukherjee K. K. 1989. *Flesh Trade- A Report.* Gaziabad: Gram Niyojan Kendra.

Nag, Moni. 1994. "Sexual Behaviour and AIDS in India." *Indian Journal of Social Work,* 55(4): 503-546.

Nandkarni, Vimla V. 1999. "AIDS Related Behavioral and Social Research in India." *AIDS Research and Review,* vol. 2, no. 1.

National AIDS Control Organization (NACO). 1995. Monthly update. New Delhi.

Pachuri, Saroj. 1992. AIDS, Seminar 396. New Delhi, August.

Raghav, Rangeya. 1993. *Kab Tak Pukaroon* (Hindi Novel), 1993. Delhi: Raj Pal and Sons.

Reid Elizabeth, and Michael Bailey. 1993. *Young Women: Silence, Susceptibility, and the HIV Epidemic Issue,* HIV and Development Program, Paper No.12. New York: UNDP.

Singh, K. S. 1993. *The People of India, The Schedule Castes, Anthropological Survey of India.* Oxford: Oxford University Press.

Swarankar, R. C. 1999. "Tradition, Tourism and AIDS in Rajasthan." In *Rajasthan,* M. K. Bhasin. ed. Delhi: Kamla Raj Enterprises.

———. 2000. *Ethnographic Study of Sexual Behaviour of Nat Community of Jaipur area, Rajasthan: A Report.* New Delhi: University of Pune/ Ford Foundation.

———. 2002. *Social Mapping of Rural Female Sex Workers in Rajasthan: A Report.* Jaipur: HEAR-ICHAP.

———. 2004. *Ethnographic Study on Migration and Mobility of Inmigrant Rajasthani Traditional Female Sexworkers in Mumbai, A Report.* Jaipur: HEAR-ICHAP.

Tod, James. 1829. Annals and Antiquities of Rajasthan. vol I. London: Routledge & Kegan Paul Ltd.

World Health Organization. 1997. *Social And Health Aspects Of STDs.* Geneva: Public Health Papers, No. 65.

Chapter 15

Gendering the Economy: Some Experiments from the Indian Sub-Continent

Sakuntala Narasimhan

With a population of 1.02 billion (one-sixth of the world's population) and a wide variety of ethnic, social, cultural, geographical and economic diversities, India offers an interesting example of social responses to initiatives for gender equity. In particular, the kind of backlash responses that traditional patriarchal perspectives manifest when projects for bringing the female half of the population into the mainstream are taken up, offer valuable pointers on the kinds of strategies that have worked (or failed) in specific situations. There could be lessons to be learnt for other developing countries from the Indian experience.

This chapter spotlights some of the more contentious experiments in gendering the economy—the move, for example, for a "gendered budget" attempted for the first time ever in India in 2002, the experiment of co-opting women through reservation of posts in local administration to give them greater participation in economic-political decision making, and the proposal to extend such reservation for women at the national level (in Parliament and state legislatures). These experiments typify the socio-economic-cultural hindrances to women's empowerment, and deserve to be shared among Asian and African women so that we may learn from each other's experiences. They also exemplify the gender-class-caste alignments and divisions that mark women's experiences everywhere.

Background

Article 15(1) of the Indian Constitution, adopted immediately after independence in 1947, forbids discrimination on grounds of sex. Article 15(3) also mandates affirmative action for promoting gender equality. But more than half a century later, any proposal for empowering women runs into not only popular opposition in the form of social hostility but also official disinterest in the form of lack of political will in implementation. While women's empowerment policies and projects are plentiful on paper and in the statute books, much of this remains as just paper promises, and the picture today continues to remain one of extreme contrasts and dichotomies—twenty Indian missions abroad are headed by women, the newly-appointed foreign secretary to the government of India was in 2002 for the first time ever, a woman (Ms. Chokila Iyer), several state governors are women, and the national airline routinely operates commercial flights with all-women crews. In spite of this, 270 million women of the rural sector who are poor, illiterate and disadvantaged are largely untouched by these advances (except for the *Panchayat Raj* experiment, as described in a later section).

For the first time ever in the history of the country, a "gendered budget exercise" was to be formulated during the budget session of Parliament in February 2001. Since this was also officially the Women's Empowerment Year for the Indian government, much was expected by way of new initiatives for removing some of the handicaps with which women are burdened. As it turned out, the budget had even less on gender than in earlier years, and the "gendered" exercise ended as a "non-event." There was no proposal, no extra emphasis, and no new schemes beyond the ritualistic one paragraph proclaiming the need for women's advancement in the course of the general overview of the nation's economy. (In contrast, women had an extra Rs5000 tax rebate announced in an earlier budget of three years ago, to enable working women to afford more home help in coping with their domestic obligations.)

In September 1996, a bill was brought before Parliament for reserving 33 percent of seats for women, to increase their participation in national decision-making processes. Currently there are just forty-nine women MPs (members of parliament) in a house of 543 members (in the *Lok Sabha* or lower house), making up 9 percent of the total strength. The number of seats occupied by women would have risen to 181 if the bill had been passed. However, in spite of the strident declarations made by every political party that it is "all for women's advancement," the bill's passage has been stalled repeatedly, under one pretext or the other, for over five years. A small minority of just three male politicians (whose support is crucial to the ruling coalition at the center) has managed to scuttle the bill every time it is introduced for debate in Parliament because they insist on sub-reservations for women of the lower castes within the 33 percent quota. (Interestingly enough, such a sub-reservation is never demanded in the case of general seat reservations for minority communities!) Tempers ran so high that the bill papers were even snatched from the law minister's hands, torn up and thrown down to prevent its passage. As women MPs say, "The men are scared that they will lose their seats if they are reserved for female candidates, it is thus an issue of seeing women's advancement as a threat to male hegemony" (Nath 1996).

Political expedience, then, rather than commitment to gender equity and justice, takes precedence. "I am all for women's progress, as long as I do not have to give up my seat," seems to be the argument of every single male politician regardless of political loyalties, right, left or center.

The reasons cited by various factions for stalling the bill provide real insights into the socio-cultural perceptions about a "woman's place" in the family and in society. A former prime minister (Chandra Sekhar) quipped, "If women come to Parliament, who will cook our food?" (Nath 1996) while another high-profile minister referred derisively to "women with cropped hair" (*kati baal*, to denote "uselessly fashionable" or "un-Indian" womanhood).[1] These same politicians, however, are not averse to putting their own wives as puppet chief ministers in their place, as Laloo Prasad Yadav (one of the main opponents of the women's reservations bill) has done, after his own position as chief minister was threatened following a corruption scandal. (The wife, now chief minister, is reported to be unlettered and inexperienced.)

Interestingly enough, similar legislation for reserving one-third of seats for women in local (village and district level) administration, introduced six years ago under a Constitutional (Eight fifth) Amendment, has worked, with nearly one million rural women getting elected to reserved posts. Despite their ignorance and inexperience, poverty and illiteracy, most of them have quickly learnt the ropes and managed to run the administration. One third of these women (around thirty thousand) have also become chairpersons of the village administration due to reservations (*Panchayat*). Many of them used to be afraid of even attending village meetings (*Gram Sabha*), and when persuaded to attend used to stand shyly on the periphery, convinced that good women should be "neither seen nor heard," especially in public. "It would bring a bad name" as one elected woman put it. (*Uma Prachar* 2001b: 7). They now come boldly to meetings, sit in front and raise questions. One such illiterate woman who was persuaded to become the *sarpanch* (village head) because the post was reserved for a woman under the new law, wears a *burkha* (a veil worn by conservative Muslim women) but flew to New York to receive a Poverty Alleviation Award from UN Secretary general Kofi Annan two years ago, whereas she had never even seen a train earlier (Narasimhan 1997).

While these are positive aspects of their success in empowerment, the stories that lie behind the *Panchayat Raj* legislation are just as eloquent as the parliamentary reservations bill fiasco in terms of mirroring social perceptions.

For example, a research team member from a social studies organization telephoned a village where the *panchayat* president's post was reserved for a female. A man answered the phone, and identified himself as the *panchayat* secretary. "Is the president there? I would like to speak to her about a field program," the researcher said. "Yes, the president is here, you can speak," said the secretary and passed on the phone—but again, a male voice answered. "Has the president been changed?" the caller enquired, intrigued. The man said, "No, the president remains the same. But I am her husband, tell me what your requirement is. I shall get it done." "But I would like to speak to the president herself," the researcher insisted, to which the man replied, "No need to speak to her, I am the one who takes care of everything, let me know what is required" (*Uma Prachar* 2001b: 10).

Men often put up their wives as dummy candidates when the law reserves a seat for a woman. They try to take charge of decision-making, thus negating the rationale behind the law but many of these "proxy" women have quickly learnt to assert themselves and seek to take charge. If this happens, a common tactic is "character assassination"—making allegations that she is inefficient or corrupt, passing a "no confidence motion" against her, and replacing her. Manavva, an illiterate tribal woman of Karnataka state (south India), became president of her village *panchayat* following reservation of the post, but her secretary (a male appointed by the government to assist her) took advantage of Manavva's illiteracy and made her sign for vouchers and payments that did not tally with actual expenditures. She was also led to believe by the corrupt secretary that her job was merely to sign papers, which she did. It was only much later, after a training workshop organized by an NGO (non-governmental organization) that she began to not only assert her right to have everything read out loud before signing, but also to complain to a higher official and have the corrupt secretary removed (Narasimhan 1998).

The women are not lacking in guts or capabilities. However, neither the men who are handing over the reins of power nor the state administration bothers to ensure that they receive adequate orientation and training. Their lack of experience becomes a stick with which to beat and deride them—and this leads to a catch-22 situation where other women become hesitant to come forward to stand for elections, and in turn women as a group never build up the core strength necessary to make their voices heard. Results are shown in table 15.1.

In surveys conducted in several villages (especially in states like Rajasthan in western India, where patriarchal culture is strong and deeply entrenched) the men have confessed that they feel humiliated in having to go to a woman ("Someone in a *sari*, with the cloth drawn over her head, as decorum decrees") to seek sanctions and benefits, and would go to any lengths to refuse to accept a woman as decision-maker. They are quoted as saying: "Why will we go to those who sit there with pallu on their heads? Never. We will go to their husbands" [2] (*Uma Prachar* 2001a: 3).

In such a situation, what we need is not merely legislation to reserve posts for women, but simultaneously a concerted effort at social sensitization on gender issues to facilitate effectiveness of the law. Passing laws to reserve seats for women is relatively easy (though even in this, the men have refused to let such a law be passed at the national level, because women in Parliament are seen as a greater threat to the patriarchal status quo than women at the village administration level). In one case, a man has been bribed in order to persuade him to get his wife to withdraw from the *panchayat* election. It is not the wife, the potential candidate, who is offered the bribe, but her husband, implying that he is seen as the de facto decision-maker, even in the matter of her candidature (*Uma Prachar* 2001a: 3)!

Table 15.1 Election Results of Panchayat Raj Institutions in Karnataka State (South India), 2000

Level	No. of Panchayat Representatives	Elected Women Representatives	Elected Men	Total
Gram (village)	5,535	35,187	43,273	78,460
Taluk (block)	175	1,343	1,997	3,340
Zilla (district)	27	337	551	890

Source: *Uma Prachar* vol. 8, no. 1, Feb. 2001. Institute of Social Studies Trust, Bangalore.

In the last five years since the *Panchayat Raj* legislation was introduced to bring women into administrative decision-making posts at the local level, a number of training modules have been introduced (mostly by NGOs) to strengthen the women's perception of their own roles in society. This training has resulted in a significant change in their self-perceptions, and also in the way the women are perceived in the community. One woman relates: "Previously, the local land owner used to call me as 'Hey, you" or as 'woman.' Now that I sit on a chair and sign papers, he is more respectful and calls me by my name, or even says 'sister,' a term he would never have used previously," says one rural woman elected to a *panchayat* post (Seminar for Elected Women 1995). In fact, some of these women are now asking why reservations should be limited to just 33 percent and not 50 percent because women form 50 percent of the population. (*Uma Prachar* 2002b). Table 15.2 gives numbers of women chairpersons in the Panchayat administration for 1999.

It is the male perception of a woman's place and role in society that now creates hurdles in the effectiveness of these one million elected women. Many of the women find that they have to continue to shoulder the same domestic burden of chores as before, in addition to the duties of an elected leader of the community. This double burden makes it difficult for her to be effective—if she attends to the community work as required, she is quickly accused of neglecting the family and children, whereas if she has to devote enough time to the household, she is equally quickly accused of not being a satisfactory leader of the community. Representation of women in selected all-India services for 1985 and 1999 are given in table 15.3. Women are underrepresented across these services.

Table 15.2 Percentage of Women Chairpersons in Panchayat Administration, India, 1999

Administrative Level	Percent Women Chairpersons
Panchayat samitis	33.75
Gram (village) panchayats	40.10
Zilla (district) panchayats	32.28

Source: Government of India, 2000

Table 15.3 Representation of Women in Selected All-India Services, 1985, 1998

	Year	Total Personnel	Women	Percent
Indian Administrative	1985	4,284	311	7.3
Services (IAS)	1998	4,991	512	10.3
Indian Police Service	1985	2,343	18	0.8
(IPS)	1998	3,115	108	3.5
Indian Foreign Service	1985	535	50	9.3
(IFS)	1998	587	67	11.4

Source: Government of India. undated.

One more eloquent example: Kerala state in south India is described as one of the best, in terms of indices for women's status and well-being (high literacy, low maternal mortality, and a social tradition based on matriarchy among communities like the Nairs). One of the elected women representatives of this state narrated at a recent south regional workshop, her experience of how women who try to assert themselves in public decision-making are accused of "being frustrated in private life and needing to be calmed down through marriage," if they happen to be unmarried. If they are married, they are said to be "having a tough time with the husband and therefore taking out her frustrations and aggression on outside work." It becomes a no-win situation for a woman worker, whether she is married or unmarried! (Seminar for Elected Women Representatives 1997).

Examples like these show that we need to concentrate not merely on sensitization and empowerment programs for women alone in our attempt to gender the economy. We also need, simultaneously, to sensitize the male component of society, to tackle deep-rooted attitudes about women's subordinate position in the community.

It is important to note that the economic hindrances to women's empowerment are not as vital as the social hindrances, especially in developing countries like India. Poor, illiterate women elected to village administration under the reservations law, are often accused of being mere "proxy" candidates for males (husbands, sons, other male relatives) who control all real decision-making. The women are found wanting on account of their ignorance—but this is true of male candidates also (from the minority communities, for instance who get elected to reserved posts. Powerful, upper caste/class males retain all decision-making powers in day-to-day functioning to manipulate them.

A recent survey among elected women representatives has shown that "irrespective of social, cultural, economic and geographical differences (among the women), the challenges and obstacles are the same for all elected women representatives" (Seminar for Elected Women Representatives 1997). This is a significant finding, which shows that the similarities (among women, in terms of gender) are greater than the differences (in education or economic well-being). Distance from her place of work to the state capital/metropolis is also seen to be only a minor factor in her effective functioning, which again underscores the fact that women, as women, face socio-cultural hurdles that reduce their effectiveness as elected representatives of the community. Strengthening their self-perception is only one part of the strategy that is being addressed. The other part—changing the socio-cultural perceptions of the community, particularly among the males—is not being addressed. And this is what thwarts the women—not their poverty, illiteracy or lack of experience. It would be interesting to compare these experiences with those of women in other regions and cultures and in other developing countries, especially on the African continent, to see what we can learn in terms of sharing strategies towards a goal of truly gendered societies.

Generalizations would be misleading in a country as diverse as India, with its wide differences in terms of regional languages, customs and socio-economic disparities. However, certain broad trends can be identified, with reference to the social responses (especially backlash) to projects women's empowerment in recent years.

Legislation for reserving 33 percent of seats for women in local administration (village and district levels) under the Panchayat Raj Act has brought nearly one million rural women into decision-making positions. Many of them have performed credibly in spite of their lack of experience, illiteracy, poverty and lack of support systems (plus male hostility because of the threat they pose to the status quo). Many have also floundered, or been taken for a ride by scheming and corrupt elements who find the idea of women's participation in community decision making culturally unacceptable. While the women's lack of experience is being tackled through training projects, the cultural inhibitions, especially in males, that prevent women from functioning as full partners in progress have not been addressed adequately as yet.

Women who try to function boldly and challenge the mindset that expects women to be unquestioningly subordinate and self-effacing are ridiculed as "disturbed because they are not married" or "frustrated in marriage," for example or maligned as "incapable" or "unsatisfactory". While a few gutsy rural women have indeed succeeded in asserting themselves, their experiences need to be publicized and shared in order to enthuse others to persevere despite the odds they face as women.

A proposal for reserving one-third of seats in parliament for women has been repeatedly stalled by four different governments since 1996, despite the Constitutional mandate for gender equality, because political considerations of each party (for holding on to power) take precedence over any considerations of equity or social justice.

Notes

1. During 1996–97, when the Bill for 33 percent reservations for women was first introduced for debate in Parliament, Sharad Yadav, a Politician, vehemently opposed the Bill, saying that such reservation will result in women "with cut hair" appropriating these seats, to the detriment of rural, disadvantaged women. The cut hair meaning fashionable urban women of westernized class. In Indian culture, women often do not cut their hair on religious or other cultural grounds.

2. In a survey in Karnataka state (where incidentally a woman was governor until recently), men were asked how they would approach the elected women representatives for claiming benefits sanctioned under state projects.

References

Government of India. undated. *Election Reports*. Delhi: Department of Women and Child Development.

Government of India. 2000. Report Presented at the 'Beijing Plus 5' session of the U.N. General Assembly, New York. Delhi: Ministry of Rural Development.

Narasimhan, Sakuntala. 1997. "Tough As Steel, Soft As Silk." *Deccan Herald*, December 7. Bangalore.

————. 1998. "Gutsy Rustic." *Deccan Herald*, August 16. Bangalore.

Nath, Meenakshi. 1996, "Cutting Across Party Lines." In *Manushi*. no. 96, p. 7–16. Dehli.

Seminar for Elected Women Representatives. *Seminar Materials*. 1995 and 1997. Bangalore.

Uma Prachar. 2001a. "Athnur at Crossroads." *Resource Letter of the Institute for Social Studies Trust*, vol.8, no 1. p. 3

————.2001b. "Any comments?" *Resource Letter of the Institute for Social Studies Trust*, vol.8, no 3. p. 10.

Chapter 16

Women as Wealth Creators and Managers in Uganda

Margaret Kigozi

The twenty-first century belongs to Africa. We have educated leaders with a vision for Africa. Resources in Africa are plentiful and include human resources, abundant arable land on which a variety of crops and livestock can grow, minerals such as gold, diamonds, phosphates and iron ore, attractions for tourism including animals, mountains and water bodies.

Africa is the fastest growing trading block in the world. There are 840 million people in Africa who offer a tremendous potential market. The vision for the continent through NEPAD (New Partnership for African Development) is Sustainable Development achieved with the millennium goal of poverty reduction to 50% by the year 2020. The vision for Uganda is more ambitious and includes alleviation of poverty by 2017 to less than 10% of the population if the economy continues to grow at current rates. The national strategy is given in the Poverty Reduction Strategy Paper (PRSCP) (GOU 2000:7).

Uganda is already implementing the PRSCP and the Poverty Eradication Action Plan. (PEAP) The PEAP is a plan put together by government, civil society, and the private sector and seeks to address provision of services such as water, education, health and agriculture for the people and economic development through a private sector led economy. PEAP identifies goals and implementation strategies and is revised annually by the stakeholders. National policies have been developed which liberalize trade, markets and foreign exchange, as well as encourage privatization and maintain low inflation. The Uganda Investment Authority (UIA) was put in place to promote investment, facilitate investors and improve the investment climate through policy advocacy (GOU 2002).

Poverty reduction in Uganda is targeted through a series of initiatives, which include services such as free primary education, free health care provision, information and communication technology (ICT) and financial services such as micro finance all over the country. Improvements in infrastructure, roads, water, agricultural practices and telecommunication will reduce poverty by increasing production and market access.

Gender considerations have influenced decisions about universal primary education (UPE) where every girl is encouraged to attend school, and affirmative action has led to an increased percentage of women in university to over 40%. Uganda Investment Authority (UIA) Women Entrepreneurs Network, which has over 200 members, encourages capacity building, networking and monitoring among businesswomen.

Foreign Direct Investment (FDI) flows to Uganda between 1989 and 2000 have grown from zero in 1989 to US$274 million in 2002. Relatively speaking, Uganda ranks eighty fourth in the world in attracting FDI; and, poverty has been reduced from 65% in 1986 to 36% in 2001. Women in that time have increasingly become wealth creators and managers in Uganda. Some have achieved success such as Wandira Specioza Kazibwe, former Vice President of Uganda; the President of the Uganda National Chamber of Commerce and Industry (UNCCI); an Uganda Revenue Authority Commissioner General; and Dr. Margaret Kigozi, Executive Director of Uganda Investment Authority (UIA). Women entrepreneurs are mainly in agriculture, education, tourism, ICT and construction.

The whole of Africa is seeing more foreign and domestic investments, which benefit both women and men. Amongst the most promising are those in agriculture and agribusiness, tourism services, education, ICT, finance, mining, energy, electronics and forestry. When developed countries invest in Africa, they access our markets, our raw materials, our labor force and our land. These investments bring new technologies, create more jobs, develop new management skills increase exports and enable our countries to substitute for imports.

References

Government of Uganda (GOU). 2000. *Poverty Reduction Strategy Paper.* (Revised PEAP,). vol. 1, draft 1 (March 14). Kampala: Ministry of Finance, Planning and Economic Development.

———. 2002. *Poverty Eradication Action Plan. (PEAP).* Kampala: Ministry of Finance, Planning and Economic Development. May.

Chapter 17

Has Affirmative Action Reached South African Women?

Vannie Naidoo

South African women have been positive change agents that stood in the forefront of the struggle against apartheid. They vigorously campaigned against inhumane pass laws, racially designed Bantu education, pathetic working conditions and child labor and countless other inequalities that were in existence during the apartheid era (Bozzoli & Nkotsoe 1991). The selfless actions of South African women have contributed to the creation of a new democratic South Africa. However, the struggle for the emancipation of the women of South Africa is far from over (Sadie & van Aardt 1995).

The stark reality in South Africa is that employment patterns are raced and gendered in ways that demonstrate white men's privilege that survived even after abolishment of apartheid laws. The Minister of Labor, MMS Mdladlana in his briefing on 15 February 1999, said that legislation was needed in relation to employment equity (Mdladlana 1999). He referred to research conducted by the Department of Labor, which completed a study of 455 employers. The study revealed that 87 percent of all management in the private sector was white 93 percent of all executive management was still white, and 89 percent of all senior management was white. Africans made up only 6 percent of all managers, women made up 14 percent of all managers and 77 percent of women managers were white (Msimang 2001).

The problem still remains that many affirmative action policies in corporate South Africa are too busy exhausting themselves over developing and empowering black managers, whilst gender equality has slipped from a low priority to a practically "non- important issue." Charlton & van Niekerk (1994: 62) emphasize the same argument by stating that to date in South Africa affirmative action has focused on racial inequalities, while the massive inequalities confronted by women have often been ignored. This chapter will highlight the need for affirmative action, its legal and social implications, as well as the possible contributions made by affirmative action in the lives of women, the problems encountered and the way forward.

The Need for Affirmative Action

South Africa is faced with a unique situation. It is the only country in the world that had apartheid laws legally legislated to protect the interests of a small white minority, whilst bringing only oppression to the lives of the black majority. Louw et. al. state that the apartheid system is perhaps one of the most extreme examples in recent history in which a racist system of social identity was enshrined in the laws and government institutions of a country (1997: 767).

After the birth of the new democracy in 1994, South African society was in dire need of social, political, legal and economic transformation. The black people of South Africa needed relief after centuries of oppression, violence, racism, gender discrimination and inexcusable dictatorship. Affirmative action was a meaningful tool, legislated by the new government to redress the horrors that apartheid had over the years injected into our racially divided society. Nelson Mandela supported this view in his address to the African National Congress (ANC) conference on affirmative action, where he goes on to say the following:

> The primary aims of affirmative action must be to redress the imbalances created by apartheid.... We are not asking for handouts for anyone. Nor are we saying that just as a white skin was a passport to privilege in the past, so a black skin should be the basis of privilege in the future. Nor...is it our aim to do away with qualifications. What we are against is not the upholding of standards, as such but the sustaining of barriers to the attainment of standards, the special measures that we envisage to overcome the legacy of past discrimination are not intended to ensure the advancement of unqualified persons, but to see to it that those who have been denied access to qualifications in the past can become qualified now, and that those who have been qualified all along but overlooked because of past discrimination are at last given their due .... The first point to be made is that affirmative action must be rooted in principles of justice and equity (1992).

Maphai states that within South Africa, affirmative action carries with it both wide and narrow connotations. At both levels, there is a great deal of confusion.

The narrow conception of affirmative action centers around the recruitment of previously disadvantaged groups. Maphai goes on to offer a juxtaposed exposition of affirmative action by saying that:

> Affirmative action is a strategy or tactic, a means to an end, the goal being black advancement. This signifies that commitment to black advancement does not require prior or simultaneous subscriptions to affirmative action. One might reject specific means on the grounds that an alternative advancement exists. Consequently, as a means to an end, affirmative action would be acceptable to the extent that it achieves what it sets out to do. Furthermore, affirmative action presupposes an existing or previously discriminatory setting and is designed to redress imbalances occasioned by that setting. It is an interim bridging device, a strategic intervention in an abnormal situation (Maphai 1992: 73).

The debates surrounding Maphai's model are that it is a too narrow conception of affirmative action, and does not capture the crisis, which was the long and hard legacy of apartheid. Moreover, the black advancement model referred to by Maphai has been severely criticized by Human (1993: 43) as a "wrong" paradigm, as it is based on a closed authoritarian system that is exclusivist and has elitist decision-making procedures. Human on the other hand advocates the "people development model." This model looks at empowering blacks to develop their skills and abilities in such a manner as to help them successfully fill higher level positions and control resources accordingly. "Affirmative action in the South African context has extremely broad connotations, touching, as apartheid did and still does, on every arena of life . . . affirmative action covers all purposive activity, designed to eliminate the effects of apartheid and to create a society where everyone has the same chance to get on in life. In terms of the ANC draft Bill of Rights, all anti-poverty ones may be regarded as constituting a form of affirmative action" (Sachs 1992).

The government in South Africa has also targeted the disadvantaged communities for issues such as education, employment, health, housing, land and nutrition. Policy must be based upon patently just, and wherever possible, universally agreed criteria of entitlement and be implemented according to widely acceptable and clearly equitable procedures. The goal of affirmative action will aim towards giving everyone a chance at equal opportunity and it will not amount to a vengeful turning of tables of oppressions, or the creaming off of the country by a small new class of exploiters (Mandela 1992).

Ngidi argues that affirmative action is a sine qua non for development and progress and he goes on further to outline three paradigmatic features within which affirmative action can be applied (1994: 3–4):

- Affirmative action can be applied to empower those communities and sectors disadvantaged under apartheid. This would entitle provision of skills in terms of whatever project is to be undertaken.

- In terms of the Reconstruction and Development Program (RDP), affirmative action must address the deliberate marginalization from economic, political and social power of black people, women and rural communities.
- Affirmative action is a program that is meant to apply broadly, by looking at racial inequality and the skill transference in preparing the beneficiaries of affirmative action to partake effectively and efficiently within the economic sphere.

Wolfgang Thomas in Human (1993: 2) argues that affirmative action can be viewed as a pro-active development tool to overcome constraints and more effectively mobilize latent resources in order to stimulate overall development. He goes on further to present the many dimensions of affirmative action, which include:

- political sphere and the decision-making process;
- education and culture;
- breakdown of segregation in social life;
- sport, entertainment and recreation;
- housing and residential infrastructure;
- welfare services;
- black business advancement and training;
- symbolism and historical perspective.

Within South African organizations the above dimensions have been incorporated by management to stimulate effective affirmative action policies and procedures that are guided towards overcoming bias of the past apartheid legacy, as well as stimulating overall development of the individual within the organization. Creating employment equity, within the organizations dominated by white males, is only one aspect of affirmative action. The government of South Africa has put pressure on organizations to increase black representation on boards, black participation in equity, external purchases from black suppliers, promotion of women within small and medium term business (SMEs) and various other positive avenues within trade and industry to help facilitate the empowerment of the previously disadvantaged communities (Human 1993).

Human (1993: 2) sums up affirmative action quite well by saying that it should be viewed as a means of overcoming barriers to equal employment opportunities rather than a means of preferentially advancing the interest of some interest groups at the expense of others. The laws that govern employment are such that they promote equity. The laws were drawn up taking all South Africa's people into account irrespective of skin color, gender, sexual orientation, ethnicity or class. Affirmative action has thus been implemented within the South African workplace to help redress the historical gender and racial inequalities that has plagued our country for centuries.

The intended beneficiaries of affirmative action according to Ngidi are those who were disadvantaged by apartheid even at the expense of those that benefited from apartheid including youth, the disabled, and rural people (1994: 4–5). Therefore, it is only fair that the major beneficiaries of affirmative action should be the African people of South Africa, as they have been worse off under the deep-rooted racial and class divisions within the labor market and society as a whole.

From a gender perspective, many women activists in South Africa argue that while all women suffered under the apartheid laws, their suffering was closely related to their skin color, class, sexual orientation, religion and ethnicity. Msimang (2001: 2) reiterates this view by saying that while all women suffered under patriarchy, they suffered in different ways. Apartheid was primarily a racial ideology, which intersected with class and gender ideologies in ways that made life easier for white women than for black women.

Legal and Social Implications of Affirmative Action on the Lives of Women

Women in South Africa have been oppressed by the society in which they live for far too long. Affirmative action is crucial as it concerns not only the identification of processes and structures which have generated gender inequalities and gender segregation, but it also devises appropriate strategies for equalizing the position of women in the workplace. The labor market has been a site of highly complex and interrelated inequalities based on both racial and gender discrimination. To add to this, gender inequalities in the economy can be directly traced to and reinforced by other areas such as women and girls' unequal access to proper education, training and development programs.

The Employment Equity Act (1998) and the Constitution both embrace women as equals in society (Republic of South Africa 1998). The existence of sexism is confirmed by the necessity of including a special reference to gender equality in the Constitutional Act of 1993 (Sec. 8, Act 200 of 1993), which states that: ". . . no person shall be unfairly discriminated against on one or more ground. . . race, gender, sex. . . .".Despite this stipulation, the stark reality is that South African women still are underrepresented at many levels within the South African workplace. According to the Employment Equity Act (1998), every employer's key responsibility should be to undertake affirmative action measures to ensure that suitably qualified people from the designated groups have equal opportunities in all occupational categories and levels within the workplace. It can be justifiably argued that affirmative action programs are needed as they offer the women of South Africa a well-recognized means of diminishing gender inequalities in the workplace. The majority of women therefore positively endorse affirmative action programs, policies, and legislation.

The key objectives of the Employment Equity Act according to the Minister of Labor (1999) are as follows:

- Firstly, to prohibit and prevent discrimination at the workplace. Direct or indirect discrimination on a wide range of issues including race, gender, disability, religion, political belief and HIV-status is prohibited by the Act.
- Secondly, it helps promote equity in the workplace. The Act spells out the process and the steps that must be taken to develop and advance groups that have been disadvantaged in the past.
- Lastly, the Act redresses past imbalances in the labor market that were created under the apartheid laws.

The Employment Equity Act (1998) also aims to break the glass ceiling that has prevented women from further accessing jobs that were once only limited to their male counterparts. The Employment Equity Act (1998) intends to emancipate women and regards gender discrimination and inequality within the workplace as an evil. It was been put in place to help women in their empowerment and upliftment. Many companies are now forced by law to employ, develop and maintain women employees. Some companies also offer female employees or prospective employees preferential treatment over male candidates when qualifications of the two groups are similar.

According to a study by SAIRR (1995), women have lower levels of education and higher rates of illiteracy. 14 percent of white women had certificates in higher education compared to 4 percent Indian, 2 percent Colored and 1 percent black women. Generally it is the African women in South Africa, specifically those living in rural areas that have the least education and are in most cases illiterate.

Gender segregation has been escalated by the media portrayal of women as being good secretaries or administrative assistants. Women have been perceived as care givers and their employment has been geared towards a very subordinate working role within the work place. According to Reskin & Padavic (1994: 9), the devaluation of women's work has existed for so long that we cannot explain its origins. It continues to occur both because it is part of the ideology in many parts of the world and because it is in men's best interest for it to continue. One survey of male managers found most of them thought that women just didn't have what it takes to be senior mangers (Charlton & van Niekerk 1994: 6). The problem with this sort of attitude, says Linda Human (1993) is that it is a 'self-fulfilling prophecy'. The belief that someone has what it takes can build self-confidence and enthusiasm, and a desire to try again, even in a situation of failure. The belief that someone hasn't got what it takes destroys self-confidence and motivation.

In many South African companies, the majority of managers, supervisors, and team leaders are still men. The ideology of male superiority is still a very potent system of beliefs and attitudes, deeply integrated into daily lives and institutions in society. This ideology sets standards, a male standard, which becomes the yardstick with which women in the workplace are judged. At one time, all posts were male dominated. Now women are flooding into the workplace. They are the new brand of worker, more sophisticated, dedicated and ambitious. The women in the working environment have brought a new perspective to the male-dominated working culture within most South African organizations. This transformation can only be effective if the company culture changes to accommodate and recognize women employees as equal within the work environment. The sad reality is that male stereotypical attitudes have prevailed despite democracy in our country; and, these vile attitudes threaten the very foundation of gender equality. Women are set up for failure. If things go wrong they are even blamed for this failure; and, through this sad demeaning process, the myth that women are failures and men are superior is reinforced. Baron et al (1990: 178) argue that traditional views about gender suggest that males tend to be more aggressive, forceful, persistent and decisive, while females tend to be passive, submissive, dependent and emotional. Growing evidence however, indicates that such differences are largely false.

In addition to the above stereotypical attitudes, race has compounded the inequalities suffered by the black (African, Indian, and Colored) working class and rural women of South Africa. These women have suffered and continue to suffer the most extreme forms of poverty. Dubourdieu (2003: 1) makes a crucial point that it is misleading to refer to South African women as if they represent one homogeneous group. There are tremendous differences within this one category, not only the obvious differences of color or ethnic group, but also major differences, which stem from class and geographic location. There is a big urban/rural divide; women outnumber men predominantly in rural areas with poor economic perspectives. Rural black women are the most impoverished group in South African society and the least likely to find formal sector employment.

The Employment Equity Act (1998) has a chapter on affirmative action that expressly includes women as a disadvantaged group for which positive steps must be taken to ensure their equitable representation in the workplace. The Act also recognizes that black women face particular disadvantage due to the inferior quality of "Bantu" education they have been subjected to, as well as the inhumane "historical black homelands" they had to grow up in. Township life has never been easy for women, with violence crime and poverty assailing all their senses every day. According to Msimang (2001: 2–3), the most common employment of black women is in the domestic sphere. Black female domestic workers subsidized the life-styles of white women under extremely exploitative conditions. Black women also occupied positions as cleaners and "tea-ladies" in office buildings. In addition, colored women in particular worked in factories in the food and clothing industry. However, in rural areas, unemployment is high and many black women rely on the paychecks of their migrant-laborer husbands, who work in the mines to sustain them and their families. Others work as farm laborers alongside their husbands but are paid less because they are women. The Employment Equity Act (1998) will go a long way to redress discrimination and exploitation that women, particularly Black (African, Indian and Colored) women have experienced under apartheid.

Other positive contributions of affirmative action to the lives of South African women include:

- The Education Department declared in August 1996, that over half of the 318 posts filled were held by blacks and that females were in the overall majority (Dubourdieu 2003: 4). South Africa ranks seventh in the world in the number of women in Parliament, and second in Africa only to the Seychelles (Msimang 2001: 6).
- The Employment Equity Act promotes the fair treatment of women within organisations, by prohibiting unfair discrimination within the workplace by employers on the basis of "race, gender, pregnancy, marital status, family responsibility, ethnic or social origins, color, sexual orientation, age, disability, religion, HIV status, conscience, belief, political opinion, culture, language and birth" (Section 55).
- According to Dubourdieu (2003: 4), Directors for Representativity have been appointed in all government departments, with the responsibility for ensuring that all appointments of staff follow the government guidelines on representativeness in all departments. Gender Equity Units have also been set up within departments and also at national level.
- Many companies in South Africa have adult based education programs for women. Some companies have extended their affirmative action programs a step further by providing female employees with mentorships and internships as well as formal tertiary education. Companies also have actively demonstrated their support for women's issues in areas such as stress, maternity issues, day-care, AIDS and women's abuse. Some companies have trained councilors in house to help women cope with these issues.
- Women's groups are mushrooming throughout South Africa with forums that help with development both as a person in society as well as an employee within the workplace. According to Dubourdieu (2003: 4), BMW in Pretoria not only has training and education programs, but it has also a self-imposed hiring quota of 70:30 in favor of previously disadvantaged groups which they defined as blacks, colored and Asian, men and women, as well as white women.

- The Government has initiated enterprise development programs, which give preference to women. Rural women are given the machinery and tools to help them grow fruit and vegetable gardens in their rural communities. They are also taught effective methods of growing these crops. This is empowerment and has a very positive effective by reaching the "poorest of the poor." Self-employment is often the only option for rural women who have limited formal schooling. Micro enterprises can be run from the home, and combined with domestic duties it can be run part-time or on a seasonal basis, fitting very well in a women's daily routine if she is a farm laborer, domestic worker or home-maker.

- Literacy programs, AIDS awareness, and abuse have also been actively taken to rural communities. In some rural villages, women are taught how to write their names for the first time. AIDS awareness and abuse issues are also discussed with poor rural women through women's focus groups and other community groups.

- Affirmative action has also played a pivotal role in identifying barriers that restrict the advancement of women in the workplace. The Employment Equity Act (1998) as well as the South African Constitution gives women a chance to come forward and legally attack their organizations if they feel discriminated against or prejudiced in any manner. Women in South Africa can now take their organizations to court for paying a male employee more for the same job. This is an important milestone in Labor Law legislation. According to Reskin and Padavic (1994: 9), the devaluation of women and their work is a key factor in differential compensation for men and women.

Problems with South Africa's Affirmative Action Policies for Women

In spite of the theoretical sides taken by different political parties, the reality is that employment patterns continue to be raced and gendered in ways that demonstrate white men's privilege. The grave danger in the South African corporate world is that affirmative action is conceptualized as a means of advancing blacks only. The battle for providing a structure of racial equality has in many respects sadly obscured another equally important issue that being the battle for gender equality in the South African workplace. Corporate South Africa in the absence of a broader vision of employment has become preoccupied with the development of black managers, and gender has slipped from a low priority to a "non-issue" (Charlton and van Niekerk 1994: 62). In Zimbabwe the issue of the advancement of women has not been afforded the importance that it deserves and, as a result, women have made very poor progress in terms of advancement in both the public and private sector (Fischer 1995: 23). The International Labor

Organization explodes the myth that gender equality is changing, pointing out that at the present rate it will take until the twenty-fifth century before men and women reach an equal status in the workplace, despite women being more qualified than their male colleagues in many cases (Charlton and van Niekerk 1994: 62–63).

In South Africa, the fact remains that gender inequality exists along with racism. Companies in South Africa must therefore provide affirmative action programs that take into account both race and gender issues and that do not privilege one issue over the other when employing affirmative action candidates. Often women have to work twice as hard to prove themselves, despite having competencies, such as empathy and interpersonal skills, that make them ideally suited to leadership positions (Charlton and van Niekerk 1994: 62).

Many companies in South Africa employ women as a "window-dressing" exercise. This is demeaning and it should not occur as it hinders the real reason behind affirmative action, for example, to develop and empower women. It should therefore follow that affirmative action programs be geared towards educating men on issues such as gender equality, gender discrimination and sexual harassment. Highlighting gender issues and male prejudice for example, can help both male and female employees change their attitudes and behavior towards each other within the workplace. It can be safely said that if men perceive women as equals, then they would have an easier task of taking instructions and working effectively under women managers. Their attitudes of fear and prejudice would be limited, if more men in industry perceived women as their equals.

Another major problem with affirmative action is the issue of double discrimination. White women are a segment of the South African population that has benefited tremendously from affirmative action. Like women all over the world, they too have been forced to accept gender discrimination within their own societies. White women however, have been fortunate under apartheid, as they have had unhindered access to the best educational institutions in South Africa. South African white women have had exposure to opportunities and economic prosperity as they were classified as being part of a privileged minority. They were not hampered in their careers by the burden of raising a family because unlike their counterparts in the Western world, most of them had at their disposal very cheap domestic "black" labor (Qunta 1995: 19). In terms of affirmative action, we are saying that white women should benefit from affirmative action programs within South Africa but not to the extent that it would disadvantage a Black person. The levels of discrimination experienced by white women, black women and black men call for corresponding levels of affirmative action policies. In South Africa, the level of sexism suffered by the white women is different than that suffered by black women. African women for example were worst off than even African men under the apartheid era. Within the South African workplace during apartheid, African women had very limited job opportunities and were forced to be either domestic workers or farm laborers, whilst white women had far better and broader job opportunities available to them. In this respect it would be proposed that black women of South Africa specifically the African women, be given more attention and preference in affirmative action programs within South African organizations than white women are given at present. Companies in South Africa find it easier to hire white women and black men. Women make up 14 percent of all management positions and 77 percent of these women managers are white (Mdladlana 1999).

Conclusion

In South Africa, the white ruling classes have possessed infinite political and economic power that has enabled them under apartheid to design social structures and create and manipulate a South African society based on racial and gender segregation. After the birth of our new-formed democracy in 1994, the government of National Unity had the hard task of cleaning up in a post apartheid era. It has not been an easy task. Affirmative action has been a strategic tactic used by government to help redress the past imbalances suffered by people of color and the female gender. Affirmative action has given South African women a new lease on life and in particular, a new victory over apartheid. Through legislation, women in South Africa have been formally welcomed as major players in the South African workplace. South African women have the power within themselves to succeed. Affirmative action is a mechanism that can help facilitate their transition within corporate South Africa. As Mahatma Gandhi once said, "the journey of a thousand miles begins with the first step."

References

African National Congress. *Affirmative Action and the New Constitution. Retrieved from gopher*://gopher.anc, arg…O/anc? Policy/affirmative action.act, updated.

Baron, R. A. and J. Greenberg. 1990. *Behaviour In Organizations: Understanding And Managing The Humanside Of Work*. Boston: Allyn and Bacon.

Bozzoli, B. and M. Nkotsoe. 1991. *Women of Phokeng*. Johannesburg: Raven.

Charlton, G. D. and van Niekerk. N. 1994. *Affirmative Action—Beyond 1994*. Kenwyn: Juta & Co. LTD.

Dubourdieu, E. 2003. "Accentuate The Positive? Affirmative Action For South African Women." *Revue ALIZE,* no.14. Observatoire De Recherches Sur Les Anciennes Colonies Et Leur Liens Avec L' Europe.

Fischer, S. 1995. "Placing Women on the Affirmative Action Agenda." *People Dynamics.* vol. 13. no. 5.

Hugo, P. and Stack, L. 1992. "Whites In South African Public Services: Angst And The Future." In P. Hugo ed. *Redistribution And Affirmative Action*. Johannesburg: Southern Books.

Human, Linda. 1993. *Affirmative Action and Development of People*. Kenwyn: Juta & Co. LTD.

Louw, D. A., D. Edwards, D. Foster, A. Gilbert, A. Louw, G. Norton, C. Plug, A.S. Jordan and J. Spangenberg. 1997. *Psychology An Introduction For Students In Southern Africa*, 2nd ed. Johannesburg: Heineman Publishers.

Mandela, N. 1992. "Whites In South African Public Services. In Redistribution And Affirmative Action." In P. Hugo ed. *Redistribution And Affirmative Action*. Johannesburg: Southern Books.

Maphai, V. T. 1992. "The Civil Service: Transition And Affirmative Action." In P. Hugo ed. *Redistribution And Affirmative Action*. Johannesburg: Southern Books.

Mdladlana, M. M. S. 1999. *"Briefing on the Employment Equity Act."* Minister of Labour Briefing in Cape Town, February 15.

Mzimang, S. 2001. "Affirmative Action In South Africa: The Policies Of Representation, Law And Equity." *Women in Action* no.2.

Ngidi, N. 1994. "The Reconstruction Development Program And Affirmative Action." unpublished.

Qunta, C. 1995. *Who's Afraid Of Affirmative Action?* Cape Town: Kwela Books.

Republic of South Africa. 1998. *"Employment Equity Act No. 55 of 1998."* *Government Gazette, 400 (193700)*. October. Pretoria: Government Printers.

————. 1995. "Labour Relations Act No. 66 of 1995." *Government Gazette, 366(16861)*, December. Pretoria: Government Printers.

Reskin, B. F. and I. Padavic. 1994. *Women and Men at Work*. London: Pine Forge Press.

Sachs, A. 1992. "Affirmative Action And Good Government." Alistair Berkely Memorial Lecture. unpublished.

Sadie, Y. and van Aardt, M. 1995. "Women's Issues in South Africa: 1990–1994." *Africa Insight*. 25(2): 80–90.

South African Institute of Race Relations (SAIRR). 1994. *Fast Facts, no 2*. Braamfontein: SAIRR.

————. 1996. *Race Relations Survey 1994–1995*. Braamfontein: SAIRR

Part III

Engendering the World of Commerce

Chapter 18

Re-thinking Organizational Theory from a Feminist Perspective

Ronit Kark

Most accounts of organizational theory and research overlook gender (Calás & Smircich 1992; Martin 2000), or at best, gender is marginalized (Hearn & Parkin 1983). This paper draws on feminist theory and research to give front stage to works that re-think and revise influential mainstream theory and research in the organizational field by applying a gender analysis. My goal is not only to demonstrate how gender had been ignored, misrepresented or under-represented in organization theory, but rather to explore how the idea of "gender" can be a strategy through which representations of organizational theories can be questioned, gendered assumptions revealed, and different ways of writing organizational theory suggested. I first present a feminist framework for analysis of organizational theories and concepts. Then I review the works of scholars working within the critical tradition of feminist theory, who offer re-readings of mainstream organizational theory, challenging some of the fundamental assumptions, and unveiling the gendered implications of apparently gender-neutral language and practices. Lastly, I conclude by highlighting the potential contribution of these perspectives, derived from feminist theory, as alternative organizing constructs for future change.

Feminist Perspectives for Analysis of Organizational Concepts

In the last decade, feminist scholars have recognized that organizations are gendered in theory, practice, and discourse (Acker 1990; Calás & Smircich

1992; Fletcher 1999; Hearn & Parkin 1983; Martin 1990). To say that an organization is gendered means that advantage and disadvantage are patterned and enacted in terms of a distinction between what is female and male, as well as what is feminine and masculine (Acker 1990). According to this perspective, while organizational logic appears to be gender neutral, underlying both organizational theories and managerial practices is a gendered substructure that is reproduced daily by practical work activities as well as in the texts of theorists of organizations (Acker 1990; Calás & Smircich 1996; Martin 1996; Martin 2000). This substructure is manifested in dynamics and practices that appear to frame and treat women and men equally but are actually male-preferential (Acker 1990; Martin 1996).

Recent organizational analysis from a feminist poststructuralist perspective is beginning to question the gendered nature of organizational theory and practice through critiques and re-reading of mainstream organizational theories. Poststructuralism calls attention to the relationship between knowledge, discourse, language, and power. Feminist post structuralism is a mode of knowledge production that aims to explore and understand existing power relations and to identify possible areas and strategies for change (Gray 1994; Calás & Smircich 1991). In this stream of work the gendered nature of the theories, as reflected in the texts, and the ways in which they emphasize and privilege stereotypically masculine attributes and overlook or devalue stereotypically feminine ones are revealed (Fletcher 1999). These works demonstrate that the current definition of work in organizational discourse is an active form of power that silences and suppresses alternative definitions and interpretations (Calás & Smircich 1992; Clegg 1989; Fletcher 1999). A feminist reading entails providing a reinterpretation in which the central issues are examined from a "gendered" perspective with explicit reference to feminist literature (Gray 1994). Different strategies of post structural inquiry are used, to reveal assumptions that relate to the suppressed interests of members of disempowered, marginalized groups (Fondas 1997; Martin 2000).

According to Martin (2000), if these gendered analyses are to have maximum impact, it is important that the work analyzed would be in some sense foundational or central. Following these lines, the current paper aims to unveil and challenge fundamental assumptions of organizational theories, by reviewing work written from a feminist perspective on influential organizational concepts and theories. Through the critique offered by the works reviewed in this paper, I will try to reveal the gendered conceptualizations offered by traditional organizational theories to central questions in the organizational field (e.g., How is work evaluated? What motivates employees? What is leadership and who gets to lead?).This body of work also permits us to re-think alternatives and re-vision the field of organizational studies.

Re-thinking the Theory of Motivation

Among management theories, Abraham Maslow's needs hierarchy (1943, 1954) is seen as a "classic among classics" (Matteson & Ivancevich 1989: 369). This theory has had a widespread influence in the field of organizational behavior, and more specifically on theories of work motivation (Cullen 1994). It has formed the basis for the assumptions underlying major motivation theories that have shaped the field, including: McGregor's theory Y (McGregor 1960), Hertzberg's (1966) motivation-hygiene theory, Porter and Lawler's (1968) model of expectancy theory and Hackman and Oldham's (1980) job characteristics model of work design.

According to Maslow's theory (1943, 1954) there are five sets of human needs, which are innate, universal needs, arranged in a hierarchy of realization. The lower needs are more basic and must be satisfied before the higher needs emerge and affect individuals' behavior. The most primary (lowest in the hierarchy) needs are physiological (i.e., hunger, thirst); followed by safety or security needs (i.e., having a job, tenure, pension plans); then belongingness or love needs (i.e., having a spouse); the need for self-esteem and the desire for reputation and prestige (i.e., confidence, independence, freedom, recognition, status and appreciation); and last there is the highest need in the hierarchy - the need for self-actualization or self-fulfillment. According to Maslow's (1954) conceptualization the pursuit of higher needs, which leads to a greater and truer individualism, is the ultimate expression of the autonomous self.

Cullen (1994) examined Maslow's theory, its basic assumptions and its common base with liberal feminist theory, by analyzing the conceptualizations of the theory, as well as the methods and studies Maslow used to develop and anchor his theory. Cullen asserted that Maslow's understanding of motivation portrays the individualized male perception of the self. This perception, that stresses the importance of hierarchy, denies relatedness and alternative perspectives of the self - such as the female self-in-relation (Chodorow 1989; Miller & Stiver 1997), that is focused on models of webs of connection (Gilligan 1982).

Feminist perceptions of the relational self (Miller & Stiver 1997; Fletcher 1999) contend that psychological growth comes from maintaining and strengthening connections with others, not from increasing one's separateness for the sake of personal actualization and fulfillment. Although these perceptions view connection with others as a source of strength and maturity, and not as a sign of weakness and deficiency, according to Maslow's conception, women who were focused on their connection to others and their motivation to meet others' needs, are perceived as less developed on the motivation hierarchical ladder (Cullen 1994). Cullen (1994) further suggested that the male bias in self-actualization is not unexpected given that Maslow refined the concept by mostly studying men whom he considered to have reached this state (e.g., Thomas Jefferson, Abraham Lincoln, Einstein, and Freud). She demonstrated the ways in which Maslow's work misinterpreted women's experience and sexuality, and valued only those women with stereotypically masculine characteristics and behaviors. Maslow's hierarchy provides management theory and liberal feminist theory with a common base. Both have their roots in a psychological theory, which focuses on the autonomous and self-fulfilled individual. The supposition of the theory, that women's and men's fullest potential can be achieved merely by individual accomplishment, leads to a person-centered approach of women in management. This approach assumed that women need to become more like men in order to achieve organizational success and argued that any women can change her situation and her organizational constraints – by merely changing herself (Cullen 1994). These assertions lead to the false perceptions that the inability of people, and more so women, to achieve self-actualization is solely dependent on themselves and their will, while ignoring the major role power relations between different social groups can have on the ability of the individual to achieve self-fulfillment. Cullen (1994) suggests that women's experience, properly used, can be a source of an alternative theory of motivation.

Re-thinking Rationality and Emotionality in Organizations

Mumby and Putnam (1992) and Putnam and Mumby (1993) challenged the dichotomy of rationality and emotionality in organizational discourse. They presented a re-reading of Simon's (1976) construct of bounded rationality using a post structuralist feminist approach. They maintained that even though "bounded" rationality provides a modified critique of "pure" rationality, this concept is grounded in male-centered assumptions that exclude alternative modes of organizing. According to Mumby and Putnam (1992), researchers treat emotional experience as either a weak or limited form of reasoning. Based on this approach emotions are devalued, trivialized or treated as inappropriate at work. Aiming to further understand the attitude of organizational literature toward emotions, they analyze the abundant recent approach to emotions, which is evident in the emotional labor literature (e.g., Hochschild 1983; Sutton & Rafaeli 1988).

Emotional labor highlights emotions as a mean to serve organizational ends. According to this approach organizations set up divisions of emotional labor in which feelings become a commodity exchanged for organizational ends (e.g., phony smiles are designed to sell products). Through a feminist deconstructive process of re-reading the "bounded rationality" and the "emotional labor" literature, Mumby and Putnam (1992) introduced the concept of "bounded emotionality" as an alternative organizing construct.

Bounded emotionality refers to a mode of organizing in which emotional expression contributes to nurturance, caring, community, supportiveness, and inter-relatedness. Under this suggested mode, positive and negative emotions are expressed at work to enable personal authenticity of employees in the workplace, not to increase productivity. This form of emotionality is bounded because it requires that individuals limit their emotional expression, while taking into account the needs, emotions and values of fellow workers. The premises and implications of this alternative understanding of the workings of emotions in organizations are discussed and illustrated by Mumby and Putnam (1992).

A study performed in the Body Shop International, a large, for-profit cosmetic and toiletries firm found support for the theoretical viability of the concept of bounded emotionality (Martin, Knopoff & Beckman 1998). This research suggests new ways of conceptualizing and practicing emotions in the organizational context.

Re-thinking Job and Employee Evaluation

Martin (1990) and Acker (1990) aim to reassess the conceptions related to evaluation of jobs and of employees in organizations, while paying close attention to gender as inherent in the evaluation dynamics. Joan Acker (1990) analyzed the organizational logic in action in the process of job-evaluation. Job evaluation is a management tool often used to rationalize the organizational hierarchy and to help in determining equitable wages. Commonly in organizational logic, both jobs and organizational hierarchies appear as abstract, depersonalized, universal categories that theoretically seem to have no occupants, no human bodies, and no gender (Acker 1990). According to this logic, filling the abstract job is a disembodied worker who has no sexuality, no emotions, and who exists only in order to do the work required. Such a hypothetical worker cannot have other commitments that can impinge upon the job. According to Acker (1990), the closest this bodiless worker comes to a real worker is the male worker whose life centers on his full-time, life-long job, while his wife takes care of his personal needs and his children. Women's bodies, sexuality, pregnancy, child-care, menstruation and 'emotionality' are stigmatized, and used as grounds for exclusion (Acker 1990). Thus, this logic is at the basis of the structure leading to the evaluation of women's work and women's jobs as lower level, lower paid and less valued work.

In a similar vein, Martin (1990) deconstructs managerial evaluation processes, by questioning the way in which masculinity continues to dominate the structure, culture, and practices of work organizations. By evaluation, she refers to assessments of others' potential, talents, legitimacy, and performance. In deconstructing the evaluation processes, she fleshes out three different frames that are affected by gender: employees attributed potential, legitimacy for power and performance on the job. The first gender-based frame used by men to evaluate men and women concerns *potential*, asserting that women and men have different traits, potential, talents, and temperaments. These perceived differences support the notion that men are seen as more fit for valued jobs, and women as 'naturally' more suited to undesirable jobs.

A second evaluational frame involves *legitimacy* and hierarchical authority, suggesting that men see women as lacking the legitimacy and the justified 'right' to hold powerful positions. Women are perceived as though they should not have authority over men. The third frame concerns the fit between performance and gender. Due to men's superior gender status, their successes and contributions may be amplified and their limitations and mistakes minimized, whereas women's successes and contributions may be minimized and their limitations and mistakes amplified. As a result of this frame, women's and men's performance on the job is judged differently, and women's accomplishments are likely to be devalued. Martin (1990) concludes that her data suggests that the context of managerial evaluation provides opportunities for men to enact masculinity(ies) in the course of doing work. She argues that this tie between masculinity(ies) and working activities has a negative affect on the ways in which women (and many men) are evaluated, rewarded, and promoted.

Re-thinking Leadership

Kark (2004) reviews the works in the field of leadership, with reference to different feminist approaches, demonstrating that most studies of gender and leadership focus on the question of gender differences in leadership style and do not critique and re-think leadership theory. Among the few studies that have attempted to re-read and critique leadership studies in the light of feminist thinking is Calás and Smircich's (1991) theoretical paper. They draw on post structuralism and deconstruction to analyze the problem of the 'female subject in leadership knowledge'. In their work they aimed to show that 'leadership' is predicated on the repression of its necessary other, 'seduction', and that this dualism is inseparable from the dualism of male/female. Their analysis examined the relationship between the concepts of 'leadership' and 'seduction' demonstrating that although the link between the concepts is concealed, 'to seduce' is the repressed underside of 'to lead', and leadership is dependent on seduction. Calás and Smircich stressed that seduction includes leadership: "Seduction means to lead (astray); to mis-lead (mis: badly, wrongly). Seduction has a bad reputation. Seduction is leadership gone wrong. Notice also that leadership includes seduction: to lead is to attract and stimulate, to overcome. Thus, to seduce is to lead wrongly, and it seems that to lead is to seduce rightly" (1991: 573). Furthermore, they argued that not only are the terms linked to each other; they are also linked to gender, suggesting that women 's influence is framed as 'seduction', whereas men's influence is framed as 'leadership'. Through this process of re-reading of mainstream leadership texts, Calás and Smircich (1991) demonstrated the role gender plays in the construction of traditional leadership theory.

Calás (1993a) also considers the ways in which organizational writing in the field of leadership makes use of the term 'charisma'. Using a textual strategy of analysis based on Derridean deconstruction (Derrida 1982), she explores the mainstream literature on charismatic leadership (Bass 1990; Conger 1989). Her analysis critiques the current notion of charismatic leadership, arguing that it defines only certain behaviors, and characteristics that are "predefined in U.S. research" (Calás 1993a: 314) and founded on the masculine heroic notion representing the "good" charismatic leader. According to Calás (1993a) this rhetoric makes it impossible to consider behaviors of other minority social groups including women, which might differ from the research norms, as demonstrating 'positive charisma'. These groups that are seen as representing 'outsiders' are likely to be ascribed 'negative' aspects of charisma.

A different approach to study leadership from a feminist perspective was perused by Fondas (1997). She examined the nature of the rhetoric used in contemporary management writings and demonstrated that an underlying thread in writings of recent management books is their representation of managerial work in terms of qualities traditionally defined as feminine. This "feminization," however, has neither been named and made explicit by the writers themselves nor identified by management scholars and practitioners. The writers produce a 'facade of gender neutrality' (p. 274) in their theorizing, which does not exist. Fondas (1997) unveiled this feminization by reviewing accounts of managerial work in three contemporary and popular management books. She demonstrated how managers invoke feminine qualities to describe managing for excellence, working in teams and re-engineering.

Fondas asserted that the failure of management writers' to label the idea by its name (i.e., 'feminization') is that it signifies 'not masculine'. Feminine words and names are problematic signifiers for management writers whose audience is predominantly male managers. To recognize and invoke feminization is a complete reversal of the subordination of femininity to masculinity in the management discourse. By elevating femininity, "...men would stand in ambiguous relationship to this universal manager, just as women have always done so in regard to the "universal" beings described in most management theory" (Fondas 1997: 274).

Similarly, Fletcher (2002) recently examined the notion of 'heroic leadership'. Accordingly, new models of leadership are moving away from the idea of a heroic leader (e.g., individual, autonomous, command-and-control, and confident 'know it all' leader) to a post-heroic image of leaders characterized by a network of people contributing to leadership, a collaborative social process, and leaders as facilitators. Fletcher maintains that the heroic notion of leadership, as well as the post-heroic notion, are clearly sex-linked and are strongly related to power and gender relations, in a manner in which the predominant image is that associated with masculinity. Fletcher notes that: "the death of heroic leadership cannot be accomplished by simply reconstructing old models with new language. Capturing the transformational promise of new models of leadership will require recognizing and naming the radical nature of its challenge and the gender and power dynamic inherent in it" (Fletcher 2000: 4). Understanding the ways in which leadership perceptions are related to gender and giving value to qualities and management skills related to femininity, as qualities needed for post-heroic leadership, are likely to support new forms of organizing for both men and women.

Re-thinking Organizational Collaborations

Barbara Gray (1994) takes on the challenge to "re-read" her own established work on 'Collaborating: Finding Common Ground for Multiparty Problems' (1989) from a feminist perspective. Gray draws on three different streams of feminist theory in order to re-think and critique her own work: standpoint feminism, ecofeminism and post structuralism. Her (1989) treatise on collaborations focuses on the relationships among organizations, while suggesting a rationale for why groups need to collaborate in order to solve pressing social problems. The book examines a wide variety of collaborative mechanisms designed to provide answers to problems that none of the groups acting alone could provide.

Using a standpoint perspective developed by Harding (1987) Gray demonstrates that the underlying premises of her theory on collaboration are consistent with assertions related to 'women's ways of knowing' in general, and more specifically to the concept of 'connected knowing' (Belenky et. al. 1986; Gilligan 1982). Gray asserts that although her theory was originally presented as gender neutral, a re-reading of her own work reveals that her work is rooted in a feminist experience of the world and portrays directly her personal experience as a woman and as a "connected knower" (1994: 289).

Her critique from an ecofeminism viewpoint raises questions about the extent to which collaborations may be overly rational and thereby privilege technocratic over ecological solutions. She explores the possibility that the (mis)use of collaboration, to legitimize decisions about natural resources and habitats, can perpetuate abuse of disadvantaged people, including women. Following the post structuralist feminist approach she further revealed the inherently political undertones of organizational collaborations and questioned its role in preservation of the current order and in stabilizing the existing gender and power dynamics versus the order-transforming potential.

Re-thinking Extra-role Behavior: Organizational Citizenship Behavior

Kark and Manor (2005) questioned the gendered assumptions of extra-role behavior or more specifically of organizational citizenship behavior. They presented a feminist reading of the concept of Organizational Citizenship Behavior (OCB) and its components, by examining the rhetorical nature of the text, language and metaphors used in the definition of OCB and by exposing the different mechanisms through which the use of this concept reproduces the gendered division of labor and inequality between women and men.

The concept of OCB was suggested to describe extra-role behaviors that contribute to the functioning of the organization, but are not explicitly rewarded or coerced by a system of formal obligations (Bateman & Organ 1983).

Most research on OCB has focused on five different dimensions of citizenship behavior: altruism, courtesy, conscientiousness, sportsmanship, and civic virtue. The first two components are considered as helping behaviors (Podsakoff et al. 2000). Altruism is characterized as a helping behavior that involves voluntarily helping others with work-related problems (Organ 1988). Courtesy implies helping someone prevent a problem from occurring, or taking steps in advance to mitigate the problem (Organ 1988). These helping behaviors, which are focused on the welfare of the other, are stereotypically associated with the female gender role (Eagly & Crowley 1986; Miller & Stiver 1997). The three remaining OCB dimensions can be perceived stereotypically as related to the male gender role. Sportsmanship is "a willingness to tolerate the inevitable inconveniences and imposition of work without complaints" (Organ 1990: 96). Civic virtue is defined as constructive involvement in the political process of the organization. The last component, conscientiousness, is defined as going well beyond minimally required levels and attendance, conserving resources and related matters of internal maintenance

Kark and Manor (2002; 2005) proposed five different mechanisms that contribute to the dynamics of devaluation or disappearance of women's OCBs.

Gendered Metaphors: The first mechanism they suggested, which contributes to the construction of OCB as a gendered concept, is that of the language and metaphors chosen for naming OCB and its components. For example, one central metaphor that has been used in the literature to describe employees that enacted extra-role behaviors was that of the "good soldier" (Organ, 1988). Using this metaphor for naming primary and influential works in the field of OCB can promote the association between OCB and masculinity. This metaphor, as well as others (e.g., citizen, sportsmanship), can contribute to a construction of a male image of the prototype employee who exhibits OCBs.

Gendered Expectations: The second mechanism is that of differing expectations for men and women. Kark and Manor (2002, 2005) suggest that on the one hand, since women are expected to perform helping behaviors to a greater extent than men (Eagly & Crowley 1986), they might be less noticeable and less valued when performed by them. On the other hand, when women behave in a way that is *incongruent* with gendered expectations, either by not performing helping behaviors or by performing OCBs that can be seen as masculine behaviors (e.g., behaving in a political manner, staying long hours), they may be penalized, whereas men performing OCBs which violate gendered expectations (e.g., altruism) are likely to be rewarded.

Differential Gendered Enactment of OCB: Men and women tend to differ in various attributes of OCBs enacted (i.e., the type of OCB, the target of action, timing, audience, and magnitude). OCBs performed by men tend to be perceived as more heroic (i.e. witnessed by an audience, targeted toward strangers; Eagly and Crowley 1986; whereas women's OCBs tend to be perceived as more common and routine (i.e., caring for others, primarily individuals in close relationships). Different social value is attributed to these types of OCBs, whereas the heroic is seen as more valuable than the routine OCBs.

Gendered Attribution of Motivation: Another mechanism through which women's OCBs can be devalued is by the misinterpretation of their actions by attribution of self-serving motivation to their behavior. According to Fletcher (1999), when people assume that OCBs (e.g., helping and nurturing behaviors) displayed by women are motivated by women's own needs to be liked and by their emotional dependence, rather than the desire to work more effectively and contribute to the workplace, their actions may be devalued.

Gendered Evaluations and Men as Managers: The last mechanism suggested is rooted in the issue of who does the evaluation, who is being evaluated and who sets the norms for evaluation. It is reasonable to expect that the target for evaluation of OCBs will most commonly be lower-level employees (i.e., women). Men, on the other hand, are more likely to be the evaluators of OCBs and to set the standards for evaluation while using the process of evaluation as an arena for enacting masculinities (Martin 1996). Such a dynamic is likely to lead to devaluation of women's OCBs.

To conclude, Kark and Manor (2005) assert that without recognition of these mechanisms by which women's OCB behaviors are devalued the theory of OCB does not attain its goal of unmasking previously unrecognized extra-role behaviors as contributing to organizational effectiveness. Furthermore, Kark and Manor (2005) took another step and considered the possible negative sides of OCB and its relations to gender, asserting that the notion of OCB, as many other organizational concepts, is grounded in the dichotomy between the public domain and the private sphere (Martin & Knopoff 1997; Fondas 1997). Theories and practices of OCB sustain this dichotomy by focusing solely on the public domain without acknowledging the effect OCB might have on the private sphere the home, the neighborhood and the wider community. By this gendered dichotomy (in which women represent the private and men the public) it is possible to overlook the question of how extra-role behaviors in the organization might affect other roles in life, as parents and community members.

Contribution of Feminist Scholarship to Organizational Theory

The works presented above, as well as research that relates to additional organizational concepts including a re-examination of the Hawthorne studies (Acker & Van Houten 1974), bureaucracies (Ferguson 1984; Martin & Knopoff 1997), stress and burnout (Meyerson 1998), field dependency (Haaken 1988) and organizational culture (Mills 1988; Ramsay & Parker 1992), serve to unveil the gendered nature of organizational theories and concepts. In the process of unveiling the gendered assumptions embedded in organizational theories, the above analyses show that gender is not peripheral to researchers' understanding of management and originations, rather it is an integral part of the very conceptualization of management, leadership, motivation, work evaluation, organizational cooperation and extra-role behaviors. All these studies not only focus on the ways in which gender is constructed in organizations, but also reveal the inherent involvement of 'organizational studies' in the perpetuation and construction of gendered arrangements (Calás & Smircich 1992, 1996; Martin 2000). The reflection, perpetuation, and reconstruction of these gendered arrangements in organizational theory further contributes to the formation and stabilization of these arrangements by providing the theoretical basis for training manuals, socialization of newcomers to organizations, for consultants and practitioners interventions within firms, and for managers' use.

According to Martin (2000), if scholars fail to notice and explore the workings of gender in their theory and research, they will take part in the perpetuation and stabilizing of gender inequalities, intentionally or unintentionally. The stream of feminist readings presented above contributes to the organizational field not only by offering an opportunity for scholars to re-examine the basic assumptions of well established theories, but this body of literature also calls for re-thinking and questioning the ideas and concepts drawn on while developing and constructing new theories. Furthermore, exposing theoretical blind spots can lead to insights that change the ways researchers think about familiar, classic theories and therefore the ways organizational functioning is theorized, studied, taught and enacted in practice. According to Calás & Smircich (1991) this type of analysis is of particular value in various fields of organizational theorizing, in which although much effort has been directed at innovative thinking and development of theory, little has changed in the field.

Organization studies can be characterized as having a 'final vocabulary' (Rorty 1989); meaning a final set of words used to justify beliefs, attitudes and actions. Mumby and Putnam (1992) advocate that organization theorists question the adequacy of such a final vocabulary and, in contrast adopt a position that understands that the final truth is not "out there," rather it is a constant unfolding discourse constructed by theorists and empirical researchers. Based on this perception it is proposed that re-reading organizational theory is insufficient. There is need to revise and re-write theory. By proposing new concepts as an alternative way of understanding and looking at organizations the current theory is challenged, possibly leading to more complex and inclusive theorizing.

Apart from the re-thinking of new vocabulary, Calás and Smircich (1993b) suggest that researchers think of new sets of images. They offer the imagery of the "frugal housewife," who can do with consuming less and saving for a rainy day and "women's gossiping," as an imagery to construct an extended network of real worldwide information. Kark and Manor (2005) suggest re-reading the literature of organizational citizenship behavior with the imagery of the "good mother" or "good nurse," rather than the "good soldier" imagery offered in the traditional theory. A playful perspective using various new sets of images may effect changes in the ways we think about organizations and management, offering new avenues to design our organizations for a better society.

The writings presented in this chapter contribute to the growing literature that is being used to revise the record of management and organizational theory drawing on a variety of feminist perspectives. Revising organizational theorizing can take several forms: First, these works correct the exclusion of women as subjects of inquiry and sources of knowledge and add their contribution and missing voices. Second, they assess gender bias in current knowledge through re-reading important texts with a different viewpoint, by assessing the extent to which the concepts used to generate knowledge are male gendered, and by reconsidering the values underlying our interpretation of data. Possibly, the most needed step at this stage is to construct new organizational theory with the creation of more diverse voices and narratives, and the inclusion of new topics that are of greater concern to women (e.g., harassment, pregnancy). Re-reading and re-thinking the grounds for organizational theorizing is not enough, there is a need to re-write the texts of organizational theories. Furthermore, it is important not only to incorporate women's voices in the re-writing of organizational theories, but also to aim for organizational theories that allow for more complex intersections of gender and other social categories (e.g., ethnicity, age, nationality and class) as a means to develop more inclusive and insightful organizational theories.

References

Acker, J. 1990. "Hierarchies, Jobs, Bodies: A Theory Of Gendered Organizations." *Gender and Society 4*(2): 139–158.

Acker, J. and D. R. V. Houten. 1974. "Differential Recruitment And Control: The Sex Structuring Of Organizations." *Administrative Science Quarterly 19*(2): 152–163.

Bass, B. M. 1990. *Bass & Stogdill's Handbook of Leadership. Theory, Research and Managerial Applications.* New York: The Free Press.

Bateman, T. S. and D. W. Organ. 1983. "Job Satisfaction And The Good Soldier: The Relationship Between Affect And Employee 'Citizenship'." *Academy of Management Journal* 26:587–595.

Belenky, M. F., B. M. Clinchy, N. R. Goldenberg and J.M. Tarule. 1986. *Women's Ways of Knowing.* New York: Basic Books.

Calás, M. B. 1992. "Re-Writing Gender Into Organization Theorizing: Directions From Feminist Perspectives." In M. Reed & M. Hughes. eds. *Re-thinking Organizations: New Directions in Organizational Research and Analysis.* London: Sage. p. 227–253.

———. 1993a. "Deconstructing Charismatic Leadership: Re–reading Weber from the Darker Side." *Leadership Quarterly 4*: 305–328.

———.1993b. "Dangerous Liaisons: The 'Feminine–In Management' Meets 'Globalization'." *Business Horizons, March-April,* p.71–81.

———.1996. "From The Women's Point Of View: Feminist Approaches To Organization Studies." In S. R. Clegg and C. Hardy & W. Nord. eds. *Handbook of Organization Studies.* London: Saga. p. 218–257.

——— and L. Smircich. 1991. "Voicing Seduction to Silence Leadership." *Organization Studies 12*(4): 567–602.

Clegg, S. 1989. *Frameworks of Power.* Newbury Park, CA: Sage.

Conger, J. A. 1989. *The Charismatic Leader: Behind the Mystique of Exceptional Leadership.* San Francisco: Jossey-Bass.

Cullen, D. 1994. "Feminism, Management And Self-Actualization." *Gender, Work and Organization* 1(3): 127–137.

Derrida, J. 1982. *Margins of Philosophy.* Chicago: University of Chicago Press.

Eagly, A. H. and M. Crowley. 1986. "Gender And Helping Behavior: A Meta-Analytic Review Of The Social Psychological Literature." *Psychological Bulletin* 100(3): 1283–1308.

Ferguson, K. 1984. *The Feminist Case Against Bureaucracy.* Philadelphia: Temple University Press.

Fletcher, J. K. 1999. *Disappearing Acts: Gender, Power, and Relational Practice at Work.* Cambridge, MA: MIT Press.

Fletcher, J. K. 2002. *The Greatly Exaggerated Demise of Heroic Leadership: Gender, Power, and the Myth of the Female Advantage* (13). Boston: Center for Gender in Organizations (CGO) Simmons School of Management.

Fondas, N. 1997. "Feminization Unveiled: Management Qualities In Contemporary Writings." *Academy of Management Review* 22: 257–282.

Gilligan, Carol. 1982. *In a Different Voice.* Cambridge, MA: Harvard University Press.

Gray, B. 1989. *Collaborating: Finding Common Ground for Multiparty Problems.* San Francisco: Jossey-Bass.

Gray, B. 1994. "A Feminist Critique of Collaborating." *Journal of Management Inquiry* 3(3): 286–293.

Haaken, J. 1988. "Field Dependence Research: A Historical Analysis of A Psychological Construct." *Signs* 13: 311–330.

Hackman, J. R. and G. R. Oldham. 1980. *Work Redesign.* Reading, MA: Addison-Wesley.

Harding, Sandra. 1991. *Whose Science? Whose Knowledge? Thinking from Women's Lives.* Ithaca, NY: Cornell University Press.

Hearn, J. and P. W. Parkin. 1983. "Gender And Organizations: A Selective Review And A Critique Of A Neglected Area." *Organization Studies (4)3*: 219–242.

Herzberg, F. 1966. *Work and the Nature of Man.* New York: New American Library.

Hochschild, A. R. 1983. *The Managed Heart.* Berkeley: University of California Press.

Kark, R. 2004. "The Transformational Leader: Who is (S)he? A Feminist Perspective." *Journal of Organization Change Management.* Special issue on Transformational Leadership Research: Issues and Implications 17(2): 160–176.

———— and R. Waismel-Manor 2002. *Unveiling the Gendered Nature of Organizational Citizenship Behavior* (02–16). Ithaca, NY: Cornell Employment and Family Career Institute, Cornell University.

———— and R. Manor. 2005. "Organizational Citizenship Behavior: What's Gender Got to Do With It?" *Organization: The Interdisciplinary Journal of Organization, Theory and Society* 12(6): 889–917.

Martin, J. 1990. "Deconstructing Organizational Taboos: The Suppression Of Gender Conflict In Organizations." *Organization Science* 1(4): 339–359.

———— 2000. "Hidden Gendered Assumptions In Mainstream Organizational Theory And Research." *Journal of Management Inquiry* 9(2): 207–216.

———— and K. Knopoff. 1997. "The Gendered Implications Of Apparently Gender-Neutral Theory: Re-Reading Weber." In E. Freeman and A. Larso. eds. *Business Ethics and Women's Studies.* Oxford: Oxford University Press.

————, K. Knopoff and C. Beckman. 1998. "An Alternative To Bureaucratic Impersonality And Emotional Labor: Bounded Emotionality At The Body Shop." *Administrative Science Quarterly* 43: 429–469.

Martin, P. Y. 1996. "Gendering And Evaluating Dynamics: Men, Masculinities, And Management." In L. C. David and J. Hearn. eds. *Men as Managers, Managers as Men*. London: Sage.

Maslow, A. H. 1943. "A Theory Of Human Motivation." *Psychological Review* 50(4): 370–396.

Maslow, A. H. 1954. *Motivation and Personality*. New York: Harper.

Matteson, M. T. and J. M. Ivancevich. 1989. *Management and Organizational Behavior Classics*. Homewood, IL: BPI / Irwin.

McGregor, D. 1960. *The Human Side of Enterprise*. New York: McGraw Hill.

Meyerson, D. 1998. "Feeling Stressed And Burnout: A Feminist Reading And Re-visioning Of Stress-Based Emotions Within Medicine And Organization Science." *Organization Science* 9(1): 103–118.

——— and J. K. Fletcher. 2000. "A Modest Manifesto for Shattering the Glass Ceiling." *Harvard Business Review*, Jan-Feb, 126–136.

Miller, J. B. and I. P. Stiver. 1997. *The Healing Connection: How Women Form Relationships in Therapy and in Life*. Boston, MA: Beacon Press.

Mills, A. J. 1992. "Organization Gender and Culture." in A. J. Mills and P. Tancred. eds. *Gendering Organizational Analysis*. Newbury Park, CA: Sage.

Mumby, D. K. and L. Putnam. 1992. "The Politics Of Emotion: A Feminist Reading Of Bounded Rationality." *Academy of Management Review* 17(3): 465–486.

Organ, D. W. 1988. *Organizational Citizenship Behavior: The Good Soldier Syndrome*. Lexington, MA: Lexington Books.

Organ, D. W. 1990. "The Subtle Significance Of Job Satisfaction." *Clinical Laboratory Management Review 4*: 94–98.

Porter, L. W. and E. E. Lawler. 1968. *Managerial Attitudes and Performance*. Chicago: Irwin.

Podsakoff, P. M., S. B. MacKenzie, J. B. Paine, and D. G. Bachrach. 2000. "Organizational Citizenship Behavior: A Critical Review of The Theoretical And Empirical Literature and Suggestions For Future Research." *Journal of Management* 26(3): 513–563.

Putnam, L. and D. K. Mumby. 1993. "Organizations, Emotion, and The Myth Of Rationality." In S. Fineman. ed. *Emotions in Organizations*. London: Sage. p. 36–57.

Ramsay, K. and M. Parker. 1992. "Gender Bureaucracy and Organizational Culture." In M. Savage and A. Witz. Eds. *Gender and Bureaucracy*. Cambridge, MA: Blackwell. p. 253–278.

Riger, S. and P. Galligan. 1980. "Women In Management: An Exploration Of Competing Paradigms." *American Psychologist* 35: 902–910.

Rorty, R. 1989. *Contingency, Irony, and Solidarity*. Cambridge: Cambridge University Press.

Sutton, R. I. and A. Rafaeli. 1988. "Untangling The Relationship Between Displayed Emotions and Organizational Sales: The Case of Convenience Stores." *Academy of Management Journal* 31: 461–487.

Valian, V. 1998. *Why So Slow? The Advancement of Women*. Cambridge, MA: The MIT Press.

Chapter 19

"Translating Empowerment": Swedish Immigrant Women and State Sponsored Employment Projects

Lena Sawyer

Frustrated over the limits of the Swedish employment offices' work with what was increasingly framed as " a problem group", the state shifted its strategy in the late 1990s to also give short term financial support to immigrants' own projects aimed at "integrating" long term unemployed immigrants to the Swedish workforce.[1] As this paper will suggest, this shift linked up competing agendas and power relations; where neo-liberal global development discourses on empowerment were strategically translated to join the Swedish state's increasing culturalization of immigrants with immigrant organizations own interests in gaining financial support and legitimacy.

One such project, that I am calling "Tigers", was often linked with the term empowerment as it was run by African women and for African women. In brochures and reports,[2] the "Tigers" project was described as ground breaking in that it had an unusually high success rate; of 265 participants, 136 of the women found employment, and 56 went into studies. The women participants were on average thirty-five years old, had lived in Sweden for eight years, and came from the Horn of Africa and/or Sub-Saharan Africa. Further, the women had varied educational backgrounds—50 percent said they had been to high school, 11 percent to university; however, there was also a significant proportion who could not read or write. Further, half of the women had on average four years of employment experience and worked in for example, health services and as secretaries, 42 percent of the women said they had no employment experience at all (Metzger 2001). In essence, the long term unemployed African women were a heterogeneous group. Yet the project was particularly lauded because it used *a bottom up* approach and was seen to be an example of *self-help* and *empowerment*. These aspects were tied to the project idea coming from the women's section of an African organization and to the fact that they employed African women as project leaders. The special aspects of this type of project are described in more detail:

> The project leaders for "Tigers" are in a very special situation, they act as so called 'bridge builders' in that they know what ethnic Swedes' think is 'strange' and foreign about African culture and can understand and tell the participants why ethnic Swedes sometimes react with fear and reservation. They feel that they know how to think both like an 'African' and at the same time they have many years of working experience in integrated workplaces in Sweden and thus have experience of the 'cultural collisions' that can occur between 'African' and 'Swedish' workplaces (Metzger 2001: 10).[3]

This role of being a so-called "bridge builder" for the long term unemployed women, is highlighted in much of the documentation about the project. Further, the project's success is also attributed to what they call the "Tiger methods" that were developed to work with the women participants; methods that consisted of creating individualized strategy plans for each woman based on her previous experience, education, and work goals, and teaching women how to look for work in computer databases, write applications, make phone calls, and behave during interviews. In the project, the women conduct role-plays, discuss, and share their experiences with the job search process. Cultural difference and understanding was, according to Metzler (2001), an important part of the project methods:

> They portray many scenes that occur in the coffee room and then turn the whole thing around when the project leader plays 'Islamic woman' or 'African woman' and the participants get to play the ethnic Swedes which gives the participants the opportunity to see the situation from 'the Others' viewpoint, 'they think to themselves - how strange you are!' This method enables you to see your own patterns and see yourself in a neutral environment, in that everyone around you is also in the same situation and often has similar experiences and background. The participants see the role that the immigrant woman often falls into at the workplace when she falls into certain patterns and behaviors . . . . The discussion afterwards often revolves around cultural collisions, how you function with your Swedish work colleagues, how to interact during the [coffee] breaks, and the different 'unwritten rules' in the Swedish workplace culture. Many of the

participants are Muslim and discussions revolve around clothing at work and why Swedes think it is 'strange' when Muslim women disappear during the breaks to pray or when they do not participate in the informal social life at the workplace (Metzler 2001: 19–20).

In these role-plays women are described as learning "cultural competence," a competence vaguely described as "knowledge of the Swedish culture" as well as the ability to reflect on one's own culture from the viewpoint of other cultures. Through such role-plays the women were pushed to view themselves from a "Swedish" viewpoint and they gain a better understanding of why they, as "Africans," can "seem strange or frightening" to Swedes.

End of the year reports and brochures produced about the "Tigers" project attest not only to the increased confidence and strength gained by the women participants but also their deepened knowledge about Swedish culture. For example in one project brochure "Rita" describes what she has learned through participating in the project by saying: "If you live in a society that is dominated by Swedes...you have to do like them . . . but if I do not know how I should behave in their society—that is what we learn at [Tigers], we learn how to meet Swedish people, 'you have to do it like this; they are like this'." Another woman participant, "Aszo" describes in another brochure that she is now more aware of how to avoid "cultural collisions," and describes the lessons of one of the "Tiger" activities. Aszo says: "In Sweden if you come to work with food that they are not used to they will say that you are strange. There was a woman who was going to warm something up, then everyone opened the windows and was going to leave the room. . . so now I try to think of these small, small, things a lot." These are all shown as examples of the self-help and empowerment that the women have encountered through participating in "Tigers." Further, "Tigers" is lauded in end of the year reports and brochures for their success in moving long-term immigrant women into employment and thus contributing to their integration into the Swedish society.

However, "Tigers" was not the only immigrant organization using empowerment discourse in relation to their work with unemployed immigrant women. I came into contact with an organization I am calling "New Start" when I was hired by an African NGO to conduct research on Africans and employment, and thus conducted interviews with some of the women in "New Start." This organization used similar "Tiger" methods of role-plays and was also often lauded as an example of "empowerment." Not surprisingly, almost all of the women I interviewed in the project described the project positively. However one interview, with a woman I am calling "Jasmine," pushed me to think more critically about how larger, uneven, power relations, such as those between immigrant organizations and national and inter-national funding agencies, *frame* discussions of social change and empowerment as envisioned in integration projects. Immigrant employment project leaders, literature, and brochures frequently invoked words like empowerment when they described themselves as building bridges for long term unemployed women into the Swedish society. Jasmine told instead of how she had decided not to walk over the bridge that such projects tried to build for her. Rather than laud project methods and goals she pushed the discussion to a critical interrogation of how empowerment and self-help was being conceptualized in "New Start" and linked empowerment to include not only individual but also structural change. Jasmine seemed instead intent on building another kind of bridge into Swedish society.

During the interview Jasmine told of how she had rejected the project leaders' role-plays and attempts that she occupy a "Swedish" viewpoint and view herself, through what she was told was their eyes, as "an African woman" and "a Muslim woman." She also questioned project leaders' suggestions that she wear a smaller hijab to job interviews. She told me with a laugh: "The project leaders told me it would be very, very hard for me to find work if I do not wear a smaller hijab, they said it is easiest if I wear no hijab at all, but why should I, it is not a problem for me to do my cleaning work with it on." And instead of discussing her clothing, Jasmine was more interested in discussing Swedish institutions and workplaces and asked me rhetorically: "Why is it, that it was ok for Swedes to take fifteen minute cigarette breaks, and why does the boss even have a special room for these workers to smoke in, but when it is about a Muslim worker who wants to pray for five minutes it is a very BIG problem?" Jasmine pushed me to consider how some immigrant project's conceptualization of empowerment had translated into it larger Swedish modernist understanding of work, gender, and "race". As such, one can wonder if projects like "Tigers" and "New Start" translated, rather than transformed power relations.

Translation Versus Transformation

This chapter raises some very basic questions about a new area of interest for me, that is: how is the discourse of empowerment, as a process of emancipation, used in specific contexts to translate rather than transform power relations? Once again, I want to stress that I am using "Tigers" and "New Start" as examples of how understandings of empowerment can be translated, that is, re-articulated, and molded, by powerful discourses accompanying economic globalization. This analysis is not meant to take away from the hard work, generosity, creative negotiations, and realized employment and study opportunities created by the "Tigers" and "New Start" project leaders and participants. Instead, the examples are meant to be an entry point into a larger discussion of how proposals for social change need to be understood as connected to larger state and international discourses of gender, work, and citizenship.

Other researchers such as Jo Rowlands (1998), Manorjan Mohanty (2001), Steven Parker et al. (1999), Gudrun Dahl (2001), and Ulrika Dahl (2002) are interested in interrogating the ambiguous ways that the categories of social change negotiate larger discourses of power. Following them, I want to suggest that the usage of terms such as empowerment and self help in NGO projects can translate, rather than transform, power relations between marginalized groups and majority societies. For example, while empowerment has been used positively in social development and social work discourse in the last fifteen years as a way to avoid paternalistic relationships between funders and NGOs (Adams 1990; 1996; Jarhag 2001), the term has lost much of the radical meanings of structural social change as envisioned by people like Paulo Freire. Researchers such as Midgely (1983) link the term empowerment to Freire's process of consciencization, a process of social change where disempowered individuals obtain a critical awareness of their own oppression and structural position in society through dialogue with others, and in turn collective action. However, through its more recent 1990s usage by The World Bank, national and local NGOs, and sometimes even activists, the term empowerment has become one way in which neo-liberalist ideas of individuality and responsibility have been translated into social development contexts and discourse (Dahl 2001: 21–22). For example, Mohanty (2001), after reviewing its usage in NGO and governmental discourse goes so far as to call empowerment a "disabling concept" and points out:

> Empowerment, civil society, and democratization comprise the new package of the liberalization discourse which at their face value respond to the long-standing demands of struggling groups. In practice, however, each of them has been given a restricted meaning and has been oriented to serve the present global drive of Western capitalism (Mohanty 2001: 25).

Within a global context of economic globalization and liberation, the advocacy of empowerment can be ambivalent (Dahl 2001). Helene Thomsson (2002) for example has done important work interrogating power relations within Swedish immigrant women's organizations and asks *who* defines the needs of the women within these organizations. She lifts up power differences when she suggests that it is often the salaried employees within organizations, who see participants as "victims", who define what migrant women's needs are and how they should be met. Indeed Swedish immigrant organizations and their projects of empowerment sometimes often contain both libratory and regulatory power, as Jasmine forcefully reminded during the interview. Jasmine's perspective pushed me to place the "New Start" project of women's empowerment as linked to employment into a larger context of Swedish modernity and specific historical discourses about employment, gender, and race.

For example, in the next ten years Sweden is expected to have an employment crisis, most specifically in the service sector, as there is expected to be a large number of elderly who will enter into institutional care. In particular there is expected to be a labor shortage in those branches of work traditionally associated with "women's work," for example, of lifting and cleaning bodies and providing company and "care" to populations on the margins of the welfare state (elderly, disabled, children, and the sick and ill). This is often physically taxing work that historically has been done by women (Fredholm & Holmgren 2002). Not only will the Swedish welfare state need more of its existing citizens to enter into this "dirty work" (i.e. women's work), but there will also need to be more citizens to do this work.

The participation of men and women in paid work has been central to modern understandings of Swedish citizenship and work has been conceptualized as a key duty that is tied to successful integration in the People's Home (Ålund & Schierup 1991). It is within this larger historical context that immigrant women's integration projects must be understood, as historical discourses provide the frame within which immigrant women's integration projects such as "Tigers" and "New Start" act. Paulina de los Reyes (2000) has pointed out the historical inter-connections between Swedish conceptualizations of gender, race, and work and discusses two different gender contracts that accompanied the Swedish project of modernity. The first contract, the housewife gender contract (husmorsgenuskontrakt), can be periodized to late 19th and early 20th century industrialization and increased class mobility, the entrenchment of new bourgeoisie ideas about men and women, and a strict dichotomous labor-division in the home and public sphere (see also Frykman & Löfgren 1987). According to Hirdman (1989), a new gender contract emerged in the 1960s and 70s, one that linked the gender equality contract to work, as this contract rationalized the large number of working and middle class women's movement from unpaid work in the home to paid work in the (mainly) service sector positions created with the expansion of the welfare state. De los Reyes (2000) includes the perspective of race and ethnicity to understand Hirdman's discussion of gender contracts and suggests that specific ideas of womanhood accompanied each of the gender contracts. These shifting norms of womanhood provide the mirror upon which immigrant women were and continue to be evaluated in Sweden. She states succinctly the repercussions for immigrant women: "In the transition period between the two different gender contracts and two different ways of defining womanhood we can see that immigrant women first represent the 'deviant' to only later be identified with the old, the old fashioned and the traditional" (2000: 39).

In other words, when immigrant women worked in the 1940s and 1950s, they were half of the employment immigrants to Sweden after WWII, and worked in industry often in monotonous low paid positions.

They were seen as "deviant" in that dominating norms of Swedish womanhood were then linked to women's unpaid work in the home. However, when in the 1970s the gender contract became tied to women's paid work in the public sphere and gender equality, immigrant women were then linked with the home sphere, and hence to the "unmodern" and to "tradition"; and perhaps most persuasive in Swedish debates, stereotyped as passive victims oppressed by their *different* and patriarchal cultures (see de los Reyes et al. 2002). Such postcolonial feminist perspectives push researchers to include the way in which immigrant women have not only played a major roll in the creation of the Swedish welfare state, but that the discourse about "immigrant women" in Sweden needs to be understood in larger historical contexts.

This brief historical backdrop provides one explanation as to why integration projects for immigrant women are so closely linked to their participation in paid employment in Sweden: through work, immigrant women enter not just into formal economy, but also modernity and hence, full Swedish citizenship. The logic of paid work as providing entry into modernity could be seen for example in how one "Tiger" project leader described the project in a brochure. Borrowing upon modernist universal rights discourse she enthusiastically proclaimed: "This is really not any kind of therapy—the project should lead to a job, and it does! To have a job means freedom—freedom to have your own money. And that is a social economic right."

At the same time this close link, between modernity, gender equality, and paid employment for women provides a persuasive explanatory frame for understanding immigrant women's absence from paid employment. For example, today, Africans and Arabic speaking immigrants (both men and women) have the highest unemployment rate in Sweden. In Stockholm in 1998 the overall employment level for African men was 47 percent and 41 percent for women, compared with 77 percent for men, and 75 percent for women employed in the cleaning sphere, the number one employer for Africans in Stockholm. Differences in employment participation are much larger between immigrant and Swedish women than between migrated men and Swedish men (Sabune et al. 2001).

At the same time immigrant women's absence from the Swedish employment sector is increasingly rationalized through the discourse of "culture." Myths about immigrant women in Sweden, produced by both non-feminist and feminist researchers alike, often represent migrated women as a homogeneous group, and all too often as passive, silent, and oppressed by their men and cultures (de los Reyes et al. 2002; Mattsson 2001). For example, Mattsson (2001) points out that the researchers focus (and reproduction of) immigrant's so called "cultural difference," and their lack of "Swedish cultural competence" are a way of avoiding discussions of structural discrimination. I would also suggest that there are gendered implications to how employment research is often conducted in Sweden; a focus on cultural difference as the cause of migrated women's absence from paid employment is also a way for images of Swedish women as modern and gender equal to go unchallenged.

Activities and role-play methods used in the "Tiger" and "New Start" projects, described as presenting a way for women to gain "cultural competence" and to avoid so called "cultural collisions" in the workplace, have in the context of de los Reyes' (2002) and Mattsson's (2001) research findings a decidedly assimilationist flavor. In asking the women to view themselves through the lens of "immigrant women" from the "Swedish perspective," stereotypical images of "Africans," "Muslims," and "Swedes" were reinforced, rather than deconstructed. Focus on the "competence" or more often "lack of competence" of migrated women in so called integration programs translate empowerment in such a way that social change becomes limited to a personal and individual project. Gudrun Dahl (2001: 20) describes the ways that development discourse is baked into some usages of the term empowerment when she says: "The term 'empowerment' has an inherent ambiguity in that it may be read either to offer capacity to deal with for example, structural constraints or to fill an assumed gap in the personal capacity to manage things according to normative standards, whereby the empowered will hopefully reach the level of the empowerer." In this context I wonder if empowerment, as translated into some immigrant NGOs in Sweden, is a form of modernist discipline that, in the words of Parker et al., "imply that power is actually power over oneself?" (1999: 150).

Conclusion

Projects of women's empowerment do not happen in a vacuum, but are molded by historically specific contexts and understandings of gender. This paper has aimed to place the discourse and methods used within two immigrant women's integration projects into a larger context of Swedish historical labor, gender, and racial politics. It is impossible to understand migrated women's visions of empowerment without taking in account how structural discrimination and racism frame constructions of gender and sexual identities. Applying the critiques and contributions of Swedish feminist writers such as Paulina de los Reyes, Diana Mulinari, Irene Molina, Helene Thomsson, Yvonne Hirdman, and Ulrika Dahl, I have given a brief background of Swedish modernization and the shifting role of gender equality, work, and full citizenship. Within this contemporary context, where migrated women have been hegemonically seen as bearers of "traditional" cultures in relation to Swedish women's self-image as "modern" and "gender equal," it is easier to understand why projects of self-help and empowerment focus on employment as integration and the development of women's so called "cultural competence." I am not suggesting that women's access to their own money through paid work cannot bring a new sense of autonomy and mobility, but I suggest that a focus on empowerment as employment also (conveniently?) overlaps with larger discourses and neo-liberalist agendas. For example, migrated women's integration into a racially and gender segregated labor market also fills larger national economic purposes in that it reduces so called "welfare dependency," fills the low status, low paid, physically taxing positions that are today difficult to recruit workers to, and finally, and perhaps most importantly, modernizes "traditional" women.

As such, Swedish immigrant women's projects envision empowerment within specific contexts and discourses and are in an unequal relationship with (state) funding agencies. These types of unequal power relations mean that project brochures and funding reports necessarily must filter out critical perspectives and questions such as those raised by "Jasmine," who instead wanted to talk about structural discrimination, rather than about how she could change herself (and her clothing) to gain employment in Sweden. Moving the discussion of migrated women's unemployment from an individual level (and questions of culture and clothing) to a structural level would mean discussing the mechanics of gender and racial discrimination, and push funding agencies and projects to delve into more uncharted territory, translating women's empowerment in ways that would engage national policy, focus on the practices of employers and workplaces, and look at the media's portrayal of migrated women in Sweden.

Notes

1. The names, and some details, of the immigrant women's projects discussed in this paper have been changed to protect the identities of the specific organizations, as well as to point out that the "translation of empowerment" discussed in these projects are not exceptional. Rather, they can be understood as examples of how immigrant integration projects are framed by, and forced to negotiate, larger national discourses about work, gender, and "race".

2. The project brochures and reports analysed and cited come from the late 1990s to early 2000s.

3. All citations have been translated from Swedish to English by the author.

References

Adams, Robert. 1996. *Social Work and Empowerment*. London: British Association of Social Workers.

Ålund, A. and C. Schierup. 1991. *Paradoxes of Multiculturalism*. Avebury: Aldershot.

Dahl, Ulrika. 2002. "Vägen till Ånge." In *Coola Böner- det handlar om kön, plats och förändring.* Jämtland: Länsstyrelsen i Jämtlandslän. p. 75–80.

Dahl, Gudrun. 2001. *Responsibility and Partnership in Swedish Aid Discourse.* Uppsala: Nordic Africa Institute.

de los Reyes, Paulina, Irene Molina and Diana Mulinari. eds. 2002. *Maktens (o)lika förklädnader: kön, klass & etnicitet I det postkoloniala Sverige.* Stockholm: Atlas.

Fredholm, Kerstin and Anna Holmgren. 2002. "Det nya Arbetsmarknaden Integration." *Alla* 2: 13–15.

Frykman, Jonas and Löfgren Orvar. 1987. *Culture Builders: A Historical Anthropology of Middle Class Life.* (Alan Crozier translator) New Brunswick, NJ and London: Rutgers University Press.

Jarhag, Sven. 2001. *Planering eller frigörelse? En studie om bemyndigande.* Lund: Lund Dissertations in Social Work.

Hirdman, Yvonne. 1989. *Att lägga liver till rätta. Studier i svensk folkhemspolitik.* Carlssons: Stockholm.

Mattsson, Katarina. 2001. "Ekonomisk rasism- föreställningar om de Andra i ekonomisk invandrarforskning." In *Sverige och de Andra. Postkoloniala Perspektiv.* Michael McEachrane och Louis Faye. eds. Stockholm: Natur och Kultur. p. 243–264.

Metzger, Johnathan. 2001. *Kvinnoprojekt (. . .) slutrapport.* Stockholm: Stockholms Stads integrationsnämnd.

Midgley, James. 1983. *Professional Imperialism. Social Work In The Third World.* London: Heinmann.

Mohanty, Manorjan. 2001. "On the Concept of Empowerment." In *Social Development and the Empowerment of Marginalized Groups: Perspectives and Strategies.* Debal K. Singha Roy. ed. New Delhi, Thousand Oaks, London: Sage p. 19–23.

Parker, Stephen, Jan Fook, and Bob Pease. 1999. "Empowerment: The Modernist Social Work Concept Par Excellence." In *Transforming Social Work Practice: Postmodern Critical Perspectives.* Bob Pease and Jan Fook eds. London and New York: Routledge. p. 150–157.

Rowlands, Jo. 1998. "A Word of the Times, but What Does it Mean? Empowerment in the Discourse and Practice of Development." In Haleh Afshar. ed. *Women and Empowerment: Illustrations for the Third World.* Basingstoke: Macmillan Press.

Singha Roy, Debal K. 2001. "Introduction." *In Social Development and the Empowerment of Marginalized Groups: Perspectives and Strategies,* Debal K. Singha Roy. ed. New Delhi, Thousand Oaks, London: Sage. p. 1–18.

Sabune, K., Sawyer, L., and Eyoma, I. 2001. *Afrikaner och arbetsmarknad. Spelar färgen roll?* Stockholm: Afrosvenskarnas riksförbund.

Thomsson, Helene. 2002. *"Feministiskt integrationsarbete-eller vem ska definiera vems behov?" In Maktens (o)lika förklädnader: kön, klass & etnicitet I det postkoloniala Sverige.* Stockholm: Atlas.

Chapter 20

The Empowerment of Women and Productive Backyard Projects in Mexico

Esperanza Tuñón Pablos

Introduction

In light of the crisis that has affected rural Mexico during recent years, rural productive projects and micro-businesses have acquired relevance as mechanisms with which to combat poverty and generate development in general. At first, these projects were led by men, as the heads of families, without contemplating women as active and productive protagonists of the campesina unit of production. This created a huge disparity within the family in terms of access to the various productive resources (land, credit, technical support and training), placing the women in an inferior and subordinate position (Zapata and Mercado 1996). Solutions were sought initially using a Women in Development (WID) focus which views the woman as the center of the maintenance of a subsistence economy in which she continues to perpetuate the hegemonic gender norms assigned to her sex. Due to her "vulnerability" the woman works a double or triple day and thus becomes a passive recipient of development.

At the end of the 1980s, Gender in Development (GID) was incorporated into the world agenda (Young 1991; Schmukler 1998). This framework departs from the concept of recognition of the subordinated relationship of women, taking into account their other essential positions such as belonging to a social, ethnic group and/or a community in general. GID promotes efficiency and the identification of opportunities for improving gender inequalities in development policies, projects and programs; analyzing gender roles and diverse tasks, responsibilities and opportunities for access to resources; and benefits to decision making for men and women (FAO 1998).

In Mexico, productive projects directed towards women have in the main had a WID focus. Nevertheless, conditions are opening up so that the central aspects of a GID focus can be incorporated into these projects. We are specifically referring to training for the management and elaboration of projects, productive, technical and administrative training and advice, research of the productive areas with economic possibilities for success and location of regions with the greatest potential for supporting women's employment (Costa 1995).

Women become involved from the first planning stages of the project, recognizing their productive role and identifying the obstacles to their own participation. This allows them to design mechanisms aimed at overcoming these obstacles via specific activities, as well as to search for ways to break down the resistance from men. They also propose structural changes in the balance of power between men and women (Rowlands 1997).

Planning with a gender perspective allows women to actively participate in the productive sphere and from there on the aim is to achieve the incorporation of the interests of women and men in the development process. This focus has as its starting point a recognition of the local reality and the identification of the problems, needs and aspirations of all involved, so as to prioritize the activities to be undertaken in the communities (Alfaro and Mendoza 1999; Blanco and Rodríguez 1999).

For this reason, productive projects with a gender perspective respond to the needs and concerns of women regarding participating actively in development, allowing them to also analyze the power relationships which occur within a society. In doing this, they strengthen the area of liberties for women and their right to make decisions in terms of their own interests. This contributes towards countering the diverse discrimination related to their sex. One objective of the GID focus is the valuing—on the part of both women and men—of women's work in the productive sphere as well as in the home. It is hoped this will provide an incentive for the participation of both in the productive and social activities of the community (Karremans 1994; Rivera 1996).

In this sense, real development must seek to find new principles and ways of relating between people and communities, and must manage to modify attitudes and practices. The GID focus seeks to contribute towards changing the position of women, proposing measures that satisfy their practical needs and leading them, in a strategic manner, towards interests that permit their empowerment. This implies giving them greater power and control over their own lives, as well as elements of consciousness-raising, the development of self-confidence and greater access to and control over resources.

We believe that one prerequisite for the process of empowerment is to get out of the house and participate in some form of collective enterprise which has the possibility of being successful, as this tends to develop a sense of independence, competency and agency among the women. As Leon (1997) points out, the creation of small voluntary groups where there is a strong sense of identification among the members is fundamental, given that the participants obtain valuable experience and confidence for leadership via the activities they carry out.

For their part, the "external agents" of this process contribute towards putting into operation the process of empowerment, simplifying the strategy of communicating women's needs and priorities, encouraging them to take a more active role in the promotion of their interests and contributing elements so that they question the practices and social orders which rule their lives. Although people who undergo this process do so at their own rhythm and according to their situation and history, it is possible that those who have enjoyed greater liberty and access to opportunities may undertake the process of change more easily than others (Alfaro and Mendoza 1999).

The facilitation process requires that the external agents adopt a focus and methodologies which are participatory (group meetings, discussion workshops and exchange of experiences. The aim is for women, as social beings, to begin to see with new eyes, viewing themselves as historical beings with the capacity for change and the ability to change themselves, deciding for themselves and demonstrating their self esteem (Zapata, Mercado and López 1994).

The application of a GID perspective requires both the individual and collective commitment of those involved in the project, for the sake of creating opportunities or situations for the empowerment of women, gradually altering the relationships of power between men and women.

Experience Developed/Gained

In 1997, we began the "Production and Gender Project" directed at 100 women in five rural communities in the municipality of Macuspana, Tabasco, Mexico. Three of these communities are of Chol origin and two are mestizo.[1] The project began by supporting ten groups of women in a backyard productive project of raising suckling pigs and, in the year 2000, it was broadened to include, in one of the communities, organic horticulture as a diversification of the backyard industry.[2]

The objective of both projects was to contribute to the health and nutrition of the women from the harvest of various products from their own backyard and to strengthen their organizational and self-management processes. Both projects incorporated a gender perspective, with the aim that the women would gradually appropriate equally the technical as well as the organizational process of their project and would thus strengthen their own organizational skills and abilities.

Throughout the whole of the first year's work the team from El Colegio de la Frontera Sur (Ecosur)[3] detected and attended to the problems that arose in these groups: problems related to organization, feedback from the technical training and the management of the financial resources of the project. A first task was to facilitate the creation, by the women, of a space of their own where they could meet, train, discuss and share experiences dealing with the various aspects related to their organization as a group where they could explore knowledge and technical skills they needed to develop and practice, as well as the management of their financial resources. They attempted to optimize the conditions to strengthen women's participation in the project and the incorporation of the family as a whole. In this way, the women gained confidence, increased their self-esteem, broadened the range of opportunities for their own development and generated family and community well being.

We began accompanying the groups, carrying out a pre-diagnosis of the situation for women in the area. We found that the majority of the women were involved in domestic and productive work and in the raising of their children; nevertheless they had no opportunity to participate as a group nor to express an opinion in their own words about the productive projects of which they were beneficiaries. It is necessary to remember that as a result of the activities for which these women were traditionally socialized, they perceived themselves and were perceived as incapable of independently carrying out various tasks which are outside those stipulated by the traditional terms of reference. This was the first time they had been presented with the possibility of organizing themselves to achieve a common objective, to interact beyond the spheres of their homes and to assume the responsibilities that are implied by a certain grade of autonomy.

The methodology designed for this task implied taking into account the daily lives of the women in their private sphere, and consisted of periodic visits to the communities to establish trust, to encourage the women's participation in assemblies and to run organizational and technical training workshops. In all these spaces the aim was to facilitate the exchange of ideas among the women themselves, always from a basis of valuing their knowledge and experiences.

This work allowed us to gradually demonstrate how the social construction of gender results in inequality with the woman being disadvantaged. As Aguilar (1999) points out, while men learn to make decisions, face the consequences of those decisions, and to value themselves, the women learn that other people decide and act on their behalf. As a result, the masculine gender is awarded many more social liberties than the feminine gender, and these liberties of movement, decision-making (personal and group), as well as the assumption of representation of the groups and ability to access the use of resources, constitute areas of inequality for women.

Here, the process of accompanying presented us with a huge challenge: to provide the women with the basic instruments and tools that would permit them to incorporate a gender perspective into their daily lives, to then lead them to the beginning of a process in search of equity in relation to the community participation of both men and women and in making decisions in relation to their productive projects—which would result in access to the services, goods and resources that said project provided. The construction of this space made it possible for these women to exchange experiences, expectations and concerns common to all of them, as well as, through the proposals put forth during the meetings and the dynamic of the project itself, to reach levels of reflection about their lives and identity which they had not previously attained.

To achieve this it was necessary to promote access to resources through the creation of instruments, the appropriation of new technologies, time, meeting places and a way of transmitting the messages that were selected as being relevant and appropriate for the women. These resources meant that we had a strategy for ensuring that the limitations (products of the existing differentiated processes of gender socialization) would not affect women's participation.

In this fashion the women gradually appropriated the porcine project which developed in two stages: one of familiarization and identification of the possible needs and priorities (via workshops which helped ensure that the recognition, potential and development of the women were explicit); and another of strengthening and consolidating the spaces for group organization and technical training for the producers, through workshops programmed according to the needs detected in the communities; and secondly, through implementing a framework for the meetings: roll call, information about activities carried out and general matters. This mechanism permitted us to promptly detect problems experienced by the groups and the specific training needs of the women, and this facilitated the process of appropriation of the project.

Another key aspect of the process has been the emergence of leadership qualities that are displayed by those influential in the process and contribute to the creation of socio-affective and work conditions between the female and male participants in the groups and organizations. This led to the realization of the stated goals and the construction of collective meanings, which in turn give meaning to the proposals for change that are the crux of the relationships between the participating individuals.

The work with the groups enabled them to acquire a momentum of their own and they began to hold their meetings without our presence. Nevertheless, each community has its own rhythm, demonstrated by the fact that just as there are groups that are barely finding their way, there are others who now resolve their internal conflicts and are in a stage of consolidation. One element that stands out in the most successful groups is the presence of natural leaders with whom we feel it is now necessary to develop a specific program of training and consolidation, and at the same time to encourage a consciousness within the group space to support the emergence of new leaderships in the medium term.

At the start of the productive projects, the situation and positions of the women in the communities were the traditional ones, with the private sphere for them and the public sphere for men. Thus, women were used to attending some meetings to listen, but not to participate, nor make decisions for themselves. This situation gradually changed in the majority of the groups, given that it is now recognized that women are capable of making decisions about their projects. In the same fashion they have developed skills they did not have before, including the appropriation of new technology both in the porcine production (management of breeding, detection of pregnancy in the pigs, gestation, assistance in birthing, feeding, caring for the suckling pigs, castration, cutting tails and teeth and weighing the suckling pigs) as well as in the production of organic vegetables (construction of beds, preparation of organic fertilizers and bio-pesticides). Even if this has not been homogenous in all of the groups, we can affirm that each day more women are developing their backyard projects.

The Impact of the Projects

To date, the pig project has had a significant social and economic impact on the communities, reflected primarily in the increase in decision-making by women, the strengthening of the technical training, participation of the women in the family economy, and learning about resources and development of skills for relating, both within and outside the community. In relation to the horticultural project there have been achievements in terms of the incorporation of new knowledge into daily life, the development of skills for adopting new technologies of production, and the benefits demonstrated by the women of having various products for consumption (chili, parsley, coriander, onions, tomatoes, carrots) near the house without having to go to the lot, or the shop, which could be up to three kilometers away.

Through the project's operation, women have developed skills considered to be "male" in appropriating technology to apply in their projects, and have fortified their capacity for decision-making and in turn their self-esteem, as is demonstrated by the following testimonies from the women themselves about their experience:

> We learned to look after the pigs, feed them, clean them, give injections and assist at births. I learned by myself, watching how they did it, I only went once to watch and then I assisted a birth all by myself . . . vaccinations, castration . . . I do it all.

> For me it is an asset having my vegetable garden closer, before we had to walk to the lot or send someone early to bring us the things, now we don't get so tired and we have more ingredients for our meals.

> Making the beds for the garden is men's work, but the women can also do it because it benefits the whole family.

The family plays an important role in these projects, especially the children, and in some cases, husbands participate in specific activities of the project. In this fashion, the productive project reinforces an interactive educational process within the domestic group.

Among the new activities that women identify as those they are able to undertake since they started their projects and which we call "features of empowerment" are: the strengthening of their participation and capabilities for decision-making and autonomy in relation to, for example, going to the bank and to meetings, signing checks, participating in assemblies and deciding how to spend the money they earn, among others.

> Before, I went to the meetings but I didn't make decisions. I was just a lump sitting there. Now thanks to the meetings that we have, I participate in the meetings at the school.

> My husband made fun of me, saying that I lead because I don't know how to keep quiet anymore. Now if I don't like something I know I can participate and they have to take me into account.

Since the women have their own income from the sale of the suckling pigs and excess vegetables, they have been able to buy things and to attend to matters for which they previously did not have the resources. Thus, some now collaborate in the education of their children by buying them school materials and clothes; they use the money earned to pay for accommodation for their children in nearby communities so they can continue their studies, contribute towards improving the conditions of their homes and acquire various goods that would be beyond their means if it were not for the income from the productive project:

> Now that I had money, I bought clothes, vegetables, and perfume. I've saved half of it to spend little by little.

> Now that I have money, I can buy what I want. I bought a little tape player. The children asked me for it, and now they'll work more happily.

> I'm happy. I like having money in my pocket and even more so because it's mine.

> I manage the money, because it's mine. I can spend it how I want and he (my husband) doesn't say anything, but when he gives me money then he wants to know.

The previous testimonials demonstrate that the productive project is increasing both the technical capabilities of the producers and the possibilities for the women themselves to become the subjects of their own personal and community development. We believe that in this process the accompaniment with a gender perspective has been a significant factor in that the space appropriated for the meetings allows the women to share their problems. They find among themselves solutions to their conflicts and develop attitudes of solidarity when problems arise due to the situation and the position they now have in their homes.

In terms of the risks and challenges for the consolidation of this experience, we must point out at least the following five:

- The continuity of government funding and/or alternative sources of resources for the productive project.
- The maintenance of technical assistance, and a guarantee for the provision of the necessary resources and of access to the market for the project's products.
- The strengthening of production of other produce in the backyard, to guarantee food security and family consumption.
- The consolidation of the organizational structure of the women's groups to allow them to become increasingly more self-managing.
- The preparation with a gender perspective of the present leaders as well as the identifying of emerging leaders.

Conclusion

We observed that the social and economic impact of the project is reflected principally through the dynamics during these years. The producers created a space of their own for reflection, organization and decision-making, which is why the women can express their sense of belonging to the project. They have involved their families in the different activities and have created a positive effect in their communities by demonstrating that the women's groups are capable of setting up and managing productive products.

The experience to date, developed through studies with a gender perspective, has demonstrated that dealing with the specifics of women's work enables making the necessary adjustments to the productive projects and their daily lives in such a way that these two areas become complementary and result in economic benefits and family integration.

Another characteristic of the work is that we defined the productive project as the main focus, and then through that focus, we incorporated the gender aspect as one more element to be considered in the operation of the project. That is, we aimed to understand and support the women in the search for solutions to the difficulties they often faced in attending to their productive project, and in doing so, incorporated reflection as to the necessity they felt to fulfill the hegemonic gender norms imposed on them as mothers, wives, domestic workers for their own family, and in many cases assistants to their husbands in their work on their lot.

At present the producers clearly express their appropriation of the productive projects, and report having managed to involve their families in the various activities, while they maintain control over the process. Another positive effect on the communities relates to the demonstration of the relevance and capability of the women's groups to manage the productive activity. Nevertheless, we believe that the consolidation of these types of projects occurs in the long term and that it is fundamental to support the day-to-day tasks of the groups in such a way that they may develop their capacity for autonomy and self-management.

We believe that incorporating the gender focus into productive projects is generating conditions favorable to equity between genders, as traditional patterns are ceasing to be reproduced in these communities, and the effects of the project are resulting in signs of empowerment in the women. This last factor, even though it is not generated in the short term, occurs gradually, from managing to get the husband's permission to work in the project to culminating in the men's recognition that female participation is a woman's right.

Achieving gender equity is a long, slow process, which furthermore requires that those who work in this field as external agents be profoundly respectful of the time and rhythms of the producers. For us, as facilitators of the process, the former implies a social commitment, and contributing with this grain of sand to the achievement of gender equity is one of the great challenges of the third millennium.

Notes

1. These communities are: Melchor Ocampo 2nd.Section, Chivalito 2nd and 4th Section, Palomas and Allende Bajo.

2. This project was supported financially by the Fondo Nacional de Empresas de Solidaridad (FONAES) (National Fund for Businesses in Solidarity) and technically by El Centro de Capacitación Agrícola y Forestal (CECAF) (the Center for Agricultural and Forestry Training).

3. The College of the South Frontier (El Colegio de la Frontera Sur) is a public research and postgraduate center located at the south border of Mexico with Guatemala and Belize a part of the Ministry of Science and Technology of México. Web: http://www.ecosur.mx

References

Aguilar, L. 1999. *Lo Que Comienza Bien Termina Mejor: Elaboración De Propuesta Con Enfoque De Género*. Serie Hacia la Equidad. no.1. San José, Costa Rica.

Alfaro, C. and B. Mendoza. 1999. *Si Lo Organizamos, Lo Logramos. Planificación De Proyectos Desde La Equidad*. Serie Hacia la Equidad. no. 3. San José, Costa Rica.

Blanco, L. and G. Rodríguez. 1999. *Candil De La Calle Y Luz En La Casa Hacia Una Gestión Y Gerencia Con Equidad*. Serie Hacia la Equidad. no.7. San José, Costa Rica.

Costa, L. N. 1995. *La Mujer Rural En México*. Beijing: Comité Nacional Coordinador Para La Conferencia Mundial Sobre La Mujer Acción Por La Igualdad, El Desarrollo Y La Paz. Unpublished.

Food and Agriculture Organization (FAO). 1998. "Género Y Desarrollo Rural: Programa De Capacitación Para Técnicos Y Extensionistas Del Sector Agropecuario, Modulos I, II y III". In *Proyecto Apoyo A Las Mujeres Productoras Del Área Rural En El Marco De Un Enfoque De Género*. San José, Costa Rica:FAO.

Karremans, J. 1994. *Análisis De Género: Conceptos Y Métodos. Informe Técnico.* Turrialba, Costa Rica:CATIE.

León, Magdalena. 1997. ed. *Poder Y Empoderamiento De Las Mujeres.* Bogata: TM Editores.

Rivera, R. 1996. *Desarrollo Rural Sostenible, Manual Para La Elaboración De Proyeotos.* Venezuela: Nueva Sociedad,

Rowland, J. 1997. "Empoderamiento Y Mujeres Rurales En Honduras: Un Modelo Para El Desarrollo." In Magdalena León. ed. *Poder Y Empoderamiento De Las Mujeres.* Bogota: TM Editores. p. 213–245.

Schmukler, B. 1998. "La Perspectiva De Género En Los Proyectos De Desarrollo y Su Diferencia Con La Perspectiva De Mujer y Desarrollo." unpublished mimeo.

Young, Kate. 1991. "Reflexiones Sobre Como Enfrentar Las Necesidades De Las Mujeres." unpublished mimeo.

Zapata, E., M. Mercado and B. López. 1994. *Mujeres Rurales Ante El Nuevo Mileni.* Tecoco: Colegio De Postgraduados.

——— and M. Mercado. 1996. "Del Proyecto Productivo a La Empresa Social De Mujeres." *Mujeres En El Medio Rural.* Año 6(13): 84–128.

Chapter 21

Mainstreaming Gender into NGO Work: A Case Study from Nigeria

Patricia Daniel

Mainstreaming gender is not a new concept: it has been discussed as part of the development agenda over the last decade and much of the pioneering work was brought together by an Oxfam initiative (MacDonald et al. 1996). By mainstreaming we mean here a systematic approach to promoting gender equality/equity, whether at the institutional or project level. The term mainstreaming has become more widely used since the Global Platform for Action on Women was published by the UN International Women's Conference in Beijing. Mainstreaming is one of the elements highlighted in the chapter on institutional arrangements (United Nations 1995). All countries who have signed the Platform for Action are required to demonstrate to what extent they have progressed on key strategic objectives and actions to improve women's well-being, status and life chances. Yet, as Page argues, "unless different interpretations of 'equality' are explored and negotiated we will not move forward on mainstreaming" (1997: 42).

The wide recognition of the principle of gender mainstreaming has led many donors to assume that the "gender agenda" has now been addressed and that funds can be spent on other areas. However, while the case for mainstreaming may have been theoretically established, actually putting the principle into practice has been a different matter. Gender cuts right to the heart of people's identity, their values, attitudes and behavior, their private and public relationships. Quite naturally, the majority of people wish to avoid confronting unacceptable truths—particularly if this is likely to affect power, privilege or protection, which they have inherited through culture, religion or class.

Many designated "Women's Officers" in non-governmental organizations (NGOs) around the world have found that working as a gender change agent often means being isolated and powerless (Gianotten et al. 1994) and there is no longer sponsorship money to attend training courses where change agents can find mutual support and exchange good practice. Kabeer's deconstruction, in table 21.1, provides a useful analysis of the different elements of institutional life that need to be addressed for change to be effected: rules, activities, people, resources and power (Kabeer and Subrahmanian 1999: 14–15).

Table 21.1 Elements of Institutional Life to Address for Change to be Effected

Element	Explanation and Importance
Rules	How things get done; official/unofficial rules; what helps things in the institution run smoothly; rules look "natural."
Activities	What is done in the institution? Activities are governed by rules; institutional practices; activities may continue social inequality.
People	Who is included and who is excluded in activities; inclusion is determined by rules and activities; exclusion reflects social inequality.
Resources	What is used or produced and what inputs and outputs are involved.
Power	Who makes the decisions; decisions are determined by rules and activities; power determines allocation of resources.

Source: Kabeer and Subrahmanian 1999: 14–15.

Yet most analyses of institutional change remain at an abstract level and we are left with little practical guidance of how to address the problem in a systematic manner in the workplace. Often, practical measures tend to address one, rather than all aspects (for example, businesses involved in Opportunity 2000, a government initiative to encourage more women into business, focused on one area such as recruitment, training, or communications), although this is not to say that such an approach may not have significant impact on other areas (Business in the Community 1992). Exceptions to a piecemeal approach include the European Commission's work on mainstreaming in the public sector. This starts the process at the corporate level and includes training as a key component in the development, implementation and evaluation of corporate plans in an iterative process (European Commission/Equal Opportunities Commission 1997). This process is similar to the much simpler Gender Quality Action and Learning cycle (GQAL) developed for a large indigenous NGO, the Bangladesh Rural Advancement Committee (Stuart et al. 1997). At a more grassroots level, the

GQAL cycle involves training workshops for each work-team to identify issues to be resolved, followed by action planning, monitoring, evaluation and new issue identification as the cycle continues.

This chapter will describe and analyze the process undertaken by CRUDAN (the Christian Rural and Urban Development Association of Nigeria) to integrate a gender perspective into its work. This took place within the framework of a DFID (UK Department for International Development) funded program: Capacity Building for Democratic Development (CBDD). CBDD comprised a series of courses over three years, designed to help build the capacity of non-governmental and community-based organizations in Nigeria to respond to the needs of the community groups and associations they work with called the Generic Training Program. The Centre for International Development and Training (CIDT), part of the University of Wolverhampton, UK, was contracted through CBDD to work in partnership with CRUDAN, which is a national training provider. The aims of the partnership were: 1) to develop training courses, materials and other support mechanisms for twenty-six member organizations in the General Training Programme; 2) to strengthen the capacity of CRUDAN itself through a Human Resource Development Strategy; and 3) to share experiences and learning to the benefit of both organizations.

Table 21.2 Workshop Objectives for Institutional Development

Objective Level	Desired Outcome
Personal	Explore personal attitudes and responses to the gender agenda and develop a personal action plan.
Team	Develop a more coherent team approach through sharing experience, values, skills and ideas.
Project	Develop a greater understanding of gender analysis and its importance within project and program development.
Community	Explore practical strategies for future work with partner agencies, CBOS/NGOS, training courses and community members.
Institution	Develop an Organization Action Plan

Source: Compiled by Author.

Gender has been one of several key areas of development which the two partners have worked on together over the past two years. Many lessons have been learned and we hope that they will be both of interest and value to other development organizations.

CRUDAN mainly serves the Middle Belt Zone of Nigeria but is developing a presence in the South and the North through the appointment of regional (zonal) facilitators. At the outset of the partnership, CRUDAN was very male-dominated, with women only in subordinate roles on the administrative/support side. Light-hearted but undoubtedly sexist innuendo and behavior was common.

Training staff worked long hours, were often away from home and the regular working week was six days. It was claimed that the nature of NGO work made it non-conducive to the recruitment of female facilitators. Early trainers from CIDT (UK) were male—with the exception of one female British trainer who was not able to deal successfully with the ethos of the organization.

Gender was identified on both sides as one focus for institutional development, as part of the Human Resource Development Strategy. All new facilitators were to be trained to deliver a gender perspective through the Generic Training Programme. As a first step, a workshop was held in October 2000 for the CRUDAN training team, designed and facilitated by one of the CIDT staff members. The specific objectives of the workshop are in table 21.2.

The overall objective was to enhance CRUDAN's capacity to equip Community Based Organizations (CBOs) and NGOs with the skills to promote gender equity and awareness in their work with poor communities in rural areas. Through this work, they hoped to help increase the capacity for poor people in rural areas to raise their own standards of living (the CBDD goal). So we hoped to see the impact of the process not only on CRUDAN as an organization itself but for CRUDAN to have an impact on other organizations.

The two-and-a-half-day workshop included a range of awareness raising, analysis and planning activities (Daniel 2000). Space was provided for exploring what Kabeer (1994: 266) calls "the personal dimensions of social change"— since experience has shown that this element has to be addressed before other issues can be taken on board. Introductory activities explored the influence of gendered socialization on participants' perceptions and their use of language, and compared myths about women with the reality. A case study was then used as a basis for analysis of gender roles, status, access and control, interests and needs. The intention was not to promote one particular gender analysis framework but to provide the chance to try out several tools that could be useful in community development work. Participants then worked together to develop checklists of changes they would like to see in grassroots communities and to suggest strategies that could be used in the short and long term. Immediate feedback indicated that the approach and content had been effective in achieving the objectives. For example, one participant said, "An excellent workshop of candid information sharing and learning," while another said, "Good to do this as a team and come up with a team action plan."

The Organizational Action Plan highlighted the possibility of gender mainstreaming CRUDAN's work through the following key areas: 1) the Generic Training Programme, 2) working through the Church to raise awareness, and 3) influencing change at the community level. Because of the additional support (the partnership) provided through CBDD and CIDT for the Generic Training Programme (GTP), this area was seen as the obvious target for the CRUDAN team to concentrate most of its efforts in the first instance. Detailed indicators were set for developments in this area of work.

The plan was reviewed after a six-month interval. Already a number of changes could be identified within the GTP, with regard to what the team *itself* did. These included: 1) an increase in the number of women attending (due to highlighting this in the invitation letter to organizations); 2) encouraging participation of women in group work and plenary sessions; 3) use of gender-neutral language by the facilitators; 4) use of gender-aware case studies; and 5) challenging overtly sexist comments and attitudes among the participants.

However, the review also highlighted the fact that the impact so far on the member organizations' practice in the field was negligible. Gender integration had been one of the indicators for the recent monitoring visits but the issue was dealt with only at a superficial level. For many organizations the concept of gender was unclear and for others it remained at the level of gender balance in numbers of staff. Some women's organizations had started to recruit men because of this misconception! The team felt that this was because the General Training Programme participants had not had the benefit of a dedicated course on gender awareness. This should start from the basics and involve learning to use some of the key tools of analysis on roles, access and control which they themselves had worked through in the in-house training. It was therefore agreed to plan a GTP course on gender.

A checklist for gender equality in organizations had been elaborated from the first workshop. This had not been used as part of the monitoring visits. While the team found the checklist was appropriate for CRUDAN itself and for some of the larger, more established NGOs on the Generic Training Programme, they felt that for many of the CBOs it was simply too advanced and threatening. It was agreed to develop a more basic list for those member organizations, which could be upgraded with time.

Review of the checklist that was developed highlighted some of the changes that needed to be made within CRUDAN itself as an organization and the second action plan focused much more on internal institutional development.

Another major obstacle to the promotion of gender equity that was identified during this review was resistance from the clergy—key partners in CRUDAN's work—and this provided a focus for future planning.

Mainstreaming

As the partnership between CIDT and CRUDAN as part of CBDD was now coming to an end, it was important to mainstream the gender strategy process so that gains made could be sustained—and built on—without external support. The team of facilitators recommended that the process now be embedded in the main management system of the organization. Essentially this consists of quarterly meetings with the whole team of facilitators, a process which sets and reviews targets for all areas of operation. This includes targets for the five geographical zones, each of which is now managed by one facilitator from the team.

Targets are recorded and reviewed in one of two systems—the Management Information System (MIS) and Organizational Capacity Indicators (OCI). Logically, from this forum, the Executive Secretary takes all decisions, actions agreed upon and performance reviews forward to the Board and the Trustees, to the Annual General Meeting and other key events with members. As part of the quarterly management meetings, the structured nature of the gender review workshops—continued reflection, analysis, action planning and target/indicator setting—needs to be retained. The importance of having an action plan was highlighted at the first workshop: "Without the plan itself the issues may get lost but the plan will act as a reminder and help to refocus us."

Table 21.3 Second Action Plan Targets

Action Plan Targets
Recruitment of more female facilitators.
Gender balance in the Board and Trustees.
Integrating gender into the five-year strategic review process.
Gender-disaggregated statistics (membership, staffing).
Gender-disaggregated evaluation of all training courses.
Family-friendly conditions of service.

Source: Workshop Discussions.

This Action Plan was reviewed after nine rather than six months because of Moslem-Christian conflict in the Middle Belt of Nigeria during the latter part of 2001. Again, while certain targets had been met, others had not. To a large extent this depended on the (lack of) full involvement of management in raising gender as a key issue to be addressed among the Board and Trustees, in a review of the constitution and the priorities of the organization. At the level of personnel management, however, promotion of female administrative staff had been effected and the right to one-week paternity leave had been established. Staff had also become more aware of the need to control their workload and spend time with their families. Analyses of the course evaluation forms by gender had been found useful both in identifying different responses between male and female participants and also in identifying other important factors affecting the level of participation in courses: one particular example is the low level of literacy of some female participants.

We can look at the impact of the strategy at different levels: on the institution itself, on the individuals who work there and on the organizations it works with. Reflection on impact was included as part of the two review workshops discussed above. Over time a number of small but significant changes can be identified at the institutional and personal level.

Generally, the staff demonstrates a higher level of confidence and commitment in addressing gender in all areas of their work. Self-perception, perceptions of gender differences and of the relative importance of men and women have been influenced by the gender strategy process and are reflected in these quotes from participants:

Increased understanding of how women can be mistreated and undervalued.

Seeing men and women as 'human beings' and not assuming stereotypes.

Understanding my role as facilitator has nothing to do with biology.

I value my wife/daughter and their role/importance in the family.

Allow (sic!) equal participation at work and at home.

With regard to their children, several staff members also emphasized a change in attitude and practice:

I am more aware of the socialization processes which could lead to gender inequality and as a result I treat my children (male/female) equally.

Educate my children on roles to be generic, not gender specific.

See our children as equals and not as male and female.

Practice what I preach.

Personal changes are reflected in the development of gender-sensitive practice within the workplace. There is now a better balance in the team of full-time facilitators between women and men (2:3) although the senior headquarters team of three is still exclusively male. CRUDAN draws on a small pool of associate trainers to help run courses and this group also includes women. Compared to many NGOs, this is an area where CRUDAN has demonstrated a certain level of success. In addition, it was felt that:

Addressing gender has enhanced the team spirit of CRUDAN.

The team approach was very rich in information gathering and effective for awareness raising.

Having had team training I now feel more confident to challenge team members on gender issues.

It is interesting to note that it is the team moving forward the gender process in the face of some managerial resistance to change—a grassroots movement supported and developed by team training.

CRUDAN promotes gender equality especially in identifying workshop participants and encourages organizations to train women too.

Women are now more involved in church activities—for example, leading prayer sessions.

Ensuring gender-balanced composition of working groups during training.

Giving opportunity for more female involvement on the zonal committee.

Conscious use of gender-neutral language in writing—for example S/he or We, They/Their etc. in all CRUDAN documents.

Reminding gender-insensitive participants about their use of words and expressions.

Greater awareness in workshops of our language and bringing value to all participants.

Greater awareness when I go into projects of the impact on women and men, and the opportunities.

More critical about the target beneficiaries in project appraisal.

Making sure that any program will be constantly reviewed for equal opportunities/distribution/participation/status.

There is more respect for women now among senior management: we (women) are not always expected to make the coffee, we're given a voice, our opinions are listened to, we're given an equal role to play in an activity. Also, senior staff will speak out about gender in workshops with other organizations—they don't avoid the issue when it arises but deal with it positively.

At the first workshop, the nature of NGO work was discussed—long hours, a lot of travel, a heavy workload—none of which is conducive to recruitment and retention of female staff, since women still bear the main responsibility for domestic tasks and family care outside of work as well. However, despite the fact that NGO work has not altered, awareness has been raised about its effects on men, women and their families. Strategies have been developed to combat some of these effects and it is not uncommon for male staff members to pick up their children from school and bring them into work as an interim care setting.

Male colleagues have begun to be more aware of family needs and their own role there. Senior management is showing a good example—A. took a couple of days off after traveling to spend time at home and provide support to his wife and new baby.

However, there are still aspects of institutional change to be tackled if we are to implement Kabeer's analysis. While significant impact can be seen in questioning and changing the rules and activities within the organization, providing greater inclusivity for female staff (for example, the secretarial staff are now sent on day-release training), control and power still tend to lie with the male staff. At one meeting, a colleague said: "Let's be gender sensitive and ask Ruth to make the speech." "Gender-sensitive" often seems to be used to mean "let's give women all the work—except, of course, the job of deciding who does the work!" Against this should be highlighted the fact that a woman has now, for the first time in CRUDAN's history, been elected Chair of the Central Zone Committee, although men were in an obvious majority at the meeting. When she noted: "But I am a woman," the men replied: "So what?"

Having benefited from the on-going gender review process, the CRUDAN team members are now beginning to develop the same process for other organizations. Until recently their influence on participants in the Generic Training Programme has been largely in the nature of "role models"—both male and female—and at the level of classroom interaction. The six-day dedicated course on gender, which was proposed at the first review, took place in March 2002. The content was enhanced to include other key areas of work for CBDD and Nigeria, and it was felt these would complement the gender focus. These objectives included: 1) highlight gender and HIV/AIDS as development issues at individual, organizational and community levels; 2) develop and practice tools for gender analysis; 3) review and practice advocacy skills in relation to gender and HIV/AIDS; and 4) begin to assess organizational capacity in relation to gender, HIV/AIDS and advocacy.

Activities included: a range of analytical tasks, role play and case studies about gender; visits to HIV/AIDS projects and the chance to examine this topic in relation to gender as a key element in both cause and effect of the disease; working in groups to develop an advocacy campaign around a gender issue or HIV/AIDS itself and analyzing problems related to change and strategies to overcome these. The objectives of the course were perhaps too ambitious.

What became very clear through the first delivery of the new course was that some of the facilitators still had much to learn about how to introduce and explore the key concepts of gender equity and development with a heterogeneous group of participants. In other words, although their own personal level of awareness and commitment had been raised, they still needed to develop specific professional skills in gender training. The lack of preparation and mentoring in this particular aspect was a flaw in the support that was provided by the partnership. Hard lessons were learned and changes were successfully implemented in the delivery of the second course. However, this experience does strongly indicate the need for on-going, in-house gender training support—especially since new facilitators missed out on earlier workshops.

A general action planning and review cycle was already integrated into the Generic Training Programme. This served as a system to support participants and member organizations to apply their learning, monitor their progress, and identify the impact of the program as it developed. During each course the participants reviewed their previous action plan and drew up a new one on the basis of the new experiences and skills gained in the present course. This plan was taken back to their organization to be implemented. Examples of action plans, which emerged from the gender training course, include the following responses by category.

For personal action, participants planned to, "Create awareness about HIV/AIDS in my family—it's not just a health issue; to carry out advocacy for girl-child education on the plateau; facilitate teamwork and equity in sharing of responsibilities, both in families and communities."

For organizational action participants planned to, "Teach members how to use the gender analysis matrix; promote gender equity—try to see that both men and women participate in decision-making. Both parties should have equal rights to develop their skills and potential, and consider gender balance even at the policy making level."

For community action, participants said, "The community I work with is highly chauvinistic. I intend to make them see they cannot depend on one leg alone since they have amongst them equally talented women; involve both men and women in planning and implementing projects targeted at women; run a meeting with stakeholders on the topic HIV/AIDS in relationship to gender; and create good home-based care for widows and orphans living with HIV/AIDS.

None of the participants was in any doubt as to the difficulty of the task. As one of them noted in their action plan, "The change envisaged may be slow. Men may be reluctant to get involved in women-oriented projects or be unwilling to allow women to freely participate. We will need continuous review of the gender analysis in our projects and activities to help women and men draw up conclusions and make decisions."

In June 2002, the CRUDAN team carried out a final field visit to assess the general impact of the Generic Training Programme on the participating organizations. This included looking at organizational capacity for promoting gender according to the checklists developed by the team and revised with participants during the course.

At this stage, the team will be able to check how far individuals and organizations have been able to put their plans into action. While it is highly likely that the member organizations will continue to need support and guidance in promoting gender equity, there is a real potential for beginning to transform grassroots communities through the sheer number and range of organizations involved—for example: YMCA, Jos Urban Ministry, Ujam Agricultural Cooperative Society, National Cashew Association, Centre for Gender and Rural Development, and the Country Women Association of Nigeria.

Another important outcome has been the shaping of the training approach. In the initial workshop, some members of the team expressed fears about the appropriacy of the training they were to receive, as it was provided by a white, Western woman from a British university. They said, "The concept will be treated in a way that is 'un-African,'" and "I want to understand how to raise awareness about gender equity in Nigerian society."

In fact these fears were not realized, since the materials used drew on Nigerian and African statistics and scenarios. The activities were highly interactive, enabling the team to exchange views, analyze situations and then carry out communal planning for their own development and training work. They were thus able to apply the concepts and tools to their own needs. Within the first action plan, one objective was to continue "to develop a Nigerian approach to gender training."

Methods, Materials and Female Role Models

Through the Generic Training Programme, the team was able to integrate case study material drawing on real situations which highlight gender roles and the impact these can have on effective development. In addition to case studies, a variety of group tasks, as well as role-plays, were already integrated into the program. These activities are well suited to exploring gender issues as long as facilitators ensure that groups are evenly mixed and that all participants feel comfortable about contributing. Sometimes working in single sex groups can be useful.

A decision was also made for trainers to work in mixed pairs to develop and deliver training modules about gender. An important element was the early identification of the role of male trainers in the process. Promoting gender equity should not just be seen as important for women to undertake; men in organizations have important insights, too. Men are often in the majority and hold powerful positions within organizations. Therefore having male champions of gender equity is even more likely to be effective. Male trainers can cite examples where they have shifted their own views and behavior, have been able to convince others, or have seen a real benefit in partner organizations where practice has changed:

> I recall Dan spoke about how gender stereotypes for boys get established and the sense of loss, or being different, that came when he was chided by an uncle for wanting to be in the kitchen with the women cooking and suddenly—age four—this was not what boys did—the sense of being cut out of that women's circle. He also spoke about men's advocacy role for women in the work place —linking it to how he wanted his daughter and his sister to be treated, his pride in their work achievements and how it irked him when they experienced discrimination on gender grounds. We had such a good debate and I felt it was very helpful—Dan's contribution gave the men who were more in favor of this thinking the chance to voice their opinions out loud despite the dominant/dominating males who were more reactionary. Also in the session it meant the women did not feel they had to be protagonists and challenge men—the men were able to do this amongst themselves because a man was opening up the topic and relating it to his own personal journey (Diana Ray, CIDT trainer, personal communication 2002).

The increase in the number of female facilitators, and the fact that they are developing the confidence to work on challenging issues with large mixed groups, has also provided good female role models for participants.

Working Through the Church

Membership figures for CRUDAN show a high male to female ratio. This raises the question: what does CRUDAN actually offer women? Is low membership related to women's lack of information or their perceived rights to take independent action? Joint membership of husband and wife has begun; this may be a promising area to pursue—thinking of more family/couples events that can also provide opportunities for raising gender awareness.

A major challenge is resistance to change among the clergy and the Church leadership itself. Unfortunately the Church accepts and incorporates into its own practice some of the worst aspects of gender discrimination, instead of confronting them. Thus, well-established cultural norms and values become even more entrenched as they are perpetuated in the name of religion. One example of this is the treatment of widows in Nigerian society. It is commonly believed that it is the woman's fault if her husband dies. She is immediately disinherited of her goods and property by her husband's brothers and turned out of her marital home. She is unlikely to remarry because of the stigma attached to widowhood. The Church condones this practice, reinforcing the stance of traditional leaders and chiefs.

CRUDAN, as an independent Christian organization, is well placed to introduce gender and development issues within the church in a non-confrontational manner, to influence theological thinking and church practice in Nigeria. Taking the plight of widows as a case study during a CIDT workshop on advocacy skills, the CRUDAN team highlighted a range of possible actions—awareness raising, good practice examples and pre-marriage counseling about wills and pensions. In addition, participants suggested:

> Advocate for widows to be treated with justice and dignity: 'valued not victimized,' and 'highlight the positive gains for the future—widow's children saved from street crime, not lost to the Church' (Qenawi and Carter 2001).

At a more general level, the issue of gender and development needs to be presented within a biblical perspective in order to make it acceptable and effective, as there are risks for the clergy in gender advocacy—losing support, creating rifts in the congregation, even preaching the wrong message. CRUDAN has developed a discussion paper that can form the basis of advocacy and education work on gender with their trustees, the new zonal steering committees, theological institutions, the clergy and church associations. The paper quotes from both Old and New Testaments to emphasize that men and women are equal in the eyes of God: "There is neither Jew nor Greek, slave nor free, male nor female, for you are all one in Christ Jesus" (Galatians 3: 28 quoted in Harvey, 2002: 6). We must question and compare everything to the Bible—this includes the way we view, value and treat men and women in our society. The main thrust of the Bible is towards leveling (see Isaiah 40: 3–4) and not the maintenance of birth-based privileges. Therefore we must assess our culture against this background. (Harvey, 2002: 9).

As another member of the team said: "The use of biblical injunctions has had a tremendous impact on the clergy." For myself, as a non-Christian, white, Western woman, I have learnt a great deal from working with the CRUDAN team. In general, though, the experience has reinforced my belief that there is more to unite us than to divide us—and that multiple perspectives can be a source of creativity rather than conflict.

Conclusion

The process undertaken with CRUDAN has been an organic one, but it is possible to step back and take an overview of objectives and targets past, present and future using a Logical Framework Approach. A great deal has already been achieved and it is hoped that CRUDAN's experiences can provide encouragement to other organizations.

Further support may well be needed in order to strengthen the work of the individual facilitators as they attempt to develop targets for gender equity work in their own geographical area, with their own steering committee and local groups. In addition, it is likely that participant organizations from the Generic Training Programme will continue to need support to embed a gender perspective into their work. However, in describing the process undergone so far, it is possible to identify some key elements to bear in mind for the future such as: 1) team training—including team planning—is a key element of developing a gender strategy; change takes time and needs a mechanism to sustain it—the on-going cycle of reflection, planning and review provides this; 2) a documented action plan helps to remind and refocus; 3) senior management needs to be fully involved and an automatic mechanism for taking team decisions forward has to be established; 4) both male and female staff are fundamental to the success of the process; 5) action strategies need to be developed from within the specific context and related to specific needs; 6) donors need to become more aware of the realities of addressing gender at a grassroots level; 7) dedicated training on gender is necessary to develop basic tools and self-awareness; a gender perspective also needs be integrated into all training courses; 8) gender trainers are not made overnight—staff needs specific training on how to deliver a gender course, and on-going support; and 9) the Church can be an important conduit for change if appropriate materials and training can be provided.

Finally, it is important to highlight the valuable role of an external facilitator in the challenging process of mainstreaming gender. She or he can—much more easily than a member of the team—insure that discussion is objective, inclusive, egalitarian and does not skirt round the difficult issues. She or he also stands as an objective arbiter and motivator of the process itself. Sometimes it is a frustrating task, but worthwhile when the team declares: "You really have made a difference." The process continues and, despite the problems, as the team says, "Never give up!"

References

Business in the Community. 1992. *Opportunity 2000 Information Pack*. London: Business in the Community.

European Commission/Equal Opportunities Commission. 1997. *Mainstreaming Gender*. Manchester: EOC /EC.

Gianotten, V., V. Groverman, E. vanWalsum and L. Zuidberg. 1994. *Assessing the Gender Impact of Development Projects. Case Studies from Bolivia, Burkina Faso and India*. London: Intermediate Technology Publications.

Kabeer, N. 1994. *Reversed Realities: Gender Hierarchies in Development Thought*. London: Verso.

——— and Subrahmanian, R. 1999. *Institutions, Relations and Outcomes*. London: Zed Books.

MacDonald, M. ed. 1996. *Reader on Mainstreaming Gender in Organisations. Oxfam Gender Learning Workshop*. Oxford: Oxfam.

Page, M.L. 1997. *Women in Beijing. One Year On*. London: Community Development Foundation Publications.

Ray, Diana. CIDT Trainer. 2002. Personal Communication.

Stuart, Rieky. 1997. *An Action-learning Approach to Gender and Organizational Change*. Dhaka: Bangladesh Rural Advancement Committee.

United Nations. 1995. *Global Platform for Action from the UN Fourth Conference on Women*. New York: UN.

Chapter 22

Rethinking Female Entrepreneurship Discourse: The Perilous Problems of Cultural Mythicizing in a Globalizing Society

Julius Kikooma

About a decade ago, the first generation of globalization theorists argued that globalization had become an influential paradigm in the human sciences; a paradigm that replaced debates on modernity and post modernity in the understanding of socio-cultural change and as a central thematic for social theory. These theorists, in an edited volume by Robertson and Featherstone (1995), treat globalization as a broad process permeating the whole world, with far reaching ramifications covering economic, political, and cultural dimensions of contemporary life. That is, they argue that as the global replaces the nation state as the discursive framework for social life, new socio-cultural processes and forms of life are emerging. In fact, Featherstone (1995), arguing from this perspective, reiterated that the inward movement of people, as well as images and information from places which for many in the West were constructed through oversimplified racist and exotic stereotypes of 'the Other', means that new levels of complexity are introduced to the formulation of notions of identity, cultural tradition, community and nation. Such is the time when global flows are assuming more centrality than national institutions. A cautionary note is in order here. Although due to globalization we necessarily have greater dialogue between various nation states, blocs and civilizations, Featherstone (1995) argued that this is a dialogical space in which we can expect a good deal of disagreement, clashing of perspectives and conflict, not just working together and consensus.

In the past, our conceptions of both society and culture drew heavily on a tradition that was strongly influenced by the process of national state formation; and now the dissolution of traditional boundaries of every kind by the globalization process has blurred distinctions that once seemed clear. Consequently the conception of independent, coherent and stable culture has been made irrelevant. Hermans and Kempen (1998) argue that in apparent contrast to these trends, contemporary conceptualizations in the discourse have continued to use a tradition of cultural dichotomies such as north-south, east-west and individualism-collectivism. Yet those cultural dichotomies do not and cannot adequately meet the challenges posed by the process of globalization. Indeed Hermans and colleagues suggest that cultural dichotomies by their nature are oversimplifying and insensitive to the tensions that are typical of the relationships between cultural groups.

In this chapter I take the view that contemporary conceptualizations of culture bear re-examination and possible revision in light of globalization. I contend that such a view is plausible given the argument that despite the magnitude of the global 'revolution', it remains the case in the discourse that the male oriented definition of reality is upheld as the legitimate world view and such processes of dichotomization, classification, codification, categorization and taxonomies have been used to further enhance the divisions among humans, race, ethnicity and gender.

In discussing research on women's experiences of entrepreneurship in Uganda, I have adopted the idea of a myth of the entrepreneur in order to examine and reflect on the ways in which women challenge and transform gender relations in their work and organizational attempts. In a note on globalization, Bakate-Yusuf (2002) made a rather sensational, if not emotional, point that myths express relations of power woven within the fabric of the human world, as well as the tears that occur within this fabric. She argued that on a cultural level, myths allow us to explain how culture is both about stasis and flows, developed out of dialogic exchange, chaotic interactions and uncertainty. Therefore, from this perspective of myths, one begins to see that what was once perceived as truth is ideologically motivated, and belongs to a specific culture and mode of perception.

The idea of a mythical entrepreneur cannot be overemphasized. Snyder (2000) in her book on women in African economies highlighted the issue of myths regarding female entrepreneurs in Uganda. For instance the following myths were revealed:

- Women simply supplement the family income which men provide;
- Women's businesses are too small to matter to the national economy;
- Husbands give start up money for their wives' businesses;
- Women who have money leave their husbands;
- No husband wants his wife to work.

In Africa a discourse that relies on such myths has dire consequences. First, Snyder explained that contributions of women are not recognized. More fundamentally however, planners have insufficient information about women's capacities to create wealth and their investment in human capital as contributions to national and household economies (2000).

Ogbor (2000) argues that entrepreneurship has long been theorized within a gendered framework corresponding to the dominant essentialist male folklore. Moreover, as Ogbor reckons, very few attempts have been made to provide an understanding of the mechanism that perpetuates this dominant ideology or its effect on entrepreneurship discourse and praxis. Instead, research continues to center on the mechanisms through which the experiences of females (both in entrepreneurship and other aspects of organizational life) can become amenable to suit the dominant paradigm of entrepreneurship or become assimilated into what is considered appropriate entrepreneurial behavior. Here I have in mind such studies as those that have constructed typologies of entrepreneurs in order to group entrepreneurial behaviors (see for instance Langan-Fox and Roth, 1995). Ogbor correctly says that these studies have repressed and neglected how societal biases created the particular conditions in which the minority (who in this case are women) business owners have found themselves. Needless to say, this has indeed sustained traditional dichotomies, oppositions and dualities (between male and female), in which masculine concepts of control, competition, rationality and dominance are celebrated.

It is important to note what Ogbor highlighted in a critical review of the discourse. He argued that female participation in entrepreneurship is reasoned to be in direct contrast to entrepreneurial norms as a result of gender qualities such as male achievement versus female subjugation and male dominance versus female submissiveness. Thus, ideologically speaking, entrepreneurial ideas in the discourse have been influenced and controlled by gender biased strategies and metaphors supporting a patriarchal conception of nature.

Changing Perspectives or Changing Africa?

In Africa, as Robertson (1997) pointed out, the history of women in trade stands at the intersection of gender, business and labor history, with all the contradictions implicit in such a location. In addition, these traders experience the full impact of an increasingly unified world economy in which some have been marginalized further and a few have expanded their businesses beyond local or national borders. However, it is important to note that from Snyder's work, as from Robertson's, we see not only the fundamental importance of women's work in creating a new world, but also how they overcome difficulties by using collective strengths predicated upon the old world and push the boundaries imposed upon women to mediate and transform the new situation. And as the two authors passionately argued, in so doing, women have offered a reconstruction of gender that has transformative value for society. These transformations have brought new ideas of self-respect among women that are helping to engender societal reconstruction.

Below I provide an abridged sample of Snyder's (2000) qualitative case study data from stories of African women entrepreneurs in Uganda that she used to analyze the ways in which women are central to the configurations of gender and entrepreneurship in Africa.

Case Study: Victoria Muwanga—A Woman Who Pioneered in a Non-Traditional Enterprise

A *matatu* (minibus) passenger bound for Ntinda from Kampala was deeply impressed with his driver's safety consciousness. "Drives carefully. Does not screech the brakes," he commented as he moved forward to congratulate the driver. Astonished, he blurted out, "Are you really a woman?"

Driver Victoria Muwanga is one of the micro-and small-scale entrepreneurs of Uganda who are trying to find new ways to enhance their productivity and income. Victoria knows that driving the most common form of transport, the *matatu*, is labeled as a "men only" job in Uganda. "You need to see the shock on people's faces, especially men, who enter my bus unknowingly and later discover a woman behind the wheel. But now they like my driving", she says.

Victoria is Kampala's first female *matatu* owner-driver. She is unwilling to be sidelined because she is a widow and determined not to become the burden to her family and community. When some men say that she is a *muyaye* (delinquent, unreliable or uncouth child) her reaction is clear:

"I do not care because I know I am not a *muyaye*; I am just earning an honest living. I have to survive. Women should not fear what people say. It is what you think, how you carry yourself that matters. Nothing is going to stop you from being a woman, a wife, a mother just because you drive a taxi!" (Snyder 2000: 187–189.)

When Victoria Muwanga decided to venture into the transport business, Snyder argued, little did she know that it would be such a big issue. She not only captured the traffic officers' attention but also won public acclaim. Out of this, arguably, highly atypical case in Uganda, Snyder was able to clarify the artfully worked nature of gender meanings, showing how Vicky, as she was fondly called, comes to sense a social, but taken for granted, world of gender expectations, and how she has to work hard to fit herself into them. Through this and other case studies, Snyder is able to produce a list of standardized expectations about gender as a social product in this society. Although most people may assume some expectations about gender in this part of the world, it is through the atypical cases like that of Victoria who finds such an assumption problematic that such a listing becomes possible. It was because of her parents that allowed some form of egalitarian upbringing that Victoria had early exposure to such skills as driving. Girls would normally not be expected to learn how to ride a bike let alone drive which would later become Victoria's critical skill in life!

It has been noted that within the household, gender relations are a critical mediating factor between the processes of capital accumulation and social reproduction (MacGaffey 1991; Obbo1980). In addition, gender relations are not static but are continually negotiated (Schoepf & Engundu 1991). Snyder (2000), using these cases, argues that women who contribute most to Uganda's economy joined the market economy formally dominated by men and became central actors in it and that is why men lost some of the power they held in the household. In other words, the economic crisis embraced the position of many Ugandan women especially poor and peasant women and weakened the basis of men's domination and as a result women came to be accepted as legitimate economic actors. However, she notes that nonetheless, the gender hierarchy that is part of 'African' culture enabled men to retain much of their control of the home and its income. In many realms of African life, this has been acknowledged as threatening to overwhelm the survivor capabilities of even the most determined (Robertson 1997). There is now a growing literature on the subject of gender-marked division of labor and other aspects of the situation of African women. However, it is my contention that Moore's (1993) three questions about the situation of women surely still need to continue to be addressed in the African context as they are elsewhere: 1) Who has control over women's lives? 2) What kind of return do women get for their labor? 3) What sorts of choices are open to women as they negotiate their positions in the world?

I explore these questions in a study which sought to construct the psychological attributes of individual females who founded new enterprises. The purpose was to group entrepreneurial behaviors necessary for entrepreneurship. During 1998 and 1999, a total of 330 establishments were founded by women entrepreneurs in Kampala, Uganda and its outskirts. Women participated voluntarily in this study. Influenced by the Langan-Fox and Roth (1995) criteria for sample selection, participants had to meet the following criteria: must be the owner of the business; must have founded the business themselves or with a partner; must have between two and fifty employees. These criteria, it was assumed, ensured that the proprietors carried the accompanying financial, psychic and social risks which entrepreneurship entails according to Hisrich (1990).

Methodology

Data were gathered by means of a largely open ended structured questionnaire based on earlier studies that had developed measures of psychological attributes (e.g. Langan-Fox and Roth 1995; Frese, Fay, Hilberger, Leng and Tag 1997; Frese 1995 and Frese & Zapf 1994). Using the questionnaire, participants were told that the researchers wanted to learn more about why and how people decide to start a business of their own. In addition the questionnaire included self-rating of the respondents' levels of satisfaction with their current entrepreneurial venture as well as questions on the form of business (e.g., sole proprietorship, partnership, and limited liability corporation) that they were pursuing. Number of initial employees, initial funding sources and financial planning processes were included. Respondents were queried about organizational characteristics, current annual sales and length of operation. The entrepreneurs were also asked to provide information about their age, education, number of businesses started and whether either of their parents had owned their own business.

Table 22.1 Initial Capital Investment

Uganda Shillings (Ush1000=US$0.55)	Number of Respondents	Percent
10,000 and less	17	5.3
12,000–52,000	39	12.2
60,000–150,000	60	18.8
240,000–450,000	68	21.3
500,000–1 million	81	25.3
1.35m–5million	33	10.3
6–10 million	18	5.6
16 million and above	4	1.3
Total	320	100

Source: Field study.

Table 22.2 Contribution of the Initial Capital Investment From Self

Uganda Shillings	Number of Respondents	Percent
No contribution	19	6.8
Below 25,000	55	19.7
30,000–100,000	71	25.4
150,000–190,000	21	7.5
200,000–300,000	43	15.4
310,000–490,000	8	3.0
500,000–1 million	36	12.9
Above 1 million	26	9.3
Total	279	100

Source: Field study.

Fifty-seven percent of the sample were sole proprietors with 18.6 percent having more than twenty employees; 21.8 percent own the businesses in partnership; 56.3 percent had plans to go into other business ventures with their businesses and 55.3 percent had other occupations in addition to their business. Age ranged from twenty-five to fifty-five, with most of them in the age range of twenty-five to thirty-five; 49 percent were married; and 7 percent were divorced; 14.3 percent had no children; 36.6 percent were secondary school educated to at least higher secondary level. All had been in business for over three years. The entrepreneurs were in the various types of business such as beauty salons, textiles, retail food stuffs, produce selling, travel bureaus, lodge, farming animal/crops and hard ware. The data were analyzed using the Statistical Package for Social Scientists (SPSS). Tables 22.1 through 22.10 report the results of the questionnaire. In terms of size and growth of the business, the majority of the respondents indicated that their sales had increased in the past year by significant percentages as table 22.5 shows.

In order to empirically make explicit the concerns in Moore's (1993) questions identified earlier on, I selected those entrepreneurs (n=91) in the database who said that other initial contributions to their start up capital came from their husbands and the statistics were revealing as the following tables show.

Table 22.3 Source of Start-up Capital

Source	Number of Respondents	Percent
Family member	75	32.5
Husband	80	34.6
Partner	34	14.7
Loan	18	7.8
Friends	24	10.4
Total	231	100

Source: Field study.

Table 22.4 Family Participation in the Business

Category of Employees	Number of Respondents	Percent
Unpaid Family Member	61	21.9
Paid Family Member	76	27.2
Other paid workers	142	50.9
Total	279	100

Source: Field study.

Discussion

Research on women and entrepreneurship has tended to follow two paths. First, although certain small businesses pose constraints on female as well as male business owners, it is women who predominantly own these businesses (Mirchandan 1999). Here structural differences are used as explanations for the situation of female entrepreneurs. That is, structural differences between the businesses which women and men operate are seen to produce the gender differences in their entrepreneurship patterns. But with the insight of the feminist lens, it is easy to see that it is business structure rather than gender that is the prime determinant. Second, the research literature is awash with studies claiming that women and men create different types of businesses and control them in different ways. In this case, women and men are seen to choose the structures and industry focus within which they work. That is, women set up different types of businesses depending on their orientation towards their businesses and their families (Mirchandan 1999).

Table 22.5 Business Size and Growth

	Number of Respondents	Percent
Number of Employees	N=242	
1–20	231	95.5
21–35	9	3.7
36–50	2	.8
Sales Growth Indicators Since Start-Up	N=315	
Increased Sales	132	41.9
Decreased Sales	23	7.3
Stable Sales	74	23.5
Fluctuating Sales	86	27.3
Annual Percent Sales Increase	N=63	
Below 5 %	4	6.3
5–10	6	9.5
10–15	0	0
16–20	14	22.2
25–35	7	11.1
36–50	15	23.8
Above 50	17	27.0

Source: Field study.

Table 22.6 Marital Status of Respondents

Status	Number of Respondents	Percent
Married	71	78.0
Divorced	2	2.2
Separated	12	13.2
Widowed	6	6.6
Total	91	100

Source: Field study.

Table 22.7 Type of Marriage of Respondents

Type of marriage	Number of Respondents	Percent
Monogamous	54	66.7
Polygamous	20	24.7
Cohabiting	2	2.5
Not married	5	6.2
Total	81	100

Source: Field study.

Table 22.8 Responsible Person for Business Finances

Responsible Person for Business Finances	Number of Respondents	Percent
Self	64	70.3
Husband	13	14.3
Accountant or Controller	12	13.2
Other	2	2.2
Total	91	100

Source: Field study.

Table 22.9 Has Your Husband or Any Other Person Encouraged You in Your Business?

	Number of Respondents	Percent
Yes	76	83.5
No	15	15.5
Total	91	100

Source: Field study.

Table 22.10 Do You Need Permission from Your Husband to Make Decisions?

	Number of Respondents	Percent
Yes	19	20.9
Sometimes	48	52.7
No	24	26.4
Total	91	100

Source: Field study.

Both of these orientations in the research literature are problematic because as Mirchandan (1999) noted, neither approach is able to provide an analysis of the interdependence of structures and gender. For instance, in the first approach, the employment structure is conceptualized as a set of variables that are independent of the gender of the business owner (e.g., firm size and industry focus). In other words, there is little analysis of how gendered processes may in fact shape the size of the firms, or the tendency to focus on certain industries. In the second approach, there is little analysis of how businesses in certain industries, for example, force individuals (both female and male) to behave in ways that typify the masculine work norm. Thus, it was Mirchandan's contention that in this approach, women and men are seen to have a set of traits and experiences that cause them to establish different types of businesses. It is pertinent to say then that such an approach does not illuminate how and why entrepreneurship came to be defined and understood *vis-à-vis* the behavior of only men.

The case study example of gender roles in Snyder's work and the results of the survey I conducted suggest that the types of women drawn to entrepreneurship vary according to the form of gender role stratification in the home and the workplace that exists in society. In addition, these findings bear directly on our understanding of how specific patriarchal constraints may lead to specific adaptations among women in the workforce. It is no wonder then that in societies that are strongly gender stratified like in the case of Uganda and where male authority is not easily negotiated, women with entrepreneurial ambitions may represent social outliers. That is why Victoria Muwanga, the matatu driver, was categorized as venturing into a non-traditional business. Such cases in Snyder's book have contributed arguably to a glamorized depiction of rising female self-employment in Uganda. This impression has tended to dominate the discourse on entrepreneurship where entrepreneurship as female self-employment has come to be taken as an alternative to some of the enduring concerns of women. But again we need to beware.

Feminist insights into gendered work have informed us that the construction of gender changes with economic shifts, and women's changing economic roles can change how women view themselves. Similarly, forms of male dominance and patriarchal ideology, like forms of racism and discrimination, mutate. The mutations are based on the changing needs of men and the dominant classes to keep control over those who have been subordinated in order to pursue economic and political goals. Can we say, then, after reading Snyder's book that female self-employment is likely to alter women's structural positions in the labor market or the household? We definitely need a continuing dialogue regarding the issue that relates female power and dominance. After all, Roberston's (1997) observation still holds. She observed that in Africa, embedded in the patrilineal, patrilocal, polygamous matrix, women were regarded by men as property. Men's categories appear to have dominated the societal ideology, which established oppositions devaluing women and justified differences in wealth. Even forms of wealth were differentiated when men had superior access to livestock, rated as most important and used as a form of currency.

The evidence from these studies suggests that there is a great deal of entrepreneurial talent, save for the constraints of societal stereotypes of what women can and cannot do. However, to the extent that entrepreneurial ideas are gendered, as Robertson (1997) argued, they themselves have become instruments of control over resources, over people and especially over the drawing of boundaries between the sexes.

The how story of entrepreneurship in Africa is of course complex. From the above explication of entrepreneurial experiences of female entrepreneurs we learn not just how aspects of culture may benefit commerce, but also how they may hinder it. The case studies provided by Snyder indicate the relative power of women and men and the wider forces they call upon in their negotiations of gender relations. By looking at entrepreneurs in 'the burning sun', or at entrepreneurs involved in roadside and market businesses as Snyder did, such studies not only expand our basic sense of the state of female entrepreneurship and how the phenomenon occurs in Uganda, but may also find some clarity about our often taken-for-granted beliefs about work, entrepreneurship and, indeed, organization in sub-Saharan Africa.

This chapter acknowledges the existence of structural differences between the economic positions of men and women. These differences are found in the uneven division of men and women's labor across the mutually dependent paid and unpaid economies. Yet it is the unpaid economy that tends to be invisible to policy makers until gender analysis uncovers it. In this case, this was made possible through the explication of the problematic nature of gender roles embedded in culture.

Conclusion

This chapter argues that a focus on gender as a process integral to business ownership, rather than a characteristic of individuals, is not only a desirable one but a plausible one. Such a focus, it is hoped, would allow researchers to pose a new set of questions about the experiences of women entrepreneurs as well as the situation of women in this part of the world. In terms of women and development scholarship, the paper responds to what Browne (2001) referred to as a large and slow moving paradigm shift related to economic growth in developing countries. As Snyder (2000) intimated, because development efforts at the macro level have generally failed to reverse or even slow poverty in the developing world, the role of micro enterprises in planning economic growth has increased in importance. Perhaps an important aspect of this shift involves a growing focus on small-scale entrepreneurs/owners of micro enterprises and specifically female-owned enterprises.

References

Bakate-Yusuf, B. 2002. "Globalization: A Note on One of the Myths of our Time." Presentation at CRD Damina School, Aug. 18–30. Kano, Nigeria.

Browne, K. E. 2001. "Female Entrepreneurship In The Caribbean: A Multi-site, Pilot Investigation Of Gender And Work." *Human Organisation* vol. 60 no. 4: 326–342.

Featherstone, M. 1995. *Undoing Culture: Globalization, Postmodernism and Identity.* London: Sage.

Frese, M.1995. "Entrepreneurship in East Europe: A General Model and Empirical Findings." In C.L. Cooper and D. M. Rousseau. eds. *Trends in Organizational Behavior*, Vol. 2. London: John Wiley & Sons.

———— and D. Zapf. 1994. "Actions As The Core Of Work Psychology: A German Approach." In H.C. Triandis, M. D. Dunnette and J.M. Hough. eds. *Handbook of Industrial and Organizational Psychology, Vol. 4.* 2nd ed. Palo Alto, CA: Consulting Psychology Press.

————, D Fay, T. Hilburger, K. Leng, and A. Tag. 1997. "The Concept of Personal Initiative: Operationalization, Reliability and Validity in Two German Samples." *Journal of Occupational and Organizational Psychology.* vol. 70 p. 139–161.

Hermans, H.J.M. and H. J. G. Kempen. 1998. "Moving Cultures: The Perilous Problems Of Cultural Dichotomies In A Globalizing Society." *American Psychologist,* vol. 53 no.10: 1111–1120.

Hisrich, R. D. 1990. "Entrepreneurship/Intrapreneurship." *American Psychologist.* vol. 45
no. 2: 209 – 221.

Kikooma, J. 1999. *Female Entrepreneurship: Findings From Successful Urban Women In The Informal And Self-Employed Sector.* Paper Presented at the Uganda Association of University Women (UAUW) National Conference. Kampala, Uganda. Nov. 25–27.

Langan-Fox, J and R. Susanna. 1995. "Achievement Motivation And Female Entrepreneurs." *Journal of Occupational Psychology.* vol. 68: 209–218.

MacGaffey, J. ed.1991. *The Real Economy Of Zaire: The Contribution Of Smuggling And Other Unofficial Activities To National Wealth.* London: James Currey.

Mirchandan, K. 1999. "Feminist Insight On Gendered Work: New Directions In Research On Women And Entrepreneurship." *Gender, Work and Organization.* vol. *6 no.4*: 224–235.

Moore, S. F. 1993. "Changing Perspectives On Changing Africa: The Work Of Anthropology." In R. H. Bates, V. Y. Mudimbe and J. O'Barr. eds. *Africa And The Disciplines: Contributions Of Research In Africa To The Social Sciences And Humanities.* Chicago: University of Chicago Press.

Ogbor, J. O. 2000. "Mythicizing And Reification In Entrepreneurial Discourse: Ideology Critique Of Entrepreneurial Studies." *Journal of Management Studies.* vol. 37 no.5: 605–635.

Obbo, Christine. 1980. *African Women: Their Struggle For Economic Independence.* London: Zed Press.

Robertson, C. C. 1997. *Trouble Showed The Way: Women, Men, And Trade In The Nairobi Area, 1890–1990.* Indianapolis: Indiana University Press.

Robertson, R. & Featherstone, M. eds. 1995. *Global Modernities.* London: Sage.

Schoepf, B. G. & W. Engundu. 1991. "Women's Trade And Contributions To Household Budgets In Kinshasa." In J. MacGaffey. ed. *The Real Economy Of Zaire: The Con-*

tribution Of Smuggling And Other Unofficial Activities To National Wealth. London: James Currey.

Snyder, Margaret. 2000. *Women in African Economies: From Burning Sun to Boardroom.* Kampala: Fountain Publishers.

Chapter 23

Women Entrepreneurs: A Challenge to a Gendered Economy

Elsje Dijkgraaff

Worldwide more and more women are entering entrepreneurial activities. What does this mean? It means that women are more likely to seek their 'own economic autonomy.' In comparison to men, women often contribute relatively more to the family income. And if you compare total earnings to spending in the family and compare who provides the direct cash flow to family expenditures women contribute more. Women often have smaller businesses due to the smaller capital inflow they can afford relative to men's business. Male owned businesses often have available more start-up capital due to the gender-stereotyped values of banking staff and moneylenders (Elan 2000).

Women's Entrepreneurship and the Economy

Women's entrepreneurship may provide a solution for women who are unemployed or underemployed, or for those who lack access to decision making opportunities or those who are underpaid.[1] If women decide to start up their own business they immediately feel the empowerment of self-determination, the ability of putting their ideas into action and experience the thrill of self-realization and economic autonomy. Economic autonomy is a major instrument in redressing the gender-imbalance of power in relationships with relatives, family and partners.

Female-headed business may promote flexibility in working time. Women's entrepreneurship contributes to the flexibility and freedom of choice women have when working on their own schedules. No outsiders direct them. They can decide for themselves where, when and with whom they like to work.

Women's entrepreneurship makes a contribution to economic development. The entrepreneurs contribute to the family income and, as such, have an impact on the development of the society. Within the Netherlands, for example, women are contributing 30 percent to the Gross National Product (EIM Research 2000). Worldwide, women's contribution to economic activities is often underestimated because it is invisible. Chambers of Commerce have just begun in the Netherlands to document the gender difference and the influence of this difference on business development. Global research on gendered success indicators for business development is indispensable for start-up activities (DEUCE 2000).

Characteristics of Women's Business

Women owned business has some unique characteristics with respect to risk, capital, growth rates and adoption of innovative business practices (e.g., flexible scheduling, IT). Women's attitudes toward risk may be the reason for lower bankruptcy rates. Women take fewer risks in business activities. They prefer to play it "safe," which may explain the phenomena of less bankruptcy among women entrepreneurs (EIM 2000). Researchers in Germany have done comparative analysis and found bankruptcy rates among male companies to be much higher than among female owned companies. Also they found that female-owned businesses had a higher success rate (Research Chamber of Commerce 2001).

Women use less start-up capital than men because a) they don't like to take risks and they make decisions on an outcome they cannot foresee; and b) banks, and lending organizations are patriarchally structured and gender-stereotyped. Because of the stereotypes, banks often do not consider women as serious business partners, which is a fallacy of judgment given the observed low rates of bankruptcy among women.

Women's businesses often start smaller, and when they grow, they grow faster (WEN 2002). If they need more staff they often choose female staff. These businesses contribute substantially to female employment and have a concrete impact on women's labor participation.

Flexibility in time is a highly valued new management policy, which takes into account the balance between work and family life. All these changing values are directly related to the participation of women in the labor force. Also, a trend in Europe is that 'output' is becoming more important than 'being on the spot'. Tele-working and new technologies are contributing to the freedom of action in work.

Female entrepreneurs are good team builders; they have an open eye for the well being of the staff; they care about personal problems; and they have an understanding of family conditions. Calamity leave and part-time work are often not points of discussion as they might be in a male dominated environment (FLEXEC 2000).

Today, every business is heavily dependent for their markets on information, communications and technology (ICT). World markets can easily be reached with ITC. Research has shown that more women than men communicate using the web and that men are more interested in using the internet in an instrumental way and women are more interested in the communicative tools provided by ICT (CONNECT E.U. project /I. T.W. 2000).

Some summary recommendations in support of these observations include:

a) Easy access to credit for women, especially when their companies have potential to grow fast; b) Reducing the stereotypical attitudes of banking staff is essential; and women need the support of lawyers (juridical support); c) Chambers of Commerce need to play an active role in de-stereotyping women's entrepreneurship and promoting women as serious business agents and agents of change; d) Successful businesswomen can act as role models for women start-ups and develop mentoring relationships and networks such as Business and Professional Women (BPW); and e) Women can use e-marketing such as *www.womenworldmarket.org* to find each others' markets and contribute to the development of Women Business Centers (WBC) where women have access to support and to the virtual marketplace.

Challenge to a Gendered Economy

The second topic relevant for women's entrepreneurship has to do with the fact that we all know women are still underrepresented in institutions of power and decision making. Women entrepreneurs, especially when they are able to play a vital role in the economy, will influence economic growth and transform an economy into a gendered economy. If we explain what is happening with women in the world through the concept of 'global gender apartheid' it may contribute to the clarification and transparency of their impact.

The International Training Center for Women (ITW) in Amsterdam, established in 1989, has always had to justify why we offer empowerment and management training to women worldwide. Many men especially from traditional sectors such as banking, accountancy and politics do not see any problem for women in business. They just don't understand what we mean when we talk about engendering the economy.

'Apartheid' was a clear concept in describing the huge inequality of access to all levels of society. We can use the concept to demonstrate that this inequality still exists with respect to women. The existing economy is built on a system of masculine values and we need persistence to transform a 'mind set' that we can define as a false mindset. The fallacy is in using the macroeconomic measure, per capita income, as the major determinant for progress and economic growth. In a gendered economy, other indicators of economic growth could be used such as: high child mortality rates reflecting a reduction of economic growth; economic growth redefined as availability of a good quality of life, long life expectancy, availability of clean water and access to schools and hospitals; investment in the public sector which would raise a country's score on the Human Development Index (HDI); measuring of 'unpaid labor' and household labor as an economic contribution to economic growth which would include gender specific work; output measured as criteria for progress and not the way of getting there.

In a gendered economy production is not focused on 'profit' for the sake of itself but stands for an economy of solidarity where 'win-win' relations contribute to economic development. The difference between short term planning and long term planning is taken seriously in a gendered economy. A gendered economy will focus on public investments; schools, hospitals, parks and the 'the quality of life' as well as the well being of humanity. In a gendered economy ethical entrepreneurship is essential and there is no place for a weapons industry. And the last tool for a gendered economy is: sharing information; don't hold back with the fallacy of 'competition'; it really brings you further if you share.

Information is very much like love: when you give it away, it grows . . . Let's do it!

Notes

1. The wage gap is a world wide phenomenon in all organizations at all levels.

References

CONNECT E.U. Project. 2000. Amsterdam: I.T.W Amsterdam. p. 5–30.

DEUCE Research Programme. 2002. "Inquiry Into the Wage Gap." European Union, p. 12–28

EIM Research. 2000. Rijswijk "Women and Gross National Product." unpublished. NL: Institute Micro Companies: 10–34.

Elan Magazine for CEOs/NCD. 2000. various issues. Amsterdam: Badhoevedorp.

EUFORA Network Organised by I. T.W at a European Level. *DG Equal Employment Opportunities.* Amsterdam: ITW. p. 3–15.

Mentorscope. 2000. *General Information Brochure.* Delft: Mentorscope Research Chamber of Commerce.

———. 2001. *Germany /Out of the Margin.* Amsterdam: Research Chamber of Commerce: 1–25.

WEN. 2002. *Women Entrepreneurs* (unpublished) Ph.D. Dissertation. Ruta Aidis: University of Amsterdam.

Part IV

Out of the House:
Entrepreneurship, Savings and
Networking as Empowerment

Chapter 24

Women in Business Networks

Catherine Komugisha Tindiwensi

Much research has been carried out and effort directed towards the empowerment of women, particularly poor rural women. The degree to which women are disadvantaged is influenced by factors such as age, social economic status, level of education, geographical location and physical ability. The category "women" does not assume homogeneity. Nevertheless women cross culturally are subordinate to men within the same groups, and this is a commonality shared by all women regardless of age, social economic status or religious background. This chapter shifts focus from poor women operating in the informal sector, normally with little access to productive resources, and representing a large percentage of the poorest of the poor, to businesswomen who operate in the formal sector and have moderate access to productive resources. The term businesswoman will be broadly used here to include professionals, consultants, farmers, processors, contractors, exporters and practitioners in any formally recognized occupation in the private sector.

The business networking model was originally developed for industrial markets where negotiations and face-to-face interactions are frequently observed. Inherent in this approach is the observation that parties engage in relationships and establish contact patterns as a basis to enhance the effectiveness and the efficiency of transactions (Hakansson 1982). Firms are linked together in a dense network of cooperation and affiliation. To suggest or even imply that firms do not have relationships is to ignore this fact. The critical factor, however, is that relationships cost time and effort to establish and maintain and are sometimes referred to as "market investments" and assets (Johnson and Mattson 1987).

Businesswomen have formed networks such as industry associations and other women's groups. The available data show that there are fewer women in such networks compared to their male counterparts except where the network is exclusively for women. This arises from two main reasons: First, most business sectors are dominated by men (except in household and domestic employment) and hence one is less likely to find women participating in business networks. Secondly, the majority of women spend most of their time on reproductive roles rather than productive roles. The reproductive sphere has prohibitive power relations within families that do not give women the opportunity to fully interact and exploit the benefits that would accrue from such networks. There is also sufficient evidence that women pay a higher "social price" in trying to balance the productive and reproductive roles and the majority end up giving insufficient time and energy to the enterprises they manage.

More often than not it is the women owned and managed businesses that suffer death or retardation at an early stage. Due to the nature of developing economies, the majority of the private firms are still small and this is more so for women owned and managed enterprises. A major characteristic of small firms is that they are owner managed, and this implies that the success of these firms mainly depends on the abilities and skills of the owners. This narrow line separating entrepreneurs from the enterprises they manage indicates that networking of the entrepreneurs is synonymous with networking of the enterprises they manage and vice versa. Research has shown that "working" women combine their industrial activities with their other responsibilities as mothers, child bearers and keepers, volunteers and homemakers. Given the access and time constraints women face, networks face the challenge of addressing network effectiveness and tackling how women owned enterprises can best be facilitated to grow amidst these constraints.

Definition and Types of Networks

Networking is the sharing and/or exchange of information, ideas, products, services, finances, resources, opportunities and social aspects. Through networks, businesswomen can advocate for policies that address their needs in addition to sharing information.

Networks have been broadly defined as a model or metaphor that usually describes a large number of entities that are connected (Easton 1992). Mitchell (1969) defined a network as a specific type of relation linking a defined set of persons, objects or events, while Van de Ven and Ferry (1980) described a network as a pattern of relationships within a group of organizations acting in order to achieve common goals. Relations are the building blocks of networks that include coordination through less formal, more egalitarian and cooperative means.

Networks have been placed into two broad categories: intra-organizational networks within organizations, and inter-organizational networks which refer to cooperation between organizational units. Studies show that networks can appear in various forms and at various levels. These may include:

- Social networks, defined in terms of patterns of communication and social interaction between and among individual social embeddedness of economic exchange. Granovetter (1985) believes that individuals may have an effective attachment for each other for its own sake.
- Strategic networks, defined as "long term" purposeful arrangements among distinct but related for-profit organizations that allow those firms within them to gain or sustain competitive advantage vis-à-vis their competitors outside the network.
- Supply networks, which serve organizations that convert raw materials into products and services. These networks evolved from the fields of supply chain management, channel management, logistics and lean supply/enterprise (Achrol and Stern 1988; Christopher 1992).
- Innovation networks, which create new products and services. Innovation networks can refer to regions which display relatively high levels of innovative activity, such as Silicon Valley in the US, or clusters of firms that engage in innovative related activity, for example, relatively large firms that share development work with their key suppliers or a federation of firms, none of which individually possess the full skill set necessary to develop, produce market and distribute a product.
- Learning networks are networks of collaborating and competing firms that help to increase the knowledge of their members within a specific technology or management practice. Such networks include industry trade groups and are formed to respond to rapidly changing environments as well as to meet the skill requirements and sustain and/or attain a competitive position in the market (Cravens et al 1996).

Despite the existence of different types of networks, the key elements of any network are actors, activities and resources (Hakansson 1982). Actors are defined by the activities they perform and the resources they control; they are connected to other actors via resources and activities. A relationship is developed as two companies build up activity links, resource ties and actor bonds.

Rationale, Strategic Issues, and Network Outcomes

Network theory is conceptually rooted in a behavioral theory of firm decision making and in a resource dependency perspective (Hakansson and Snehota

1990). Goals are achieved through social bargaining with existing participants, and organizations are dependent on the external environment for acquiring their resources.

Businesses are not independent, free-thinking, and free-acting individual units. They operate interdependently with others in complex networks. Their planning and thinking processes are affected by the past actions of those around them and evolve over time as they interact with other companies. Hakansson and Snehota argue that companies in business markets depend on their own internal resources and those external resources that exist in companies elsewhere in the network (1990). In *No Business is an Island*, Hakansson & Snehota (1990) observe that there are a "limited number of identifiable organizational entities (actors) in business to business networks between which there are exchange relationships."

Relationships developed in the networks are significant to the participants. In many countries, women's networks have resulted in policy reviews that have led to affirmative action for women. In addition, these relationships may reduce costs of exchange and production, promote development of knowledge of the respective parties give the parties some control over each other be used as bridges to other firms; be used when mobilizing partners against third parties (Johnson and Mattson 1987); and be used as bridges in accessing better markets, skilled labor and product development techniques.

Networks are formed to respond to rapidly changing environments as well as to meet the skill and resource demands to sustain a competitive position in the market. There are strategic issues that must be addressed at the network level to ensure that expectations of the network members are met. These include identifying specific competitive advantages networks can deliver. It is argued that networks are a source of competitive advantage. Networks have the ability to create a net of relationships with a potential for mutual complementary action, the ability to harness synergistic potential to the net in pursuit of a common goal, and the ability to identify how these advantages can be achieved by collective actions and the coordination of resources and skills at the level of the network (Cunningham and Gulligan 1991).

Relationships may be purposefully developed to achieve strategic goals, to gain competitive advantage and to strengthen the participants' core competencies. Network members attach value to network relationships that are in turn related to the expected outcomes and are a measure of network effectiveness. The major network outcomes are categorized into (1) Economic, which includes cost reduction, value engineering, investment quality, risk reduction and financial performance; (2) Strategic outcomes, which include time to market, core competencies, market position, strategic fit and customer satisfaction; and, (3) behavioral outcomes, which include flexibility, trust, social bonding, accountability, adaptation and dependability.

The African Centre for Women (ACW) of the Economic Commission for Africa listed the following as benefits that accrue from networks: access to market channels at national, regional and international levels, business opportunities within the region, sharing technologies, promotion and publicity, facilitating joint ventures, access to global business, exchange of skills and e-commerce (ACWECA 2001). Successful networks normally provide these benefits to the members. In Uganda, we collected testimonies from the Uganda Women Entrepreneurs' Association (UWEAL) members at a July 20, 2001 business breakfast. UWEAL is an organization that brings together women entrepreneurs. One member said, "[Networking] is the best thing that happened to me" (UWEAL Pers Com. 2002).

Barriers to Networking

In a network, modes of resource allocation transactions occur neither through discrete exchanges (markets) nor by administrative fiat (firms) but through networks of individuals engaged in reciprocal, preferential and mutually supportive actions (Powell 1990). The basic assumption of network relationships is that one party is dependent on resources controlled by another and that there are gains to be had by the pooling of resources. In essence, the parties to a network agree to forge the right to pursue their own interests at the expense of others (Powell 1990). Business relationships premised on the need to achieve bargaining power may be more aggressively competitive than is in their best interest. Keys et al. (1996) identified the major challenges facing networks as: uneven development, overly aggressive support, competition and conflict and the need for sustainability. Kenichi Ohmae (1989) suggests that a problem for managers when contemplating (or when involved) in strategic relationships is that of relinquishing or sharing control.

Biong et al. (1997) articulated why some firms do not want to engage in partnering relationships: (a) when they fear unilateral dependency on the other due to loss of flexibility in strategic choices, fear of opportunistic behavior of the partner and loss of personal or organizational control; (b) unless significant added value is proposed in terms of cost reductions, new sources of revenue, superior market position, development of new competencies and social rewards; (c) when other companies do not display the ability and motivation to fulfill the objectives of the relationship; (d) when partnering companies are small, unimportant, unreliable, lack an innovative outlook and generally have a low reputation; (e) if companies have low relational orientation due to inhibitive company policies, transaction-based reward systems, corporate belief systems, rigid organizational structure and restrictive flow of communication; or (f) in industries with rapid technological changes, large growth and many actors.

Major gender challenges also exist that would impede the success of the networks if not addressed. These issues are dependent and interactive and form a multiplex, socio-economic and cultural setback to enterprise growth and competitiveness. These include: (1) Companies with low relational orientation will be less inclined to engage in partnering relationships. From the gender perspective, low relational orientation could be due to restricted flows of information (Gemunden, Ritter and Walter 1997); (2) Women who do not participate fully in the networks in our study give a number of reasons. For example, lack of time due to heavy workload at home and lack of support from their husbands. The cost of "disobedience" is so high, particularly in the social context, that women opt not to participate. "In general, by relating to theories of inter-firm cooperation, the results suggest that companies (women) will not engage in cooperative relationships if the costs are perceived to be too high to alternative marketing arrangements" (Ritter and Walter 1997); (3) Women combine their industrial activities with their domestic responsibilities. This spread of efforts cannot allow the commitment required for networks to be beneficial. This divided attention explains partly why some women's enterprises are relatively unresponsive to competition, sales and size of employment, and ultimately tend to consume current profits and surpluses (Natukunda 1990); and, (4) Several women's networks have been formed and registered little success. They tend to be characterized by petty quarrels, lack of good leadership and selfishness over money matters. Conflict retards growth of an enterprise.

Networks and Affirmative Action in Uganda

Among the strategic issues women's networks need to address is affirmative action for women-owned organizations. Affirmative action always brings mixed reactions, but despite the problems the cost of affirmative action is outweighed by the benefit. Uganda's affirmative action at the university level is a success story from which a lot can be learned.

Our research indicates that women in every sector lag behind their male counterparts and that the magnitude of this disparity is significant. According to the UWFCT 1989 estimates, the overwhelming majority (about 95%) of women's businesses in Uganda fall below the staffing level of twenty persons. They tend to be linked to "petty" household related subsistence and retail trade activities (Natukunda 1990). The available information on small scale industries in Uganda shows that in Kampala women represent seven percent of the shareholders, seven percent of the management, and nine percent of the workforce in production units (Natukunda 1990). This is pathetic in a country where women comprise more than fifty percent of the population. The situation is not very different for developed countries. According to a study carried out in the U.S., only five percent of Fortune 2000 industrial and service company managers in U.S. businesses are women. The same study notes that over one half of the American population and 57 percent of the working population is female or minority or both, and a woman still earns seventy-nine cents for every dollar earned by a man (Ellis 1995).

The term affirmative action, because it is "loaded and tends to create strong reactions in people, negative and positive," is avoided in Uganda and elsewhere (Ellis 1995). It often creates mixed and extreme views. To some it may imply hiring a woman regardless of competencies while to others it implies extra efforts to increase the number of women in the pool of candidates under consideration in order to increase the chance of finding a woman. Some entrepreneurs argue that you don't need government policy to be competent saying,

> I've got a superior product, and I can compete on the strength of the product; I don't want to weigh in with a small business woman-owned category in order to win the business.
> —President, Boulder Software Development Firm

> I've never gotten anything because of being a woman-owned business. We should self regulate rather than having government regulate hiring practices to try to force people to do the right thing.
> —Susan Routt, President, Fibrotek Industries Inc. (Ellis 1995)

Some women entrepreneurs believe that underachievement of women is a matter of self-esteem and that as women gain confidence in their ability, they will have more confidence in (male dominated) business.

Stephanie Allen (Chair, Colorado Women's Chamber of Commerce) says that although small, the gains achieved through affirmative action are substantial enough that women and minorities aren't willing to go back. "The principles of affirmative action are valid; we still have sexism and . . . it is not ok for half of our citizens to be second class citizens" (Ellis 1995).

Way Forward For Women in Business Networks

There is need to create a greater awareness that business networks are market investment assets but that they have positive and negative aspects with regard to specific individuals. The pertinent issue for women in business is the balance between those positive and negative aspects. Women should join and form several business networks compatible with their special roles. By joining several networks they create more contacts and can establish strategic business relations in their supply chain that will enhance their growth and competitiveness.

Most policymakers have suggested that in order for women to have access to improved techniques and achieve economies of scale they reorganize and form themselves into small groups for the purposes of solving the problems of supply of inputs and product marketing. Women's groups alone are seen as less likely to improve the situation, though they can strategically act as "incubators" for this purpose. The ultimate goal, however, should be to bring more women into mainstream business networks that are currently dominated by men.

Efforts should be put into engendering the activities of business networks, particularly where males are the majority. This will facilitate both women's participation and the preservation of social harmony, particularly in families.

Networks are strong avenues for businesswomen to achieve and maintain competitiveness. It is important that proper selection of collaborative partners is done by ensuring that one joins the right network. Women's networks are very supportive and can be useful in boosting one's confidence, business focus and communication skills.

Women's networks facilitate the mentoring process. Mentoring can be a shortcut to career success because it provides a safe, protected environment in which one can learn. One benefits from the mentor's experience and being mentored by the right person is an important and viable bridge to success.

Networks provide the leverage/bridging capital that one needs to get ahead or change one's opportunities. Boissevain (1974) says this is about access to clout and influence and is the key to mobility. The problems of inadequate resources and social exclusion require connecting women to mainstream resources and services.

Women can form strategic alliances and valuable chain networks. This is done through establishing business relations as suppliers, buyers, distributors, marketing agents and service providers of the others' business in the network. Efforts could be made to include spouses of the women in the network. This will help them see the benefit to their part; they will gain a better understanding of network activities, and this understanding may reduce the antagonism in the form of prohibitive power in personal relations.

Networks as a collective unit can influence government policies that affect business growth and competitiveness. Women-owned firms should be facilitated to enable their organizations to reach maturity earlier. This will enable them to separate management from ownership, hence availing women time to attend to other roles without jeopardizing organizational growth and competitiveness. Affirmative action for organizations where women are decision makers should be sought and implemented. This will facilitate access to markets for goods and services produced by women-owned and women-managed organizations. There are still several cultural barriers that prevent women from owning property and hence productive resources and inputs. Policies that enable women's access to major productive inputs like land, skills and credit finance should be strongly advocated.

References

Achrol, R. S. and L. W. Stern. 1988. "Environmental Determinants of Decision Making and Uncertainty in Marketing Channels." *Journal of Marketing Research.* vol. 25 no. 1: 36–50.

African Centre for Women (ACW) of the Economic Commission for Africa (ECA). 2001. *Report on the Development and Reinforcement of Networking Among Women Entrepreneurs.* Togo: ACW

Blois, K. J. 1997. "When is a Relationship a 'Relationship'?" In G. H. Gemunden, T. Ritter and A. Walter. eds. *Relationships and Networks in International Market.* London: Elsevier.

Biong, H. 1997. "Why Do Some Companies Not Want to Engage in Partnering Relationships?" In G. H. Gemunden, T. Ritter and A. Walter. eds. *Relationships and Networks in International Markets.* London: Elsevier.

Boissevain, J. 1974. *Friends of Friends.* Oxford: Basil Blackwell.

Christopher, J. G. 1992. *Logistics and Supply Chain Management.* London: Pittman.

Cravens, David W., Nigel F. Piercy and Shannon H. Shipp. 1996. "New Organisational Forms for Competing in Highly Dynamic Environments: The Network Paradigm." *British Journal of Management* vol. 7: 203–218.

Cunningham, M. T. and K. Gulligan. 1991. "Competitiveness Through Networks of Relationships In Information Technology Product Markets." In S. J. Paliwode. *New Perspectives on International Marketing.* London: Routledge.

Easton, G. 1992. "Industrial Networks: A Review." In B. Axelsson and G. Easton eds. *Industrial Networks: A New View of Reality.* London: Routledge.

Ellis, Caron Schwartz. 1995. *Affirmative Action? Business Women's "Views Mixed".* Boulder CO: Boulder County Business Report.

Gemunden, H. G., T. Ritter, and A. Walter. eds. 1997. *Relationships and Networks in International Markets.* London: Elsevier.

Granovetter, M. 1985. "Economic Action and Social Structure: A Theory of Embeddedness." *American Journal of Sociology* vol. 91 no. 3: 481–510.

Hakansson, H. ed. 1982. *International Marketing and Purchasing of Industrial Goods,* Chichester UK: John Wiley Sons.

Hakansson, H. and I. Snoheta 1990. *Developing Relationships in Business Networks,* London: Routledge.

Johnson, J. and L. G. Mattson. 1987. "International Relations in Industrial Systems: A Network Approach Compared with a Transaction Cost Approach." *International Studies of Management and Organisation* vol. 18 no. 1: 34–48.

Keys, L.G., Alex Schwartz, Avis Vidal and Rachel Bratt. 1996. "Networks and Non Profits: Opportunities and Challenges in an Era of Federal Devolution." *Housing Policy Debate.* vol. 7 no. 2: 201–229.

Mitchell, J. C. ed. 1969. *The Concept and Use of Social Networks in Urban Situations.* Manchester: Manchester University Press.

Natukunda, Edith R. T. 1990. *Background Definitions and Role of Women in the Development of Small Scale Industry.* Kampala: Freidrick Elbert Foundation Workshop.

Powell, W. W. 1990. "Neither Market nor Hierarchy: Network Forms of Organisation." *Research in Organizational Behavior.* vol. 12: 295–336.

UGADEV/ACCORD. 1989. *Survey of the Small Scale Industry,* Kampala: UGADE/ACCORD.

Uganda Women's Entrepreneurs Association. 2002. Personal Communication. Kampala.

Van de Ven, A. H. and D. L. Ferry. 1980. *Measuring and Assessing Organisations.* New York: John Wiley Sons.

Chapter 25

Women's Entrepreneurship: The Empowerment of Women Through Enterprise Development Training

Angela Beigaruraho Bazaare and Juliet Nazziwa Musoke

There are many schools of thought about entrepreneurial behaviors. One school defines entrepreneurship as a management process and organizational philosophy that helps the entrepreneur to pursue opportunities and overcome obstacles in the open market environment. It can further be viewed as the process of starting a new or continuing an existing venture (Fry 1995). In this view entrepreneurship involves the thrill of taking an idea from concept to reality. The outcome is gratifying and fulfilling, either to the psychological needs, self-ego (e.g. through the accumulation of wealth) or by meeting social needs through interacting with people of all calibers.

Another school of thought defines entrepreneurship as the dynamic process of creating incremental wealth by individuals who assume major risks in terms of equity, time, and career commitment in order to provide value for some products or service. The products and services may not be new, but the entrepreneur, who secures and allocates necessary skills and resources, must infuse value (Ronstadt 1985).

Entrepreneurship is possessing the know-how to find, organize, and control resources as well as fulfilling personal goals through interaction with customers, suppliers, investors, workers and the people in the community and the government. It is a discipline that can be learned. Owning a business, investing one's personal capital, making executive-level decisions and maneuvering past the competition involves the thrill of risks and challenges. In this chapter the term entrepreneurship refers to the act or skill of setting up, managing and growing a business enterprise. The action of setting up an enterprise, although purposeful, should have a risk, emphasize innovation and new ways of doing things.

Our concern in this paper is why there are few women entrepreneurs in the formal sector and whether women's business activities reflect the entrepreneurial skills and spirit of starting, growing, and harvesting their businesses.

Ugandan Entrepreneurs

Women the world over have started enterprises and used the income to support themselves and their families. In Uganda, since 1986 there has been increased self employment among women, mainly because of wars, the AIDS epidemic, and a liberalized economic policy.

Women-owned enterprises in Uganda can be categorized into informal, micro-small enterprises and a few formal small-medium enterprises. Many of the informal enterprises are owned by non-professional and "semi-educated" women who have a limited appreciation of a structured form of business conduct, hence qualifying their businesses as informal. The informal enterprises are started as household and home activities to supplement family income; for example, many engage in tailoring, food preparation and processing, trading in surplus agro-based products and petty trade as well as traditional health care.

A good number of women-owned enterprises are also micro in nature, with a capital base of less than three million Ugandan Shillings ($US 1,677) and one to five employees. Some of these businesses are operated at home, such as animal husbandry, which includes poultry, piggery and zero grazing. Others are in market vending and cross-border trade in textiles and crafts. About 75 percent of women in this category are said to be in the trade sector (ILO/SLAREA 2001).

The few women in small-medium income levels are generally urban, fairly well educated, and culturally disposed towards the concept of business. Their enterprises are specialized with capital and include consultancy firms, law firms, clinics, education and schools, nurseries, import and export trade, printing, food processing and textile and garment making. Very few women have ventured into manufacturing and those who have are restricted to the traditional food processing sector: production of ghee, oil from groundnuts, sunflower, sim-sim and soap. However, even manufactured products are crude and are sold to large enterprises to be refined.

Information and statistics on the success of women in the informal, micro, and small enterprises (MSEs) are difficult to obtain. This sector plays a vital role in employment creation, improving the socio-economic status of women, as well as contributing to the economy of Uganda (Kasente 2002).

Some of the strengths of women's entrepreneurship in Uganda according to the Federation of Uganda Employers (2001) include: (1) Enterprises provide self-employment and means to earn a stable income to women who are unskilled, illiterate and have limited opportunities to join the formal sector. Over 70 percent of proprietors in MSEs work in their own enterprises; (2) Entrepreneurships enhance the socio-economic status of women. Women's MSEs contribute tremendously to the family income, to the education of their children and general welfare of the home and extended family. In urban areas the number of women owning property is growing. Women in MSEs now act as role models and mentors to the girl children who work as hand-help in the food and beverage enterprises; (3) MSEs act as a safety net to women in the formal sector who wish to supplement their income. They also support those who continue to lose employment in the formal sector due to restructuring and retrenchment in the now liberalized and privatized state-owned enterprises; MSEs absorb school dropouts and women from rural areas; (4) Women-owned enterprises have contributed to the economy by providing employment to family members and unskilled labor. It is estimated that 10 percent of workers in MSEs are family members while over 12 percent are hired labor. In addition, according to the ILO publications (ILO/SLAREA 2001) on the structure of small business in East Africa, women dominate the food, beverage and textile sector with 66.2 percent of business. 70 percent of women-owned MSEs are in the trade sector. These do contribute indirectly to tax revenues, for example paying for market stalls, trading licenses, and daily market fee dues; (5) The informal enterprises act as a seedbed for women's entrepreneurship.

Although there is a high rate of failure for women's enterprises in general, this is compensated for by a high rate of entrance of other women entrepreneurs. The high rate of entry and exit is because the nature of the enterprises started requires little or no capital investment initially.

The entrepreneurial skills of women are yet to be harnessed and reflected in starting and running growth-oriented enterprises. This is because women face a number of challenges which inhibit the growth of their enterprises. These include the following:

Women's enterprises are not growth oriented. Most of women's enterprises are started and operated to meet physiological, economic, and social needs. According to a baseline study done by the council for the Economic Empowerment of Women in Uganda, (CEEWA-U) for the year 2000, 60 percent of all micro entrepreneurs depend on their business to meet needs such as housing, clothing, food, security and transport (Musoke 2001). Hence, the enterprise is started for survival purposes. Much of the time and resources are spent this way and do not allow women to build a vision for their enterprises, let alone rise to aspire to other needs such as achievement and self-actualization (as per Maslow's needs hierarchy).

Socio-Cultural Factors. Existing socio-cultural factors are still a barrier to women's entrepreneurship. Most women are perceived as "weak, passive, and home oriented." In a lecture series, one of the students described characteristics of an entrepreneur as "masculinity," and "positiveness," while femininity was equated with "negativity" (UPK 2002). There is stereotyping surrounding women's roles as maternal, healthcare providing, and housecare-providing. Family ties and household duties also burden women. In addition to the multi-faceted roles, women's work is not recognized or valued and is taken for granted. This is made worse by lack of belonging, identity, and ownership in the home. The socio-cultural conditioning of women may have eroded their confidence; they may be unable to assert themselves, to persist when faced with obstacles, and to mobilize resources and seek opportunities outside the home environment. Hence, many women may have a tendency to underestimate their own abilities, talents, dreams and vision, all which need to be reflected in the entrepreneurial activities. However, independent women like single mothers, widows and strong-willed women with supportive husbands have overcome such cultural constraints to build strong enterprises (Kasente 2002).

Self Confidence. Due to lack of self-confidence, women tend to choose enterprises that reflect their reproductive roles. Many women-owned enterprises are in the traditional sector and very few women have ventured into the non-traditional enterprises, which can raise their income level as well as become a source of achievement and self-actualization.

Dual Gender Roles. Women are burdened by the dual responsibility of managing the home and the enterprise with little or no support from family members. The biggest percentage of their income is spent on household obligations such as food, health, school fees and little or none is saved for reinvestment and expansion of the enterprise. In addition, managing an enterprise requires commitment, hard work, competitiveness, and dedication. As a result, many women do suffer from stress caused by "role overload" and role "conflict" as they strive with the demands of the home and the enterprise. For example, for women whose businesses require frequent international trips, there is a misconception that married women should not travel frequently, whereas men who travel regularly are socially and culturally accepted.

Lack of Business Experience. Despite the large number of women in business, many of them lack business management skills; they are not literate in business transactions such as identifying and planning for a viable enterprise, mobilizing resources, record keeping, banking and saving culture. This is made worse by the low literacy levels of women who start enterprises.

Business Not a Career Option. Typically, women start enterprises as a last resort. Going into business is viewed negatively, for example, because one did not finish formal education, lost a job in formal employment or a breadwinner (husband) through death, or because family income needs a supplement. Therefore, from the beginning, managing an enterprise is not seen as career option but as means of survival. Many women do not envision their enterprises growing into a profitable, long-lasting enterprise that can create jobs, extend goods and services to an area, advance the well being of the proprietor and workers, and contribute to the growth of the economy.

Unsupportive Business and Policy Environment. Because there is a good, engendered political environment there is a tendency to believe that this power will eventually be transformed into economic empowerment. This is unrealistic, especially when the existing social structures that perpetuate inequalities have not been dismantled. Without specific policies on the economic empowerment of women, considering the large number of women in MSEs, women will not be groomed and empowered to either build growth-oriented enterprises or compete favorably in a competitive business environment. Hence, there is need for a deliberate move to encourage women in managerial and leadership positions in both public and private enterprises in order to gain experience, exposure and a wide scope for their vision. All of which can be used in creating growth-oriented enterprises. In her paper, "The Status of Gender Equality in Employment in Uganda," Kasente highlighted the under-representation of women in decision making positions in government with 16 percent women compared to 84 percent men. However, she noted that the situation was better balanced in the private sector than in the public sector (2002).

One of the main deterrents to growth of women's enterprises is a lack of ownership and effective control of resources. In many cultures the girl child's identity and ownership is vested in the male lineage. She cannot inherit land or property in her own right, even when she is married. The delay in Uganda to enact the Domestic Land Bill that seeks, among others, rights for co-ownership of property by wives, continues to perpetuate women's inability to provide collateral security in banks in order to get additional funding for their enterprises. In addition, it affects access to land and security of tenure of women's enterprises, given that most female MSEs are started in the home and/or are an extension of the home. For example, "most women-owned enterprises operate in semi-permanent roof-only structures; the quality of these physical structures tends to be poor depending on the security of tenure, whereas the male counterparts own titles or have customary ownership and can construct permanent structures" (Taigha 2001).

Even though the constitution in Uganda recognizes the equality of both sexes before the law, legislative discrimination still exists. For example, under current legislation the husband is by law the head of the family and is given superior legal authority. Whereas administration of property is a joint responsibility, the husband's decision prevails unless the wife goes to court.

The following quote from Ngajja (1993) highlights the constraints that a typical woman faces when she initiates a business activity.

Edith Kagino is married with seven children. Before marriage, she developed an interest in dairy farming while helping her mother look after the family's dairy herd. After marriage she worked in her husband's workshop. From 1991 she was a regular saver with the Uganda Women's Finance and Credit Trust and acquired a loan in 1992 to buy two in-calf heifers and for the construction of a small cow shed. She planted napier grass to feed the cows. Edith started off very well, with the first cow calling normally. Problems started when her husband instructed her to go back to the workshop. She could no longer take care of the cows, and eventually she lost one of them. Despite her protestations, her husband insisted that she remain in the workshop. Eventually, her husband chased her away from her home and she had to find shelter for herself and the children. The husband claimed ownership of the calves and so she was not allowed to take them with her. After some months, with the intervention of in-laws, the husband called her back. But he had already sold the roofing sheets and construction materials of the cowshed and all the grass was gone. She got pregnant again, then her husband decided to live with another wife. Edith is recovering from the shock, trying to start all over again. Her project is marked by debt for credit of doubtful value. Her debt to UWFCT is not fully repaid. (Ngajja, E. B. J; (1993) Uganda Women's Finance & Credit Trust: Evaluation Report 1991–1993. Kampala, UWFTC cited in Taigha 2001.)

Other constraints include the quality of the women's products and services. Much as there is improvement at the domestic level, the quality is not good enough or standardized enough to meet regional and international standards. Few of the products are patented or given a quality certificate. In addition, many women's enterprises use low or crude technology due to lack of technological skills and lack of financial resources to invest in capital equipment. There are also legal requirements for establishing a business. For example, it is now a requirement to use a lawyer to register the business and this is expensive for most women in MSEs. The bureaucracy in public offices often is a constraint since many women do not have information and are not familiar with many business transaction procedures. Banks and financial institutions still have the "traditional" attitude towards women borrowers. This attitude constrains them. Loans that women can easily access, especially from micro finance institutions (MFIs) are always small, with high interest rates and no grace period. They require a group guarantee/security. And lastly there is lack of access to markets.

Is Enterprise Development Training An Empowerment Process?

"Empowerment" is a process with many dimensions and may mean different things to different people. In this context empowerment is seen as a process that involves creating conditions that enable, encourage, and allow women to become economically independent through enterprise development. Empowerment through enterprise involves "access to resources and markets, actual ownership and active control of these resources" (Rani and Raju 2000: 9).

The current gains in the empowerment process of women in Uganda have been mainly positional, in terms of political participation, representation, decision making and education. In education, the girl child now has an opportunity to receive basic primary education, hence raising the literacy level of women in general. However, she may not be able to continue to the post-secondary level if the same facility is not available. In most cases, she will eventually join the many women in the informal and MSE sector. The increasing number of female students joining tertiary and institutions of higher learning, due to the additional 1.5 admission points for female students at the University, does provide a much higher knowledge base for women that can enable them to tackle the challenges of setting up and managing enterprise.

The importance of training cannot be underestimated, especially if it is the means through which women can be empowered to get ownership, access to and effective control of resources. In addition, the integration of women into the on-going development process and acknowledgement of their contribution to the economy in Uganda have led to specific programs and activities that empower women who own enterprises as well as potential women entrepreneurs.

In general, most tertiary and institutions of higher learning offer a wide range of business related courses at the certificate, diploma, degree and masters level. It is hoped that women in business, especially those in the middle class with small enterprises, take advantage of these courses. In the long run, this training will provide business management skills to women. For women who have not gone up the formal education ladder, Makerere University Business School (Kampala) has a variety of short courses for small businesses that are offered after working hours. The women in the Uganda Women Entrepreneurs Association (UWEAL) and others have benefited from such courses. However, the number of female students in institutions of higher learning is still very small.

The trickle down factor of starting enterprises as a result of this training is still difficult to determine because there is no follow-up of students. Also, the training in these institutions is not tailored to the needs of the private sector and to the MSE in particular. Hence it is not responsive to the needs of women and the economy in general such as building confidence in enterprise creation and creating employment opportunities. Worse still is that the programs are not language sensitive. The courses are offered mainly in the English language, hence marginalizing those who do not have a good command of English, a majority of whom are women.

The private sector and related associations have initiated entrepreneurship development programs for their members and the general public. Examples of programs from which women entrepreneurs have benefited include: The Entrepreneurship Development Program (EDP) organized by the Uganda Manufacturers Association (UMA) in 1997, 1998 and 1999 for existing and potential entrepreneurs; The Business Skills Development Program (BSDP) aimed at unemployed youth which was created by Private Sector Development (PSDP) under United Nations Development Program (UNDP) sponsorship with UMA as an implementing agent in 1998. This program is on-going in the regional districts. Some of the youth in these districts received seed money to start enterprises. This was timely, considering that females are over represented among the youth, and when employed in enterprises are always confined to marginal and poorly remunerated activities. Currently, there is the Entrepreneurship Development Program for growth-oriented enterprises being offered by Enterprise Uganda, which was started in 2001. The Entrepreneurship Development Program for unemployed female graduates was organized by the Uganda Entrepreneurs Association (UWEAL) and begun in August 2002 (Nazziwa 2001).

Most of the training organized this way does not have monitoring or follow-up activities in order to evaluate the responsiveness and effect of the training on the enterprises of women. Many women in the micro sector do not attend these courses because there is no immediate financial assistance attached to them while some cannot afford the fee.

It is mainly the development agencies and micro finance institutions which offer training. The training is tailored to meet the needs of women related to income-generating activities and improve access to resources, especially financial resources. Development agencies like FINCA-Uganda, and the Uganda Women's Finance and Credit Trust pioneered this kind of training. It is in these institutions that women in the informal and micro sector have greatly benefited and been empowered in terms of leadership, group formation, decision making, saving and banking procedures, managing loans and basic bookkeeping skills.

Many women have benefited from product development and technology improvement programs organized by the Uganda Small Scale industry Association (USSIA) and UN Industrial Development Organization under the Master Craftsmanship Program. The programs have a technical, business management and training of trainer's component. Women in the craft, textile, and food processing sector have especially benefited. The demand-driven courses tend to be flexible to the needs of women, especially in acquiring modern technological skills at a low cost, at a time convenient to them and in a language-friendly atmosphere. These courses have improved the quality of products produced by women-owned enterprises, ensuring that now they have a competitive advantage in the globalized economy.

Since 1997, an entrepreneurship course has been integrated into the curriculum of all technical courses at Kyambogo University. The main aim is to motivate and change attitudes of students to start looking at owning a business and self-employment as a career option. Originally the technicians and engineers were trained to fit in middle-management cadre positions in industries.

In a 1999 baseline survey of students on the benefit of the entrepreneurship course on the industrial training exercise, it was revealed that the training had changed the students' outlook to employment and enterprise building. Before this, they looked at the employer as one who took full responsibility in managing the industry and enterprises. The students revealed that industrial training offered an opportunity to learn the process of production and business management with the hope of starting their own in the future. The following is an extensive quote from the report on the training course.

> On the importance of competition in sustaining a business, the report revealed that success in business depends on hard work, putting in long hours of work, and producing quality products and services. Students acknowledged that knowledge and skills are motivating factors when starting a particular business and that these minimize costs and risks in business. They appreciated that with-

out businesses/industries one would not be able to do industrial training. They realized that the entrepreneurial skills in management they had acquired enabled them to handle and attract customers and determine what to produce to meet the customers' needs and understand the proprietor's vision.

In addition, the entrepreneurship training they had acquired empowered them to identify business opportunities and emphasized that creativity is the basis for technology advancement. The students further stated that they were in a position to use electronic data processing skills in the identification of a need and in meeting that need. Students offered the idea that a need for production of local oil could be met by creating a machine to make the production easier, faster, and less costly.

Students highlighted the importance of motivating workers if you want to get things done —by involving them in decision making, open discussion and understanding the administrative set-up of companies. The students were now in position to take supervisory/managerial responsibilities confidently and solve the problems that affect business and workplace management.

Personally, students could now identify with the entrepreneurs in industry by understanding the process involved in entrepreneurship and adjusting accordingly. For example, being conscious of minimizing losses by being efficient and mindful of resources available to accomplish a task; setting short term achievable goals; focusing on the long term benefits of training and the need for expansion and growth of businesses in phases. (Uganda Polytechnic Kyambogo 2001.)

There are many women's organizations in Uganda whose aim is to empower women. These include umbrella organizations like the National Association of Women Organization in Uganda (NAWOU), the Uganda Women Entrepreneurs Association (UWEAL), the Centre for Economic Empowerment of Women in Uganda (CEEWA-U), the Federation of African Women Educationalist (FAWE), Federation of Uganda Female Lawyers Uganda Chapter (FIDA-U) and many other women's groups. These organizations appeal to one of the motives that lead to entrepreneurial behavior and that is the need for affiliation. Through these organizations, women with enterprise have been able to create networks, influence and mentor others, share experiences, debate and discuss current issues, lobby for changes in policy, get informed and participate in local and international trade fairs and exhibitions.

Conclusion and the Way Forward

In conclusion, women's entrepreneurship is successfully finding a firm root in Uganda. The success of women within the informal sector has encouraged many of them to join the formal sector. However, few women's enterprises are growth oriented. Women are still ill prepared to meet the varied business challenges which result into their early exit and return to informal businesses.

The private sector has done a commendable job of empowering businesswomen with entrepreneurial skills. Many women organized groups and individuals have benefited from the training and are encouraged to become economically independent through enterprise development.

Entrepreneurship skills training is now integrated in the curriculum of institutions of higher learning and will strengthen entrepreneurial competencies of female students and changing their attitude towards self employment as a career.

References

Namaki, E.L. 1990. *A Cross Country Examination of Barriers to Women's Entry and Continuity in Business and Efforts Aiming at Barrier Waiving*. Research Papers. vol. X no. 2, December. The Netherlands: Maastricht School of Management.

Federation of Uganda Employers (FUE). 2001. "Position Paper on Micro and Small Enterprises in Uganda." Presented At ILO/SLAREA East Africa Sub-Regional Workshop On Strengthening Labour Relations For Small Business Employers. August 12–13. Nairobi p.5.

Fry, Fred. 1995. *Entrepreneurship: A Planning Approach*. New York: West Publishing Co.

Kasente, Deborah. 2002. *The Status of Gender Equality in Employment in Uganda*. Presented at a Women in Management Workshop Organized by the Federation of Uganda Employers (FUE). July 12–13. Kampala.

Maclachiac, Rob. ed. 1999. *People And Management Magazine*, April vol. 5, no. 7. London: Personnel Publication Ltd.

Nagajja, E. B. J. 1993. *Uganda Women's Finance and Credit Trust: Evaluation Report, 1991–1993*. Kampala, Uganda.

Nazziwa, Juliet Musoke. 2001. *Uganda Women Entrepreneurs Association's Networking Experiences and Challenges*. Togo: ECA/ACW Workshop, June.

Nazziwa, Juliet Musoke. 1999. *A Report on Reponses of Second-Year Students Regarding Several Aspects of Industrial Training Exercise*. Kampala. unpublished.

Rani C. and U. B. Raju. eds. 2000. *A Trainers Handbook for Developing Enterprises Among Women*. New Delhi: Tata McGraw Hill Publishing Company Ltd.

Ronstadt, Robert C. 1985. "The Educated Entrepreneurs: A New Era of Entrepreneurial Education is Beginning," *American Journal of Small Business*. vol. 10, no. 1.

Taigha, Edward A. 2001. "The Structure and Performance of Small Business Sector in East Africa: The Case of Kenya, Uganda and Tanzania." Presented at the East African Workshop on Strengthening Labour Relations for Small Business Employers. August. 12–13 Nairobi. p. 37.

Uganda Polytechnic Kyambogo (UPK). 2001. "Gender Roles and Entrepreneurship Development." Discussion Paper Presented by the Department of Human Resource Development, School of Education at a workshop on Curriculum Development in Technical Education Institutions in Uganda.

Chapter 26

Empowerment of Women Through Credit Facilities: A Case of FINCA in Jinja District, Uganda

Harriet Muwanika Kiwemba

Women, especially rural women, are regarded as the poorest of the poor. Devereux (1990) highlighted the fact that the very poor in developing countries commonly lack funds to increase production and improve their living standards. Concern for poverty alleviation and recognition of credit as a constraint for self-help by the poor have caused some governments, non-governmental organizations and the private sector to devote considerable resources to the provision of credit targeted at the poor. Many development agencies have begun to turn their efforts towards utilizing credit as a development tool.

Musoke and Amajo (1989) observed that early on, credit facilities targeting the poor adopted conventional bank procedures of availability of collateral as security for a loan. However, very few women benefited from these facilities since the lending principles of the financial institutions continued to be inclined to possession of collateral, which most women lacked. Shapiro and Maynes (1990) held that collateral requirements are the major stumbling blocks for most businesswomen. This brought the realization that there was a need to assist women with an emphasis on increasing their opportunities to earn money. This was crucial, especially for those in the informal sector who formed the majority and had the potential, the entrepreneurship, and the experience which were being inadequately tapped and under utilized. Some organizations came up with strategies to increase women's access to credit so as to meet the credit and savings needs of the poor women without the condition of collateral. They specifically targeted the small and micro entrepreneurs.

In Uganda, much informal effort has been made to devise strategies to enhance the status of women through poverty alleviation. Government and several non-governmental organizations have come up with various strategies to facilitate the empowerment of women. Provision of savings and credit facilities has been identified as one of the best strategies towards enhancing the status of women, and thus extensive resources have been invested in this strategy by government, non-governmental organizations, and local groups at formal and informal levels. These organizations include: the Women's Finance and Credit Scheme and the Foundation for Inter-National Community Assistance (FINCA). They aim to provide small credit to women, which can be channeled productively into a variety of micro enterprises promoting the growth and profitability of women's activities that are usually hindered by lack of capital.

FINCA started its activities in Uganda in 1992 in Jinja District with the objectives of helping women get gainful employment, be educated on the need to save money and be empowered both at the individual and community levels. Today FINCA operates throughout the country. FINCA provides small credit to identified groups of women micro entrepreneurs, with social accountability and peer pressure as a substitute for collateral. These women must be engaged in an income-generating activity with the ability to immediately utilize the money and pay it back in weekly installments during the loan cycle of four months or sixteen weeks, and they must also have money to meet their household and personal needs. FINCA enforces two types of savings, which must be realized by the client on a weekly basis during the loan cycle. One is the programmed or "forced" savings, which is a percentage of the loan amount, and the other one is the voluntary savings program whereby the client saves any amount based on her weekly income. Credit is offered to individual women in the form of small loans after they have satisfied certain requirements set by FINCA. They must be members of a group of thirty women who meet on a weekly basis. Each member must be engaged in an ongoing economic activity from which she earns money on a daily or weekly basis. The group must be approved and trained by the FINCA staff in the appropriate financial and management techniques. They must have a bank account at a commercial bank with each member having saved at least 20 percent of the loan amount. Loan repayment is done through weekly installments for a period of sixteen weeks, with an interest rate of 12 percent. In addition, each client must meet the programmed savings, which is a percentage of the loan, and also make other savings on a voluntary basis.

FINCA also provides training in financial management and accountability, leading to keeping accurate records of payments and receipts and a better understanding of the program procedures involved and purposes for which credit is given. The FINCA credit officers who ensure the weekly meetings of the individuals and the group-at-large supervise all the groups' activities regularly. FINCA counts more on local pride and peer group pressure as the reason for paying back the loan, and it depends on group liability as a guarantee of financial responsibility rather than on property. It is believed that peer group pressure acts as a means of reducing defaults on small loans and helps to avoid the need for collateral as security.

The FINCA credit facility, therefore, involves three major aspects: provision of credit in the form of small loans to individual women who are members of a group of thirty women, training of the women in administration and financial management prior to the loan disbursement and provision of an opportunity to the women for social interaction through the weekly meetings. These are believed to play a vital role in the empowerment of individual women clients within a group.

Development practitioners further realized that with the enlargement of the productive bases through the provision of the financial and physical resources that women lack, together with the resources to which they have access, their living conditions could be made better. This would contribute to the women's economic, psychosocial and political empowerment and reduce the gender inequalities in society.

As more women enter the cash economy, more decisions must be made regarding the purchase of food, clothing, household supplies, and equipment. Skills must be developed to facilitate the necessary decision making and ensure the efficient use of the scarce resources. It was thus important to find out whether the women clients of FINCA had gained the capacity to meet their own needs and those of their dependents as a result of the credit facility. Furthermore, women's income may be increased as a result of the micro finance facility, but there are questions about how much this income benefits or is controlled by the women (Wheat 1997). Another issue, therefore, was to establish who controlled the economic activity and the use of the income generated, given the power relationships whereby, traditionally, men have the power to control the finances generated in the household, even if they are earned by women. An important factor was the extent to which these women were involved in decision-making, including decisions concerning the allocation and control of benefits.

Therefore, the study examined the extent to which the above aspects of the credit facility contributed to the empowerment of women, economically, psycho-socially and politically by identifying specific ways in which FINCA as a credit facility had empowered women clients in Jinja District. Secondly, it aimed to identify the factors constraining or facilitating the empowerment of women clients through access to credit. For the purpose of this study, the term empowerment refers to gaining the capacity to earn an independent income, being able to plan, organize, manage and carry out activities and make choices and decisions affecting the individual, one's family, and community. Furthermore, empowerment refers to the ability to own and control resources and also the acquisition of knowledge and skills.

Findings and Discussion

The population of study included women clients of the FINCA program from the sub-counties of Mafubira, Busedde, Kakira, Buwenge and Jinja Muncipality East and West. These were purposively selected because FINCA had been operating in those areas long enough to have effects which could be assessed. They also have a representative range of respondents from the rural and urban areas of the district with varying socio-economic backgrounds.

The main sources of data were in-depth interviews and discussions with the women clients of FINCA. These were supplemented by informal conversations that were held with key informants who included women, local leaders, and FINCA credit officers in charge of some of the selected groups. These were presumed to have relevant, balanced, and objective information about FINCA activities and the clients. Additional information was generated from the focus group discussions with a rural and an urban women's group.

The socio-economic background of the FINCA women clients plays a vital role in facilitating or constraining the empowerment process of the women with respect to the intervention of the credit facility. The socio-economic factors considered in the study were: age, marital relationships, education level, occupation, number of children and dependents and type of economic activity.

The study findings revealed that the majority of the women clients were between thirty-five and forty-five years of age and that very few youths below thirty-five years were actively involved in the FINCA activities. The focus group discussions revealed that the youths, especially those who were still single, did not want to team with older women whom they thought did not always respect their ideas and regarded them as inexperienced. On the other hand, the elderly clients had the responsibility of looking after themselves and the orphaned grandchildren left by their children due to the AIDS scourge. Access to a credit facility, such as the one provided by FINCA, was therefore important for these women. This explains the high number of elderly clients.

The majority of the sample population (73%) was married while 1 percent had never married, 7 percent were separated, and 19 percent were widowed. About 43 percent of the married were in polygamous and 57 percent in monogamous relationships. Furthermore, 53 percent of the married did not live with their husbands most of the time, while 47 percent lived with their husbands.

The presence of more married women could on one hand indicate the cultural importance attached to marriage, but also indicates the amount of responsibilities and financial demands a married woman may have. The widowed and separated had to cater for themselves and their families and thus had to look for ways of economic and social survival by indulging in economic ventures. This indicated that the responsibilities of the more elderly women arose from marriage or by virtue of more advanced age.

Individual reports revealed that those who were married but did not stay with their husbands most of the time had the burden of catering for most of the daily family needs and welfare. Even those in polygamous marriages had to find ways of supplementing the household income and meet the daily family and personal needs. Polygamous families are usually large and the husband may not be able to meet all or most of the family needs. This is in agreement with the World Bank country study report, which revealed that:

> In polygamous relationships, only the richest men are able to provide adequate financial, let alone emotional support to more than one family. Most women in polygamous marriages are for all practical purposes, heads of their households, in the sense that they are principally and often solely responsible for the welfare of the family (1993: 20–21).

Education or literacy level facilitates the effective administration of the program, which always needs minimum skills of reading, writing, and basic numeracy for proper understanding and active participation. Education also boosts self-confidence, which is an important aspect in facilitating the empowerment process. About 64 percent of the sample had attained post primary level, 30 percent primary junior level and 6 percent never went to school. The majority of the women could read and write, but even those who could not depended on their long-time experience in their businesses, and, therefore, had access to the credit facility.

With regard to the women's major occupations, the study considered what took most of their daily time. The majority of the women (61 %) spent most of their time in general businesses which involved commercial undertakings on a retail basis such as retail shops, groceries, tailoring, textiles, food vending, local brewing, produce, and charcoal selling. Others involved service provision such as clinics, maternity services, hairdressing, nursery schools, medical and veterinary drug shops. About 21 percent of the women were in salaried employment as nurses, primary teachers, and copy typists. These occupations are in the lower echelons with low status and meager incomes, and the women needed ways of supplementing their incomes in order to meet most of their personal and family needs. About 17 percent were in agriculture-based activities, such as animal keeping (poultry, piggery, zero-grazing heifers), and crop farming (sugarcane, mushrooms, vegetables).

The fact that the majority of the women were engaged in non-agricultural activities concurred with the report by Nelson, MK Nelly, Stack and Yanovitch that:

> Frequent payments encourage a net shift away from agricultural activities to income generating activities, which produce a steadier flow of income than the primary cropping activities of households (1995: 30).

The type of activity where women earned some income on a daily basis facilitated their access to FINCA credit facility and a step towards their empowerment. The study sought to identify specific ways in which women clients had been empowered economically as a result of the credit facility, in terms of changes in income, individual savings, utilization of the savings, property acquisition and ownership and management and control over financial and physical resources.

Findings revealed that most women (80%) realized increases in their incomes over the five years of the program despite their differences in education levels, marital status, and location of residence. However, 20 percent of the women had unstable incomes due to the seasonal nature of their income-generating activities, such as supplying school uniforms, sweaters and operating school canteens. Some businesses, such as textiles and poultry, picked up during such seasons as Easter, Idd el fitri, and New Year's Day. Yet still the women took care of the unexpected or unforeseen expenses incurred on such things as medicine, weddings, and burial ceremonies. Although increases in incomes were observed, reports from informants revealed that female-headed households had more responsibilities than other families. It can therefore be inferred that marital status is closely related to the disadvantages and advantages women face, which influence their capacity for empowerment.

Personal savings can form an internal source of funding for small enterprises, which can contribute to the empowerment of women. Looking at the individual's savings as an indicator of economic empowerment, the majority of the women reported making cash savings on a weekly basis and learned to value saving as a discipline, not only as a FINCA program requirement. The saving requirement of the FINCA program had contributed much towards the adoption of a savings culture, which was originally lacking among most women. One respondent said:

> I would never think of setting apart any savings. Every money I made, I would spend on immediate family and personal needs. I have now learned that saving is a discipline, which must be cultivated.

As to how the women mainly utilized their savings, 65 percent reinvested it in their businesses as working capital, expanding on them and acquiring business-facilitating equipment, while 27 percent invested in new business undertakings to diversify their income sources. Some reported indulging in multiple businesses as security for their weekly financial demands. A forty-eight-year-old teacher reported that she dealt in buying and selling produce, and also made pancakes and maize flour, which she supplied to schools. At the same time 15 percent reported having banked their savings to have access to larger future working capital and to gain credit worthiness in other lending institutions. About 17 percent purchased business-related and non-business-related property as family and personal assets, while 59 percent used their savings to meet family needs and 7 percent used it on personal needs. Overall, 32 percent of the women used the loan and savings for the intended purpose of investment. However, a large number spent their savings on meeting family needs and their personal needs (66%). This is a result of the socialization process whereby women are raised as caretakers of everyone else but themselves.

Reports indicated that some women had achieved a bit of self-sufficiency. They could meet their children's clothing and bedding needs and also purchase essential commodities such as sugar, soap, salt and tea leaves. Some reported being able to meet educational and medical expenses and also to meet expenses for ceremonies and other eventualities. A twenty-eight-year-old woman from Masese said, "I can now meet my children's school requirements, provide some pocket money for their snacks, lunch and transport."

The conclusion is that with access to credit, women may become more economically independent. This helps to reduce, break or end economic dependency on the husband or a male relative. Findings also disproved the traditional belief that the role of a woman is that of a mother, housewife and homemaker and that the man is the "bread winner."

Acquisition and ownership of property is one of the indicators of women's economic empowerment. The women were able to acquire family and personal properties, over which they reported having full rights of use and control. Among the personal property, immovable properties ranked highest with 19 percent, as compared with 31 percent acquired for the family. These included plots of land, as well as residential and commercial buildings locally known as "mizigo," used as a source of income. About 11 percent acquired personal domestic utilities such as household crockery (dishes, plates and saucepans), furniture (beds, tables and chairs), mattresses, television, radio, and tap water. These properties were mainly for commercial and domestic use. Some personal savings acquired business-facilitating equipment such as bicycles, machinery such as sewing machines and hair dryers for salons. Another 6 percent acquired domestic animals such as heifers, goats, and pigs and 10 percent acquired properties and facilities for the family.

In focus group discussions, women revealed their feeling of insecurity if they did not own in their individual capacities properties such as land, houses and animals, which they believed were a source of security in life. Women are gradually acquiring properties such as land and buildings for their own development through purchase, as a forty-two-year-old woman from Wairaka put it:

> The only way we women can be assured of owning personal properties is through hard work and purchase of these properties ourselves since most of these are usually acquired through inheritance, the laws of which have always favored men.

Some of these properties were reported to provide income and others provided for the improvement of their standard of living. Some women, especially those with children, purchased properties for the family as security and for children's future use. One widow from Jinja Municipality said:

> I work for my children's well being. No mother would like to see her children suffer. I know I am going to die soon; I would like to leave something tangible as a source of income for my four children, to see them through their education which I believe will be the foundation of their lives.

It seems that the FINCA credit facility has created a sense of security through property acquisition, ownership, and self-reliance, which contribute to the economic empowerment of women.

Access to and control over financial resources is another indicator of economic empowerment. Full access to, control over, and management of productive resources facilitates women in exploiting their potential to the maximum within their households and the community. Longwe (1991) emphasized that the levels of participation and control are crucial yardsticks for empowerment. In order to assess the women's extent of access to and control over the financial and physical resources in the household and the income-generating activities, it was necessary to look at the type and location of the activity, establish who started the income-generating activity (initiator), and who was responsible for the daily management of the income-generating activity. These were believed to have an influence on the level of the women's access to and control over the financial and physical resources.

Fifty four percent of the women in the study used their own money to start the income-generating activities, while about 11 percent used money from their husbands, 16 percent used the FINCA loan, 13 percent used money from other sources such as relatives and friends, and 6 percent did not use cash as capital. Furthermore, 70 percent of the income-generating activities were started by the women themselves, 10 percent by husbands, 9 percent by both the women and their husbands, and 13 percent by friends and relatives. Where the women used their own money and initiated their income-generating activities, they had full access to and control over the activities and the finances from these activities. In cases where the woman with her husband jointly began the income-generating activity, especially where the husband was the source of capital, some women reported having full or partial access to and control over the activities and the finances. However, key informants revealed that in most cases, the husband had full control over and managed the activity. Some women gave the loan to their husbands who solely managed the business and in some cases gave the women the finances required by the program so that they continued benefiting from it. This deprived some women of the opportunity to develop their own management skills, participate in decision making, and enjoy fully the proceeds accrued from the business. Often where women work with men, gender-power relations work to the detriment of the women. They lose control and hardly participate effectively in the income-generating activities. The majority of the women (66%) operated their businesses outside their households in commercial or trading centers, schools, hospitals, markets or hawking and 34 percent operated from their households. Among those who operated from their households, 58 percent were rural-based compared to 13 percent who were urban-based. About 67 percent of the urban dwellers operated from the commercial centers. This indicates that more women were venturing from the "private" to the "public" sphere, which has long been the domain of men. The domestication of women has been a major hindrance to their empowerment.

Venturing outside the home has enabled women to gain access to independent sources of income, cash and to exposure to learning opportunities and also to competition in the market mostly managed by men. This contributes to the socio-economic empowerment of the women.

Forty-one percent of the women were responsible for the daily management of their income-generating activities and were physically participating in them and about 24 percent used hired labor, 9 percent relied on husbands and 26 percent on family labor. Individual respondents who had full-time salaried employees did not participate fully in the economic activities. Those who participated fully had full access to and control over the activities and proceeds from these activities. Where the husbands were in charge, most women had partial or no control over the activities. In cases where decisions were jointly made, the woman was the junior partner and the husband made the final decisions. However, with the support of their husbands, women gained confidence and made a contribution to the family and personal welfare.

Sixty-six percent of the women's income was used on the education of the children and dependents in terms of school fees, stationery, transport, pocket money, snacks, uniforms, and visitation for those in boarding schools. 17 percent was spent on rent, 9 percent on medical services, 5 percent on food, and 3 percent on children and personal clothing. High expenditure on children's education was reported as a result of having appreciated the value of education towards social development and empowerment. A forty-six-year old local council leader from Wairaka said:

> Education is necessary for self-advancement and is a lifetime investment. When you give a child fish, you solve her immediate problem of hunger but when you teach that child how to fish, you would have provided a lifetime solution to many more problems.

With regard to the women's perceived achievements as a result of the FINCA credit facility, respondents said that improvement in the acquisition and application of new knowledge and skills through training, exposure and interaction in such areas as business planning, budgeting, communication, public speaking, financial management, leadership, mobilization, record keeping and priority setting. Most of the women learned to manage their finances properly through budgeting for expenditure. Other respondents revealed improvement in the day-to-day management of their income-generating activities and the households.

About 77 percent of the respondents reported a feeling of improved self-confidence exhibited by reduced shyness, increased free participation in group discussions, improved ability to speak for oneself in public and among colleagues. A thirty-two-year-old woman from Wairaka said, "I can now speak among my colleagues with confidence, participate in the group discussions, and share ideas on any topic I know."

About 80 percent of the women reported having gained social and emotional support by getting "true" friends who always provided financial and material support during times of need such as when they lost their beloved ones or in sickness and also during times of joy. One respondent from Masese revealed

that her colleagues helped her and her husband with their introduction (engagement) ceremony by providing material and physical support. This helped to improve their marital relationship and earned the group respect and support from
the husband and the community. This was affirmed by the local council leader
who said:

> Social support promotes solidarity and team work. This has earned women re-
> spect and recognition. However, lack of support from fellow women hinders
> women's advancement. When women support one another, negative attitudes
> towards women in the community change.

Some women reported having been able to improve on personal character
through improvement of their self-control and patience. This contributed to the
improvement of personal relationships, which in turn promoted good working
relationships within the group. Others reported reduced quarrels and improved
marital and family relationships. Some women revealed that they had learned
proper personal care and hygiene. A forty-eight-year-old woman from Mafubira
said:

> The weekly meetings, the visits and the interaction with other members have
> enabled me to learn to care for myself through self-grooming, proper hair care
> and dressing. Several people have told me that I now look younger than before.

A positive attitude towards oneself builds confidence and contributes to psychosocial empowerment.

About 55 percent of the women reported having gained financial independence, leading to reduced dependence on their husbands and other male relatives.
This reduced quarrels and brought peace of mind and happiness in their families.
Some women reported using their own money to operate and own personal bank
accounts they had never owned before and thus break some of the barriers to
their personal welfare and male dominance. A forty-four-year-old woman from
Buwenge proudly said:

> Using my own money I now operate a personal bank account without the
> knowledge of my polygamous husband. I can now meet household needs and
> attend to any financial and material needs of especially my teenage girls.

Gaining access to other lending institutions improves the women's access to
capital resources, which in turn facilitates the empowerment process.

Sixty-nine percent of the women contributed to family and personal welfare
through increased access to social services by being able to meet medical bills
and pay for the education and clothing expenses of their children. One respondent revealed that she was able to take her handicapped child to the school for
the physically handicapped and another was able to take her children to boarding
schools.

Better feeding and permanent and comfortable accommodation brought
happiness to their lives and homes. Some respondents revealed contributing to

the husband's welfare in terms of providing financial support, which in turn contributed to more happiness in their homes. Other women reported being able to purchase household necessities such as sugar, paraffin, salt and soap without waiting for their husbands. Contributing to family and personal welfare increased women's self-confidence and earned some women respect from their husbands, family members, and the community. This further cultivated in some women a feeling of self-worth and motivation to work harder. Some women revealed that their husbands listened to them more and they had a "say" in family matters now that they contributed to the household income. A forty-four-year-old respondent dealing in second-hand clothing, and an active member of Munakukama Women's Group, said:

> My financial contribution has helped to educate our children up to university level. This has earned me respect from my husband and the children and has cemented our relationship, and promoted cooperation and unity among the family members.

When asked how their neighbors and members of their community had benefited as a result of their being FINCA clients, reports from individuals revealed that as a result of their improved incomes, they had been able to provide financial and material support such as salt and tea leaves and sometimes lending them money in case of eventualities. Some of the women had mobilized others to join FINCA women's groups after seeing the benefits the clients enjoyed and the changes in their lives and households. In this way, FINCA clients have acted as agents of change in their communities. Credit facilities encourage social development and empowerment. Nelson, MKNelly, Stack, and Yanovitch (1995), when discussing village banking, established that "Even relatively small increases in income can have a positive impact on women's self esteem and status within the household and a greater self-reliance."

With regard to gender-household relationships, among the married women, 47 percent of the husbands were supportive of their activities and 18 percent were not supportive. While 2 percent of the husbands were not aware of their wives' activities, 10 percent were not concerned and 24 percent were at first not supportive but later became supportive of the women's involvement with the credit facility. This was due to the fear of losing their power status and also their properties, in case of failure to repay the loan. Others were suspicious of their wives' being away from home and attending the weekly meetings, thinking they could indulge in "gossip" and immoral behavior. After witnessing the benefits, their negative attitudes changed to positive ones. The partner's support facilitates women's participation in the development activities and enhances their empowerment process.

Women's participation in decision making levels in the community can be measured in terms of the numbers of women elected to occupy leadership positions in the community. Fifty-five percent of the women participated in leadership positions in the local councils, religious and community-based groups and women's groups, while 45 percent did not participate in any community leadership. When the women were asked how they had been helped as FINCA clients in their leadership roles, they cited improved self-confidence, time management and the ability to mobilize others. Other women referred to teamwork and improved interpersonal communication. Furthermore, solidarity and support from FINCA group members enabled some women to confidently compete with men for leadership positions in their communities. Reports from key informants and individual respondents revealed that women played a more active role in the community, and some had taken up leadership positions in the local councils, religious and local women's groups, and yet others were aspiring to leadership in the forthcoming local council elections. This shows a change of attitude from the traditional view that public life is a male domain. One respondent confidently reported that she represented her group in public functions. Some women affirmed their intention to stand as candidates in the forthcoming local council elections. The women's groups function as a source of support, social interaction and a vehicle for women to develop and exercise their own leadership potential, which contributes to their political empowerment.

Alongside the success of the credit facility intervention, there are a number of constraints that limit the empowerment process. Some constraints or problems pertained to timely loan repayment, making inadequate savings, having inadequate capital, heavy workload, and heavy responsibilities. However, most of the women cited the problem of not having adequate training and access to information concerning their income-generating activities. About 71 percent affirmed experiencing these constraints, and 29 percent did not.

Fifty percent of the respondents revealed having experienced problems with loan repayment. The four-month loan term was set to attract women who were engaged in short-term, rapid-turnover trading activities. However, women who had major agricultural investments encountered problems with the weekly loan repayments and realization of savings. Some invested the loan but had to look for cash from other sources, such as borrowing from husbands or relatives to fulfill the weekly financial demands and maintain their membership. Those who failed had to forego some of their properties to raise funds to meet the financial obligations. Others had to miss some cycles without getting the loan, and some had to drop out completely, thus missing out on the other benefits accrued from group membership.

About 21 percent reported having had problems with realizing reasonable savings. This was attributed to the high household financial demands, coupled with the short-term program financial requirements. Some of the married women reported making low savings as a result of having many responsibilities: larger families, caring for their parents, orphans and other dependents. Some of their husbands were unemployed and had to be catered to. A forty-year-old respondent from Wairaka said, "My retrenched husband does not want to work. I have to work hard in my brewing business in order to cater for the family welfare and his personal needs."

Reports revealed that the savings could have been more if the women were not using the same money as capital to keep their businesses going and also to meet their family and personal needs. Others reported lacking support from their husbands and having to meet most of the financial needs of their families. A forty-four-year-old respondent from Jinja Municipality had this to say:

> Since my husband got another wife four years ago, he stopped caring and providing for our household needs. I have to meet all the household, children's, and my personal needs.

Some women lacked full control of the proceeds from their income-generating activities, which was a constraint to their empowerment. A thirty-five-year-old nurse said:

> My husband who decides on the use of it takes most of the money made from the clinic. This has helped to bring peace in our marriage and has enabled me to continue as a client of FINCA.

However, some reports revealed that operating away from the household was a great sacrifice and not favorable to the married women and those who had very young children, who they had to leave the whole day under the care of a relative or hired worker. This was an expense and most times their children were not well cared for. This affected the participation of especially the young women with children, some of whom had to drop out, as they could not afford to leave their children at home or go with them to where they were operating their businesses. A twenty-four-year-old said:

> I was operating a salon in the trading center away from home. During some seasons, I would spend longer hours away from home leaving my two children with the house helper. Later I found out that my children were ill treated, not well fed and were sick most of the time. I decided to shift the salon to my household where I can keep an eye on my children. This has reduced my income.

Some women revealed that it was easier to control activities within their households than those outside where they had to rely on hired labor or a relative. The empowerment of women sometimes occurs at a cost. Venturing into the public life may be a constraint to their empowerment. However, others felt that, though practically they were experiencing those problems, it gave them the "drive" to work hard, to be creative, and to plan their work. Other women reported that they were now able to set priorities in order to fulfill the financial obligations and maintain their membership in FINCA because of its diverse psychosocial, economic, and political benefits.

Thirty-four percent of the women reported having had problems of inadequate capital. The amount of savings determined the new loan size. Therefore, inadequate savings affected the size of the loan received in the subsequent cycles and thus affected the amount of capital. Focus group discussions revealed that the short loan-repayment periods tended to "eat" into their capital, which curtailed the level of self-sufficiency and promoted dependency on husbands for some of those who were married.

Nineteen percent of respondents reported not having had enough time to attend the weekly meetings, especially those women who had full-time salaried employment. These thought the weekly meetings were too demanding and costly since they had to pay fines for late coming and for the missed meetings. They reported having experienced difficulties in fulfilling the demands of the full-time employment of their businesses, the group and domestic obligations. On the other hand, some women appreciated the weekly meetings in that they learned to plan for and utilize their time effectively through proper time management at individual and group levels. Others reported having learned to work hard and also to set priorities in order to fulfill the program and family obligations. The weekly meetings took strictly one to two hours as agreed by the group members. This indicates that disciplined time management is important in the empowerment of women. It also dispels the traditional belief that women, once in a group, waste time indulging in idle talk and "gossip," which leads some men to refuse to allow their wives or children to join women's groups and in so doing frustrates the agenda for the empowerment of women.

Thirty-one percent of the women revealed having had a problem of inadequate training and access to information concerning business. They reported that they had received some training in mobilizing savings and keeping records concerning loan repayments and savings prior to the loan disbursement. However, they were encouraged to identify their needs, utilize resource persons, and meet any expenses involved. But this was expensive on their part due to the various financial demands they had. Some reported having had to rely on their own experiences, information, and advice from their friends and colleagues. Many expressed the need for more training in business skills. Lack of adequate training and information is a constraining factor to the empowerment of women.

Conclusion

The empowerment of women involves an interaction of many factors, access to credit being one of them. The process of empowerment occurs at both individual and group levels and involves personal initiatives. The credit facility played the role of facilitating the empowerment process among some women in varying levels through the provision of loans, training and social interaction.

Some recommendations can be drawn from these results: 1) More organizations that access credit to the individual women within deliberately formed groups should be promoted and supported by the government; 2) Specific programs targeting women and youths should be put in place by government and non-governmental organizations with the aim of training in business skills, accessing credit and employment creation; 3) There is a need for networking and collaboration between organizations that address the plight of women; and 4) There is a need to lobby for men's support and cooperation through gender awareness alongside the efforts put in place for the empowerment of women.

References

Devereux, S. and Pares H. 1990. *Credit and Savings for Development*. Oxfam: Oxford.

Longwe, Sara Hlupekile. 1991. "Supporting Women's Development in the Third World: Distinguishing between Interventions and Interference." Presented at a Training Programme in NID issues for FINNDA staff. unpublished.

Musoke, M. and M. Amajo. 1989. *Women's Participation in the Existing Credit Schemes in Uganda*. Kampala: University Field Staff International.

Nelson, C. MK Nelly, B. Stack, and K. Yanovatech. 1995. *Village Banking: The State of the Practice*. SEEP Network (Small Enterprise Education and Promotion). New York: United Nations.

Shapiro, J. and G. Maynes. 1990. "Report of International Workshop of Women in Banking and Finance." Amsterdam, March 12–15. unpublished.

Wheat, S. 1997. *The Future for Micro Enterprises: Banking the Unbankable,* Panos Media Briefing, no.21. London: Panos.

World Bank. 1993. *Uganda Growing Out of Poverty, A World Bank Country Study.* Washington D.C.: World Bank

Chapter 27

Possibilities for Saving Money?
Female Slum Dwellers in Bangalore

Signe Ekenberg

This chapter presents empirical examples that illuminate the saving situation for women slum dwellers.[1] The empirical data are collected from six women and their families. These six women are all different, but representative of women in these circumstances. The differences among them show the diversity among the slum dwellers in addition to the diversity in modern urban society. They represent both young and old women, married, widowed and separated. The data were collected through an intensive field survey using informal interviews and supported with participant observation over a period of five months. The study used a translator for the local languages, Kannada or Tamil. A local woman in the slum translated through all five months of the study.[2]

The majority of the residents in this slum area are Tamils who have migrated from the neighboring state of Tamil Nadu, but some of the residents are also Kannadigas, people from the state of Karnataka where Bangalore (population about 7.2 million) is situated. Most of the inhabitants are low-caste Hindus who in the past, converted to Catholicism. Most of the group of residents shares therefore a common culture, caste and history. Primarily they speak south-Indian languages, but the majority speaks Tamil. In spite of the fact that most of the slum dwellers are technically illiterate they often have some knowledge of several languages. As in other parts of Indian cities the nuclear family is prevalent in the slum. In this society women have authority in the domestic domain, but that does not imply that women have any power.

A local non-governmental organization (NGO)[3] had started self-help groups for women where this fieldwork was situated. The self-help group is a part of what is called micro-credit. Self-help groups who work with micro-credit will inform women about banking and savings and the project aims at creating an alternative credit program for the urban poor.

The fact that poor women want to save and have some capacity to save is not self-evident. The poor spend their income and still do not get enough to eat, so how can they save? The fact is that even though the women are poor, they have knowledge of an informal system through their habit of lending each other small amounts of money, rice and kerosene. This kind of system is a reciprocal lending system wherein I lend you something today and you lend me something some other time.

The income of a woman and her family may be tiny or irregular, and there are occasions when the family needs more money than the sum they have in hand. Such occasions might be birth, education, marriage, death, and emergencies. The only suitable way they can obtain these sums of money for bigger expenses is by saving. Poor women are at a disadvantage here because banks and insurance companies and other financial institutions don't want them as customers or they charge interest rates too high to manage. To give poor people a chance to save, micro-credit was made as an alternative to banks. In this case the group of people who gather to organize loans is called a self-help group.

Micro-credit projects are popular with NGOs these days. The goals of micro-credit projects are diverse and include: micro-credit is a tool with an undiscovered force that can take the poor out of poverty; micro-credit can reach the poorest of the poor; most of the micro-creditors are able reach a good repayment level, mostly through social networks; and almost all micro-credit is used for building micro industry, which is a secure source of income.

The reason why most of the self-help groups only are for women is because NGOs and others consider women as having the least access to financial resources. Research shows that women will spend money on food, clothing and education for their children. Husbands, on the other hand, tend to spend money on themselves, buying alcohol and tobacco. Women are also considered serious borrowers and have a high repayment rate. In the group under study here, the most important goal was to save money to form a basis for bigger loans. Each group has no more than twenty members and each member must save ten rupees[4] every week to qualify as a member of the group. During the meeting, money is collected in a pot and the members can take a loan from their self-help group. The group will collectively choose who will get the next loan, but the leader of the group has the last vote. The members of the group choose the leader. The interest on loans is as low as possible. Normally it is not more than 2 percent every month, which is bearable for the slum dwellers.

In the slum the women not only work towards making their self-help groups a bankable institution, they also go beyond the financial perspective and through these groups, reinforce positive aspects of their culture and community. The group aims to become an effective vehicle for transforming their communities as a whole. They will fund money for building latrines and other necessities in their area. In other words micro-credit projects seem to be good opportunities to empower woman and to give women economic and social benefits. But only two of the women in the slum out of the sample of six, were members of a self-help group, while the other four were not. This chapter explores why so few women are members of a micro-credit project.

Profile of the Sample Group

One of the women who was a micro-credit member was a sixty-year-old Kannada-speaking Hindu, who came to Karnataka when she was young after migrating with her parents from Tamil Nadu. She lived with her two daughters (both without a husband for different causes), her only son and her husband. Her third daughter lived in a neighboring house together with her husband. This woman had been a member of the micro-credit group since it started two years earlier, and before this she had been in a similar project. All her daughters were also members of the self-help group. Her family lived in a rather big house with all the vessels they needed, including television, a telephone, and even some furniture. She also owned a small shop and a wood shop not far from her house and her family owned five houses in the slum area that they had put out for rent. The old woman worked in her shops everyday while her daughters were at home doing the housework and looking after their small children. Because of her age she did not have as many duties at home as she used to and was allowed to stay outside her home alone. Her husband was an old man, and did not work any longer. Normally he was sitting outside their house talking to neighbors.

To expand both the shop and wood shop she got a loan from her self-help group. But to make the shops the way she wanted she was in need of a bigger loan. She could not take more loans now; she had to repay the one she already had first. She reported that she wasn't happy with the situation in the self-help group. She meant that the only women in her group who got bigger loans were the ones who had the nicest saris and gold rings and necklaces. By this she was implying that the group did not want her to have success in her business; they only wanted to help those who already had plenty, she said. But even if she did not agree with the other women in her group, she did not want to quit. Her membership in the self-help group had also helped her in other ways. The same NGO sponsor of the self-help group sponsored an eye operation for one of her grandchildren and she still wanted to keep in contact with the NGO because of this kind of help.

The second woman who was a member of the self-help micro-credit group was a widow. She was a mother of four, and a Kannada-speaking Hindu who had lived her whole life in Karantaka in a village and then in Bangalore, when she married. Her oldest daughter was married and had moved away to live with her husband. The other two daughters and one son lived with her. The oldest daughter at home was also a widow and she had a one-year-old daughter herself.

The other two, the boy (fifteen) and the girl (thirteen), were in school. Her oldest daughter living at home was nineteen and also a member of the self-help group. Her family's income comes from renting out the second floor in her self-owned house, and from her daytime job as a maid in a middle-class family. In addition, she sold milk in her neighborhood from her own stock of three cows and three goats. She started to build a house for her widowed daughter across the street from her own house. To do this she had both a loan from the self-help group and a loan from her brother. To finance the repayment of her loans she was planning to rent out the new house, which wasn't finished during the research period. She said that she did not have enough money to finish it and she could not take more loans from the group before the other was repaid. The money she had left she wanted to spend on her two youngest children's school fee. She especially wanted her son to go to school; according to her he would be the one who would take care of her when she grew old. She wanted her widowed daughter to re-marry so they would most likely move to their in-laws when they got married. By giving her son the best education possible she participated in securing her old age.

She herself had started a micro-credit project many years earlier. Before that she used to work as a moneylender.[5] She stopped working as a moneylender because she found it hard to get the money back. But she would be a part of the micro-credit project because she looked at it as security for her future. Because she did not have a husband to take the financial responsibility for her family, the self-help group, she said, was a way for her to do this.

The last four women in the sample weren't members of the self-help group. They were all Tamils and Tamil was their mother tongue. One of them was the translator for the interviews. She was thirty years old and had a six-month old son. She had only lived in the slum for two years. Earlier she had lived in a much better area with her family, but because of some unfortunate family situations she now lived in the slum, which was the only place she could afford. Her son's father had left her just after the birth. She used to sweep apartments for a living and her brother's wife looked after her son while she was at work. When she was translating she could take her son along with her. She was renting her house that consisted of one room from her next-door neighbor. The neighbors were a family of six: husband, wife, and their four sons. The wife in this house was also one of the women in the study.

The translator's background was different from most of the other slum dwellers. She had spent twelve years in a relatively good Catholic school, which is rather unusual for women slum dwellers. She had knowledge of Kannada, English, and Telegu in addition to Tamil. As she was living alone it was hard for her to make the ends meet; she had sold all her jewelry to pay the hospital bill when she gave birth to her son. Her monthly wages for translating for the study were one thousand rupee (this was said to be an average income) which was what she asked. Compared to the other women she was free to do mostly as she pleased; she did not have anyone else but her son to take care of. She had a brother whom she sometimes visited and from whom she borrowed and lent money. Because she was living alone with a child the neighbors were gossiping.

She said she did not care what they said because she was not like them anyway. She did not look at herself as a slum dweller; she said she was going to move out of the area as soon as possible. She had no intentions of staying in the slum. This was also one of the reasons she gave for not taking part in the self-help group. If she took part in the group she would be engaged in the slum and that was not something she wanted. Her situation was in clear contrast to the others who built more houses for their families in the same area and were planning a future there. Another reason for not participating was, of course, her income. She did not have money to put away in the weekly savings pot, so this meant that she was not qualified to be a part of the project.

Her neighbor from whom she was renting her home had four sons. This neighbor was a thirty-five-year-old Hindu and her sons ranged in age from twelve to nineteen. Her husband was a drunkard and a troublemaker all over the neighborhood. He was violent and beat both his wife and sons. None of her sons had more than four years of school. She did not force them to go to school because she had no money to pay for the materials, and besides the two oldest boys had seasonal jobs that helped her family have enough money for food. Her husband had a vegetable trolley from which he, when sober enough, walked around in the slum selling vegetables. This was not a very stable source of income because a lot of people did the same and her husband often let the vegetables rot in the sun while he was sleeping, trying to sober up.

She never left the house; she did not even have sandals. She said she didn't need sandals because she was not going anywhere. She had a sewing machine that she got from her father for her wedding. On this she made sari blouses for women in the neighborhood. Because of the income received from this work she did not need to ask her husband for money to buy spices for food preparation. She could go and buy them herself. The shop was only ten meters from her house. She said she had never heard of any micro-credit projects or similar projects in the slum before. She wished she could get a loan somewhere because her house was missing one wall and because of this it was getting very wet inside during the raining season. But because of her family's income she could not take part in the self-help group. She did not have money to put aside and her family did not have a stable income to repay a loan.

The last two women were mother and daughter; they were Catholic and the mother was from Tamil Nadu along with her husband. They had four daughters, all born and raised in the slum. Her husband was ill and for that reason he spent most of the time staying in bed. They had given their two oldest daughters the possibility to go a school driven by the NGO that also organizes the micro-credit project. Because of this they knew of the self-help group. During this study, the two youngest were no longer in school because after their father's illness they could no longer manage to pay the school fees; their money was mostly spent on hospital bills and a new house that they are building. Their new house consisted of two big rooms, and each room was to be considered one house. The new house was for the two oldest daughters and their husbands.

Only one of the rooms was finished during the study period and the whole family moved in there, except the eldest daughter and her husband, who just had a newborn baby girl and needed to stay in her parent's house because it was closer to the water pumps. When the baby was older they would move to the new house and her parents would move back to their own house. The daughter's husband worked as a chef in a small restaurant and had one day off work every week. Since their marriage, he refused to let his wife have a job. She had taken an electronics course at the NGO's school and had been working as a radio repair person. She often said she wanted to have a job but he would not let her. After the baby was born he had become even stickier on this matter. He wanted her to stay home and look after their child. Most of all he wanted her to move to his parents' home in a village in Tamil Nadu. But because of their housing situation in Bangalore she and her family had persuaded him to let her stay.

The family knew the NGO well because of its school. The women had been offered participation in the micro-credit project, but their husbands would not let them. First the men said it was because of the money; they said they could not afford it. Then they both said that they did not want their wife to wander around the slum and go to these meetings. They said they needed their wives at home because they had lots of duties to take care of.

Women's Space of Action

Generally poverty is a factor that reduces interest in formal education in India. A tiny economy, illiteracy, and lack of education have had an impact on women's space of action. Women slum dwellers who lack education reduce their access to a number of jobs. Positions that require literacy and specialization skills are hard to get. Most of the poor parents don't have money to pay for the school fees; in addition many parents don't see the use of school in the long run. If they decide to send their children to school, the traditionally patriarchal ideology makes it more attractive to send boys to school. Parents look upon their sons as the future heads of the household. Daughters, they perceive, will marry and move to their husband's family and not benefit the parents.

Space of action defines what a woman can and cannot do. Even though women encounter many barriers, they have a relatively large space of action. Some have more opportunity to influence their own situation and by that increase their own and their family's space of action. Women in the slum have a large space of action because of different resources such as money, knowledge, social resources and status in the home. Rosaldo (1974) says that for women to obtain influence in the society they have to leave the household sphere or make a "women's community." The self-help group can be an example of such a community, as it consists of women only. The self-help group in the slum and this common ship that the women share makes the geographic space of action as well as the economic space of action larger. By participation in the self-help group women are directly participating in expanding their space of action. The loans they took to build their own houses are part of improving their living conditions.

The informants, very attached to their domestic domain, joined a self-help group to expand their social arenas. The space of action is on a higher level. These women will meet other women, maybe some they did not know before. In addition women who are members of the self-help group may obtain a higher status in the community. Their financial situation might improve, and their influence over the family economy may increase. Women gain a wider perspective of the household's finances and therefore they can control it, and for that reason women become less dependent upon their husbands and fathers. After receiving a loan in the self-help group many build new houses and start their own business, which gives them an appearance of being successful.

Not all of the women who have this opportunity want to take part in the project. One of the informants looked at the project as an obstacle for her self-development and the possibility of moving out of the slum area. For her it was a conscious choice not to be a part of the project. She was not interested to taking part in the group; she said that the more she got involved with the local area the more ties she would have to the slum, and this was not her desire. This woman's opportunity to say no to the program, shows that she already has a relatively large space of action, compared with the other women in the sample. This independence may have originated with her background and level of education. We must not forget that her independence was being reduced by the other slum dwellers' views on honor, which is important in the Indian society. Honor is a dominant value in people's understanding of reality; without one's honor the individual is nothing. Honor is both collective and individual—collective honor is the sum of the lineages' honors and through respectable behavior in daily life one will obtain individual honor. So for this woman one way to obtain respect was to not attend the program because she then avoided walking outside alone which would be viewed as dishonorable.

The self-help group is an important step toward the empowerment of women, which is the strengthening of the women's autonomous control of material and immaterial resources and an increased self-esteem (von Bülow 1996). The self-help group encourages the women to take part in what happens in her local community. It also makes her leave the slum area and see other parts of the city where other self-help groups meet. In this way women in a self-help group get a wider perspective on what there is outside a slum. In the meetings, even though they are outside the slum, the women will only meet other women from other slums with the same background as themselves. Typically, the women from one self-help group gathered together at these meetings and did not seek to meet people from other groups.

The women at the beginning of the study had an extreme attachment to their domestic domain. They hardly ever left their houses. Some would never leave the slum area, not even their street. If possible they would spend the whole day inside their own houses. "What is there for me to do outside?" they wondered when asked questions concerning the outside world.

One reason why the women are not participating in the micro-credit project is because women are prevented by their husbands from joining. Women in self-help groups have a "women's community" in which men directly cannot take

part. Men are the possessor of power and look upon women's participation outside the domestic sphere as a menace to this power. The self-help group can be
seen as a kind of "pillow power." "Pillow power" illustrates the situation where
men have the official role in the house while women have power to a certain
degree inside the house (de Wit 1996). Men are not threatened by cooking
classes and tailoring classes, but contributing to the family's finances is part of
men's traditional sphere. Women entering men's sphere are considered threatening.

The sexual division of labor is one of the most hard-programmed ideas in
society and as a result, there is no opening for men to enter the domestic domain
to do some of the housework while their wives are at meetings. A hard programmed idea according to anthropologist Gregory Bateson, is an idea, confirmed many times, through different situations, and is therefore considered as a
matter of course and becomes a reference for other ideas. It is hard to make any
changes in these ideas, because that involves change in the whole related con-
stellation of ideas (1987). There exist hard-programmed ideas both in men and
in women about what makes them gendered and in what kinds of activities they
can participate. For example, it is not imaginable that a man can do housework;
except for helping to carry water, men do not participate in housework activities.
Women feed infants, they are nurturers, and it becomes natural that they have
the task of staying home with the children. In this way women's spaces of action
are reduced and their responsibilities for children will be used as a good reason
for not letting them leave the house, not even for an hour. The idea that a woman
should stay home and take care of her children becomes a hard-programmed
idea.

Why do women accept being prohibited from participating in self-help
groups and other activities outside their homes? An explanation can be the father
figure. The father figure is an authority that doesn't need a reason. It is culturally
understood as a matter of course that the husband represents a father figure and
challenging that authority is similar to a sin. According to the anthropologist Jan
Brøgger, the female role is complementary to the male role and this positive
aspect in the distribution of authority can be an explanation for the fact that
many women appreciate their husbands' authority and masculinity, even when it
can seem unreasonable (1999).

Access for the slum dwellers to information from the government or others
according to the situation in the slum is small, unless they are connected to an
NGO in the slum. One of the women in the slum said she had never heard about
micro-credit for women or other similar savings projects. Leaflets and other
information do not reach the women slum dwellers. NGOs distribute leaflets but
they are mostly written in Kannada. Yet, the majority of the women are illiterate
and Tamils, and because of this they are excluded from accessing this type of
information.

Even when the husbands could see that they were in need of stronger financial security, the men did not seem to like the self-help group as it caused their
wife to leave the house. Some men said that a self-help group would take too
much time because the women would have to go to weekly meetings. They

meant that their wives were needed in the house to make food, wash clothes, and clean the house. But the biggest problem seemed to be bigger meetings outside the slum, where all of the self-help group from the whole city were represented. To go to this kind of meeting the women had to go by bus, which the men did not like. The women could be approached by other men on the bus as they traveled. According to the husbands, that is not considered proper. The best thing for a woman would be to stay at home and do housework, they stated several times.

Many of the women who participated in the group did not live together with their husbands or were widows, living without a man. The women lived with their children and got money by borrowing from relatives and had income from renting out rooms in their house, selling milk from their own stock or from working in a small self-owned shop. These women also had no grownup male family member living in their house who could interfere with their membership in the self-help group. These womens' reason for joining the self-help group were in fact that they did not have a husband, and they looked at themselves as suffering more then others because they didn't have a husband to provide for the family. In reality, they all had a reasonable income, valuables, and residential properties, more than those women with husbands.

Both the two women who were members of the self-help group got in contact with the NGO through relatives who had joined other projects with the same NGO. Both had daughters who were members of the same self-help group. As a result, these families could take out more loans and have better opportunities to reach their goal of building houses or carrying on their micro-business. But at the same time they had more debt to repay. Both these women were relatively well off compared with the other informants. Both had big houses, and an extra house for rent; one of them had two small shops. Both families spoke Kannada, which is the language used at the self-help group. They owned their houses and didn't have any plans to move from the slum area. At the self-help group they were involved in improving their local community by building latrines and cleaning the area.

What is the Effect of Micro-Credit?

Participation in self-help groups means an increase in status. At home, women's authority can increase when they have an overview of the household's expenditures and finances, and this enables them to exercise more control over the family's economy. Other women who are not members look at these women as strong individuals with a good husband. After a loan from the self-help group their social status may increase depending upon what they use the money for. Some may start a small shop or build a new house, which gives them the appearance of being successful. Some do actually succeed in their business.

The women might want to be independent and to some extent the self-help group makes them so. On the other hand, the self-help group also contributes to making them dependent on the slum, as with this kind of group there is no urgent need to take part in the community outside the slum. They do not have the need to seek people or institutions outside for information or assistance for banking. Their lack of knowledge of what is on the outside will be even greater and does not give them a chance to achieve a higher status.

There is relatively little research on the effect of these kinds of groups in very, very poor areas. Some research of self-help groups in Tanzania shows that the groups has increased the women's income and with that led both to improve the women's self esteem and their status at home. Other research shows that projects changed both the power relations inside the family and the local area. In other areas, women's income and employment situation worsened, they became more dependent on their husbands, fathers, and local government, and in the worse cases women became even poorer. In Bangalore the consequences of the micro-credit project are not quite clear because the project is still rather new. But two of the members of the self-help group expressed a certain skepticism towards the loans they had gotten without being able to reach their goals.

The self-help group forms a "women's community" where men cannot participate directly, and for this reason, the "community" is protected. This exclusive "community" can give women a strong offense in this male-dominated society. But the "women's community" can also be the reason why men are not letting their wives and daughters attend the micro-credit project. Traditionally men have the power in the family and therefore women's participation outside their domestic domain can be a threat that men might see as a threat to the honor of the family.

More women might have access to micro-credit projects if they included men. In the slum it is obvious that besides the economic aspect, men are a major reason why women cannot participate in micro-credit. For slum dwellers these traditions are not going away in the near future, so an alternative solution will therefore be to include men more in micro-credit projects. The more knowledge men have about micro-credit, the more they can see what good their family can get from it.

The absence of men is a theme among the assistance aid workers nowadays. The South African scientist Robert Morell (2003: 6) said, "You are forgetting the men." He said that the focus solely on women leads to negative consequences. From his studies on Africa, Morell shows how men lose their position in society when the focus is on women. This has led to situations where the man is not longer the provider for his family. The number of households led by women increases, the women have now both the resources and the power in the household. Men are left with only one manner to express their maleness, their sexuality. In their marriage men still have power and it is often expressed by violence, concludes Morell (2003).

Conclusion

Women slum dwellers meet many obstacles to participation in self-help groups that would increase their space of action. In this society where these women live, being a woman is an obstacle itself. The status, gender, is an obstacle that prevents women from expanding their space of action. The women in this study are born in a role that is inferior to the male role in their society. Traditional understandings of the tasks of men and the tasks of women are thoroughly integrated into their minds. The traditional understanding of being a woman in this society includes taking care of children, doing housework and obeying the husband (or other male members of the family). Performing these tasks prevent a women's physical space of action from expanding, since her tasks are all closely connected to her physically being at home. The women, whose husbands did not allow them to participate, sometimes explained this by referring to the other women's husbands as "better husbands."

Micro-credit and the self-help group's aim is to give empowerment to poor women. However, it is difficult for them to join in. There are several reasons for the inability to participate, some of which occur separately and others that occur together. There is the need to save for occasions such as birth, weddings, death, widowhood and old age and so on. Women's financial burden stops them from saving, but also the women's families, ethnicity and social problems are factors that prevent them from attending micro-credit meetings. Even though the projects seek to empower women, it is very hard for women to gain access to the projects, at least in this case of the slum in Bangalore. Their tradition will not allow them to take part in the public arena even when it is in their own community. One of the reasons why NGOs do not reach out to the poorest of the poor is because husbands prevent these women from joining the group. Often the women who are already relatively well off and empowered are able to attend micro-credit projects. The evidence from the interviews in the small sample shows that it is those women who already have their own houses and money who are members of the self-help group. In addition they have also taken part in similar projects before. Participation in the micro-credit is based on having a regular income. This is an obstacle for those without financial security because irregular income makes it impossible to save on a regular basis. The ones who have money get even more and this creates differences within the slum as well as differences with those on the outside of the slum.

Notes

1. For my master's degree in Social Anthropology, I did fieldwork in a slum in Bangalore in South India. This paper is based on my Master's Degree Thesis, which is called "Mikrokreditt for noen. Livsvilkår og handlingsrom bland kvinner i en slum i Bangalore, India" (Micro-credit for a Few. Living Conditions and Space of Action among Female Slum Dwellers in a Bangalore Slum, India).

2. My translator had been in school twelve years and her English was satisfactory for the work which I needed her to do. She, being a local woman, made it easier for the research to be done closer to the women interviewed.

3. NGO is a term that includes all non-profit organizations.

4. Rupee is the Indian currency. In 2001, one hundred rupee was about 1.5 British pound.

5. Moneylender is a person who lends out a sum of money and collects it after a week or a month with a rather high interest rate.

References

Bateson, Gregory. 1987. *Steps to An Ecology of Mind: Collected Essays in Anthropology, Psychiatry, Evolution and Epistemology.* San Francisco: Janson Aronson.

Brøgger, Jan. 1999. *Psykologisk antropologi.* Oslo: Cappelen Akademisk Forlag.

von Bülow, Dorthe. 1996. "Dyrekøbte erfaringer: Formel kredit til kvinder." In *Den NY verden No 2.* Copenhagen: Center for Udviklingsforskning.

Morell, Robert. 2003. "Afrikanske Menn er Taperne. Sørafr kansk Forsker Stiller Spørsmålstegn ved Bistandens 'Kvinnemote'." In *Bistandsaktuelt nr 6,* NORAD.

Rosaldo, Michelle Z. 1974. "Women, Culture and Society: A Theoretical Over-view." In M. Rosaldo and L. Lamphere. eds. *Women, Culture and Society:* 17–42. Palo Alto: Stanford University Press.

de Wit, Joop W. 1996. *Poverty, Policy, and Politics in Madras Slums. Dynamics of Survival, Gender and Leadership.* London: Sage Publications.

Chapter 28

Analysis of Factors Influencing Women's Economic Group Survival in Tanzania

Aurelia N. Kamuzora and Faustin R. Kamuzora

Women's economic groups (WEGs) are formulated for the purpose of generating income for family members and women themselves. Traditionally there are many types of women's groups in Tanzania. Some of these are religious groups, ethnic groups, "help each other groups," credit society groups and *Upatu* groups. Through this practice of group formation, some women decide to transform their traditional groups into WEGs. Others are formulated as WEGs from the beginning. Many WEGs are formed to receive credits responding to the conditions provided by credit service providers, including the government (Kydd and Kashuliza 1996; Makombe et. al. 1998).

Women's economic groups are very important because they are usually involved in various types of small private enterprises. Private business is now viewed as an engine of economic growth; therefore these WEGs can be vehicles for alleviating poverty in society. Since the majority of Tanzanian women are relatively poor (Mbughuni 1993; URT 2001), WEGs provide an opportunity to fight poverty. In addition, gender discrimination and stereotyping prevail in many spheres in the country, for example, in the employment sector. This is evidenced by the majority of women being subjected to low positions in the workplace in addition to their respective traditional (family) roles (Makombe et. al 1998; URT 2001). In order to reduce these disadvantages faced by women in Tanzania, economic empowerment is considered one of the ways to emancipate women. One of the methods of economic empowerment is to utilize WEGs (Meghji 1987). However, as noted by Kamuzora (2000) the majority of WEGs do not survive for a long enough period to accomplish the objective of economic empowerment. The majority of WEGs die within the first two years. This chapter presents information on WEGs and determinants of causes for their failure and success.

Background and Hypothesis

In 1991, the government of Tanzania issued a policy statement on financial sector reform designed to stimulate competition and lessen government interference (Narayan 1997). Women in Tanzania were encouraged to establish small credit groups. For example, in the Morogoro region all councils were supposed to set aside 10 percent of revenues that they collect to use for "soft" loans. About 2.8 million Tanzanian shillings were set-aside for that purpose in 1998.

However, many businesses that were started survived for only a short time, and many of the groups disintegrated in less than two years time. (Kamuzora 2000) Only 17 percent of the groups started between 1992 and 1999 were still in business in the year 2000. Similarly, only about 16 percent of women in Tanzania who applied for a loan, for example, from the Credit Regional Development Bank (CRDB) in the year 1998 got it. Rutashobya interviewed a sample of women who had applied for loans and 91 percent of the respondents reported that there were problems in receiving the loan. This mainly emanated from complicated procedures and a bureaucratic system (Rutashobya 1998). Such an environment would not help WEGs to survive.

Innovation can be measured in terms of the presence of new products and improved product quality, new services, new markets, marketing methods and new methods of operation. Also, innovation allows adaptation to new market conditions. Many authors consider innovation to be characteristics of entrepreneurship (Schumpeter 1934; Druker 1985; Burns and Dewhurst 1996; Stokes 1995; Spring and McDade 1998). Therefore innovation is regarded as the introduction of a new good or improving the existing one, the introduction of a new process, the opening of new markets especially exporting, the identification of a new supply of raw materials, the creation of new sources of the materials or the creation of new types of industrial organization (Schumpeter 1934; Druker 1995). We assumed that a group, which is innovative, would remain in operation for a period of more than three years. According to Schumpeter (1934), innovation reinforced by today's changing and competitive environment is a source of success in the market economy. An organization such as a WEG that is not creative and innovative may not survive (Kristiansen 2001). This is because innovation enhances the entrepreneurial spirit (Druker 1995). The hypothesis we tested was as follows: There is a positive relationship between innovative characteristics and the women's economic group survival rate.

Gender imbalances in Tanzania are a cultural and an institutional phenomenon, deriving from Tanzanian history. Mbughuni (1998) shows that the colonial economy and educational system had a negative impact on policies for women. This negativity has been entrenched within the societal values and has increased the work burden on women. This situation eroded women's power base, channels of communication and organizations and access to resources needed to maintain a family. The resources in question include fertile land, trained labor, and finance. This situation has resulted in the majority of Tanzanian women being marginalized in the commercialization process.

Gender refers not only to men and women but to the relationship between them and the way this is socially constructed. Gender relations are context specific and often change in response to altering circumstances (Moser 1993). Similarly, studies like the one done by Williams (1994), found that self-concepts of men and women were differentiated in countries and within regions in the same country. Thus, businesswomen vary from one country to another and from one cultural group to another. Narayan (1997), in a study conducted in Tanzania, showed how women have been marginalized as far as business undertakings are concerned. A woman in Tanzania is also influenced by the impacts of colonialism and cultural practice. In addition, the Tanzanian economic institutional framework, structural adjustment and other policies are impacting women differently relative to men (Mahigi et al. 2000). In order to investigate how these issues affected the longevity of WEGS, we hypothesized that gender imbalance in Tanzania has a negative impact on women's business groups.

Other researchers also unveil the selective highlighting and reinterpretation of cultural forms of expression to bolster patriarchy (proverbs, stories and songs). For example, according to Kazmaja (1996), in most Third World countries women are prepared to be housewives from their childhood. Given the values of Tanzanian women received from their parents and society as a whole, women tend to be marginalized in several societal aspects including assets ownership. A woman owns very few items in the household. For example, in her study on resource ownership conducted in Tabora, Tanzania, Narayan (1997) found that during marriage a woman has rights to use almost everything except those possessions a man identifies as his, either because he bought them or uses them exclusively. Men said that the radio, bicycle, cattle and house are owned by the man and cannot be used by others without permission of the husband even though the wife contributed her efforts to acquire the properties. Traditionally, men own other properties like spears, beehives and children because they have paid the bride price. Women own kitchen pots, ornaments and vegetables because they make them or they are primary users. To determine the influence of cultural values in WEGs, we hypothesized that cultures that value women (gender stereotypes) are positively related to women's business group survival.

The majority of women in Tanzania lack business skills. These skills could enhance survival of women's economic groups. The low level of education among women in Tanzania has had an adverse effect on business skills. Narayan (1997) revealed that more girls are pulled out of school than boys and when parents were asked why they were pulling girls out of school, they gave many reasons, such as: girls will get married so no need of investing in them (25%), risk of pregnancy (24%), boys bring income (12%), boys are home guardians (8%), and educating girls was a waste of money (7%). These parental attitudes reduce the chances of girls and women receiving a sufficient education. Entrepreneurs with higher educational standards stand a good chance of surviving economically in a "turbulent" business environment. Business training takes many forms such as on-the-job training, off-job training, seminars, workshops and talks by guest speakers invited to address special topics and information dissemination. The best training takes place through the transfer of practical knowledge in ongoing relationships between buyers and sellers and through subcontracting. Therefore, women's groups are vehicles through which women can be developed. To test the impact of the presence of business skills among group members on WEGs survival, we hypothesized that the presence of business skills has a positive impact on women's businesses.

Business networks are a mode of handling activity independently but within the relationships created among several business actors (Hollensen 1998). In a business network the actors are linked to each other through exchange in relationships, and their needs and capabilities are mediated through the interaction taking place in the business world. Networks operate best when their organization and activities are not fixed, but are flexible (Castell 1996). Similarly, Wathne, et. al. suggest that, implicitly or explicitly, the assumption is made in the literature that the presence of social bonds protects existing relationships from competition (2001). The structure of an individual's social relationship with an exchange partner will determine how a potential new partner is viewed. The stronger the pre-existing social bonds, the greater is the investments in social capital, and the greater the likelihood that the existing relationship will be maintained. To test the effect of a social bond on the survival of WEGs in Kibaha district, we hypothesized that the stronger the social bonds (social capital) of women with the existing competing firms, the more the likelihood (probability) of women's business survival.

According to the analysis of Mbughuni (1998), women have a history of negative experience with group and/or cooperative projects. For example, Rayeski and Bryant (1994) found that the top five conflict causes in groups were as follows (ranked from the highest to the lowest): goal and priority definition, personality, communication, politics, administrative procedures. Conflicts in WEGs reduce cohesion among members. To test whether cohesion among members of WEGs is important in influencing WEGs' survival, we tested whether a group cohesion influences women's businesses.

The socio-political environment in Tanzania has changed remarkably since the first two decades post-independence that were dominated by the *Ujamaa* ideology. Market liberalization has influenced the current epoch. In the *Ujamaa* era, political leaders would easily interfere with business operations by requesting various contributions and favors. To small enterprises such as WEGs these favors and contributions sometimes eroded the capital base resulting in the demise of the business. To test whether this trend is continuing and impacting the WEGs, the last hypothesis we formulated was whether the outsiders' interference influences women's businesses.

Results

In order to evaluate these hypotheses, we collected both qualitative and quantitative data.

Qualitative data was collected using a questionnaire in Swahili where respondents ranked their answers with a Likert scale. The sample was randomly selected. In our case, Kibaha District Community Development Officer's (CDO) office had the list of the women's groups who had ever started in business. There were 149 women randomly selected members from both surviving groups and non-surviving groups.[1] The results in this paper are based on quantitative data from 139 respondents since ten of the respondents were not involved in any WEG at the time of the study because their's had died and they had not joined a new one. The Likert scale was constructed as: 1 = Not important at all, 2 = Not important, 3 = Somehow Important, 4 = Important, 5 = Very Important. In the coding process and data analysis, the researchers used the statistical software package, Statistical Package for Social Sciences (SPSS) version 9.0, to analyze the collected data.

The qualitative data[2] indicated that more than half (52%) of the respondents' WEGs had been in operation for only two years or less (see table 28.1). Whereas, 15 percent of the respondents' WEGs had been operating for over four years. There were five groups, 3.6 percent of the total, which survived for more than thirteen years.

Table 28.1 Number of Years for Surviving WEGs in Tanzania

Years	Frequency	Percent	Cumulative Percent
1	26	18.7	18.7
2	46	33.1	51.8
3	25	18.0	69.8
4	21	15.1	84.9
5	16	11.5	96.4
13	5	3.6	100.0
Total	139	100.0	

Source: Kamazora and Kamuzora 2002

The few WEGs that survive for more than three years must have specific survival characteristics.[3] In depth interviews on credit services, conducted between the researchers and the District CDO, revealed that the government and international community do support women's development in Kibaha. In the District there are many women's economic groups funded by various agencies. Some of the agencies are CARITAS; UNDP; Presidential Trust Fund (PTF), and the Women's Development Fund (WDF). Every WEG has a right to receive loan money from the District based on the requirement that the District set aside tax revenues for this purpose; there are no other conditions except to adhere to the credit rules. From the available records, in 1989 four groups were initiated by

Women's Appropriate Food Technology (WAFT) project. Table 28.2 summarizes information about these early WAFT groups.

Women's Development Fund (WDF), according to the government directive, was established in 1997. District Councils were required to allocate 5 percent of their gross revenue for women's development (similarly 5% to youth development). These totals are shown in table 28.3.

Table 28.2 Women's Appropriate Food Technology Groups Established in Kibaha District, Tanzania, 1989

Location of Group	Funding Agency	Project Activity	Status
Mkuza	UNDP/UNIFEM*	Milling machine	Still living
Visiga	UNDP	Chicken project	Dead
Misugusugu	UNDP	Gardening	Dead
Bokotimiza	CRDB**	Milling	Dead

Source: Kibaha District Council (KDC) records 2001.
Note: *United Nations Development Programme/United Nations Development Fund for Women; ** Credit Regional Development Bank

Table 28.3 Amount of Loaned Funds in Kibaha District, Tanzania by Group, 2001

Name of Group	Source of Funds (Tanzanian Shilling)		
	CRDB*	UNDP/UNIFEM**	Other
Mkuza	54,000	387,000	1,200,000
Visiga		208,000	
Misugusugu	50,000		
Bokotimiza	980,000		

Source: Kibaha District Council (KDC) records 2001.
Note: *Credit Regional Development Bank; **United Nations Development Programme—United Nations Development Fund for Women;

Table 28.4 shows for 1996–2000, the contributions to women's economic development by the Kibaha District and the Central government. Between 1996 and 2000, the actual contribution of KDC falls short of the estimated amount of available revenues.

KDC's contribution was less than one quarter of the estimated amount for every year except 1999 when it was only 28 percent of the estimate. Reasons for the above scenario include poor collection of estimated revenue by KDC and little importance accorded to women's economic development in the Council by policy-making organs. The contribution of the Central government to WDF in Kibaha District Council has been declining from its inception in 1997. This decline in funding has occurred simultaneously with efforts to motivate women to form economic groups.

Table 28.4 Contribution to Women's Development Fund (WDF), Kibaha District, Tanzania, 1997–2000 (Tanzanian Shillings)

Year	Estimate	Contribution	Percent of Estimate	Contribution to WDF from Local Government Sources	Yearly Percent Decline
1997	-	-	-	2,840,000	
1998	4.3 mil	50,000	1.2	1,225,000	56.9
1999	3.6 mil	1,000,000	28	700,000	42.8
2000	6 mil	1,186,000	20	0	100.0

Source: Kibaha District Council 2001.

Table 28.5 Type of Activities Supported by Women's Development Fund, Kibaha District, Tanzania, 2001

Activity	Percent
Agriculture/Gardening	22
Selling wood/Charcoal	14
Food kiosk/Mama Lishe	13
Selling buns (bites)	11
'Genge'	11
Selling fried fish	5
Tailoring	3
Local brew	3
Maize/chicken retailing	1
Used clothes (mitumba)	3
Total	100

Source: KDC 2001.

Table 28.5 indicates that the major activity supported by the WDF is agriculture. The reason for this is the comparative advantage Kibaha District Council has for market access. There is a potential market for the sale of garden products in nearby Dar es Salaam.

These are the steps of the WEG loan process: (1) Awareness creation. Women in villages were informed about WDF followed by organizational meetings in villages using the assistance of village governments. (2) Village governments recommended interested WEGs (each group comprised five members). (3) Every member had to fill out the forms requesting a loan. (4) Then, a selection committee discussed the names of recommended groups at the district level, after which, the groups selected for a loan are informed and members are usually advised to open a bank account; and, lastly, (5) balances are deposited in bank accounts or cash is granted to those without accounts.

Table 28.6: Loan Amount and Repayment, Women's Development Fund,
Kabaha District, Tanzania, 1999

Ward	Amount Loaned*	Loan repayment rate (%)
Soga	880,400	92.1
Ruvu	880,400	81.8
Magindu	880,400	75.0
Visiga	880,400	91.2
Kibaha	1,326,800	97.5
Tumbi/Vikawe	979,600	56.7

Source: Kabaha District Council records 2001.
Note: * Tanzanian Shillings

Table 28.6 indicates that the WDF repayment for most of the loans is quite impressive. More than half of the wards have loan repayment rates of above 80 percent. Only one ward was below 50 percent. Many women in Kibaha received loans to start a business, but when they return home they find other economic hardships. Sometimes the economic hardships force women to reallocate the loan towards other consumption in the households like buying school uniforms for their children or buying food.

In order to further assess women's economic group survival, we interviewed the chairperson of the longest surviving group. The business operated a mill from 1988 to 2001. The chair indicated that the business began in 1988 in response to the TANITA government program that encouraged business formation. When we asked where the group received training to run the business and the technical know-how to run the milling machine, they responded: "A man, working with TANITA, trained us. We also had different seminars on how to operate the milling machine and the business side too." They explained the difficulties they faced during training, as the business was more technical than physical and financial management. "There was neither electricity transformer in this village nor electricity line. Through small businesses we were able to get electricity and then we could install our machine. In the village people thought we couldn't be able to survive as they could see us turning on and off (operating) the machine, others thought we were crazy and they waited for our failure, but we didn't," she added. Through training they obtained skills for running their business.

Asking the same questions to the members of a non-surviving women's economic group, lack of business skills led to their failure, although the group member did not directly admit it when she said: "We secured the loan from the government, then we bought chicks. The chicks continued well, but later they died of unknown disease." "Then what else did you do," we asked. Interviewee: "Nothing." Interviewer: "Did you know that you could receive another loan, if you have genuine reasons, to leverage your small business?" Interviewee: "We didn't know before, but after we stopped our activities, CCM members decided to take our building, which was on their premises. We decided to report the matter to the Women's Welfare Department, the DCO decided to help us. The CCM members have now returned our building." Interviewer: "Why do you think the

CCM members decided to take your building?" Interviewee: "The building remained idle for many years; the CCM members hired someone who had a VCR and a television set and used it as a video show house. He rehabilitated it and he was paying Tsh500 per show to CCM. After getting that information the women went to the DCO's office and that helped us to get it back. The building is now idle; nothing is taking place there. We are planning to continue hiring it if they get another person who can use it for the same purpose."

It seems these women lacked the necessary business skills to continue in business after their chicks died. The CCM members have shown them the way; the building could be used for something else. However, this group had only one member left, who used to be the chairperson.

How does group dynamism affect women's economic groups? When asked the importance of cohesion in the group as a factor for surviving, the group members admitted that the group couldn't survive without unity. In order to get an indicator of group cohesion, the interviewer asked, "Had you some misunderstanding from the day you started working together?" The woman answered, "Yes, we were thirty people at the beginning, but we are now ten. The others who couldn't conform with the group norms left the group." "We started by cultivating vegetables, and selling them in the streets. The only thing that made us able to survive is unity and cooperation among the remaining ten members. Also we appreciate the leadership offered by our chairwoman."

The non-surviving women's group indicated that group cohesion was a big reason for business survival. The women who formulated the group were twelve at the beginning, later they remain six. The six members help each other on a traditional basis with events such as wedding ceremonies, funerals and at planting time, but they don't have any group investment. It seems that the women in Kibaha groups, surviving and non-surviving, understood the importance of adequate group cohesion.

Does institutional framework contribute to women's group business survival? The Tanzania government institutions are a barrier for business survival. Even though the government provides loans specifically for women. When we interrogated the women in a surviving group, the group member said, "We have obtained support from different individuals and groups. We remember the Regional Commissioner came with other government officials to see what we were engaged in; he was impressed and he sent us Tshs 100,000 as support." She continued to say, "Our milling machine was not only for business purposes, but also it helped the villagers to have a milling machine in the neighborhood. For that matter, everyone was ready to help." "We faced the cultural problem, where the men were thinking that we were going against their expectations. Some men could come to the place of work and laugh at us and they said, 'these women are crazy'. Because the men did this many women decided to get out of the group. Our husbands started to discourage us from working during the night. But, after realizing the benefits we obtained from the business, they relaxed the stringent cultural division of labor and gender roles. They started to help us in cooking, taking care of the children, and other domestic chores." Another said, "A man should respect our job, because they see the benefits from this business. We were able to send our children to school and build corrugated iron houses that the family couldn't afford without our milling machine."

Even the non-survivors group also appreciated the support from the government. When the interviewer asked about marriage institutions effect on business, the woman said, "Marriage institutions didn't affect any of us who were not in marriage. However, one of our members was in marriage and her husband prevented her immediately after starting the business."

How does the business network (social-capital network) of women affect their business? The business network was not seen to affect the surviving group; they had a good social capital network in the village. Everybody in the Mkuza village needed their service because villagers had no milling machine for a long time; they used to travel a long distance to another village to look for this service. Community members were excited to get that service, so they provided the necessary cooperation and they helped to educate the skeptics that women can run such a business successfully. The social-capital network facilitated the success. "There was a male technician in the village who was working with TANITA, and he couldn't skip even a single day without passing by to see if they had a problem to solve or any need of advice." When there was any machine defect, the technician, an electrician, could show them how to resolve the problem. "When there was some kind of electric leakage, we could put it off and wait for him. In the long run we solved some of the electrical problems ourselves." He encouraged them to rely on themselves and his words were "you can do everything, you are strong as the men."

The non-surviving group had nothing to relate to a social network except the CCM members who decided to take away their business house and rent it without informing them. As long as these women did not stay in business for a long period, they couldn't explain exactly how a social network hindered or leveraged their business. "We cannot blame the interference of outsiders, because during seminars we were told to use our money for running our businesses, not for welcoming the guest."

How does gender stereotyping as a cultural value affect women's business? The surviving group explained the gender stereotype to be a problem in Kibaha district. They explained the negative attitude that people had at the time they installed the milling machine and operated it themselves without employing men. "They called us names such as crazy, uncultured and so on," explained the woman. "The disgrace they showed to us made some of our group members run from the group," she added. Ten women or 33 percent of women remained while 67 percent dropped out over time. When the group members who left were asked why they decided to stop membership, they replied, "We cannot operate the business that our husbands are not interested in."

The non-surviving group cited the influence of a husband who stopped his wife from being in the business. He supposedly said to his wife, "Working together with unmarried women will make you to be a prostitute." The woman stopped the membership in the business immediately.

In order to test our hypothesis quantitatively, we used a regression analysis. WEGs business survival, the dependent variable, was measured as number of years of active operation. Independent variables were lack of innovation, credit policies, culture, gender imbalance, group cohesion, business skills, social bond and interferences, measured with a Likert scale on the questionnaire.

The linear regression model we estimated was as follows: Longevity = f (Inno, Gend, Credit, Cult, Gro, Busi, Soci, Interf); Where: Longevity = Years of survival of Women's Economic groups; Inno = Innovative characteristics (expected sign is positive); Gend = Gender imbalances (expected sign is negative); Credit = Conducive credit policies (expected sign was positive); Cult = Cultural values (expected value is positive); Gro = Group cohesion (expected value is positive); Busi = Business skills (expected sign is positive); Soci = Social Bonds or Business Networks (expected sign is positive); Interf = Interference by outsiders.

The variables were operationalized in the questionnaire as:

- Innovation was indicated if a member of the group responded positively on the innovation indicators such as WEG participation in a new market, new ways of operation, diversification, changing the product in the course of business operation, modification or other additional business technique.
- Gender imbalance was measured by asking about perceptions by woman as to whether she thinks that if she wasn't a woman she could have done better in business and if she thought that being a woman was considered as a handicap in business.
- Credit policies: Women were asked to assess how credit policies hinder or help their possibilities of having access to loans so they are able to acquire capital.
- Culture: The women were asked how overall cultural values in Tanzania contributed or not to the successful operation of business.
- Business skills: Women were asked about their acquisition of business skills from school, on-the-job training, seminars, meetings, and learning from each other.
- Social bonds: Social bonds were measured by asking how the social network helps them in business. The business network is the relationships with outsiders and how those relationships give benefits towards their success.
- Group cohesion: Because WEGS are business groups we wanted to measure the group cohesion as a variable and determine how unity and togetherness led to their success.
- Interference by the outsiders: We asked respondents to measure their perception of the impact toward their business of outsiders such as party leaders, politicians and other non-group member.

The eight variables explain about 32 percent of the variation in years of survival (see table 28.7). Business skills positively and significantly contributed to the longevity of a WEG while Innovation was inversely related to longevity perhaps reflecting groups taking on increased risk in the face of strong cultural constraints. The rest of the variables proved insignificant. Despite the relatively low predictive power, the overall model is significant as depicted by the F statistic, which is significant at the .05 level. The low R–squared and the possibility that some variables are correlated with others suggests a need for further investigation about the other factors that can affect WEGs survivability. Therefore we can conclude that women's economic empowerment through group investments has a complex set of determinants of success. Innovation and business skills have strong impacts on survival.

Table 28.7: Determinants of Longevity of Women's Economic Groups in Tanzania, Ordinary Least Square Results

Variable	Coefficient		t	Sig. Level	R2	F
	Beta	Std. Error				
Constant	4.110	1.145	3.591	.000		
Innovation	-.814	.232	-3.513	.001		
Credit Policies	.0603	.268	.225	.822		
Culture	.159	.392	.405	.686	.324	7.078
Gender Imbalance	.461	.398	1.158	.249		(sig. 000)
Group Cohesion	-.204	.228	-.894	.373		
Business Skills	1.426	.227	6.288	.000		
Social Bond	.0262	.253	.104	.917		
Interferences	-.316	.446	-.709	.480		

Source: Authors' results.

Conclusion and Policy Implications

Based on the results from the study, the policy plans and strategies towards WEGS need to be directed into women's training in business skills, which would also include sensitization to innovative strategies for the business. There have been many seminars conducted to improve women's economic activities in Tanzania, but these trainings have not been need-specific. One has to conduct Training Needs Assessment (TNA) at the individual level, then at the WEG level. After capturing the gaps in what each individual WEG needs, the training should be tailored to the single group with its specific investments. At present, a certain NGO or an interested organization and some government bodies at the district level conduct training. The qualitative data indicates that it is relatively easy for Tanzanian women to form groups and start their group businesses. This research opens other avenues for future research such as the following: 1) The need to conduct training needs assessment amongst Women's Economic Groups; and 2) The need to investigate further the other variables which might have an impact on WEGs and their survival.

Notes

1. Because of migration, it was not easy to get the group members who had been in non-surviving groups.

2. The qualitative data was collected using in-depth interviews with twelve respondents before collection of the quantitative data. The composition of these twelve respondents included respondents whose WEGs had died and did not join new ones, those who had joined new WEGs after the disintegration of the old ones and those who were in the very few WEGs that had survived for thirteen years. The in-depth qualitative information assisted us to design the questionnaire and clearly elaborate the questions during the survey where the questions seemed hard to be discerned by the respondents. Thus, even though the results presented in this paper are based on quantitative data, it should be borne in mind that the qualitative data were as important in the research.

3. Before running the ordinary least square regression, we first performed the Exploratory Data Analyse (EDA) as recommended by Mukherjee and Wuyts (1998) to ensure that the data possessed the characteristics suitable for OLS. The results from the study are presented in this paper from three statistical methods, namely, OLS, stepwise regression, and Factor Analysis.

References

Burns P. and J. Dewhurst. 1996. *Small Business and Entrepreneurship*. London: McMillan Press.

Capozzoli, T. K. 1995. "Conflict Resolution: A Key Ingredient In Successful Teams." *Supervision*. vol. 56 no.12: 3–5.

Castells, M. 1996. *The Rise Of The Network Society; The Information Age: Economy, Society And Culture*. Malden MA: Blackwell.

Drucker, P. F. 1985 *Innovation and Entrepreneurship Practice and Principles*. London: William Heinemann Ltd.

———.1995. *The Practice of Management*. London: HarperCollins.

Ghauri, P., and Gronhaug, K. 2002. *Research Methods in Business Studies*. London: Financial Times—Prentice Hall.

George, D. and Mallery, P. 2003. *SPSS for Windows Step By Step: A Simple Guide And Reference. 11.0 update* . 4th ed. Boston: Allyn & Bacon.

Hollensen, S. 1998. *Global Marketing*. London: Prentice Hall.

Huber, J. ed.1973. *Changing Women in a Changing Society*. Chicago: University of Chicago Press.

Kamuzora, A. 2000. "Lack of Innovation in Women's Economic Groups: A Cause of Low Business Survival Rate: A Case of Morogoro Region." Paper Presented at a Workshop on System Innovation Organised Jointly by the Institute of Development and Planning, Aaborg University, Denmark and the Institute of Development Management (IDM), Mzumbe, Tanzania at IDM-Mzumbe, Sept.

Kazmaja, V. 1996. "Strategies For Women in Science & Technology." *Proceedings Papers from GASAT 8*. Ahmedabad, India, January.

Kristiansen, S. 2001. "Geography and Innovation: Regional Contexts and Small-Scale Entrepreneurs in Tanzania and Indonesia." *Entrepreneurship and Regional Development* vol. 13: 24–35.

Kydd, J. G. and A. Kashuliza. 1996 "Determinants of Bank Credit Access for Small-holder Farmers in Tanzania: a Discriminate Analysis Application." *Savings and Development*, vol. XX No. 3: 285–304.

Mahigi, B. A., A. Ryen, and A.M. Stocken. 2000. "Women and Labour Markets in Tanzania: Impacts on Gendered Lives." Agder University College.

Makombe, I. A. M., E. I. Temba and A. Kihombo. 1998. "Credit Schemes and Women's Empowerment for Poverty Alleviation: The Case of Tanga Region, Tanzania." *Research Report No. 99.1*. Dar es Salaam: REPOA.

Mbughuni, P. 1998. "Gender and Poverty Alleviation in Tanzania. Recent Research Issues." In M.S.D. Bagachwa. ed. *Poverty Alleviation in Tanzania. Recent Research Issues*. Dar-Es-Salaam: Dar Es Salaam University Press.

Meghji, Z. 1987. *A Study of Credit Facilities to Women in Tanzania*. Dar es Salaam: University Press: Dar es Salaam.

Moser, C. O. N. 1993. *Gender Planning and Development. Theory, Practice and Training*. London: Routledge.

Mukherjee, C. and Wuyts, M. 1998. "Thinking With Data." In A. Thomas, J. Chataway and M. Wuyts. eds. *Finding Out Fast: Investigative Skills for Policy and Development*. London: The Open University and Sage.

Nachmias, C. F. and D. Nachmias. 1996. *Research Methods in the Social Sciences*. London: Arnold Press.

Narayan, D. 1997. *Voices of The Poor: Poverty and Social Capital in Tanzania*. Washington D. C.: World Bank.

Nunnally, J. C., and I. H. Bernstein. 1994. *PsychometricTheory*, 3rd ed. New York: McGraw-Hill.

Rayeski, E. and J.D. Bryant. 1994. "Team Resolution Process: A Guideline For Teams To Manage Conflict, Performance, And Discipline." In M. Beyerlein and M. Bullock. eds. *The International Conference on Work Teams Proceedings: Anniversary Collection. The Best of 1990–1994:* 215–221. Denton TX: University of North Texas.

Rutashobya, L. K. 1998. "Women's Entrepreneurship in Tanzania: Entry and Performance Barriers." Addis Ababa, Ethiopia: *OSSREA.*

Schumpeter, J. A. 1934. *The Theory of Economic Development*. Cambridge MA: Harvard University Press.

Spring A. and B. E. McDade. 1998. *African Entrepreneurship: The Theory and Reality*. Gainesville: University Press of Florida

Stokes David. 1995. *Small Business Management: An Active Learning Approach*, 2nd ed. London: D P Publications.

URT. 2001. *Household Budget Survey*. Dar es Salaam: Government Printer

Wathne, K. H. 2001. "Supplier Choice in Embedded Markets: Relationship and Marketing Effects." *Journal of Marketing,* vol. 55: 54–66.

Williams, S. 1994. *The Oxfam Gender Training Manual*. London: Oxfam.

Index

About the Editor

Linda E. Lucas, professor of economics, Eckerd College, St. Petersburg, Florida has teaching and research interests in women and labor and the gendered impacts of globalization. She has been a Fulbright professor at ITAM (Mexico City) and in the department of women's and gender studies, Makerere University; and a visiting professor at the department of economics at Thammasat University in Bangkok and at the department of women's studies at the University of South Florida; a visiting researcher at the Thailand Development Research Institute, the East-West Center in Honolulu and the Economic Policy Research Center in Kampala. She is a founding member of the International Association for Feminist Economics (IAFFE) and has published several book chapters and articles in her fields.

About the Contributors

Noor Rahamah Hj. Abu Bakar, associate professor, school of social development and environmental studies, Universiti Kebangsaan, Malaysia, completed her Ph.D. in 2003 at Universiti Kebangsaan Malaysia in Development Studies. Her research interest is in the area of women and gender in the labor market. She has published journal articles and presented at several national and international conferences.

Angela Beigaruraho Bazaare, principal lecturer, Kyambogo University, Kampala, Uganda, has twenty-five years experience in teaching and is an accredited trainer with Uganda Manufacturing Association in business skill development programs. She holds a postgraduate Diploma in Management from Maastricht school of management in the Netherlands. Her research area is in language, communication and entrepreneurship.

Marta B. Chiappe, professor agregado in the department of social sciences, college of agriculture at the Universidad de la República in Uruguay, has a Ph.D. from the University of Minnesota. Her research and activist interests focus on rural women, women farmer's organizations and the view and attitudes of farmers towards the environmental management of their farms and rural areas.

Patricia Daniel, senior lecturer in social development at the Centre for International Development and Training (CIDT), University of Wolverhampton, UK, has edited a number of publications including a special volume of *Equal Opportunities International* on Women's Literacy and Power and the *University of*

Wales (Bangor) Women's Studies Monograph Series. She specializes in participatory methodology, impact assessment and conflict prevention.

Manisha Desai, associate professor of sociology and women and gender in global perspectives, associate program director in South Asia and Middle Eastern Studies, University of Illinois at Urbana, Champaign, Illinois, is currently working on a Gender and Globalization book for the Gender Lens Series. Her most recent edited book is *Women's Issues in Asia and Oceania*, Greenwood (2003).

Elsje Dijkgraaff, director, International Training Center for Women (ITW), Amsterdam, holds a Ph.D. in anthropology from the University of Amsterdam. She is founder of ITW which has trained hundreds of women in entrepreneurial and management skills in eastern and western Europe, Asia, Africa and Latin America. She has extensive experience in evaluation and assessment of business skills in different cultural contexts.

Signe Ekenberg, Ph.D. candidate, political science, University of Tromsoe, Norway, is currently working at the United Nations Association of Norway, northern region. Her master's thesis from the University of Tromsoe was on slum women in Bangalore, India.

Aurelia N. Kamuzora, lecturer, department of economics, Mzumbe University, Tanzania, holds an MBA from Agder University College, Norway. Her research interests are in gender issues, small and medium enterprises as well as marketing and globalization issues. She has published several papers in her fields.

Faustin R. Kamuzora, lecturer, department of economics, Mzumbe University, Tanzania, holds an MSc. in agricultural economics from the University of North Carolina A&T State University. His research interests include livelihood issues, systems thinking as well as information and communication technologies for development.

Ronit Kark, lecturer, department of sociology, Bar-Ilan University, Ramatgan, Israel is affiliated with the graduate gender studies program. She has a Ph.D. from the Hebrew University of Jerusalem and undertook postdoctoral studies at the Institute for Research and Gender and at the Department of Psychology at the University of Michigan.

Margaret Kigozi, executive director, Uganda Investment Authority (UIA), Kampala, Uganda,is a medical doctor who practiced in Uganda, Zambia and Kenya before she was appointed in 1999 as Executive Director of UIA. She is chancellor of Nkumba University, a director of the boards of Uganda Export Promotion, Enterprise Uganda and Crown Beverages Limited; chief commissioner of Uganda Scouts Association and multiple other advisory councils and decision making bodies both nationally and internationally.

Julius Kikooma, lecturer, department of organizational and social psychology, Makerere University, Kampala, is a Ph.D. student at the University of Cape Town. He has presented many papers at international conferences and teaches in the area of women and minority resources development.

Fatoumata Badini-Kinda, holds a Ph.D. in sociology and is lecturer (maître-assissante) on the Faculty of Sociology at the University of Ouagadougou, Burkina Faso. Her fields of teaching and research include urbanization, local social security and old age, migration and poverty among women. She is engaged with a social security project sponsored by the Swiss National National Science Foundation.

Harriet Muwanika Kiwemba, manager, FINCA, Jinja, Uganda, received her B.S. from Makerere University in 1988 and was a student in the M.A. program in the department of women's and gender studies researching micro credit institutions and the impact of such programs on participants. Harriet passed away on May 1, 2004, leaving three children, and her husband, Stephan Kiwemba of Jinga, Uganda.

Meg Luxton, professor and director, graduate program in women's studies, York University, Toronto, Canada, has research interests in women's work—paid and unpaid; international initiatives to measure and value unpaid work; and the politics of the women's movement in Canada. Her previous books in clude, *More Than a Labour of Love: Three Generations of Women's Work in the Home* (1980); and the award winning *Getting By in Hard Times: Gendered Labour at Home and on the Job* (2001). She is currently working on a book on informal caregiving and social policy.

Emma Zapata Martelo, professor, Colegio de Postgraduados en Ciencias Agrícolas, Montecillo, Mexico, studied sociology at the University of Texas at Austin and has long worked with poor rural women in Mexico. Her books include, *Women and Power; Mujeres Rurales Ante el Nuevo Milenio;* and *Desarrollo Rural y Genero.*

Mahua Mukherjee, holds a Ph.D. from Jadavpur Univeristy and is currently a faculty member in the department of architecture and planning in the Indian Institute of Technology. Her speciality is in sustainable human habitat and has research interests in disaster mitigation using a sustainable model and climatic issues in building and construction.

Juliet Nazziwa Musoke, senior lecturer, Kyambogo University, Kampala, holds an M.A. from the University of South Wales and certificates in entrepreneurship training, business development services, empowerment of women through enterprises and business counseling. She is a program officer in the Council for Economic Empowerment for Women in Africa (CEEWA_U).

Ngila Mwase, senior economic advisor, UNDP, in Maputo covering Mozambique and Swaziland, holds a Ph.D. in economics from Newcastle upon Tyne University; and has served UNDP in Uganda, Kenya, Zambia and Malawi; worked for COMESA, EAMI and as senior research fellow and deputy director, Economic Research Bureau, University of Dar-es-Salaam. He has published more than fifty scholarly papers.

Vannie Naidoo, holds an M.A. in finance and is currently a faculty member at the University of KwaZulu Natal Westville campus. She has also taught at the University of the Free State, Qwaqwa Campus and is a sixth generation South African Indian. Her research areas are AIDS and workplace dynamics, marketing, management issues and small business issues and finance.

Sakuntala Narasimhan, is currently an Associate of the National Institute for Advanced Studies. She is a senior Indian columnist, author, and activist specializing in gender. She wrote a fortnightly, award winning column, "On Women" in the Deccan Herald paper, Bangalore from 1984 to 2001. Her writings have been translated worldwide. Of the ten books she has published, *Empowering Women: An Alternative Strategy from Rural India* (1999) is a "bestseller."

Esperanza Tuñón Pablos, Ph.D. in sociology is researcher and director of population and health at El Colegio de la Frontera Sur, México. She has been a gender specialist for fifteen years, published four books and more than twenty-five papers. She is research level 2 in the Research National System (SNI) and a member of the Mexican Science Academy in the Area of Social Science.

Claudia Roth, holds a Ph.D. in social anthropology and is a researcher and lecturer at the department of social anthropology, University of Zurich. Her fields of interest include gender, old age, anthropology of development and ethnopsychoanalysis. Since 1989, she has been doing regular research in bobo-Dioulasso, Burkina Faso and is actively engaged in a research project financed by the Swiss national Science Foundation and the Swiss Development Cooperation.

Saskia Sassen, Ralph Lewis Professor of Sociology at the University of Chicago, Chicago, and Centennial Visiting Professor at the London School of Economics. She is a member of the National Academy of Sciences Panel on Cities, and Chair of the Information, Technology, International Cooperation and Global Security Committee of the SSRC. Her latest book is *Denationalization: Territory, Authority and Rights in a Gloal Digital Age* (2003).

Lena Sawyer, holds a Ph.D. in cultural anthropology from the University of California at Santa Cruz. She is an Assistant Professor in International and Intercultural Social Work, Mid Sweden University, Östersund, Sweden. Her research interests include identify, migration and diaspora, and anti-racist feminist social work.

Margaret Snyder, is Founding Director of UNIFEM, a co-founder of the African Centre for Women of UNECA in Addis Ababa, and member of the committee to Organize Women's World Banking. She is a Fulbright scholar. Her books include *Transforming Development: Women, Poverty and Politics, a History of UNIFEM* (1995); *African Women and Development, a History* with Mary Tadesse (1995); *Women in African Economies: from Burning Sun to Boardroom* (2000).

Ramesh Chand Swarankar, Assistant Professor and Head, Department of Anthropology, University of Rajasthan, has areas of research interest in HIV/AIDS, forced migration, rehabilitation and resettlement, water and common property resources. He has published four books and over a dozen articles in national and international journals.

Kristen Timothy, Senior Research Scholar, National Council for Research on Women, was deputy director of the UN Division for the Advancement of Women and co-cordinator of the Beijing Women's Conference. She has an M.A. from Harvard's Kennedy School and in African studies from Makerere University. She was a founder and board president of the Association for Women in Development.

Catherine Komugisha Tindiwensi, lecturer, Makerere University Business School, holds an M.B.A. and teaches entrepreneurship development and small business management. She is a businesswoman and carries out research relating to small and medium enterprise development and growth. She is a member of the expert group ow women and agriculture of CEEWA and a Board member of Uganda Women Entrepreneur's Association Limited.

Akello Zerupa, part-time lecturer, department of women and gender studies, Makerere University, has research interests in gender and poverty in the agricultural sector, gender and sports in secondary schools in Uganda and monitoring the impacts of government support programs in Uganda. She holds a B.S. in education from Kyambogo Unversity and a diploma from the National Teachers College in Laliro.